BUILDING THE DEVIL'S EMPIRE

BUILDING THE DEVIL'S EMPIRE

French Colonial New Orleans

SHANNON LEE DAWDY

The University of Chicago Press ⅌ Chicago and London

The University of Chicago Press, Chicago 60637
The University of Chicago Press, Ltd., London
© 2008 by The University of Chicago
All rights reserved. Published 2008
Paperback edition 2009
Printed in the United States of America

18 17 16 15 14 13 12 11 10 09   2 3 4 5 6

ISBN-13: 978-0-226-13841-1 (cloth)
ISBN-13: 978-0-226-13842-8 (paper)
ISBN-10: 0-226-13841-0 (cloth)
ISBN-10: 0-226-13842-9 (paper)

Library of Congress Cataloging-in-Publication Data

Dawdy, Shannon Lee, 1967–
    Building the devil's empire : French colonial New Orleans /
    Shannon Lee Dawdy.
        p.   cm.
    Includes bibliographical references and index.
    ISBN-13: 978-0-226-13841-1 (cloth : alk. paper)
    ISBN-10: 0-226-13841-0 (cloth : alk. paper)
    1. New Orleans (La.)—History—18th century.   2. New
    Orleans (La.)—Social conditions—18th century.
    3. French—Louisiana—New Orleans—History—
    18th century.   4. New Orleans (La.)—Colonial influence.
    5. Ethnology—Louisiana—New Orleans—History—
    18th century.   6. New Orleans (La.)—Ethnic relations—
    History—18th century.   7. City planning—Louisiana—New
    Orleans—History—18th century.   8. Louisiana—History—
    To 1803.   I. Title.
    F379.N557D39   2008
    976.3'3502—dc22

                                                    2007047693

In memory of my roguish Dad, James Hayward Dawdy

being neither of the two Americas map   or thing itself
buoys clanging in the chop buzzing flies abyss on tape

we talk about what is as if our dominion barks at infinity
I need to plug my ears with spun cotton against what is

     to happen elsewhere if it doesn't happen here
a night on the town all the murderers   wear Venetian
                          masks of spun gold

it's a trumpet Monod hears when he wakes
after a while the snakeskin left behind becomes translucent

we are left behind too stitching one end to another
worried that a friend was cold that time   alone   on earth

ℱ Duncan McNaughton, *another set of circumstance*

Contents

Illustrations & Tables

TABLES

Preface

This is a different preface than the one I had once imagined writing for this book. As individuals, each of us can probably identify certain events that have changed the course of our lives. The same can be said for the life of a city. There is no question that Hurricane Katrina has been one of those events for the city of New Orleans. There is no question that it has been one of those events in my own life. After a summer of research, I had left New Orleans just a few weeks before the storm in August 2005. I am extremely fortunate in that the change I have experienced is not one of deep loss, as experienced by so many other Louisianans. I did not lose family members, or many worldly possessions, to the levee breaches. What I have experienced is a radical shift in perspective. My world has been turned upside down—if only inside my head. I see, and prioritize, my life differently. My strong emotional reaction to the disaster made me realize how attached I had become to New Orleans, not simply because I have been an on-again, off-again resident for thirteen years, but because I identified with the city. In my imagination, it had a personality I had come to know, love, even emulate. This is a risky admission for a researcher to make. I think Katrina has also emboldened me to take more risks.

I am passionate about my work. But the love I offer New Orleans is much like that I offer my family (much to their annoyance)—a questioning, demanding, but ultimately, I hope, forgiving one. Intellectually, Katrina has in some ways radically altered my perspective on the history of the city, but in others it has only sharpened my previous impressions. In the fall of 2005, I spent three months in post-Katrina New Orleans conducting street-to-street surveys, attempting to help assess damage to the city's historic architecture and archaeological deposits. I learned more than I had ever known about neighborhoods such as the Lower Ninth Ward, Pontchartrain Park, and Lakeview. This experience has forced me to think of the city more as a patchwork of communities and neighborhoods than the coherent whole I had once imagined. At worst, personifying the city, as is done in so much tourist literature and even historical writing, requires glossing over the differences and divisions between these neighborhoods. At best, it requires finding the stitches that knit the patchwork together without disregarding the diversity of experiences the patches represent. I now try to be more careful to do the latter.

In other ways, Katrina has convinced me of the coherence and longevity of certain patterns. National (even international) media reports painted New Orleans as a highly racialized, backward place where public disorders such as looting and shooting were sadly expected, even natural. The prurient interest of these reports, but also the grains of truth obscured by their gross distortions, gave me an intense sense of *déjà vu*. I had seen it all before, heard it all before. It felt as if the city was reliving its French colonial past, the words of eighteenth-century ministers being channeled by twenty-first-century television news anchors. The combined moral and material failure of New Orleans, and the shameful abandonment of the city by its parent nation, was likewise headline news in the Atlantic world of the 1720s and 1730s.

But my research on the French period has also been a source of hope for the city's future. The New Orleans that I describe in this book is largely gone, materially destroyed except for that which remains underground as archaeological strata. The French Quarter is not really French. Almost the entire city burned down in 1788 and 1794, and was rebuilt in the Spanish colonial period (1769–1803). Only a couple of buildings from the French period now survive. Despite this, certain social and cultural features of the city—its *joie de vivre* and dedication to entertainment, its self-deprecating humor, its political insularity, its simultaneous intimacies and inequalities of race and class, its everyday aesthetic sensitivity and the ability to find beauty in disorder—these imponderables seem to persist despite many episodes of destruction, abandonment, and rebuilding from the French period down to the present. These stitches that knit together the lives of New Orleanians extend through both time and space. Still, the long-term perspective destroys a cherished myth of New Orleans—that it is lost in history, stubbornly traditional, and culturally conservative. It has, in fact, constantly adapted to environmental challenges, dramatic population fluctuations, and global economic shifts. There is no reason to believe it will not improvise and adapt again after Katrina, while retaining much of its unique cultural stitchwork. Adaptation and preservation, after all, need not be opposing strategies.

New Orleans has undergone tremendous demographic, economic, and cultural changes over the course of its history, so the historic patch I write about here—French colonial New Orleans (1718–69) is in many ways a different place than the New Orleans that came to exist in the Spanish, antebellum, or reconstruction eras. What has not changed much is its public persona. First impressions and legacies from the French period have contributed to this continuity.

New Orleans began to gain a special reputation in the early eighteenth century that has endured and become part of the lore of the city. By the early nineteenth century, travel writers were describing New Orleans fairly consistently as a "splendid bedlam of a city"—Louisiana's Babylon. At first glance it appeared charmingly European, but on closer look, it seemed foreign and even uncivilized. Some emphasized "splendid" pleasures, others moral "bedlam." William Darby claimed, "There are few places where human life can be enjoyed with more pleasure," while J. Benwell called it "as vile a place as any under the sun" occupied by "renegades of all nations" who made "violence and bloodshed indigenous." These were not just the views of English-speaking visitors. Alexis de Tocqueville wrote in his diary on January 1, 1832: "Arrival at New Orleans. Forest of ships. Mississippi 300 feet deep. External appearance of the town. Beautiful houses. Huts. Muddy, unpaved streets . . . Population just as mixed. Faces with every shade of color . . . Incredible laxity of morals." It is difficult to tell where reputation and true character overlap. One undoubtedly feeds the other. In the imagination, New Orleans has been fixed as a dangerous and delightful wild town, *une ville sauvage.* In the streets, New Orleans has been a place of constant reinvention and creole improvisation.[1]

As with its reputation for sexual license and libertine drinking, the image of New Orleans as a violent place is still very much with us in the present day. The greatest trepidation I have about presenting this work to the public eye is that the passages in which I trace the "disorders" and legal deviations of French colonial New Orleans will be misappropriated as a genealogy of the city's criminality. I do not, in any way, believe that the roots of violent crime in New Orleans are either so old or so entrenched that they cannot be addressed with social care and political ambition. Both the rate and the causes of violent crime in New Orleans have fluctuated over its complex history. In fact, the long time I have spent thinking about this topic has convinced me that the causes are tied more to structural conditions of the present than to any cultural inheritance of the past.

Thus, the phrase *rogue colonialism* as used in this book is not meant to substantiate the myth of New Orleans as a wild, roguish town by giving it even deeper roots. In material and social terms, the city has changed tremendously over the years, and such claims for essential qualities are more rhetorical than real. But certainly, the surprisingly old public image of the city has influenced the way I approach the problems of colonialism. I suggest that there is a self-fashioning, and a utility, in taking on the "rogue" label that has benefited New Orleanians from the town's earliest days. It is an invention partly of their own making, to serve their own interests—but it can backfire.

In some ways this book has been evolving since I first moved to New Orleans in early 1994. The friends I made, the food I ate, the education I received in local customs and dialect—all fed my decision to reorient the focus of my research from the historical archaeology and ethnohistory of southeastern Indians to that of my new home town. As director of the Greater New Orleans Archaeology Program at the University of New Orleans, I undertook several research projects that deepened my archaeological and archival knowledge of the area, but also confronted me with a barrage of unanswered questions. I was especially struck by the conundrum that New Orleans is still identified as "French" in so many ways, yet this was by far the least well preserved and least understood period of the city's history. The opportunity to excavate the courtyard of Madame John's Legacy, a National Historic Landmark located in the French Quarter, deepened my curiosity. The main house stands as the only representative example of domestic architecture from the French period, although it too was rebuilt in the Spanish period. Both the archaeology and the archival materials associated with this house were intriguing, not least because it had served as an inn owned by a smuggler's wife for the entire French period.

The subfield in which I was trained is a thoroughly interdisciplinary one. Historical archaeologists are a breed of historical anthropologist. They typically conduct background regional histories in libraries and "micro" property histories in archives to contextualize the interpretation of materials they excavate. One thing I soon realized was that no one had yet written a contextual history of daily life in French New Orleans that could help me make sense of the material I was getting out of the trash pit at Madame John's Legacy. I would have to write it myself. Second, I realized that although early deposits remain intact below the streets of New Orleans, I had many years of excavation ahead of me before I could amass the amount of artifactual evidence needed to flesh out the material history of the city in the French period. So this book is the first part of a two-step ambition. Although I have integrated the scant archaeological data we have on the French period where it makes sense, the hat I wear here is that of a historical anthropologist. Historical anthropologists bring a theoretical orientation that causes them to ask different sorts of questions than most historians would ask of the same material. In my case, I am interested in how New Orleans informs us more generally about the nature of colonialism—how colonies are established, how they are ruled, how they produce new societies, and how these societies are organized.

Much of the research and writing of this book was completed at the University of Michigan, where I was enrolled in the Doctoral Program in Anthropology and History between 1998 and 2003. The primary archival sources I used are the Louisiana Superior Council Records, the Louisiana administrative correspondence of the French National Archives Colonial Section (particularly the C13 series), and a grab-bag of historical *mémoires* and maps. Except where otherwise noted, I have offered my own English translations of the documents. For space considerations, I have here omitted the original French quotations, but the interested reader will find most of these reproduced in the footnotes of the dissertation.[2] Earlier versions and offshoots of this research have appeared in the journals *French Colonial History* and *Annales*, and in the edited volumes *Haunted by Empire*, *Discipline and the Other Body*, and *Coastal Encounters*.[3]

One outcome of my new perspective on the "patchwork" nature of the personality of New Orleans can be seen in the narrative strategy employed in this book. I have tried to be true to the diversity of the historical actors and their distinct experiences in French colonial New Orleans. The historian-philosopher Hayden White tells us that most historians provide a narrative of events that follows the storyline of one of five basic plots: tragedy, romance, comedy, satire, or (now rare) epic.[4] If that is so, then most historians have told the story of early Louisiana as a comedy ending in the self-defeat of French absolutism. It is about the absurd failure of imperial hubris. There is some truth to this story. In it, scholars will recognize French New Orleans as a precocious but disastrous experiment in modernity and venture capitalism. The participants themselves applied no such terms, or neat packages, to what they were doing. However, through the letters and reports exchanged between Louisiana and Europe in the eighteenth century, we can detect a spirit of experimentation, of adventure and individualism, of designing ambition and political idealism, as well as the danger and confusion of wide-open possibilities and comedic cases of mistaken identity.

I will admit that my first impulse was to write this story as a romance about Louisiana's triumph over imperial will. After all, the final act was a gallant action scene, one of the first creole revolts of the eighteenth century. In 1768 a motley crew of creole merchant-planters, second-generation colonial farmers, and urban tavern-goers of the maritime trades took to the streets of New Orleans in revolt against the Spanish government's peaceful takeover of Louisiana. They sent the appointed governor packing for Havana. The revolt, however, failed when nine months later Spain sent a more assertive governor backed by 2,600 troops. The local resistance movement disintegrated with finger-pointing and evasion, leaving only a dozen or so radicals to stand trial and be executed. It would be a rather embarrassing, anticlimactic ending to a romance.[5]

Rather than rewriting the early colonial history of New Orleans as a tragedy (or tragicomedy) to fit the ending that historical events have given us, I would like to escape these standard emplotments. One thing I have learned from reading the literature of eighteenth-century France and its colonies is that our present-day categories of genre—those of romance and tragedy as well as history and science—did not yet exist. In their place were incipient forms that combined these elements, but also some well-defined genres that have now become all but extinct, such as the epistolary travel narrative and the picaresque novel. The archival fragments I have pieced together to create this picture of early New Orleans attempt to give voice to those who actually experienced it, so in a way this collection of quotations, letters, and postcards sent from the colonial frontier forms a type of epistolary history. However, the story I tell in my own voice comes closest to a picaresque tale.

A picaresque novel puffs up the protagonist to make him look like a ridiculous buffoon, but also recognizes his humanity. If tragedy recounts the folly of individuals trying to willfully (and futilely) direct the course of history despite large impersonal forces in their way, and if romance allows them to triumph in some meaningful way, then the picaresque allows both to be true. Thus, I offer a picaresque history of New Orleans that accounts both for the grand plans that created it on an imperial scale and the individual follies, creative shenanigans, quotidian rebellions, acts of God—and of the devil—that thwarted it.

The picaresque novel is usually episodic. Rather than build up one major plot, the author presents a series of adventures or travel stories that coalesce to present a characterization of the protagonist and his or her society. This episodic (rather than linear) approach to relating history reflects my ethnographic orientation. Ethnographic history employs an ensemble cast whose conflicting voices can be framed together in the same context and in relationship to the same events. To preserve this multivocality, I have chosen to open each chapter with a biographical sketch of a different actor from French Louisiana. The multiple perspectives produced from this ensemble cast are difficult to reconcile into a simple "whodunit." Thus, one might say the historical narrative I have composed takes literary inspiration from the multiple voices of *The Canterbury Tales* as well as the comic epic arc of *Don Quixote*. I hope this narrative strategy helps make the work speak to both general New Orleans curiosity-seekers and academic colleagues. That ambition has perhaps been my own bit of personal hubris. Whether it is folly or not, only the reader can tell.

Acknowledgments

One measure of a project crying for completion is when the list of debts becomes embarrassingly long. My partner in life, Dan McNaughton, has suffered through the many iterations and deadlines of this project, and helped with everything from proofreading to preparing mind-sustaining meals. I am grateful to him for dragging me to New Orleans in the first place, though I know he must regret it just a little. My son Asa has had to schedule his life around this book, but I am grateful that he himself is such a bookworm that he didn't seem to mind *too* much. My parents, Jim and Arletta Dawdy, and my brother Jess have supported, if not always understood, my work obsession at critical junctures. Genie and Duncan McNaughton have helped to keep both project and family going. I am grateful for their empathy. For shared food, laughter, and love of the city, I have no better friends and muses than Patrick and Lydia Rogan, and Kelli Ostrom.

Researchers in New Orleans are fortunate in having access to an incredible cadre of knowledgeable and cordial professionals. I owe special thanks to the librarians and curators at the Williams Research Center of the Historic New Orleans Collection, especially Pamela Arceneaux, Siva Blake, Mark Cave, Mary Lou Eichhorn, and John Magill. Leon Miller, Bill Meneray, and Ken Owen at Tulane's Special Collections made the cold, quiet research of the archive fun. I also benefited from the expertise of staff at the Newberry Library, especially Patrick Morris in the map division. Attendants at the Bibliothèque de l'Arsenal in Paris were patient with my rough Louisiana French and the staff at the Bibliothèque Nationale were likewise understanding and helpful.

I am grateful to staff at the Louisiana State Museum, including Jim Sefcik, Kathryn Page, Michelle Fontenot, and Alecia Long, who supported a very early phase of this research, as well as the Friends of the Cabildo, who underwrote it. During that time, I was working at the College of Urban and

Public Affairs at the University of New Orleans, which enthusiastically supported the peculiar endeavor of outreach archaeology and public history. I do not know if that job, or this project, would have come to be without the firebrand of New Orleans archaeology, Bettie Pendley. I am indebted to all the volunteers who have helped me over the years. I wish I could name them all, but Joan Bruder has a special place in my heart. My colleagues in Louisiana have given me tremendous support, training, and feedback over the years. I am especially grateful to Nancy Hawkins, Tim Joder, Chip McGimsey, Paulette Simon, Juana Ibáñez, Ben Maygarden, Louise Fergusson Saenz, and Ruben Saenz. Jill-Karen Yakubik was my first mentor in Louisiana archaeology; she taught me how to lick ceramics, a skill I am now passing on to my graduate students, much to their amusement. More than to anyone else, I owe my career to the late Tom Eubanks. My life path would have lain in some other, probably less exciting, direction if he had not had faith in me as a newbie archaeologist.

The final stages of the dissertation were supported by fellowships from the Institute for the Humanities at the University of Michigan and the Rackham School of Graduate Studies, as well as an ACLS—Society for Eighteenth-Century Studies short-term fellowship at the Newberry Library of Chicago. I received support and feedback also from members of Ann Stoler's Tense and Tender Ties Workshop and participants of the Mahan Symposium on Gulf History at the University of Alabama—Mobile. It's difficult to overstate the value I put on the interdisciplinary training, material support, and intellectual spirit I found within the University of Michigan's doctoral program in anthropology and history. At the University of Chicago, I've benefited from the comments of participants in the America before 1900 Workshop, the Comparing Colonialisms Workshop, and the Workshop on Early Modern France.

During the dissertation phase of this project, I received the generous advice and feedback of committee members Rebecca Scott, Julius Scott, Dena Goodman, Ann Laura Stoler, Norman Yoffee, and Henry Wright. They each made a mark upon this project and have continued to be superb interlocutors. As the book developed, many other colleagues have read or heard bits and drafts and helped me make sense of the material, as well as of my own thoughts. Thanks go to Philip Boucher, Carl Brasseaux, Paul Cheney, Emily Clark, David William Cohen, Fernando Coronil, Laurent Dubois, Sylvia Frey, Virginia Gould, Christopher N. Matthews, Lawrence Powell, Jane Schneider, Julie Skurski, Daniel Usner, and Greg Waselkov. I am especially grateful to Jessica Cattelino, who has the dubious honor of being the first to have read the revised manuscript from beginning to end. Her friendship has meant as much as her collegial service. Other colleagues have, knowingly or unknowingly, helped me along in other ways. I want to single out especially Mickey Dietler, Gayle Fritz, T. R. Kidder, Gordon Sayre, Elizabeth Scott, Adam T. Smith, and Carla Zecher. I'm grateful to John and Jean Comaroff for their bounty of kind mentorship and to all my colleagues in the Department of Anthropology at the University of Chicago for creating a lively professional home that helped nurture this project into a more mature and ambitious work.

In the final throes of this project, I am indebted to my graduate students. Rebecca Graff and Megan Edwards pulled the illustrations together, and Rebecca overall helped me keep my head on straight. Richard Weyhing was a generous colleague with informed readings and suggestions. I thank Zach Chase and Zada Johnson for letting themselves get bitten by the Louisiana bug so I have people around who understand.

I also thank the unnamed peers who reviewed the prospectus and manuscript, and made strategic suggestions that helped me improve the work. Finally, my editor David Brent's bemused patience has been *just right*. Mary Gehl, Elizabeth Branch Dyson, Laura Avey, and Lys Ann Weiss made the editorial process a pleasure. I may not have incorporated all the sage advice I have been offered, but any fool's errands or errors that remain are due to my own stubbornness and should not reflect upon my friends.

Introduction

In 1727, a young Ursuline nun named Marie Hachard from Rouen, France, embarked on a New World adventure. After a harrowing, five-month journey marked by storms, pirates, shipwrecks, and thirst, Marie and her fellow nuns entered the muddy mouth of the Mississippi. Necessity forced them to temporarily set aside their vow of seclusion. Marie's eyes were wide open as she emerged from the sailing ship that had brought them across the Atlantic, and stepped cautiously into the large canoe in which they would complete their journey. As they made their way through the strange, steamy landscape of gnarled cypress trees dripping with Spanish moss, one imagines polite, restrained conversation occasionally interrupting the buzz of insects and the flutter of water birds taking sudden flight. The pilot may have pointed out their first alligator sighting or explained the eerie sound of the sheep frog. Perhaps he apologized for the putrid swamp vapors that assaulted their senses. After seven days, with their habits of black serge alternately soaked by rain and baked by the August heat, they arrived at their long-anticipated destination—New Orleans. Their mission in French Louisiana's new colonial capital was to take over the operation of the hospital and found a new school for girls. Established just nine years earlier, the town was a frontier settlement where the sounds of tree clearing and construction still clanged through the day and where muddy streets defied the pretenses of civilization. Before the sisters once again cloistered themselves at their temporary convent in the former governor's house, Marie took the opportunity to survey the town, and pronounced to her father in a letter that it was "very pretty, well constructed and regularly built." Within a few months of her arrival in New Orleans, however, her impressions began to sound less sanguine. Informed by the enslaved laborers, food vendors, and catechism students who came to the convent, the twenty-three-year-old began to make more ethnographic observations on the social and moral life of the town. Shocked by the painted faces of colonial women, offended by the malfeasance of the local economy, and dismayed by the lack of regard for religion, she pronounced: "The devil here possesses a large empire."[1]

Marie Hachard was neither the first nor the last observer to characterize New Orleans as a devilish, disorderly place. With incredible rapidity following its founding by the French in 1718, New Orleans gained a reputation as a wild town and a colonial failure, a reputation that has endured. Its untamed nature was evident in the ways in which it veered away from the neat, civilized plans designed for the colony's economic development, social structure, and political order. By the 1720s writers were describing Louisiana as a failure and the French crown's reaction as one of "abandonment." In 1722 Jesuit traveler Père Charlevoix remarked that the town was a disappointment inflated by overambitious plans. His characterization derived from his visit to New Orleans in 1721, just after the Mississippi Bubble had burst. The colonization of Louisiana teetered upon an elaborate financial pyramid scheme invented by the brilliant but overreaching Scottish financier, John Law. As a result of the collapse, shipments of foodstuffs and other survival necessities abruptly stopped before colonists had had a chance to achieve agricultural self-sufficiency. Hundreds, possibly thousands died of starvation and disease in the early 1720s. A second devastating event sealed the colony's reputation as a failure. In 1729 several villages of the Natchez Indian nation rose up to expel the French settlers, whose encroachments on their land and resources had become high-handed. In a surprise attack, over two hundred French settlers were killed at the colony's "second city" of Natchez, 100 miles upriver from New Orleans. Despite the obvious hardships and setbacks that might have overwhelmed any colony, French writers insisted that Louisiana's failure was also an internal, moral one. In 1730 another visitor to town remarked that "disorders are so frequent in this colony and vice here triumphs unpunished." In 1731 novelist Abbé Prévost chose by then notorious New Orleans as the perfect backdrop for his final tragic scenes of *Manon Lescaut*, portraying it as a bedraggled town of abandoned Frenchmen living more like "wild natives" than civilized Europeans. Admirably, according to Prévost, they encouraged natural love and ignored the artifice of social rank. But they could also fall victim to dangerous passions and capricious local leaders.[2]

The simple question that drove my own original expedition into French colonial New Orleans was this: how did the town get (and maintain) this wild reputation, and what does it say about both Old World perceptions and New World realities? Because the accounting of "failures" makes clearer what the expectations and challenges for particular projects might have been than do taken-for-granted successes, the New Orleans story has the power to deepen our understanding of colonialism and empire in the eighteenth century, as well as in a broader perspective.

New Orleans was the "Devil's Empire" in several ways. Marie Hachard and other observers remarked upon its predilection for "disorder" and what appeared to be a corrupt moral economy. It was a devilishly difficult corner of empire to control. Instead of developing into an exemplary French-dominated "opulent metropolis" as intended, New Orleans quickly became the untamed hub of a Mississippi-Caribbean frontier. From the view of *ancien régime* France (Bourbon France of the pre-Revolutionary period), the town had a savage and disorderly quality due to its smuggling activity, ethnic diversity, social mobility, "spirit of insubordination," and the confusing animosities and intimacies of slavery. New Orleanians in the French period (1718–69, see chronology p. 247) were prone to be pragmatic rule-breakers and undomesticated travelers, independent-minded and imaginative in their strategies for survival. Some were chameleons with many aliases, others were self-made social climbers who tried to pin down competitors also aiming for a "masterless" existence. The French had established Louisiana with the intent of enforcing a state monopoly on smuggling with the Spanish colonies, but the skilled workers they enlisted for this enterprise—Caribbean freebooters (*flibustiers*, those who worked for plunder), professional privateers, experienced salt and tobacco smugglers, Indian traders, and enslaved Africans— were not the sort to be easily contained. Many French convicts (*forçats*) sent to the colony to reform themselves refused to do so, while Africans and Native Americans, for whom the city was never intended, made it their market town. On hot nights, contraband deals and fistfights involving a multihued crew of travelers and petty traders spilled out of New Orleans taverns into the muddy streets.

This book has two basic aims. First, it aspires to provide a historical ethnography that makes the characters, smells, struggles, and banter of this eighteenth-century community come alive in the imagination. Second, it grapples with the nature of colonialism itself and theories regarding its strategies, technologies, and ideologies. Although often depicted as remote or exceptional, New Orleans is significant to our understanding of colonialism and the development of creole societies. Its peculiarity is helpful because certain undercurrents of colonialism became mainstream in New Orleans, and thus remain more visible for study. I explore the "tensions of empire" that operated in the French period and make a series of claims about the nature of colonialism itself.[3]

The narrative device that serves both aims—describing the lived experiences of New Orleanians in the French period and theorizing colonialism—is the picaresque, a tragicomic adventure tale with overtones of social critique. I present a cast of characters making history, but not exactly as they pleased, nor exactly as their superiors planned. This tale is not a simple story of revolutionary romance or political tragedy, nor is it just an exposé of the comedies of the state, though it offers episodes of each. The entry for *picaresque* in the *American Heritage Dictionary* reads: "1. Of or involving clever rogues or adventurers. 2. Of or relating to a genre of usually satiric prose fiction originating in Spain and depicting in realistic, often humorous detail the adventures of a roguish hero of low social degree living by his or her wits in a corrupt society."[4] Picaresque tales such as *Don Quixote, Moll Flanders, Robinson Crusoe,* and *Huckleberry Finn* are stories of misadventure characterized by heroic travels, tragic failures, endearing pathos, and accidental comedy.

Looking beyond the always colorful story of New Orleans captured in the picaresque, I suggest that studying the "devilish" side of colonialism—its failures and its underworlds—reveals the contradictory forces that drove colonialism and shaped lived realities on imperial frontiers. Colonial societies were created by a combination of imperial designs (a drive for gold, a civilizing mission, a utopian vision of a city on a hill, a demand for tropical imports, a plan to resettle dissenters and troublemakers) and local contingencies (inept or insubordinate officials, unexpected strength of resisting natives, corruption, smuggling and piracy, an unpredictable natural climate). Colonial designs often contained the seeds of their own destruction. The history of the Atlantic world since 1450 is about the spread of empire, but it is also about the spread of revolution, rebellion, and resistance. The Americas, in particular, were dotted with counter-colonial fiefdoms and syndicates just as likely to be operated by disloyal Europeans as by indigenous natives, creoles, pirates, or maroons. My local argument is that New Orleans in the French period was one of these pockets of resistance. But it was not isolated. A study of New Orleans material and textual archives shows that these pockets were connected by intricate, intercoastal networks that in many ways disregarded the mainstream of the Atlantic world. Thus, my more global argument is that colonialism frequently creates conditions that foster not only cultures of resistance, but also circuits of seditious power and contraband flow—what one might, without irony, call *rogue colonialism.* In their organizational strength, political savvy, internal conflicts, far-flung networks, use of exemplary violence, and oligarchic tendencies, these rogue forces resemble organized crime syndicates. While from the view of some European officials such syndicates were, in fact, criminal entities, my point is not to exoticize these circuits and their participants, nor to discredit certain colonial enterprises by exposing practices of corruption and deviance. Naming the phenomenon "rogue colonialism" certainly risks echoing the condemnations of peevish metropolitan ministers or, contrarily, placing charming antiheroes upon a fragile pedestal. But rather than taking either side, my intent is to maintain an omniscient point of view and invite the reader to do the same. In the end, this strategy helps us see that in many colonies legitimacy and legality were of little relevance to daily operations, and the boundary between banditry and statehood was difficult to draw.

Rogue colonialism, I argue, flourished in many contexts due to the quintessentially experimental nature of colonial projects. This experimentalism was encouraged from two directions. The first was formal and abstract planning initiatives originating in Europe that mobilized people and resources on an ambitious scale in a deliberate effort to engineer landscapes, economies, and even societies through colonialism. The second impulse toward experimentation was local, arising from what James C. Scott calls *mētis,* or the practical knowledge and flexible survival strategies the colonial frontier necessitated. These two factors helped create an environment that encouraged many actors to individually refashion themselves and to collectively invent new institutions.[5]

A Greek word meaning "cunning and craft," *mētis* has a kinship with common definitions of creolization, although its roots are distinct from the French *métis,* meaning "mixture" (when capitalized, it refers to French Canadian–Indian parentage, from Latin *mixtīcius*). In a linguistic mode, creolization represents the creative adaptation of a native grammar to an imported vocabulary. It also connotes hybridity among diverse peoples and, in the Americas, the rise of a distinctive and independent social class. Many authors associate creolization with an inventive, improvisational aesthetic and a clever working of the colonial system.[6] The social formation of New Orleans in the French period might evoke any of these forms of creolization. However, in this work I define *creole* using the eighteenth-century Louisiana meaning of "native born" rather than either of the competing racialized definitions that date to the late nineteenth century (e.g., the mixed-race descendants of free people of color *or* the all-white descendants of the original French colonists). Louisiana creoles in the French period could be free or enslaved, black or white, or any combination.[7] Based on this local understanding, I define *creolization* as the birth of a new native society. The term describes the process of transition from an experimental colonial enterprise, in which the rules structuring social, moral, economic, political, and even material life are uncertain and in flux, to a more stable, locally adapted society created through *mētis,* in which actors come to share a basic set of understandings about who's who and how things work. Cultural creolization marks a gradual adaptation measured by the emergence of distinct new world practices. By "new world," I do not mean the geographical territory Europeans thought they had "discovered" in 1492, but rather the new mental, physical, and social dimensions of the colonial setting experienced by both natives and newcomers. Creolization does not produce a suddenly harmonious or smooth-running society free of conflict or ambiguity. Instead, it can be thought of as the sociological equivalent of a creole lingua franca arising out of the babel of early colonial encounters. Misunderstandings are still common, but actors reach for a common grammar and vocabulary of social, economic, and political forms.

From this I hope it is clear that I do *not* mean creolization as an equivalent for hybridization, or the creation of "mixed" offspring from "pure" parents. Hybridization is a concept based on ideal types that exist neither in nature's gene pools nor in human communities. When applied to cultural contexts, it makes even less sense. Contemporary anthropological thinking has abandoned the model of culture as a bounded box, yet many scholars fail to realize that the premise behind the popular idea of hybridity requires its resurrection by imagining an earlier period of cultural purity enjoyed by the parent societies (for example, in calling Trinidadian culture a "hybrid" between East Indian and West Indian cultures, one artificially fixes these entities as stable categories without their own complicated histories and circulations of diverse languages, religions, and genes). A revised model of culture imagines a series of overlapping webs (of social relations, of political-economic institutions, of belief systems). The densest intersections of these webs form nodes in a three-dimensional network. Culture, then, resembles the constantly evolving nerve structures of the human brain. This means that from certain temporal and spatial perspectives, every culture might be thought of as a hybrid connected to other hybrids. This model does not offer the same heuristic clarity as "container culture," but it does resonate with the real world. Certainly, there exist degrees of boundedness, and human groups can and do proclaim the limits of their culture and the moments at which it was influenced by, or mixed with, that of another. In defining the creolization of Louisiana as the emergence of "new natives," we cannot escape the fact that some sectors of the founder generation came from starkly different cultures, and that each passed on bits of memory, tradition, and habit to the next generation in some recombinant way. I want here simply to caution the reader against conflating creolization and hybridity because first impressions of New Orleans always seem to invite it, and as I hope this early history of the city will demonstrate, the transition from a colonial to a creole culture did not necessarily result in a well-blended, harmonious mixture. While syncretism in language, material culture, and religion undoubtedly took place, there also developed a new system of inequality that segregated subgroups and created new measures of difference. These were sometimes subtle and intimate, but therefore all the more powerful.[8]

The utilization of *creole* as the dominant designation for native New Orleanians dates at least to the 1740s. Virtually abandoned by France in 1731, Louisiana saw no significant new immigration from Europe or Africa until the beginning of Spanish rule thirty-five years later. As a result, the city presents an unusually clear picture of the generational transition from colonial to creole society. New Orleans quickly came to be dominated by locally born natives and a highly mobile class of "nationless" traders who plied the Mississippi–Caribbean waters. The chaos of the early years gave way to new hierarchies, understandings, and organizations under creole rule. Although local society became more stable and coherent in the second and third generations of settlement, it grew ever further from metropolitan designs.

The demographic profile of New Orleans is an important, though not all-determining, factor in its development. By the end of 1731, approximately 5,700 Africans and 7,000 Europeans had been sent to Louisiana. Many died before reaching the colony or jumped ship somewhere en route; many more died shortly after arrival. Others who had the means turned around and returned to France within a few years. By 1732 only 6,000 African and European immigrants remained—perhaps half of all those who had embarked for the shores of the Gulf during the height of immigration between 1717 and 1725. The period from the 1730s to the 1760s has been characterized by both contemporaries and historians as one of "abandonment." Although the population of New Orleans grew steadily in this period and the economy actually improved significantly, few French immigrants arrived, and the town's garrison was chronically undersupplied.

In this book, I frequently refer to the "founder generation" (or "charter generation") and the "creole generations." Although defining the parameters of a generation can be tricky, I follow a common convention tied to the average age of inheritance, modified by a consideration of Louisiana's unique immigration history.[9] Although a handful of second-generation children were already inheriting humble legacies from pioneering *coureurs de bois* (unlicensed fur traders, see glossary p. 249) as early as the 1710s, they were quickly overwhelmed by a massive wave of European and African immigration that peaked in the early 1720s. The children of these immigrants began inheriting property in large numbers by the late 1730s, and their children in turn by the late 1750s. Thus, I have stretched the "founder generation" to span the years from around 1699 to 1736.[10] The first creole generation dates to approximately 1737–57. The second creole generation comes to prominence around 1758, but I follow them only until the transfer of power to the Spanish administration in 1769.

The end of the French period was as peculiar as its beginning. In 1762 Louis XV secretly offered New Orleans and western Louisiana to his cousin, King Carlos III of Spain. The transfer was confirmed the following year by the Treaty of Paris, ending the Seven Years' War.[11] In 1766, the Spanish belatedly began taking steps to occupy New Orleans by sending Governor Antonio de Ulloa to the city, but he arrived with neither supplies nor troops to back the transition. Unhappy with his leadership, the still operating Louisiana Superior Council, dominated by local creoles, ousted him in 1768. In 1769 the Spanish government retaliated by sending a new governor, Alejandro O'Reilly, with 24 ships and 2,600 troops. Following a brief court trial, O'Reilly placed the leaders of the revolt in prison or in front of a firing squad. New Orleans and western Louisiana then continued under more peaceful Spanish rule until 1800, when Napoleon Bonaparte won it back from the Spanish in the secret Treaty of San Ildefonso but held it in name only before selling it to the United States in the Louisiana Purchase of 1803.

The story I focus on here is that of the first New Orleans, a French colonial *ville*. New Orleans came to see such major shifts in its political, economic, and demographic landscape under its subsequent Spanish and American administrations that it is in many ways difficult to speak of it as the same city in subsequent periods. Yet events, ideas, and material structures of the French period had a lasting effect upon the city. Even today the heart of the town—the French Quarter—has changed little from the 1721 grid, although the buildings themselves may owe more to creole innovation and Spanish zoning law than to French architectural tradition. And the reputation of New Orleans as a place where social order is barely maintained—or in the case of Bourbon Street on Mardi Gras, not maintained at all—is alive and well. The city is depicted, and depicts itself, in novels, plays, and tourist material as an exotic, licentious, dark, and decayed place. This imagery can be traced back to the realities and ravings of the French colonial period.[12]

This work is the first full-length study since 1917 devoted exclusively to New Orleans in the French colonial period.[13] Most of the existing historical literature collapses New Orleans into a general narrative of the Louisiana territory or discusses the French period as background to the "golden age" of sugar and cotton in the Spanish and antebellum periods. I believe it is important to understand French New Orleans in its own spatial and temporal terms.

Also, as an ethnographic history rather than a linear historical account, this book is less concerned with explaining certain events and their development (such as the Mississippi Bubble, the Natchez Rebellion, or even the New Orleans Revolt of 1768) than with filling out a detailed picture of the cultural categories and social dynamics that pertained during a particular place and time, and exploring what lessons they teach about colonialism in general. I focus on drawing out social geographies, life histories, and the texture of everyday life. Anthropology and history have long been on converging paths, and many works in the subfields of social history, cultural history, and microhistory closely resemble what I am here calling ethnographic history. Disciplinary distinctions are a provincial concern. Ethnographic history explains what makes people tick by examining micro-events, social networks, street-level conflicts, and shared cultural understandings.[14] Like any ethnographer, I arrived in the "field" (in this case, the archives) with a general problem that interested me: how to account for the reputation of New Orleans as a colonial failure and what this meant to the participants. Still, I was prepared to surrender myself to whatever patterns emerged out of a thorough immersion in the culture, trying to remain self-aware of my own biases. I set out with an idea of debunking the image of New Orleans as a site of disorder. But at the end of my research trek, I was forced to abandon my original revisionist stance, not because my hypothesis was wrong, but because the question was wrongheaded. Asking "just how disorderly *was* French New Orleans?" traps us in the evaluative language of European planners and sends us down the foolish path of attempting to quantify an abstraction. The picture is much more complicated than the simple binary trope "order/disorder" can capture. That binary itself is a figment of an eighteenth-century European worldview. It is interesting as an ethnographic fact that had a profound influence on colonial New Orleans, but is not very helpful for understanding the dynamics at work on the ground that rarely break along simple black-and-white lines. Like visions of heaven and hell, or God and the Devil, the idea of order/disorder tells us something about the guiding beliefs of historical actors, but not much about the rich texture of their daily lives.

Responding to self-critiques within history and the interdisciplinary field of colonial studies, I have tried to unfold the story of French colonial New Orleans freed from the teleology of later periods and the just-so story of modernity.[15] In other words, much of history is written backwards, working from a major event (such as the French Revolution or the onset of industrial capitalism) to uncover the conditions and causes that seemed to make it inevitable. This mode of historical explanation encourages us to skip over those factors not privileged as causal. Elements of accident, coincidence, or the influence of singular personalities drop from view. Factors that pushed society in the opposite direction from the forces that eventually won out, and those historical trajectories not ultimately completed, are usually ignored in conventional historical narratives. Modernity itself seems to insist on a constant search for its own genealogy, and wishes for this genealogy to have pure, straight lines of descent. According to this way of thinking, the "failure" of Louisiana makes it a dead-end branch of the family tree. Thus, my commitment to writing a less linear, event-centered history also comes from my belief that New Orleans played important, though forgotten, roles in Enlightenment intellectualism, in the development of colonialism, in the revolutionary movements of the Atlantic, and in the uneven evolution of modernity. It may have moved off-stage during the final acts of these dramas, but it nevertheless had a part to play that contributed to the whole.

"Modernity" can mean many things, so let me be clear about how I am using the term here. I mean it as a description of political forms, and the ideas and practices that supported them, that came to dominate the language and landscape of Europe and much of the Americas by the mid-nineteenth century. Dipesh Chakrabarty's description works well for my purposes: "The phenomenon of 'political modernity'—namely, the rule of modern institutions of the state, bureaucracy, and capitalist enterprise—is impossible to think of anywhere in the world without invoking certain categories and concepts, the genealogies of which go deep into the intellectual and even theological traditions of Europe. Concepts such as citizenship, the state, civil society, public sphere, human rights, equality before the law, the individual, distinctions between public and private, the idea of the subject, democracy, popular sovereignty, social justice, scientific rationality, and so on."[16] According to James Scott, when states institute these political forms, they are guided by a set of aesthetic preferences for simplicity, straight lines, and minimalism (an aesthetic complex he calls "high modernism"), more than by verifiable efficiency or sound science.[17]

The field of colonial studies that has emerged since the early 1980s focuses disproportionately upon colonies of the late nineteenth and early twentieth centuries.[18] As a result, the explanations and narratives scholars use almost always entail some engagement with the emergence of modern political forms and struggles over whether colonized subjects (particularly nonwhite "natives") were capable of "modernity." Colonization and modernization were simultaneous processes in Europe and the rest of the world. Thus, they create a confused tangle in which explaining one in terms of the other adds little clarity. Much of colonial history is written either as a tragedy ending with the colonized subsumed by modernity, or as a romance with the colonized resisting modernity—or better yet, co-opting it for their own ends. Interestingly, studies of the French Caribbean have recently begun to lead the way to escape these standard emplotments. Work by Michel-Rolph Trouillot and Laurent Dubois shows how slaves[19] and free people of color in Saint Domingue (Haiti) and Guadeloupe did not simply seize the ideas of liberty, equality, and fraternity proclaimed by the French Revolution. Rather, they were instrumental in defining what these terms *meant* for revolutionaries on both sides of the Atlantic, and what modern political forms they were to take in the next century. Like these authors, I insist that that colonies were key sites of production for political modernity, though I focus more on the material practices and socioeconomic structures that birthed "new worlds" than on the discursive outcries of revolutionaries.[20]

In this picaresque history, I invoke three archetypes—the engineer, the creole, and the rogue—to represent the three major factors I see contributing to the character of New Orleans in the French period. The first was the role of Enlightenment rationality and experimentation in engineering the city. New Orleans was established at a time when Enlightenment absolutism was perhaps at the peak of its effort to restructure French society and devise new methods of social control. The early plans for the city and the profile of the French immigrant population were deliberately experimental creations. Second, as a direct result of the specific experiments designed for New Orleans—and their unexpected failure—New Orleans rapidly developed a self-identified creole society, aided by the diversity of its Native American, African, Caribbean, Canadian, and European population as well as by the crown's virtual abandonment of the colony after 1731. By the second generation of settlement, France was exerting little of its political or economic will over Louisiana. The third major factor affecting the character of New Orleans was what I call *rogue colonialism*—the influence of those individuals on the ground who pushed colonial frontiers in their own self-interest. Reviving their role in the story underscores how colonies were created as much by military entrepreneurs and piratical vagrants as by monarchs and ministers. These three factors—engineering, creolization, and rogue colonialism—are interconnected. While metropolitan authorities may have been tempted to blame "rogues" for the failure of colonial experiments, independent and self-interested agents (rather than state agents) were those most likely to propose bold new schemes and volunteer to personally oversee their implementation in the new territories. Creoles, or those born in the colonies one step removed from national fealty, were even more prone to practices of rogue colonialism than the adventurous immigrants of the founding generation.

The establishment of New Orleans in 1718 coincided with a pivotal time in the *ancien régime* when the Bourbon government was experimenting with new forms of social control and Enlightened absolutism, characterized by a drive to discover the most "rational" means of operating an empire. An experimental spirit influenced Bourbon ministers to view the colonies as a laboratory for social, economic, and political reforms. The crown came to view New Orleans as a failed experiment when it became apparent that without massive investment it would be very difficult to control conditions or test subjects in the remote capital of a vast hinterland. In the latter part of the French period (c. 1731–69), intellectual currents that we call the Enlightenment continued to be a significant factor in shaping colonial life, but the influence of rational royalist scholars gave way to a common ground emerging between Louisiana elites and radical humanist *philosophes* in Europe.

Members of Louisiana's first creole generation did not re-create the old worlds of their parents. They formed new alliances that knitted them together in the intimacy of the home, the haggling of frontier markets, and the heat of the street. In contrast to the situation in many of the Spanish colonies, Louisiana's creole identity did not arise so much out of a resistance to metropolitan authority as out of an opportunism created by metropolitan neglect. The networks of relations and shared interests that the creole generation created in Louisiana set its members apart from those born in Africa, Europe, and preconquest America. These networks were still crosscut by internal divisions and inequalities, but even these were along new lines. In Louisiana, a social hierarchy arose fraught with its own tensions and divisions, distinct from those of the Old World. The French state had by its colonial policies intentionally tried to avoid the conflicts of the three estates system (clergy, nobility, and commoners) that plagued *ancien régime* society. However, in doing so it helped create a society that operated under such a different set of understandings that it drifted away from the social practices and political sentiments that wed the people to the king.[21] The crown's own experiments fostered one of the first colonial revolts against absolutism in the New World, the New Orleans Revolt of 1768.

New Orleans formed its own kind of "middle ground" in the lower Mississippi valley in the eighteenth century, which helped foment a strong creole identity in Louisiana.[22] The efforts of French designers to develop a civilized metropolis in the swamp actually helped create an environment where the colonial population could meet on new terms. Like many port cities, New Orleans fostered the interaction, negotiation, and refashioning of a diverse population. Among the French immigrants, a significant number of ex-convicts, exiled ne'er-do-wells (targets of *lettres de cachet*), and illegitimate orphans had strong personal motivations for reinventing themselves in the New World. Slaves and Afro-Louisianans had even more obvious motivations for carving a space of independent action, if not freedom, out of the busy ambiguities of a market town. To Native Americans, the urban environment was not necessarily a new experience, but it did represent an opportunity to bypass white middlemen in the Mississippian trade network, as well as a refuge of sorts for those individuals whose cultural group had been scattered by war or decimated by disease. In the founding generation, internal dissent among elites, the fact that most settlers were unwilling exiles, and the lukewarm support of the metropole meant that the authorities were not very effective in determining the rules of interaction. In the creole generations after 1731, the rise of a politically independent merchant–planter oligarchy and the daily operations of a pervasive smuggling economy further undercut metropolitan authority. New Orleans underwent a transition from a motley crew of adventurers and captives scrambling for position in a society with few clear structures to a place governed by violence, the social facts of slavery, and the strong will of local despots who eventually led a revolt against Bourbon rule. Between 1718 and 1768, Louisiana went from being a colony of rogues to a rogue colony.

The contribution of New Orleans to our developing image of modern empire has much to do with its timing. New Orleans was established at a high point of collaboration between the Enlightenment and French absolutism in the first decades of the eighteenth century. Both movements are identified with Louis XIV (reigned 1661–1715). Absolutism refers to the concentration of political power in one person, which Louis achieved through massive efforts to centralize the French state and its diverse provinces under one system, as well as numerous initiatives to weaken the power of the French parliamentary system, the Catholic Church, and the old noble families (*noblesse d'épée,* or "old sword nobility"). Although the late Enlightenment is associated with the French Revolution and regicide, its spirit of intellectualism had emerged a hundred years earlier under the direct patronage of Louis XIV. The Sun King generously funded and expanded the French Academy, the Royal Academy of Science, and the Academy of Painting. He also sponsored the training and development of a sophisticated corps of army engineers who exercised skills in mathematics, architecture, geography, urban planning, shipbuilding, navigation, astronomy, metalworking, and the development of new technologies. While many of these initiatives had been launched by Louis XIII and a series of remarkable seventeenth-century French ministers (Cardinal Richelieu, Cardinal Mazarin, and Jean-Baptiste Colbert), Louis XIV brought both absolutism and the French Enlightenment to full fruition. His achievements in both realms, as he fully intended, are symbolized in the construction of Versailles, which concentrated all the new offices of the state and court in a setting that expressed the rational aesthetics of the age in its symmetrical gardens and baroque chambers.

Louis XIV had laid claim to the territory of Louisiana when the explorer René-Robert Cavelier, Sieur de La Salle, reported back that he had successfully navigated down the Mississippi River from Canada and had established a cross and plaque at the river's mouth. La Salle was an impoverished lower noble from Rouen who had left the Jesuit order for the reason of "moral weakness" before immigrating to New France, where he engaged in land speculation and fur trading before lobbying the state to back a series of expeditions. The first effort to colonize Louisiana failed in 1685 when La Salle could not re-locate the mouth of the Mississippi from the Gulf of Mexico. No further attempts were made until the Canadian adventurer Pierre LeMoyne d'Iberville convinced the crown to try again. He brought a collection of French soldiers, Caribbean buccaneers, and Canadian *coureurs de bois* to the Gulf Coast in 1699. For the next decade and a half the colony continued to be little more than a small outpost in search of a decent mooring, moving between Biloxi, Dauphin Island, and Mobile under the leadership of Iberville's younger brother, Jean-Baptiste LeMoyne de Bienville. Called the "father of Louisiana," Bienville was to rule as governor or military commandant four times: 1701–13, 1716–17, 1718–25, and 1733–43.

In 1712 the ailing Louis XIV handed the rights and responsibilities for the colony (including its civil and military affairs) to a businessman named Antoine Crozat. Crozat began to fulfill his obligation to settle the colony, but his real interests lay in mining and trade with the Spanish; he never invested enough to spur significant immigration. When Louis XIV died in 1715, he was succeeded by his great-grandson, Louis XV. Since the young king was only five years old at the time, his grand-uncle Philippe, Duc d'Orléans, ruled in his name as regent until 1723. It was during the Duc d'Orléans's energetic leadership that the city of New Orleans was founded and thus named in his honor. Historian Gwynne Lewis refers to the 1718–23 period of the city's founding as "the authoritarian phase," during which the regent, with close advisers such as John Law, redoubled Louis XIV's early efforts to clamp down on the powers of the nobility and the French *parlements,* while at the same time attempting to "modernize" the economy and rescue the treasury from the appalling state in which Louis XIV's wars and luxuries had left it.[23]

It was the regent who handed over the Louisiana monopoly to John Law, a dynamic Scottish financier who virtually took over the entire French economy in the late 1710s after convincing his friend the regent that he could make both the state and penniless nobles rich once more. His ambitious financial scheme involved centralizing and tying together national banking operations, the royal treasury, and the colonial companies. The Mississippi Company was a stock-backed venture based on huge claims about the wealth to be made in Louisiana. Stock prices quickly soared, at first delighting the many noble purchasers who had been convinced to try their hand at capitalism for the first time. There was no separation of public and private venture. Law's bold plan was roughly the equivalent of a scheme to eliminate the U.S. budget deficit by selling stock in a government-owned company that held a monopoly on a new, untried technology; the ensuing financial flows would then be managed by a nationalized bank, returning additional profits to the state. This bank also managed the national budget for the military, public works, and all other state services and institutions. The liabilities as well as the revenues of the state and stock company were bound together. They would rise and fall together. Failure of such a clever, "modern" plan was inconceivable, but inevitable.

New Orleans was founded under Law and the regent in 1718 and became the colonial capital in 1722. During this period, French and African immigration to Louisiana began in earnest as investors advanced huge sums to ensure the colony's future, money that was funneled through the state-sponsored company monopoly. But it was too much, too fast. Stock plummeted from 15,000 French pounds (*livres*) a share to 500. The crash of John Law's multi-tiered financial scheme in late 1720 became known as the "Mississippi Bubble." A reorganized Company of the Indies continued to operate Louisiana until 1731. The Company surrendered its charter to the crown in 1731, but few French ministers retained any enthusiasm for the colonial project.[24]

Still, the legacy of the "Enlightened" absolutism of Louis XIV and the modernizing verve of the Regency was a creative push to colonize the Louisiana territory. A spirit of scientific experimentation and an impulse toward bureaucratic control went into planning not just the physical layout of New Orleans, but its social, political, and economic structures as well. Through engineering, mercantilism, census-taking, mapmaking, and natural history writing, French officials made an attempt not only to render Louisiana "legible" but also to track a grand colonial experiment, the outcome of which they only dimly imagined.[25] Their failure was due as much to a lack of follow-through as to state hubris. Their experimental, ambivalent steps illustrate an important phase in the development not only of modern colonialism, but also of modern statecraft. Although theorists such as James Scott, Benedict Anderson, and Michel Foucault have credited the eighteenth century with being a formative period for the articulation of modern forms of power, examples illustrating its contributions have been thin, or have focused on the late eighteenth century, when revolutions were already well under way. French Louisiana, and especially its capital town, provided a canvas upon which early sketches of modernism were drawn.²⁶

But focusing exclusively on planning and regulation would be a dry, short story in Louisiana. The colony was considered a failure so early (by 1731) that the rest of its history is largely a local story. Of course, local histories also contributed to the development of modernity. Eighteenth-century New Orleanians belong to the ranks of what Benedict Anderson calls "Creole Pioneers," those residents of the New World who developed a distinct cultural and social identity that propelled them toward political independence from Europe.²⁷ The intercolonial smuggling network developed by New Orleans creole pioneers helped break apart mercantilism, while plantation agriculture propelled capitalism into the countryside. Creoles, too, experimented—with new forms of representative government, discipline, and social classification. Although even their revolt can be termed a failure, its early date of 1768, at the dawn of the "Age of Revolution," is consistent with Louisiana's precocious, if halting, development.

New Orleans was a planned colonial city. French ministers intended to plant a "metropolis" in a remote and sparsely settled territory dominated by Native Americans. In recent years scholars in colonial studies have begun to address the questions of urban planning and social control in the colonies.²⁸ These studies have concentrated on the period of late imperialism, from the mid-nineteenth to the mid-twentieth century, when both colonial administration and urban planning were more self-consciously theorized activities than they had been in the eighteenth century. A capital city planned for a settlement colony at the height of the Enlightenment presents a different picture. New Orleans was meant to be a new and improved *French* city, not a city designed to control foreign natives. Creating a metropolis was considered a vital step to establishing an imperial hold on the territory. The idealism incorporated into the plan for New Orleans and the lessons learned from its implementation suggest an old and intimate relation between empire building and city planning.

As the example of urban planning indicates, there was an experimental quality to many of France's early policies toward Louisiana that contributed to a self-conscious accumulation of knowledge by Bourbon ministers and encyclopedists alike. A spirit of experimentation, observation, and knowledge building was a significant feature of the Louisiana experience. While ministers may have been learning the hard way how *not* to run a colony, they did strive to collect as much information as they could on the flora, fauna, and people of Louisiana. Thousands of official letters and reports flew from the pens of Louisianans to superiors and friends at court, many of them filled with natural history, ethnographic descriptions of Native Americans, and suggestions for the economic development of the colony. Specimens of cardinal feathers, native plants, and medicines were shipped back; so were Indians. Some colonists reported on their careful agronomy experiments with tobacco and silk crops; others wrote treatises on how to "manage" slaves. Printers in France published dozens of these *mémoires, histoires,* and letter collections, many of them showing the hand of metropolitan editors who viewed one colonist's account as the continuation of another's. The colonial narrative was a collaborative, accumulated *oeuvre.* Despite all this intellectual effort, Louisiana's critics often cited its policy-makers' "insufficient knowledge" of the region as an explanation for the colony's failure. Perhaps administrators learned more from their mistakes. The inquisitive, bureaucratic, and philosophical tendencies within *ancien régime* culture helped establish a substantial base of knowledge useful not only for its particularistic descriptions, but also for its ability to instruct the state on how to run a colony. The eighteenth century was an encyclopedic period critical to the development of later colonial regimes. In 1903, as France was attempting to complete its drawn-out conquest of Algeria, historian Marc de Villiers du Terrage prefaced his book on French Louisiana with these words: "Let us hope that these dissensions or similar rivalry will no longer hamper the development or, indeed, the maintenance of the French colonial empire. May this sad tableau [of Louisiana] . . . serve as a lesson to our fellow Frenchmen living in the new countries."[29]

Viewed over the long term, imperial schemes more often falter than result in total or even effective domination. Fissures in colonial control and "tensions of empire" create a complex relationship between metropole and colony. Fred Cooper and Ann Stoler observe that "colonial regimes were neither monolithic nor omnipotent. Closer investigation reveals competing agendas for using power, competing strategies for maintaining control, and doubts about the legitimacy of the venture." In eighteenth-century Louisiana, the colonial regime was particularly weak and the struggle for control particularly desperate.[30]

Although the political and economic designs for Louisiana, like other Atlantic colonies, possessed many elements of calculated cruelty in relation to Native Americans, Africans, and the laboring classes of Europe, and although these plans rarely accomplished what they set out to do, colonies were dynamic enterprises that moved and repositioned thousands of people. They did succeed in creating a new society, or at least a diverse population of peoples living under new conditions that eventually took on the sort of coherence and order we would call a society. What sort of society was created? What were the currents, factors, and processes of its formation?

Colonies do not simply import cultures, ideologies, economies, or political structures and recombine them. They create them. I am not saying colonial administrators or planners in the European metropolitan centers were the masters of creation. They played their role. However, many factors unforeseen and uncontrolled by those drawing up military plans and urban blueprints shaped colonial societies. It is the conditions of the colonies themselves that are generative, with multiple agents and creators participating, from Versailles ministers to local bureaucrats, Indian traders, field slaves, and baker's wives. Thus, I shall resist the tendency in colonial studies to credit the imperial center (in this case France, or more conceptually early modern Europe) with too much vision, intent, or even power.

The case of French colonial New Orleans has convinced me of three general points that I think are worthy of broader consideration in discussions about colonialism:

1. *Colonialism is fundamentally experimental and usually poorly controlled.* Although there is certainly variation across time and space in terms of how colonies were planned, ruled, and managed, recent critiques by David Scott and Fred Cooper have highlighted how those at the nominal political helm struggled to maintain control over the material returns of colonialism and even over the most basic ideologies of social inequality (savage/civilized, black/white) intended to underwrite it.[31] Even when they did have specific and well-backed designs for the colonies (such as the *Code Noir* and mercantilist policies of Jean-Baptiste Colbert), they often had to compete with other metropolitan advisers and schemers to get their plans enacted, or win arguments with peers who held opposing philosophies. As a result, colonial initiatives were halting, uncertain, often contradictory, and almost always experimental. Fred Cooper calls imperial power "thin" even in the later, more militarized initiatives in Asia and Africa in the nineteenth and twentieth centuries.[32] Due to this thinness, colonial representatives often failed to enforce policies or follow through with new policies. Rarely recognizing the scale of enforcement as the problem, distant metropolitan ministers would respond by faulting the original policy or the qualifications of the personnel sent to implement it. Influenced by competing ideas, another trial balloon would be floated, another method tried. Failures both big and small were endemic to colonialism. The parameters of the experiment were always being adjusted because the expected outcome was rarely achieved.

2. *Despite their frequent failures, early modern colonies of the seventeenth and eighteenth centuries were important laboratories for the package of ideas and practices we call modern statecraft (that is, bureaucracy, legibility, planning, centralization, applied science, and a highly ordered aesthetic).* Because colonial space was perceived as "virgin territory," state ambitions in social engineering and economic manipulation went far beyond what was thought

feasible at home. Although scholars frequently draw on parallels, precedents, and passing examples of modern statecraft and urban planning in the colonies, by and large the dominant narrative is that modernity originated in Europe and flowed outward to the colonies.[33] I think there is a strong case to be made for early and significant counter-flow. The difficulty has been that experiments in modernism were even more likely to be failed and short-lived in the colonies, so they have been left out of the dominant historical narrative. In some cases (though certainly not in that of Louisiana), the archival record of these developments can be ephemeral.

3. *Colonialism was as much a creation of rogues and independent agents as it was the project of imperial states.* It was actually rare for those at the center of state power (such as a monarch and his close advisers, high-level ministers, or powerful legislators) to take the initiative in launching colonial projects, and even rarer for them to pay close attention to how the projects were managed. "Colonial power" has become too abstracted and too overstated, in my view. Although colonialism, particularly in the Americas, is characterized by unfathomable depths of genocide and dehumanizing slavery, this brutality has too often been attributed to a nearly faceless state power located in Europe. In fact, these acts were perpetrated on the ground by local militias, slaveowners, and colonial administrators often acting on their own initiative and in pursuit of their own interests—in short, by private citizens and rogue politicians.[34] I argue that we need to reintroduce the explorers, conquistadors, and cavaliers into the colonial picture and understand in what ways they were agents of the state, and in what ways they were independent agents who manipulated the resources of the state. I want to bring them back in, not to romanticize them, as was done in an earlier historiographic era, but to look at them as dispassionately as possible to understand their role in the colonial experiment, whether in creating cultural strains of violence and repression, or in promoting entrepreneurialism and individualism.[35]

Beginning with Christopher Columbus and continuing with subsequent conquistadors as well as several generations of slave traders in Africa, actors whom we might call explorers, entrepreneurs, big men, and con artists were the most active and important agents in pushing colonial frontiers. Such descriptors fit nearly every high-placed operative in French Louisiana. In pursuit of their own personal interests and ambitions, they worked patronage networks within the European states to get ships, supplies, immigrants, and military backing. They sweet-talked, lobbied, bullshitted, bullied, and wheedled their way into the chambers of power, either directly or through letter writing, to sway European power-holders to value their colonial enterprise. Once they gained this backing, they may indeed have successfully created imperial ambitions and diplomatic embroilments (such as the new contest for territory and trade between France and England in the Americas that exploded with LaSalle's pushy exploration of the Mississippi River in the 1680s). The idea of rogue colonialism provides a way of thinking about forms of agency beyond and beside those that follow the transcript of "domination and resistance" between colonizers and the colonized. Rogues are improvisers. Improvised and "masterless" forms of agency were crucial to the founding, making, and undoing of colonies.

Grand political ambitions for the glory of king and country were secondary to the personal gain that motivated rogue agents on the ground. Once they received the backing that allowed them to secure a territory and establish an economic flow, their interests might become better integrated with those of the imperial center. But they could also begin to deviate more sharply from metropolitan direction. A roguish colony might then grow under the shadow of the official one, characterized by profits from smuggling, cooperation with imperial enemies, and/or a duplicitous disregard for official directives on how to civilize natives or build city walls. The different possible trajectories (diverging or converging) depended upon the contingencies of local conditions, personalities, and historical events. When local interests significantly diverged from those of the metropole and metropolitan powers attempted to rein in their rogue agents, resentful seeds of independence might begin to sprout. Counter-colonial impulses, syndicates, and pockets of resistance were as much part of the messy colonial story as metropolitan blueprints.

Intercolonial collaboration held out another set of possibilities. Rogue empires arose in the long eighteenth century. They were highly organized entities that channeled power, goods, and ideas over long distances, often using state resources and flowing along "official" circuits. Understanding how these networks articulated with official empire is important to our understanding of colonialism. There are many forms of power. They do not all emanate from a legitimate polity, or even a polity at all. Separating out legitimate business from illegal trading, or imperial power from criminal tyranny, is, upon closer inspection, a difficult task. Rogues and states were bound together in a volatile interdependency.

Examining documentary and artifactual evidence in this dark light reveals the trans-colonial circulations, organizations, and illegitimate forms of power that underlay official colonialism, sometimes abetting it and sometimes undermining it. As I will explore more fully in chapter 6, there are instructive parallels between rogue colonialism, banditry, and organized crime, particularly in relationship to revolutionary movements and the modern nation-state. The idea of rogue colonialism helps jump the gap between an overarching trend in colonial studies engaged with the scripts of domination emanating from imperial policies, and the common historical observation that many colonies "failed," or inadvertently nurtured the seeds of revolution. It also allows for other types of agency beyond the binary of despotic bureaucrats and romantic revolutionaries. These opposing caricatures are insufficient for portraying the motley crew that created colonialism.

While my first two general points about the experimental nature of colonialism and the impact of early colonial endeavors on modern statecraft are not yet common themes in the scholarship, I expect they will be accepted without great controversy. In contrast, my emphasis on "rogue colonialism" may be riskier, which is why I have given it more space here and develop the idea further in chapter 6.

In the chapters that follow, I look at the local elements of Enlightenment experimentation, creolization, and rogue colonialism within five realms: intellectual life and literary discourse, urban planning, trade, social status, and law. In chapter 1, I consider the ways in which people talked about and imagined New Orleans, and how certain words and ideas shaped its destiny before the first trees were felled. Its "disorder" was in part a literary creation. I look at the personal correspondence, official reports, and published accounts written on, to, and from New Orleans, with attention not only to content, but also to the material context of their making. The sheer volume of writing about New Orleans, and the themes regarding observation, experiment, and social critique running through it, show how much Louisiana participated in the movement we call the Enlightenment. It also demonstrates how the city's reputation for moral disorder was a joint production of *ancien régime* imaginings and local literary input.

The *ancien régime* had greater success in some areas than others in its attempts at control. The remaining chapters expose imperial blueprints and track various colonial experiments as they developed on the ground, first with the colonial founder generation, and then with the creole generations. As traced in chapter 2, many of the innovative plans for the urban design of New Orleans and its intended place in the territorial economy were realized, although designers had hoped the careful physical ordering of the town would have a more direct impact on the social order. In other areas, "disorder" and the failures of the crown were more complete. Chapter 3 argues that the original economic impetus for the establishment of Louisiana was a state monopoly on smuggling with the Spanish colonies. However, this monopoly was soon undercut by the activities of individual smugglers and profiteers (including several Louisiana governors) who created a significant black market in New Orleans. While multi-tiered, most of this activity was oriented toward the Gulf of Mexico and the Caribbean, funneled through the station at La Balize (meaning "beacon"), the port of New Orleans at the mouth of the Mississippi. New Orleans merchants not only violated exclusive privileges granted by the crown, they in some ways turned their backs on transatlantic trade altogether, subverting two of the basic principles of mercantilism.

Chapter 4 examines social engineering efforts, their effects, and the emergence of a creole social order. Early colonial administrators did a remarkable job of tracking the immigrant population by maintaining dossiers of identity through detailed, door-to-door censuses, precursors to later bureaucratic efforts in the nineteenth century. However, the censuses did not altogether freeze social status, nor did they prevent mobility. Free people of color and forced exiles were among those who found a niche in New Orleans that had not been envisioned by metropolitan planners, and whose numbers until now have been undercounted. The censuses, however, do document the ambitious self-fashioning of individual colonists and the evolution of new categories, both of which went into the creation of a new local hierarchy governed by an increasingly endogamous creole oligarchy of merchant–planters. Social positioning and class formation was a highly fraught process, as evidenced by libel cases from the New Orleans notarial archives.

Chapter 5 presents the French crown's experiments in law, justice, and political organization and several creole innovations in these same areas. Through Louisiana's *Code Noir* (the law regulating slavery) and the shifting strategies of colonial discipline we witness a divergence between the racial ideology of the state and the practices of slaveowners and freemen in the colony. One of the more puzzling failures of Louisiana's planners was the absence of a formal police force. Creole elites took justice into their own hands in the mid-1730s and also adopted legislative and executive powers never granted them, through their usurpation of the Louisiana Superior Council, the colony's governing body. During this period, New Orleans society became increasingly violent and the crown lost its monopoly over the terms of race and class. What seems to tie these trends together is the consolidation of a creole oligarchy increasingly invested in smuggling and slavery.

The political independence of this group turned to insubordination in the Revolt of 1768, an event I analyze in chapter 6, where I look back on the forces of Enlightenment engineering, creolization, and rogue colonialism that peaked during this moment of regime change. The revolt also invites us to look forward, to explore the idea of rogue colonialism and how it articulates with theories of crime, statehood, and revolution.

Although many French writers of the eighteenth century saved their strongest scorn for New Orleans, the entire colony of Louisiana shared a reputation for disorder. In fact, some collapsed the town and its territory into a single symbolic geography. This book will at times venture outside the city, but for the most part it focuses on residents of the colonial capital. The most important justification is that the historical actors themselves viewed New Orleans as the center of the colony's social, economic, and intellectual life, as well as the source for much of its "disorder." They also viewed it as an urban space, perhaps out of proportion to its small population, which probably numbered no more than 3,000 when the Spanish took over in 1769. Nevertheless, the town had a character quite distinct from that of settlements in the surrounding plantation zone or the "Indian country" of Louisiana's vast hinterland. In addition, New Orleans represented simultaneously one of the most deliberately planned aspects of the colony's development, and one of the least controlled, at least as viewed from the metropole. The flow of slaves, Native Americans, runaways, sailors, and soldiers into the town's markets, streets, and taverns created a colorful hustle and bustle that probably would have startled even the most worldly residents of France's port cities. The *petits gens* of New Orleans, or the "little people," as the French called the dispossessed and laboring classes, were an extremely diverse lot. Another reason to focus on New Orleans is its status as the center of the colony's administration and justice system, its communication network, and its economy. Of the colonial population, the majority of poor free people, and nearly all of Louisiana's elites, both French-born and creole, lived in town at least part of the year. Owning a townhouse in New Orleans distinguished a planter of means from a mere farmer.

French colonial New Orleans was what anthropologists call a "face to face" community, meaning that permanent residents probably recognized each other on the street and could quickly place one another within family trees and social geographies. It is a place where one can become reasonably intimate with the community through archives and artifacts. Its small scale makes historical ethnography feasible, giving us the means to imagine scenes of everyday life, peopled with a cast of familiar characters. In each of the chapters that follow, we are welcomed into this world by one of these real-life characters.

1

"A VERITABLE BABYLON"
Enlightenment and Disorder

"Les petits" are led along by the example of "les grands" and "les grands" have no power to repress the unruliness of "les petits" since they take part in the same disorders. This entire colony is a veritable Babylon.
⟊ Father Le Maire on Louisiana, 1717 (Bibliothèque Nationale, Ms. Fr. 12, fol. 105)

One of Louisiana's earliest intellectuals was also one of its most interesting characters: Father Le Maire, who spent fourteen years in Louisiana (1706–20). He had taken this missionary work out of a curiosity fostered by a mentor in Paris. Le Maire's secular leanings caused him to attend more to the temporal than to the spiritual world. He has been called by one historian "by far the best educated man in the colony." What Le Maire lacked in religious zeal he made up for in literary and scientific accomplishments. At least four *mémoires* and numerous sketch maps by his hand survive. These documents reveal an active mind concerned with colonial politics, Native Americans, flora and fauna, geography, and the potential of Louisiana to fulfill metropolitan dreams. The reportedly rotund and bearish priest had a keen sense of the value of his secular mission. In one of his *mémoires* he wrote, "I flatter myself, that I am the only one here to work on a natural history of Louisiana." His work in this field involved long descriptions of native plants and their uses, as well as an attempt to collect botanical specimens for the royal garden. Yet when it came to reporting on the colony's social and moral order, his facility for cool observation left him and he ranted on poetically about its "disorders." He is even accused of having written a scathing satire of members of the colony's military elite that became the basis for one of the top-selling novels of eighteenth-century France, Abbé Prévost's *Manon Lescaut*. Later the source for two famous operas, the plot moralizes on the dangers of licentiousness and experiments that jumble the social order. Its final tragic scenes are set in New Orleans.[1]

In 1717, when Father Le Maire was writing from "Louisiana Babylon," New Orleans was as yet a meager encampment located at an old Native American crossroads. As the settlement slowly acquired the urban character its planners intended, New Orleans became the subject of new comparisons to Babylon. Some residents and visitors described New Orleans as though carnival's lords of misrule reigned every day of the year. By the 1720s writers were characterizing the colony of Louisiana with a language of "failure" and "abandonment," although the colony was to survive another forty-five years under French rule. From the view of the metropole in Europe, Louisiana was a colonial experiment gone awry. Distracted by wars in Europe, pinched by financial worries, and discouraged by early difficulties, France was an ambivalent, if not "reluctant," imperialist in eighteenth-century North America.[2]

Despite the crown's wavering support for the colony, many French observers placed the blame for Louisiana's perceived failure upon its land and its people. In their eyes, the failure was in part a moral one. One anonymous writer described the "State of Louisiana" in 1720:

> I dare say that one should not be deluded into believing that it is possible to establish the colony with persons who were incapable of discipline in France, especially since it is noted that a man who was an excellent subject becomes a mediocre subject in America and a mediocre subject becomes very bad. We do not know the reason for this deterioration. Some attribute it to the food which does not have the same substance as in Europe, to a greater dissipation of the mind, or to other causes. Regardless of the reason, the fact is certain. What can one expect from a bunch of vagabonds and wrongdoers in a country where it is harder to repress licentiousness than in Europe?[3]

It is hard to imagine how the reputation of any colony could overcome such fatalism. What actually happened after the immigrants disembarked barely mattered.

Within ten years of its founding, New Orleans began to appear in literary descriptions as a dark, primitive, and abandoned place, governed by immoral pleasures rather than by rationality and law. The darkness resonates in derogatory comments of the day regarding the populace's lack of education or interest in letters. In these renderings, New Orleans is the shadow of Paris, "the city of light." Decay and ruin are omnipresent in descriptions of New Orleans. Observers as early as the 1730s described dilapidated buildings sagging under vines and sinking into mud. They then made a quick literary leap from architecture to society, implying that New Orleans had been in a state of moral and intellectual decline almost from its inception. Indeed, its time of youth and innocence were quite brief. The bursting of John Law's Mississippi Bubble in the early 1720s, the Natchez War of 1729, periodic food shortages and epidemics, and a policy of exiling French convicts, orphans, and elite delinquents to Louisiana had all done their damage to the colony's reputation. In just over a decade, New Orleans had plummeted in the French imagination from an aspiring "opulent metropolis" to an untamed and degraded outpost.

These oft-told stories tend to overshadow the ways in which the French created New Orleans in a spirit of Enlightenment experimentation. The unrealistically high expectations they placed on this new kind of colonial capital were almost destined to be disappointed. After France had ceded Louisiana to Spain, the *philosophe* and historian Abbé Raynal wrote with sad retrospection: "Louisiana has shared the fate of those extraordinary men who have been too highly extolled, and are afterwards punished for this unmerited fame, by being degraded below their real worth . . . This enchanted country was now held in execration. Its name became a name of disgrace."[4] The tropes of abandonment and decay speak more to French perceptions of a failed experiment than to life in New Orleans, which was soon thriving with a vivacious jumbling of peoples coming and going through a far-reaching Mississippi–Caribbean network.

The questions I pursue in this chapter pull at the order/disorder thread, drawing it back to its sources to help us understand eighteenth-century modes of thought. How did New Orleans acquire a reputation for "disorder" so early in its colonial history? What did "disorder" mean to eighteenth-century observers? To what degree did this perception reflect the metropole's own internal anxieties? To what degree did it reflect Louisiana's deviation from an imperial plan? Answering these questions requires putting a remote colonial town back into the context of the *ancien régime* and its ongoing experiments in eliminating disorder of various kinds. It requires understanding the mentality of Enlightened absolutism. The result is a curious juxtaposition between the dark and disorderly reputation of New Orleans and its Enlightenment intellectual practices. If academics and *philosophes* had not taken such a genuine interest in the colony, both on the ground and from the armchair, it probably would not have been scrutinized and critiqued quite so thoroughly. As this chapter will show, New Orleans was an intellectual experiment and this was the very condition that informed its disorderly reputation. It is important to underscore the connection between colonial Louisiana and the Enlightenment because otherwise we can easily be seduced into thinking New Orleans *was* a savage other-world that fell off the map of modernity.

Désordre (disorder) was a word used with increasing frequency in the *ancien régime*, indexing an Enlightenment-era desire to classify, organize, and rationalize the natural world, to order society, and to discipline the individual. The *Dictionnaire de l'Académie française* of 1798 offered six definitions of *désordre*: (1) disarray of things without rank or organization; (2) disarray of the moral order; (3) depravity of a person; (4) confusion of the mind; (5) pillage and havoc; and (6) unexpected dissension in a group. The compilers also noted that it was occasionally used in a poetic sense—*désordre lyrique, un beau désordre.*[5]

The public image of New Orleans in the French period seemed to reflect all these forms of disorder. Under the influence of the "disorder" vocabulary embedded in the archive, the historians of Louisiana have used a language of disorder, misrule, and failure to describe the colony's social, political, and economic conditions. Struggles for control and stories of things not going exactly according to plan form a trope running through Louisiana historiography dating back at least to Gayarré's *Louisiana: Its Colonial History and Romance* (1851). Works such as Herbert Asbury's *The French Quarter: An Informal History of the New Orleans' Underworld* (1938) reiterated the sensationalism of *Manon Lescaut* 200 years later, reinscribing the city's licentious image for a new generation. Contemporary historians cannot escape the disorder theme in one form or another. Most seem to agree that it refers to a disconnect between metropolitan expectations and local developments in French Louisiana, or to a particularly inept effort to install colonial power.[6]

I do not fundamentally disagree with these characterizations. There was certainly a straying from imperial plans, at least those conceived within the halls of Versailles. However, I would argue that the intentions of major agents on the ground, such as those of the famous LeMoyne brothers (Sieurs d'Iberville and Bienville), were actually quite successfully enacted, and that by the second generation of settlement Louisiana had a functioning social hierarchy, political structure, and economic system. None of these, though, followed the approved blueprints for colonialism as imagined in France. As will become apparent in chapter 3, although they acted with legitimate titles, Iberville and Bienville were among the most roguish of early colonials.

Examining how these disorder narratives arose and were circulated is key to understanding the construction of New Orleans as a dark place, and how this reputation helped widen the gap between European idealism and American pragmatism in the colonial endeavor. It would be simple to say that Louisiana's roguish early Canadian founders created the town's reputation through their actions. And it is just one more step from there to say that rogue colonialism emerged in Louisiana after Europe abandoned the colony to a throng of criminal characters. But the relationship between reputation and on-the-ground possibilities is more complex. In some ways, the disorder trope applied to New Orleans was prefigured before the first tree was felled, attributable to forces within French culture that had little concern with colonial realities. Once launched, however, the rogue reputation could be useful in attracting smuggling business and in creating a political separation between metropolitan ministers and local agents. Time and again diligent officials (particularly those filling the role of *ordonnateur*, the colony's chief financial officer) held back from getting their hands dirty in a reputedly corrupt operation. But by holding back, they allowed local interests to evolve ever further into an independent, if not seditious, political economy.

New Orleans was from its beginning rife with tensions between an *ancien régime* dream of order that administrators attempted to impose, and a social jumbling characteristic of both frontiers and cities. The terms that Le Maire used to describe the basic social order, divided between "*les grands*" and "*les petits*," created a distinction approximating "elites" and "commoners." *Les grands* encompassed the first two privileged estates (or recognized classes) from the medieval Etats-Généraux system of France, the clergy and the nobility, but was probably also meant to include wealthy merchants and landed *bourgeois* who were on their way to becoming noble. In France, *les petits gens*, or the laboring classes (literally, "the little people"), technically belonged to the Third Estate of commoners along with wealthy and influential nonnobles. However, in the eighteenth century the French increasingly viewed the tripartite class system as anachronistic.[7] In Louisiana the crown's own policies bound together bureaucrats, noble military officers, large landholders, wholesale merchants, missionaries, and trading company employees as colonial administrators—*les grands*. As a group, this new amalgamated class was set above *les petits gens*, who in New Orleans comprised an unfamiliar mixture of soldiers, slaves, Indians, ex-convicts, and "vagabonds" of all kinds. To Le Maire's outrage, even the most basic social boundary—that between *les petits* and *les grands*—became blurred within the ranks of Louisiana's "deteriorated" subjects.

New Orleans was not alone in its reputation for "disorder" and "licentiousness." Colonial life was often imagined as such by distant observers in the metropole, as well as a few on the ground. Contemporary literature depicted colonies such as Saint Domingue, Mauritius, Jamaica, and even New France (Canada) as sites of moral corruption, sexual promiscuity, cultural degeneration, and social chaos. Literary critic Doris Garraway argues that French colonialism and Caribbean slavery were partly the products of European sexual longing. Thus, many contemporaries equated "creolization" with descent into moral disorder, the result of primitive passions and illicit liaisons.[8] But the colonies were not the only sites of imagined moral and social corruption. A growing number of critics in the eighteenth century saw the cities of Europe as dark, out-of-control places. Rapid urbanization had caused a reshuffling of population in ways not unlike that of colonization. Although the scale of urban living meant that strangers were always about, in the eighteenth century cities suddenly became densely populated by diverse and displaced people uncertain of their neighbors. Cities became synonymous with disorder, an anxiety that (as we will see in chapter 2) prompted the birth of urban planning as a discipline in the same period.

Some of the disorders that administrators complained about in the colony were identical to those they complained about in the homeland—wanderers, smugglers, loose women, bickering clerics, corrupt bureaucrats, vicious political intrigues, and uncontrolled borders. Early eighteenth-century France was tense with class conflicts, religious rebellions, and major transformations.[9] The French exported some of these domestic problems to the colony, and projected others onto it with exaggerated shadows. The colonial situation did bring about new types of perceived "disorder" as a result of slavery, racial and ethnic diversity, and the large number of soldiers permanently stationed in a civilian town. But since the perception of *désordre* comes from the language and thoughts of eighteenth-century Frenchmen, I will try to refrain from evaluating whether or not the colony actually *was* a "disorderly" place according to some contemporary understanding. It is probably impossible to establish any agreement on criteria for measuring "orderliness." Interestingly, the handful of non-French visitors who wrote about New Orleans in the early period did not comment so much upon its disorder as upon its provincialism.[10]

Complaints about the reign of disorder dogged New Orleans throughout the French period. A 1722 report on Louisiana by a French military commander pointed to collusion between a corrupt Canadian governor (Bienville) and a rabble of criminal immigrants and pirates:

> The Company as well as the colonists are plundered without mercy and restraint; revolts and desertions among the troops are authorized and sanctioned; arsonists who commit whole camps, posts, settlements, and warehouses to the flames for the purpose of pillage remain unpunished; prisoners of war are forced to become sailors in the service of the Company, and by either criminal negligence or conspiracy they are allowed to run away with ships loaded with merchandise; other vessels are purposely run aground or wrecked, their cargoes lost to their owners; forgers, robbers, and murderers are secure of impunity. In short, this is a country which, to the shame of

France let it be said, is without religion, without justice, without discipline, without order, and without police.[11]

Although complaints about disorder in New Orleans persisted throughout the French period, they reflected a shifting set of worries and a rotating cast of perceived troublemakers. In the early years, French administrators worried most about the "disorders" of the town's *petits gens*—its slaves, sailors, convicts, and indentured servants. They fretted over moral and criminal disorder, fraternization, and the maintenance of class distinctions. These preoccupations reflected the absolute monarchy's efforts to gain more thorough social control in France itself. But by the 1750s and 1760s, what alarmed metropolitan ministers more than the disorders of *les petits* were the disorders of *les grands* in the colony. Complaints came to focus on the malfeasance of local officials and a general spirit of "insubordination and independence." These worries may have contributed to France's decision to transfer Louisiana to Spain. The first Spanish governor of Louisiana reported in 1768 that "the inhabitants of that colony live in an independence so general that once a man retires to his home he sees himself as absolute lord without subjection to any authority. From this is born the liberty that reigns among them to do whatever they wish and treat their superior with so little respect that he is governor in name only."[12]

In that same year the colony's local governing board, the Louisiana Superior Council, launched the ultimate disorder by revolting against the new Spanish governor and expelling him from the colony. The rebels printed and distributed in New Orleans several "manifestos" appealing to theories of popular sovereignty, natural rights, and the benefits of free trade, clearly influenced not only by self-interest, but also by late Enlightenment *philosophes* such as Rousseau and Diderot. The most radical among the New Orleans rebels pushed for an independent republic.

To understand the impact that literary images and the disorder discourse had on New Orleans, one must be willing to place the colonies firmly within the Enlightenment and the Republic of Letters. By "Enlightenment," I do not mean any set body of ideas or literature; rather, I mean a self-conscious social movement dating from the reign of Louis XIV in the late seventeenth century until the French Revolution in 1789. This movement involved an exploding literacy rate and an almost evangelical belief that any problem (moral, political, technical, or social) could be solved with the application of knowledge and human ingenuity. Although in critical hindsight the Enlightenment tends to be associated with protoscientific rationality and the rise of bureaucratic modernity (and thus wrongly conflated with one of its major chapters, "the Age of Reason"), humanist and romantic strains were also present, represented most famously by the writings of Jean-Jacques Rousseau. The Enlightenment, which French-speaking contemporaries referred to as Les Lumières (The Lights), was first and foremost a social movement. Knowledge-building and the formation of new ideas were imagined to be collaborative efforts that took place in salons, coffeehouses, and the social space of an international community of letter-writers which participants referred to as the Republic of Letters.[13]

Eighteenth-century France was a place where intellectualism was *en vogue* and individuals with ambition considered themselves philosophers, scientists, and writers. Those bound for Louisiana were no exception. They appreciated that the colonial experience would present opportunities to apply their observational skills. They hoped it would produce interesting material for letters, reports, travel accounts, even novels, which would be eagerly consumed back home. Some prepared for their journey by reading from a proliferating literature on Louisiana. A generation before the ground for New Orleans was cleared, La Salle's explorations of the Mississippi Valley in the 1680s had produced at least ten well-circulated accounts, some factual, some plagiaristic, some truer to fiction.

When New Orleans became established as Louisiana's capital, it became a frontier of the Republic of Letters—the community of readers and writers knitted together by common debates and shared knowledge of the latest publications. In France, members met in coffeehouses and salons, but they also carried on dialogues across space by letter writing and the wide circulation of manuscripts and publications. As in present-day online communities, participants could be fairly well known to one another and carry on lively conversations without ever meeting face to face. They could spawn artistic or political movements without meeting in the same room. The spaces of this community crossed national and linguistic borders (such as that between France and Switzerland or France and England). This, the first Republic of the Enlightenment era, also spread across the Atlantic.[14]

French New Orleans was an outpost of the Republic of Letters. It was Louisiana's port for the importing and exporting of books, ideas, letters, news, and learned people. Quite literally, Louisianans lived and died by the words written on paper letters sealed with red wax. The writing of letters and reports formed one of the most important infrastructures of colonialism. As we shall see, the town had its share of colonials who fancied themselves men of letters participating in a great experiment, or living out the plot of a gallant novel. Many of these same literary and scientific activities ended up contributing to the colony's reputation for disorder. Titillating narratives of disorder seeped into the "science fiction" of colonial literature as metropolitans filtered colonial reports through their own fantasies.[15] Uncontrolled letter writing carried news reports about political dissension and economic anarchy in Louisiana. And no amount of "natural history" could yield mastery over a formidable river and a volatile climate.

In this chapter, I draw out the ways in which Louisianans participated in the Enlightenment's intellectual community and how different forms of literature created, corrected, and recycled the public image of New Orleans. Many colonists arrived with scientific missions or propensities that encouraged them to approach life in the New World explicitly as a knowledge-gathering and experimental endeavor. They constructed libraries, laboratories, and observatories, and wrote encyclopedic natural histories. Louisiana colonists helped create a new genre in the eighteenth century, pasting together *mémoires*, letters, military reports, natural history descriptions, and travel accounts into a useful kit of colonial knowledge called *une histoire*, or "history." Literate colonists also participated passionately in France's developing epistolary culture through private and official letter writing. Contrary to their reputation for darkness and ignorance in the years of "abandonment" after 1731, New Orleanians provided for the education of creole children both at home and in Europe. Through their children, correspondents, and growing libraries, New Orleanians maintained ties to a Republic of Letters that was becoming increasingly critical of the French state. The participation of Louisianans in Enlightenment practices reveals how colonialism was an explicitly experimental and intellectual endeavor, and how the colonial experience in turn informed public discourse and intellectual debates in Europe.

Libraries, Laboratories, and Observatories

At the time New Orleans was founded during the regency, efforts were being made to investigate and document the colonies of France. As Regent, the Duc d'Orleans took an interest in geography, the natural sciences, and travel writing. In the 1710s he backed a scientific voyage to the West Indies to record the region's natural history, while he ordered the king's doctors in Québec and other colonies to send back botanical specimens. The Ministry of the Marine launched several new map-making expeditions to Canada, Guyana, the Canaries, and the Windward Islands during the same period.[16] The colonization of Louisiana coincided with this movement, heightening an intellectual curiosity about France's newest colonial endeavor and demanding extensive documentation of its progress. In a cartouche from a royal almanac made for 1720, "Missisipy" (as the Louisiana endeavor was

FIGURE 1. Detail from lithograph in royal almanac showing "Missisipy" flanked by figures of Arts and Sciences, 1720. (Courtesy of Bibliothèque nationale de France, Estampes et Photographie, IFN-6700387.)

popularly called) is flanked by the reclining figures of Arts and Sciences, an allegory expressing the fact that the colony was imagined as an absolutist intellectual experiment (fig. 1).

Many of Louisiana's original administrators, concessionaires (or land-grant planters), and military officers were well-educated petty nobles or bourgeois who applied their knowledge and training to establishing a colony in the new world. They brought their books. They built laboratories and observatories. Ministers and Company officials selected some of these individuals specifically for their academic talents. As will be discussed in chapter 2, engineers educated in drafting, cartography, mathematics, and architecture played a vital role in mapping the colony and designing New Orleans. They were among a significant number of men and women in Louisiana who saw it as their duty to design, observe, experiment, and record the colony. Some explicitly viewed their colonial work in Enlightenment terms. Many kept up an active correspondence with friends and families in France. Others, either by request or on their own initiative, kept daily journals of their experiences, some of which were transformed into literary or scientific publications consumed avidly in the metropole. Members of Louisiana's literate class participated in an active investigation of the lands, environment, peoples, and potentials of France's vast new province. Many followed directives from the crown or sponsors. Intelligence gathering and knowledge building were important components of the colonization project. But the task was monumental. When attempting to explain Louisiana's failures, both colonials and metropolitans cited "inadequate knowledge" as a leading cause, although they undoubtedly had different ideas about where the gaps lay.

Louisiana was a topic of interest in Parisian salons in the 1710s and 1720s. Le Maire's efforts in cartography allow us to see how the circuit of knowledge flowed through both formal and informal channels. Le Maire was a devoted letter writer, and it was through his personal correspondence with Father Jean Bobé, a chaplain at Versailles, that his work was passed on to the court. His skillful maps of the uncharted Gulf Coast made their way to the respected Delisle brothers' mapmaking house. In the eighteenth century, mapmakers were not simply craftsmen, they "were regarded as leading figures in Parisian intellectual circles." From the early 1700s to the late 1720s the Delisles published nearly a dozen maps of Louisiana, many credited to Le Maire, to satisfy a growing intellectual and popular fascination. Due in part to the influence of Le Maire and the Delisle brothers, Louisiana began to "outclass the older colonies in the mind of the world of learning."[17]

Another man of letters with inclinations toward natural history was Alexandre Viel, a surgeon and botanist whose pharmaceutical "experiments" were encouraged by royal authorities. Beginning his sojourn at the Kolly concession on the Gulf Coast in 1720, he was reassigned to New Orleans in 1723. From there he corresponded with "savants of the Académie des Sciences and the Jardin Royal in Paris concerning plant life in Louisiana."[18] He set up a laboratory and study garden in New Orleans to test the efficacy of botanical remedies. Other men acted on their own initiative to study and record the colony. Both the concessionaire Le Page du Pratz and the soldier Dumont de Montigny included long natural history sections in their published *histoires.* Entries for many of the species include notes on medical uses or the best methods for cultivation. While they undoubtedly collected some of this information from Native Americans and other settlers, they each designated one of the outbuildings on their plantations as a "laboratory," where they passed much of their time experimenting, writing, and drawing.

Ironically, the one person sent to the colony with the sole mission to conduct scientific research never did publish his findings. The Royal Academy of Sciences appointed Pierre Baron in 1727 to go to Louisiana and "make observations on astronomy and navigation and to conduct research on plants, vegetation, minerals, and all matters concerning natural history." He quickly got sidetracked in the capital when his superior, Governor Étienne de Périer, appointed him engineer and architect in the city. Baron is credited with the architectural design of the original Ursuline Convent and the prison on the Place d'Armes, among the few monumental buildings in the early city. In 1730 he built his own house in New Orleans, which contemporaries referred to as L'Observatoire (The Observatory), due to two unusual lookout alcoves built into the second floor, where he positioned telescopes

FIGURE 2. Pierre Baron's house in New Orleans, called "L'Observatoire." One of the two observation alcoves is visible, marked with arrow. (FR.ANOM. Aix-en-Provence. F3/290/20. All rights reserved.)

for stargazing (fig. 2). Baron said in a letter to the Minister of the Marine that he spent his days building and his nights examining the skies. From his lookouts he also had an unobstructed view of the center of the city and a large decorative garden he shared with the governor's residence. New Orleans visitor Caillot said of Baron: "This is a man of superior intelligence who lives like a true philosopher, not taking the trouble to do anything else but think." Baron considered himself an Enlightened architect of the colony. He embodies the colonial impulses both to study and to build. New Orleans itself was an observatory over the rest of the colony, from which the powerful and the erudite could conduct their studies.[19]

No public libraries, bookstores, or printing presses operated in New Orleans until near the end of the French period, but literate colonists did bring books with them to the New World. The founding sisters of the Ursuline Convent brought numerous volumes of religious and philosophical texts on their first voyage; other works were sent later from France. Individuals such as Viel and Baron undoubtedly carried personal libraries in their luggage. At least one of the early engineers must have brought French engineering and architecture books, for many New Orleans buildings and Louisiana fortifications follow published structures so well, they appear to have been cut from a pattern book. Even minor officers such as Dumont de Montigny brought reading material with them and shared it with their friends. Dumont tells of being attacked by a lone Chickasaw hunter while reading a book under a tree in the woods. Some of these books may have been books about Louisiana itself. Years earlier, during his explorations of the Gulf, Iberville packed two books claimed to be based on the earlier La Salle expeditions. In his journal, Iberville complains bitterly about the authors' bad sense of geography. In fact, these accounts by Hennepin and the "false" Tonti were a mixture of poor plagiarism and pure fiction.[20]

The size and content of private colonial libraries proves that spending thirty years in a remote outpost did not prevent colonials from continuing their education, nor from imbibing the most current thinking in the metropole. Estate inventories of major Louisiana concessions taken between 1729 and 1769 list collections of books and pamphlets numbering from 36 to 300.[21] The most impressive inventory from the later French period belongs to Jean-Baptiste Prévost (not to be confused with Abbé Prévost, the author of *Manon Lescaut*). J.-B. Prévost began his colonial career in New Orleans as an agent of the Company, but grew wealthy through his own business ventures. When he died in 1769, Prévost left a library of over 300 volumes. The collection is remarkable for the selection of titles associated with the Enlightenment, especially political works credited with laying the cultural ground of the French Revolution. They include Locke's *Essay on Human Understanding* in a French translation, Montesquieu's *L'Esprit des loix*, and Françoise de Grafigny's *Lettres d'une Péruvienne*.[22] Also present is a pamphlet with the intriguing title *Patriotisme ameriquain* (American Patriotism). The library shows a depth and breadth not only of topics, but also of dates of publication, with some published just a few years before Prévost's death. Perhaps unsurprising given their popularity in France, as well as the ingenuity of the members of the New Orleans smuggling economy, at least ten of these books were outlawed by the crown at the time of the Prévost inventory. This rogue literature included Rousseau's *Emile* (1762) and *Oeuvres* (1756), Voltaire's *Oeuvres* (1728), Crébillon's *Oeuvres* (c. 1763), *Testament politique* (1762), and *Secret de l'ordre des franc-maçons* (1745).[23]

Via legitimate or illegitimate trade, books were clearly making their way across the Atlantic to this so-called "illiterate outpost." So, too, were metropolitan images of Louisiana itself. Prévost over the years had collected twenty volumes of the literary magazine *Le Mercure* from the 1750s onward, which frequently featured pieces on the colonies. He also owned a title, *Relation de la Louisiane*, which could be one of several books on Louisiana published between the 1710s and 1750s.[24] Prévost stayed current with European literary and philosophical trends by importing reading material, but he also maintained a lively correspondence with friends and family in France. His inventory lists several bundles of letters stacked in his office. Prévost was not unusual among Louisiana's literate elite for whom letter writing was a favorite pastime.

Colonial Letter Writing

Letters—whether official, private, secret, or open broadsides to the public—were a vital part of colonial life, perhaps even more so than in France, where literate members of society were in the throes of an epistolary craze. Given Louisiana's small number of troops and the sparseness of settlements, letters sent from the outposts to the capital were the main administrative tool the governor and *ordonnateur* had for coordinating diplomatic and military efforts. Likewise, letters to the Ministry of the Marine, the Company of the Indies, or influential friends and family were the means by which colonists attempted to curry favor, affect policy, seek material aid, and broker business deals. In both personal and official accounts of Louisiana, so many references are made to letters written, sent, and received, that one gets the impression of a postal deluge emanating from the colony. In fact, the French colonies' "volume of correspondence far outstrips England's contact with its colonies." In 1713 alone, over 700 official letters passed between France and its American colonies, while the parallel British correspondence averaged just 52 per year.[25] The dependency upon letter writing for long-distance absolutism meant that colonial administration was a particularly literate affair. Letter writing was also the method through which many colonials participated in dialogues with other members of the Republic of Letters despite their remote location. Letters had the capacity to collapse the geographical space between colony and metropole along social, intellectual, and political lines.

French Louisianans were avid letter writers. They often complained that metropolitan friends did not reciprocate in kind. Colonials anxiously waited for responses and sent multiple copies of their letters in hopes of a speedy response. Many letters begin with an allusion to this lopsided state of communication. For example, Jean-Charles de Pradel, writing to his brother in response to a family letter that took eight months to arrive, noted: "You must have already received many of mine [letters], since I have written via all the ships. The arrival of this ship that we have been expecting a long time, gives us an unspeakable joy."[26]

Colonial *mémoires* often mention how travelers headed from outlying settlements to New Orleans were expected to collect letters from the communities along their route. In town, residents anticipated the arrival of ships with great excitement, not only for the provisions and informal news carried by the crew, but for the anticipated packet of letters from colleagues, superiors, and family members. The departure of a ship was no less momentous, as all those who could write hurried to finish letters on their own account as well as for illiterate acquaintances who dictated their messages.[27]

Homesickness and an insecurity in the colonial situation undoubtedly enhanced the importance of personal correspondence. Letters helped maintain both logistical and sentimental ties to the continent. In Louisiana's climate of political dissension, letters served as appeals to a higher court, channeling attempts to resolve conflicts or thwart foes. Letters to patrons substituted for the personal audience at court, and they were the means through which Louisiana's *ordonnateurs* and governors fought their many battles. A convincingly written letter addressed to the right person could, and sometimes did, reverse political fortunes in Louisiana.

The *mémoire*-writer Dumont de Montigny had a special appreciation for the importance of the letter in colonial politics. After he inadvertently insulted Governor Bienville, both men raced to write letters to their sympathizers at court. Dumont appealed to a metropolitan superior to mitigate the effects of having angered the colony's senior official; Bienville wanted his vengeful actions interpreted as reasonable and appropriate. Similarly, when Dumont got into hot water with his supervisor, the engineer Le Blond de la Tour, they also engaged in an indirect epistolary duel, both writing to the Minister of War, Le Blanc. The minister wrote back, probably with some annoyance, that the two "complain well of one another." Dumont later learned that Delatour had intercepted his letter to the court and as a result had crafted a plan to demote him. Although Dumont undoubtedly felt persecuted by powerful figures in the administration, the interception of letters, which he says occurred to him personally on this and at least one other occasion, was not the figment of a paranoid imagination. Le Page du Pratz took the trouble of traveling from Natchez to New Orleans in order "to send my letters to France myself, which I was certainly informed, were generally intercepted." On another occasion, Dumont was carrying a packet of letters for various people from the upriver posts down to New Orleans when his boat overturned. The names on the envelopes were washed out and unreadable. In a solemn ceremony, he burned the letters and had witnesses sign a formal document attesting that no one had read their contents. He did this, he said, because there could have been dire political consequences if letters were delivered into the wrong hands.[28]

Information, like cargo, could be legitimate or smuggled, inspected or pirated. A remarkable account of the importance of colonial letters in shaping public opinion of Louisiana comes from an event that occurred on a return voyage Dumont made to France in 1719. After his ship docked in Port Louis on the coast of Brittany, officials from the Company of the Indies (then in control of operations in Louisiana) prevented anyone from leaving or boarding the ship. They ordered the passengers and crew to turn over all the letters they were carrying. Dumont said their purpose in doing so was

> to see if anyone had spoken badly of the country. Mr. de Valdeterre [Dumont's travel companion] had many letters, and I too had some. All of us were quite surprised by such an order. Each one went to obey. By each one I mean, sailors, cabin boys, carpenters, and others. But as for me, upon this announcement, I began to think of how I could be exempt from this order. I went down [below deck] and opened my trunk and took out my letters and those of Mr. De Valdeterre and his journals as well, I put them in two fat bundles and put them in an envelope, addressing them to Megr. Le Blanc, Minister of War, and I put these two packets back in the trunk. I calmly went back up deck, without letting anything show in my face. A short moment later, Mr. de Saint Martine asked me if I didn't also have some packets of letters. I responded yes, but that it was necessary that I deliver them myself by my own hand, it being customary. This took him aback and he demanded the key to my trunk. Making protests of one kind and another, in the end I brought up the two packets. I said to him, "Monsieur, for handing them over to you, give me not only a receipt, but also the weight, so that I can inform Mr. Le Blanc, my patron." He looked at me and said, "You are affiliated with the Minister?" "Yes, Monsieur," I responded. "Ah, in your case, you can keep the packets, letters to such persons are exempt." It was thus through a little trick of deception that I saved not only four or five letters than I had but more than 80 belonging to Mr. de Valdeterre and others.[29]

This interception and attempted censorship of letters going between Louisiana and the Continent underscores what a powerful tool they could be in shaping a colony's fortune or sealing its fate. Representatives were perhaps attempting not only to intercept politically damaging letters to important figures such as Le Blanc (though they were thwarted in this case), but also to monitor personal correspondence in order to manage public opinion back in France. Dumont's shock at the order suggests that such personal correspondence was normally (in France) considered private. It is also notable just how many letters travelers were carrying—between them, Dumont and Valdeterre had at least eighty-four. Assuming that other passengers and crew (including the lowly cabin boys who could act as couriers even if they could not read) carried at least a few letters each, one imagines that the diligent Mr. de Saint Martine and his staff had a formidable task of combing through hundreds, if not thousands, of letters before allowing the passengers to complete their journey. This example demonstrates how port cities acted as custom houses of information. New Orleans, as one of those cities on the French colonial route, was the port of information for all of Louisiana.

Jean-Charles Pradel's letters to his family in France, preserved in the family château and published in 1928, compose a remarkable portrait of colonial life. Pradel was a younger son of a struggling noble family. He began his colonial career as a cadet in the navy, but eventually became a private colonial entrepreneur, amassing one of the largest estates in Louisiana through his import/export business. Through his letters he cajoled, begged, and sweet-talked his older brother in France to act as a backer and agent for his business deals. His correspondence comprises a mixture of business dealings and family affairs. Most of his fifty-four surviving letters from Louisiana span the years from 1729 to 1762.[30] However, many letters are missing, and since the collection does not include letters Pradel sent to friends or associates, it probably represents but a small fraction of his total correspondence. Pradel often wrote letters to the same person just days apart, never missing an opportunity to send a letter on an Atlantic-bound ship since he did not know when the next one would arrive. Official transatlantic ship arrivals in New Orleans fluctuated wildly due to wars in Europe and economic downturns—one year only four vessels docked, while another year new ships arrived almost weekly.

Pradel was among the more literate members of the New Orleans establishment. He attended the Collège Saint-Michel in Paris until age twenty-one, and many of his letters are ornamented with literary references. As he became more secure in his finances, his letters reflected a keen curiosity about the latest economic theories and political happenings in France. He requested that his family send him books, and he carried on epistolary conversations with his brother about their contents. He shared these books with his children. And when the children were old enough, he sent them to France for further education; from this, his number of correspondents grew.

Although Pradel's letters were not published until the twentieth century, many letters from Louisiana were transformed into literature during the French regime. In the early period, it is difficult to separate letters from literature. The Jesuit *Relations*, widely read throughout Europe since the late sixteenth century, were a serialized collection of letters from Jesuit missionaries used to promote the activities of the order. The *Relations* were arguably Europe's earliest genre of colonial literature and as such they undoubtedly influenced subsequent forms.[31] The transformation of colonial letters into published accounts also reflects the popularity of epistolary tracts and novels, which began to take off in France not long after La Salle's exploration of the Mississippi in the 1680s and continued up through the French Revolution.

Science Fiction and Natural History

French scholar John Carpenter remarked in 1966 that "the literary production of Louisiana resembles modern works of science fiction: they represent a very curious melange of the genres of travel account and utopian novel." The strands of fiction and fact, of fantasy and science, that went into writing about Louisiana can be difficult to disentangle, but it is important to understand how literary currents rippled back to the shores of the Gulf. Fiction could be as powerful as fact in driving policy, making fortunes, or ruining lives—in short, in writing colonialism. Novelists and colonial historians wrote with "imperial eyes," to use Mary Louise Pratt's term for a set of common European perspectives on colonized peoples and places, although in Bourbon France there were also many who wrote with "anti-imperial" eyes.[32]

Considering the relatively small population of Louisiana and its reputed illiteracy, the dozens of known journals, reports, discovery accounts, and histories the colony produced, from Marquette's 1673 exploration of the upper Mississippi to the end of the French regime, is remarkable.[33] Some of these were published soon after they were written, while others were circulated in manuscript form, but became well enough known to be plagiarized and cited by continental authors. The impulse to record created a complex colonial genre that may be distinguished from travel writing by its forward-looking character. While writing about the "present state of Louisiana," many authors were also trying to imagine or promote a future state, resulting in a "science fiction" or "utopian" quality.

It is important to understand how Louisiana literature responded to metropolitan demands and took shape within a transatlantic dialogue. In some cases, writers contributed to an appetite for stories of disorder and mishap, and in others they attempted to "correct" the French public's misconceptions and poor opinion of Louisiana. Several Louisiana writers saw themselves not so much as contributing to a local tradition as participating in the cosmopolitan Republic of Letters.

Taking a close look at Louisiana's early literature helps us see the strands of science and fiction that went into constructing the public image of New Orleans. In terms of the volume of publications, the Company period marks the high point of literary production on Louisiana, spanning the years from about 1717 to 1731. Some of these writings were purely promotional, produced by associates of John Law and the crown to attract investors and colonizers. Others had more of a journalistic quality through their attempts to investigate and report back on how the venture was going. Some took the form of adventurous picaresques that allowed their authors to play out fantasies in an exotic place. By the early eighteenth century, French travel writing had already begun to depict the colonies of the West Indies as "libertine" places of laziness, indulgent drinking and eating, and a racially charged sexuality. These qualities were even more likely to be ascribed to creoles than to first-generation settlers. Thus, the reputation of New Orleans as a place of debauch and disorder was in some ways scripted long before the streets were laid down.[34]

Two structural features of the writing from this period are remarkable: nearly all works were written in the epistolary form, and the majority were addressed to women, suggesting that Louisiana was a fashionable topic in Parisian salons at the time. Women were important navigators of this cultural institution. In addition, writing to a female correspondent allowed male writers to exhibit their gallantry. In the French imagination, Louisiana provided an appropriate setting for noble adventure.[35]

One of the earliest examples from this period demonstrates how ambiguous the lines could be between journalism, promotional tract, and epistolary picaresque. A long article appeared in a February 1718 edition of *Le Mercure de France*, written in the form of a letter from an officer to a lady. It gave a detailed description of the geography, natural resources, and economic potential of the colony. The author speaks of the active pelt trade, lists useful animal and tree species, reports the existence of gold and silver mines in Illinois country, and mentions the possibility of a huge silk industry. Louisiana would be "one of the most beautiful and fertile countries of the world, if the inhabitants work hard to take of advantage of what it can offer."[36] The *Mercure* author ends with an imaginary stroll with his lady through the "garden" of Louisiana. "Before leaving Louisiana, permit me, Madame, to take us on a promenade of five or six leagues through a charming terrain. In a woods where we are walking we come upon grapevines and wild indigo that hardly need to be cultivated, and then come to a hill or find ourselves in a vast plain agreeable with its lush greenness and variety of flowers, or then along the banks of an infinite number of creeks and streams that flow to the river. You will see that Nature has not lavished its treasures and charms on our Europe alone."[37] The colony is already a picturesque garden rather than an imposing wilderness.

Two full-length accounts of journeys to Louisiana written soon after this article in *Le Mercure* use the same form—letters from an officer to a lady. As evidence that the epistolary form was part of both the fantasy and the reality of the colonial experience, one of these was a fictional account, and one appears to be the actual private correspondence between a ship captain and a female friend. The first, written in 1720 by the fictitious "Chevalier de Bonrepos," is a plagiaristic composite of previously published and well-circulated relations. The author's aim appears to be to summarize the current state of knowledge of the colony in a digestible form, highlighting its most interesting features. The opening lines suggest that his readership is the salon: "You want, then, to shine among the ladies of your clique and show your wit in speaking knowledgably about the Mississippi cause which now is so much the talk of the Companies, in the hope that the Realm will draw immense profits from its commerce."[38]

Written the same year, though not published until a generation later, Vallette de Laudun's *Journal d'un voyage à la Louisiane, fait en 1720 par M. ***, capitaine de vaisseau du Roi* also takes the form of a long letter to a female friend, organized as a diary. The author makes references throughout the letters to her request for a detailed account of his journey, and he apologizes for the "dryness" that characterizes a sailor's journal.[39] His correspondent is either a wife or a lover; he closes many of his entries with a poetic reference to love or comments how jealous he is that she might be dancing with other men. It is clear that she is active in the salon scene. When he mentions the Tropics of Cancer and Capricorn, he instructs her to check with a mutual friend (identified as "Madame X***") to learn what these are. Vallette occasionally spices up his daily lists of onboard happenings with dramatic storms and encounters with other ships that cast him in a heroic light.

Although given to some literary exaggeration, Vallette is not himself an invention. He was the actual captain of the *Toulouse*, which made a 1720 trip to Louisiana. Despite the publisher's emphasis on the final destination, the great majority of Vallette's entries date from his Atlantic crossing and stops at other ports of call. When he did arrive in Louisiana, he was forced to stay several weeks due to illness among the crew and a lack of provisions in the warehouses. The authenticity of his account is confirmed by the sad dissonance he finds between the propaganda of the Company and the hungry and diseased settlements he sees during his layover on the Gulf Coast. Although he remains optimistic about the agricultural and mining prospects for the colony, he summarizes his disappointment with urbane irony: "Regarding the balconies and the ladies that ornament them, you can hardly overlook the fact that these are purely imaginary things . . . All the houses are of wood and have but a single story."[40]

Vallette does do his best to investigate the state of the country, though he must rely on secondhand accounts for the interior. He can see that things are not going according to plan. The Company had deposited great numbers of colonists, both rich and poor, on Louisiana's coastline, supplying them with dreams of gold and little else. He evaluates the situation in a combination of economic and moral terms: "[W]hen one has too vast a vision, one neglects the essentials. It seems to me that one must apply oneself principally to two things: the first is the cultivation of the land which then requires people who know about this, and not to send, as has been done until now, forçats and bandits who are good for nothing . . . The colony could subsist on its own with maize, rice, and vegetables planted there."[41] Vallette's call for agricultural investment is a repeated motif in the Louisiana literature, but the emphasis on subsistence and food crops (as opposed to profit crops, such as tobacco or sugar) really begins with the Law-period collapse, which Vallette witnessed firsthand. He was concerned that too many criminals and smugglers were being sent to the colony and he (somewhat naively) did not believe they could help the colony's economy. While he believed that the "excessive heat" had caused the sickness he witnessed, Vallette is less sanguine about environmental causes of another rumored medical condition: "It is said as well that the Europeans transplanted to this country become sterile. If that were the case, the colony could not long survive. I believe rather that the women sent here are so unhealthy and ill-used by trysts they have had that they were sterile even before they left."[42]

Vallette shows us that already in 1720 two theories were forming to explain Louisiana's failure. The first held that it could be blamed on a particularly inhospitable province of Nature where flooding, disease, and heat sabotaged efforts to build a respectable community. The second claimed that the colony represented a moral failure on the part of the French themselves—the blame falling not only on loose women in Louisiana, but also on the men who sent them there. How could France expect an orderly colony when it was peopled with criminal rejects from the home country? Vallette was not the last to express concern about the moral quality of Louisiana's immigrants, and its women in particular.

The first book published by a New Orleans resident was that of the young Ursuline nun, Marie-Madeleine Hachard, whose arrival scene opened the introduction. Like Vallette, Hachard wrote letters at the request of a continental correspondent. Her father had asked her to send detailed reports of her journey and experiences in the colony. He apparently had intentions of publishing her letters from the very beginning, perhaps excited by the association of Louisiana with his native town of Rouen through one of its most famous sons, the explorer Robert de la Salle. Monsieur Hachard published his daughter's first five letters within one year of her arrival in New Orleans in 1727. In her letters, the twenty-three-year-old Hachard (also known as Sister Stanislas) provides an account of her travels and a description of New Orleans. Her letters combine her own reflections on the morality and educational needs of the city's residents with specific responses to her father's queries. Among the latter are an account of local La Salle lore, an inventory of the colony's natural resources, and an assessment of its economic potential. Hachard was enthusiastic about her vocation to serve New Orleans for the rest of her life, and she clearly wanted both her mission and the colony to succeed. Some of her passages sound like straightforward promotion, echoing the *Mercure* articles: "[I]f the soil were cultivated, there would not be any better in the world." Other passages make it clear that the Ursuline sisters had their work cut out for them in terms of "correcting" the town's moral disorders.[43]

Hachard's firsthand descriptions of New Orleans alternate from "very pretty, well constructed and regularly built" to a place where women wear so much makeup that "the devil here possesses a large empire." While certainly her father and the reading public were curious about the colony's landscape and potential, she may have also been appealing to their appetite for scandal and the exotic. Hachard painted scenes for an immorality play, set in a city that residents proudly compared to Paris in the lyrics of a local song. Before she ever arrived, she expected to encounter a scene of "disorder." She says that on at least two occasions before her arrival, the nuns had been told things that gave them a bad impression of the city and the "corrupt and scandalous" conduct of the lay populace.[44] After living in the city for some months, she confirmed these rumors through her own anecdotes and commentary. One passage is particularly striking: "[N]ot only do debauchery, godlessness, and all other vices reign here more than elsewhere, but they reign with an immeasurable abundance! As for the girls of bad conduct, they are watched closely and severely punished by being placed on a wooden horse and flogged by all the soldiers of the Regiment that guards our city. In spite of all this there are still more of these women than would fill a house of refuge."[45] Hachard claimed that the town was overrun with prostitutes and loose women. It is difficult to assess whether this passage reflects reality, Hachard's own anxieties, or her readers' appetite for titillation.[46]

"New Orleans is the place to come to," I often told Manon, *"for people who want the true joys of love."*[47] A book published just three years after Hachard's account provides further evidence that the French public had formed an idea of New Orleans as a place where passions ran wild. The novel *Histoire du chevalier DesGrieux et de Manon Lescaut* was the most widely read book about Louisiana in the eighteenth century. It was published in 1731 by a man who had never been there, Abbé Antoine-François Prévost. The story begins in France and ends in New Orleans. Given that even Iberville had trouble distinguishing between real and fictional accounts of Louisiana, the influence of this novel on New Orleans cannot be discounted. *Manon*

Lescaut deserves a place in this discussion for what it tells us about the public image of New Orleans in 1731, an image that the novel helped perpetuate for decades to come.[48]

Prévost's introduction to New Orleans, in fact, resembles a classic arrival scene from historic ethnographies and travel accounts, only with a twist—here "the natives" are abandoned fellow countrymen. Prévost's description combines facts garnered from travel accounts and the workings of his own imagination.

> After a two-month voyage, we finally reached the desired shore. At first sight the land had nothing pleasant to offer, just barren, uninhabited expanses with no more than a few reeds and some trees stripped by the wind. Not a sign of man or beast. However, once some of our cannon were fired on the captain's orders, it wasn't long before we saw a troop of citizens from New Orleans coming towards us with visible signs of joy. We hadn't seen the town, which is hidden from the sea by a small hill.
>
> We were received as if we'd descended from heaven. These poor people crowded around us, asking endless questions about the state of France and the various provinces where they'd been born. They embraced us as their brothers and dear companions who'd come to share their poverty and solitude. We made for the town in their company but were surprised to discover, as we got nearer, that what had been portrayed to us until then as a flourishing township was nothing but a collection of mean cabins occupied by five or six hundred people in all. The Governor's house appeared to be slightly distinguished from the rest by its height and situation, having earthworks and a large circular ditch to defend it.[49]

Prévost intends to disabuse his readers of the image of New Orleans offered by Law's propaganda in *Le Mercure*. Rather than a sparkling city, it was a lonely hamlet of ramshackle huts. As expressed through its architectural inadequacies, New Orleans failed as a capital to provide three things essential to the name: protection, power, or culture. It even failed to provide that most simple of urban amenities, a salve for loneliness. New Orleans was a disappointment. The pathetic arrival scene foreshadows Manon's tragic ending, but Prévost's tableau merely fleshed out a reputation New Orleans had already acquired. His poetic associations would have been less effective without an established referent.

While Prévost showed his ignorance of the colony's geography (there are no hills within fifty miles of New Orleans), he chose Louisiana not for its physical landscape but for its moral climate. It provided the perfect setting for his story of adultery, downfall, and social isolation. *Manon Lescaut* is the story of a gullible young man of noble birth, named DesGrieux, who falls passionately in love with a professional consort, a feminine rogue. Despite the fact that she quickly moves on to conquer wealthier men in her pursuit of luxury, he remains faithful and follows her. His constancy eventually wins her true heart as he becomes embroiled in her schemes. After escapades, duels, and stints in prison, she is eventually put on a ship to Louisiana as one of the women of "ill repute" to be sent to the colony. He books passage, determined to free her. He convinces first the ship's captain, and then the governor of the colony, that they are actually married. Manon and DesGrieux then live for several months free and blissful in the colony.

When speaking of the anticipated journey to Louisiana, DesGrieux says that the colony will be a better setting for their "natural love." This he knows from reading accounts of the colony:

> I imagined us already in some wilderness inhabited by savages. "I'm quite sure," I said, "no savage could be as cruel as G*** M*** and my father. At least they'll let us live in peace. If what people say of them is true, they observe the laws of nature. The furies of avarice which possess G*** M*** and the fantastic notions of honour which have turned my father into my enemy are quite unknown to them. They won't trouble two lovers leading as simple a life as theirs."[50]

The two lovers never do encounter any Indians. They do not need to because New Orleans possessed the same "natural savage" character as the Indians. In the French imagination, savagery and the colonial city were barely distinguishable.

> America . . . seemed to me a land of sheer delight. "New Orleans is the place to come to," I often told Manon, "for people who want the true joys of love. It's here that people love each other without self-interest, jealousy or infidelity. Our fellow countrymen come here looking for gold. It doesn't occur to them that we've found treasures which are far more worthwhile."[51]

Prévost was writing ten years after the John Law debacle. A critique of the quixotic search for gold in Louisiana began soon after investors in France and adventurers in the colony faced the realities of the collapse. It became one of several repeated motifs in Louisiana literature. Most authors, like Hachard and Laudun, suggested that true Louisiana "gold" lay in the land— that the rich fertility of the Mississippi Valley could be the source of agricultural riches if properly worked. Prévost, though, had his character say that Louisiana's treasure is less tangible—a city of "natural love" where colonists can give free rein to their hearts and their passions. This freedom of the heart was permitted by the social disorder of New Orleans, where rank became muddled and identity was more self-determined. DesGrieux elsewhere says that it is "in America, where we depend on no one but ourselves, where we don't have to worry about the arbitrary rules of rank and deco-rum."[52] The perceived disorder of New Orleans satisfied an Enlightenment fantasy about natural love in a society free of strict hierarchies.

But the savage city had a dark side. DesGrieux and Manon were not the only ones free to let their passions rule. Other inhabitants were possessed by passions of a more brutal kind. When desires come into conflict, the powerful, not the romantic, win. Hachard's image of a place where women are both marketed and abused haunts the background of DesGrieux's story. Upon their ship's arrival, he describes how the governor "one after the other, looked over all the women who had come on our ship . . . After examining them at length, he sent for various young men from the town who had long been waiting for wives. He gave the prettiest women to the most promi-nent men and the rest were drawn by lot." The governor plays the protec-tor of DesGrieux and Manon until he discovers that the two are not legally married. Since his nephew has been smitten with her beauty, he decides to "reassign" Manon. The chaplain informs DesGrieux that the governor is "absolute master here." DesGrieux then realizes that the governor is a "bar-barian," not the noble kind of savage. This "obstinate tyrant" believes that Manon is "at his disposal." The loneliness of New Orleans reemerges: "We found ourselves in New Orleans as if in the midst of the ocean, separated from the rest of the world by vast expanses. Where could we seek refuge in a land that was unknown, deserted or inhabited by ferocious beasts and equally fierce savages?"[53] Manon and DesGrieux find that they are not quite as savage as other New Orleans inhabitants. They decide to flee and live among the Indians, making their way toward the English colonies. But just six miles outside the city, Manon falters and dies. She was not equipped to live outside her dream of urban luxury.

Manon is a tale about passion, scams, false hopes, futile efforts, and the consequences of living in "social disorder," as DesGrieux himself calls their affair. The two are not only exiles *in* New Orleans, they *are* New Orleans.

Histoires

By the 1740s the founding generation had grown gray enough to deserve a history. We begin to see a formal coalescence of colonial knowledge through compendia called *Histoires*, published by Charlevoix, Dumont-Mascrier, and Le Page du Pratz between 1744 and 1758. Bossu's two works, dating to 1768 and 1771, although entitled *Voyages*, also belong to this group because he published retrospectively, after Louisiana had been ceded to Spain. He relates his experiences as travel through a place of the past. The writings of these authors provide further evidence of the experimental and intellectual nature of colonialism, and in two cases, its roguish qualities as well.

The French term *histoire* should be understood in its double meaning as both "story" and "history." Although these works share certain formal characteristics, they are not exactly "histories" in the contemporary sense. Each of the authors spent a period of time in the colonies, from two years for Charlevoix to nearly twenty years for Dumont. Their works combine, to a varying degree, autobiography, travel narrative, natural history, and colonial how-to manual. Despite the individual personalities of the authors, as a set these works represent a group effort. Paraphrasing, borrowing, and outright plagiarism create a complex field of authorship. This literary repetition demonstrates a desire to collect, reorganize, and emphasize an essential set of facts and recommendations on the colony. Despite their plagiarisms, the authors do at times dispute with one another in an effort to assert "truths" and correct misconceptions. And despite their disagreements, they are working toward a consensus on the colonial project. Both this spirit of skepticism and the shared goal of accumulating a useful body of knowledge signal that Louisiana continued to participate in the Enlightenment during its encyclopedic phase, despite the negative publicity of the Law-period literature. These colonial authors were minor *philosophes* who presented their knowledge and experience in the literary fashions of the day, and also contributed to important debates.

In Louisiana's eighteenth-century *histoires*, we see a gradual accumulation of ideas, lore, and facts about the colony. Many of the opinions and recommendations of the authors arise directly out of their colonial experience. But through time a *philosophe* influence becomes more tangible, particularly where the texts touch on natural history, economic policy, despotism, civilization/savagery, child rearing, and paternalistic slavery. These Enlightenment themes in the Louisiana literature, as well as the influence of this literature on writers such as Raynal and Diderot, have been addressed in other studies, although the richness of the intellectual dialogue between colony and metropole has yet to be fully explored.[54] My goal here is to look more specifically at how these *histoires* show New Orleans as both an Enlightenment experiment and a roguish corner of empire. To differing extents, these *histoires* advanced a collaborative project of knowledge building at the same time that they provided new evidence of the ways in which life in New Orleans deviated from an ideal colonial order. Some of these "disorders," such as an embrace of free trade and a spirit of insubordination against "despotic" governors, had revolutionary overtones that resonated with *philosophe* critiques of Bourbon France coming to the fore in the mid-eighteenth century. Recognition of these Enlightenment connections helps us reposition the town at the center of Enlightenment thinking, not at the periphery where it has usually been placed.

I focus my discussion on the three historians who were long-term residents of lower Louisiana: Dumont, Le Page du Pratz, and Bossu. (Charlevoix was a through-traveler who expanded his account with armchair history.) Their work displays a common desire to serve the public with a complete, truthful, and useful account of the colony. Yet we can see that these men attempted to live out different fantasies of colonialism. Le Page was a naturalist living out the experiment. Dumont and Bossu imagined themselves as gallants living out a picaresque. For each, committing their experiences to paper completed the fantasy.

DUMONT

A self-described noble *forçat*, Dumont had a rakish sense of humor, a quick temper, and, as we might put it today, problems with authority. Well educated and politically well connected, but of uncertain nobility and little wealth, he was a man extremely sensitive to matters of status, *honneur*, and gentlemanly conduct. Beset by one misfortune after another, usually imposed by Mother Nature or his villainous archenemy, Governor Bienville, Dumont perseveres sometimes heroically, sometimes pathetically with his clothes in tatters, being resurrected when someone recognizes his good name or rewards his conduct as an *honnête homme*. Dumont consciously strives after a literary effect. At the beginning of his text, he introduces himself as a *"un robinson françois"*—a French Robinson Crusoe.[55] Having returned to France after being shipwrecked (both literally and figuratively) for many years during which he lived by his wits alone, he offers his protector a "confession" of his life and an entertaining account of the "island."[56] His autobiographical narrative moves through one adventure, or more often misadventure, after another. They include many of the key events in early Louisiana history, such as the attack on Spanish Pensacola, the establishment of New Orleans, a 1722 hurricane, devastating epidemics, the development of the Natchez post, and the Chickasaw campaign of the 1730s.[57]

Dumont's literary activities are part and parcel of his self-image as a nobleman.[58] His happiest days were those spent at the Yazoo post when he was able to enjoy the leisure of an officer's life, which he spent drawing, reading, and working in the garden. Dumont proudly tells how he entertains others with his poetry. As mentioned above, his plantation house downriver from town included a "laboratory" (or private study) where his books, drawings, and papers were kept. His manuscripts are illustrated with watercolor drawings of New Orleans, the posts where he served, exotic Louisiana fauna such as alligators and rattlesnakes, and Native American musical instruments (color plates 1 and 2). Dumont clearly enjoyed the process of writing an autobiography, but he was also conscious that his readers wanted an account of the resources of the country and the customs of Native Americans. He dutifully added a long section toward the end of the manuscript that provides these, though it exudes a love of pleasure rather than scientific curiosity. His descriptions of Native Americans emphasize their physical appearance and arts. Almost all his descriptions of plants and animals include a review of their taste and texture, and many include a recipe.

Dumont's description of New Orleans occurs in passages associated with the early 1720s, but it is architecturally a pastiche of his twenty years there. He sings the praises of the town that he claims to have helped build: "New Orleans [is] now the capital of the whole country. It can with reason carry this name because of its beauties: pretty and well-built buildings all in brick or half-brick, its perfectly straight streets . . . The Place d'Armes is quite attractive and spacious, surrounded by fat square posts set side by side and gates between, facing the square is the parish church managed by the Capuchin fathers . . . [I]n a word, it is well arranged and divided, and well built, but not at all fortified."[59] Dumont soon goes on to describe how a visit to the city cured him of a fever (possibly malaria) that had racked his body for nineteen months. Dumont's "cure" may have been his own invention, but his depiction of town life celebrates its pleasures. He eats a good meal of salad and curdled milk, then drinks "at least" two bottles of Bordeaux wine and smokes three or four pipes of tobacco while taking large gulps of the local crude rum called *eau de vie*. After vomiting violently for two days, he finds his body purged of its illness.[60] In contrast to Laudun, where the local climate exacerbates the ill effects of a libertine life, the pursuit of pleasure in New Orleans "cures" Dumont.

LE PAGE DU PRATZ

Antoine Simon Le Page du Pratz (c. 1695–1775) arrived in Louisiana in 1718 at the age of twenty-three to seek his fortune as one of John Law's concessionaires. He stayed sixteen years, at first on his own tobacco plantation at Natchez and later as manager of the king's plantation across the river from New Orleans. Years after his return to France in 1734, he began to write memoirs of his colonial experience, culminating in the 1758 publication of *Histoire de la Louisiane*.[61]

As a minor man of letters, Le Page provides a rare view of the colonies informed both by his personal experience and by Enlightenment ideas. Other than what he himself provides in *Histoire de la Louisiane*, we have little biographical information on Le Page. We know that he graduated from a French *cours de mathématiques* and that he considered himself a professional architect and engineer. Le Page's writing is sober and precise, and his intellectual orientation tends towards natural science. His only other known published work is a treatise on astronomy.[62] His *Histoire de la Louisiane* comprises three volumes covering French colonial activities and military campaigns, Louisiana's natural history and economic potential, and descriptions of the customs and conditions of Native Americans in the region, particularly of the Natchez, among whom he lived for many years. Le Page was generally optimistic about prospects for economic development of the colony and provided detailed descriptions and recommendations for tobacco and indigo cultivation, as well as silk and tar production.

Where Dumont's frame of reference was Robinson Crusoe, Le Page uses the language of reason and clearly places himself within French salon life. In his original preface, Le Page positions his work as a correction to the rumors and false impressions of Louisiana that have biased the "République des Lettres" (his own words) against the colony and misled learned men about its properties and possibilities. Le Page offers instead, he tells us, "researches, observations, discoveries and experiences." Le Page often cites his wish that his work be "useful to the Public." For him, however, learning comes not only out of the practice of letters, but out of experience and living in the world. It is literally earthy: "The Enlightenment that I came to acquire during my travels in the country was aided greatly by knowing the nature of the soils in Louisiana."[63]

Le Page's description of New Orleans is rather dry and engineer-like, simply describing the layout of the town, its principal buildings, and the system of levees and ditches designed to keep it drained. He rarely mentions French settlers or politics, although he is politely critical of Bienville's choice of the site for New Orleans and his handling of Indian affairs. His true feelings surface briefly when he relates how he lost his post as manager of the king's plantation due to a "sycophant," coincident with Bienville's return as governor in 1734. When he does mention Louisiana colonists, Le Page generally praises them in terms as favorable as those he uses to describe the natural climate, which he insists is beautiful and fertile. He argues explicitly against the impression of want and starvation that prevailed in France, saying the colony never once experienced food scarcity during his whole time there. He also discounts the impression that Louisiana's French minority were at the mercy of bellicose natives and their own unruly populace: "[T]he settlers, by their martial character, and their zeal for their king and country, aided by a few troops, commanded, above all, by good officers . . . will be always match enough for the Indians."[64]

Drawing on his experience as a colonist, Le Page was an early advocate of physiocracy, an economic philosophy of the late Enlightenment that advocated agriculture and free trade as the keys to true wealth. The wealth of Louisiana lies in its natural fertility (he calls it "the most fertile colony in the whole world") and in its potential to produce—under conditions of free trade—tobacco, indigo, fruit, silk, wax, and other products that France might otherwise import from foreign sources. He rejects the mercantilist idea of a colonial "mine" of wealth for the mother country, both literally and figuratively: "A country fertile in men, in productions of the earth, and in necessary metals, is infinitely preferable to countries from which men draw gold, silver, and diamonds . . . I therefore boldly aver, that Louisiana, well governed, would not long fail to fulfil all I have advanced about it."[65]

No doubt, Le Page was in part reacting against the John Law debacle and the shadow it cast over the colony in the French imagination. But his devotion to agriculture ran deep. During his time in Louisiana, he actively experimented with different ways of growing and processing tobacco, and his detailed botanical descriptions have earned him a place among America's early naturalists.

According to Le Page, only the lack of "good government" stood in the way of Louisiana's prosperity. By good government he meant free trade, support of agriculture, population increase, and some "inventive and industrious geniuses" from Europe to make it all work.[66] Perhaps what Louisiana needed more than anything else was the steadfast dedication of more men of letters like himself.

BOSSU

Jean-Bernard Bossu served as a military officer in Louisiana from 1751 to 1762, primarily in Arkansas, Illinois, and Alabama. In 1768 he published his first book, *Nouveaux Voyages aux Indes Occidentales*, which, despite its broad title, mainly describes his Louisiana experience.[67] Bossu presented his work as a series of published letters in the genre of an epistolary travel account, although he incorporated several historical events he could not have witnessed, and borrowed liberally from Le Page du Pratz on subjects such as Natchez culture and the 1729 uprising. His writing has picaresque and libelous characteristics akin to those of Dumont. His text contains several stories meant to amuse and titillate, about superstitious Native Americans, charming women, drunken mishaps, and sodomy. Still, Bossu was even more explicitly allied to a *philosophe* point of view and an Enlightenment vocabulary than was Le Page du Pratz. He speaks in terms reminiscent of Rousseau about "natural law," "natural sentiment," and "natural understanding" that he witnessed among Louisiana Indians.

Bossu attempts to correct some misconceptions about Louisiana and emphasizes positive attributes such as its fertility and the sophistication of both its Native American and creole inhabitants. In other ways, though, his purpose was to write an exposé of the disorders reigning at the top of the administration and the colony's deep involvement in smuggling.

At several points in the text, Bossu implies that Governor Kerlérec's character was less than upstanding and that his malfeasance had caused mutinies, shortages, and difficulties with the Indians. Bossu depicts him as aiding and abetting not only smugglers, but pirates who boarded ships and raided cargoes with insufficient legal cause. His attacks on Kérlerec's "criminal depotism" caused Bossu to be hauled into the Bastille almost immediately after his book's first printing of 2,000 copies. The Paris police searched and seized his private papers, looking for evidence of collaboration with other accused Louisiana libelists, Bossu's friends Grondel, D'Erneville, and the creole Marigny de Mandeville. These men also wrote *mémoires* on Louisiana, but their works did not meet with the same popularity as Bossu's. In his papers, police found a copy of an undated letter from Bossu defending his decision to publish on the grounds of "liberty" and the "rights of citizens." The police also added to his dossier a review from *Le Mercure de France* dated April 1768. The reviewer thought the natural history sections and accounts of Native Americans to be complete and useful. He also appreciated Bossu's "simple" style: "After all the romances that have appeared under the title 'Accounts of the Mississippi,' it is a pleasure to see a work in which the author speaks only of what he has seen and hesitates to abuse the truth by ornamenting it." While the reviewer seems to have been taken in by Bossu's "simplicity," he found a grain of desirable truth in Bossu's revisionism and political critique.[68]

Bossu presented New Orleans as a place already well known to his French readers. But he revised its image, depicting it as a healthy, thriving creole city. Upon his arrival he wrote to his correspondent,

> I shall describe the capital of Louisiana, but I do not think that it is necessary to speak of the city at length, since you are doubtless familiar with most of the maps and articles published on it. I simply want to call to your attention that New Orleans, with its well-laid-out streets, is bigger and more heavily populated today than formerly. There are four types of inhabitants: Europeans, Indians, Africans, and Negroes, and half bloods, born of Europeans and savages native to the country.
>
> Those born of French fathers and French, or European, mothers are called Creoles . . .

This country offers a delightful life to the merchants, artisans, and foreigners who inhabit it because of its healthful climate, its fertile soil, and its beautiful site. The city is situated on the banks of the Mississippi, one of the biggest rivers in the world, which flows through eight hundred leagues of explored country. Its pure and delicious waters* flow forty leagues among numerous plantations, which offer a delightful scene on both banks of the river, where there is a great deal of hunting, fishing, and other pleasures of life.

*[This water also has the power to increase fertility in women].[69]

The city was no longer the *bicoque*, or shabby shanty town, of earlier writers. Merchants, artisans, and foreigners people the streets, as they should in any successful port city. Its waters are healthy and its women fertile rather than overused and sterile. In contrast to the sickly founder generation of criminals and depraved Frenchmen, creoles are robust and inclined toward Enlightenment: "They are generally very brave, tall, and well built and have a natural inclination toward the arts and sciences. Since these studies cannot be pursued very well because of the shortage of good teachers, rich and well-intentioned fathers send their children to France, the best school for all things."[70] Bossu offered a counter to the prevailing ideas that creoles were both ignorant and isolated.

Creole Education

The anti-intellectualism of colonial New Orleans is one of the stratigraphic myths of the city, built layer by layer over the years. The city's supposed lack of interest in the mind was only natural for a place so engaged in the pleasures of the body. One of the most prominent contributors to this myth was Thomas Jefferson, who in his *Account of Louisiana* stated that "[n]ot more than half of the inhabitants are supposed to be able to read and write; of whom not more than 200, perhaps are able to do it well."[71] Jefferson wrote this at the end of Spanish rule (1803), although other observers credited the Spanish for having improved educational opportunities through publicly funded schools. Many historians have supposed that conditions under the French must have been even worse. However, other scholars have examined the history of education in colonial Louisiana and found evidence that a significant proportion of colonial Louisianans were interested in education and literacy. The town's literacy rate compares quite favorably to *ancien régime* France and other Catholic communities of the period.[72]

Jefferson's numbers are a dubious exaggeration. Thirty-four years earlier, just before the Spanish takeover in 1769, the New Orleans rebels printed 300 copies of their manifesto to be distributed around the town, which at that time was one-third the size of Jefferson's New Orleans. The imprint presumed a minimum readership of 300 individuals, or at least 15 percent of the free population. Considering that neighbors and literate members of the same household would probably have shared copies, the readership of this one document was probably higher. Thomas Ingersoll found in a sample of slave baptism records from the 1730s that 84.4 percent of male and 57.8 percent of female sponsors (godparents) could sign their names. In another sample, it was found that 42 percent of the colony's soldiers between 1727 and 1730 could sign their name and 7 percent had received some sort of higher education. About the same percentage (40 percent) could sign their names to the oaths of allegiance required by the new Spanish king in 1769. More intriguing are the results of Emily Clark's analysis of marriage contract samples. She found that 32.5 percent of free women and 47.5 percent of the free men in a sample from the New Orleans founder generation could sign their names (1731–32). But by the creole generation of 1760–62, these figures had jumped to 72 percent for women and 70 percent for men. On average, creole New Orleanians were twice as literate as their parents or grandparents and much more likely to be able to sign their names than contemporaries in France.[73]

Still, there were criticisms in the French period regarding the colony's intellectual and educational shortcomings. Father Le Maire condemned his enemies on the Superior Council (many of them Canadian born) as "ignorant and scandalous people."[74] The purported lack of interest in education went hand in hand with a perception of moral disorder. Father Raphaël, a Capuchin in New Orleans, convinced the Company of the Indies to support a college in order to correct "the ignorance and bad conduct" of the young. Raphaël struggled to keep the small school open between 1725 and 1731. The difficulties were due not lack of interest, but to lack of funds, as he was dependent on the contributions of private citizens to pay for the building, and their fortunes undoubtedly were insecure during this difficult time in the colony. The school had about fifteen students, and no tuition was charged.[75]

In his final term as governor, Bienville recognized the need to reestablish a school for boys after Father Raphaël's had apparently faltered. In 1742 he wrote to the French government requesting funds for a school:

> [F]or a long time the inhabitants of Louisiana have made a case for the need to establish a college for the education of their children . . . [I]t is essential that there be one, at least for the study of the classics, of geometry, geography, pilotage, &c. There, the youths of the colony would be taught the knowledge of religion, which is the basis of morality. Parents cannot help but see how the young people raised in idleness and luxury are found later to be

useless and how those inhabitants who are in a position to send their children to France to get an education go through their funds quickly. It is even to be feared that those young people thus educated abroad will form a dislike of the country [Louisiana], and will come back to it only to cash in what property their parents left them.

Many persons in Veracruz would rejoice at having a college here, and would send their children to it.[76]

Bienville's letter is remarkable from several angles. First, he ties education to morality and cleverly exploits the metropole's perception of Louisiana's dark side. Not only would schooling help improve the quality of Louisiana's youth, but the very fact that they would be occupied and not "idle" within the luxury of a slave society would go far to correct colonial character. Bienville's fear that children sent abroad for their education would "imbibe a dislike to their native country" derives from the poor reputation that Louisiana had in France at this time. His comments also mark a creole switch of allegiance, since "Louisiana," not France, was now considered the native country of these children. Finally, Bienville's suggestion that parents in Veracruz would send their sons to New Orleans indicates that the city strove to be a cultural center not only for Louisiana, but for a larger Mississippi-Caribbean sphere.

Girls' education in French New Orleans was better supported than that for boys due to the institutional devotion of the Ursuline nuns who arrived in New Orleans in 1727.[77] Although according to their contract with the Company, the Ursulines' first mission was to establish and run a hospital for the poor (for which they received funds from the Company, the government, the church, and private donors), they quickly took up a second mission to educate the girls and women of New Orleans. The nuns reported that on their arrival they were enthusiastically received by the townspeople, who were eager to have their children educated. Within a year they had twenty boarders, in addition to numerous day students. In 1728 Marie Hachard wrote: "Our little community is increasing from day to day. We have twenty boarders, of whom eight have today made their First Communion, three are lady boarders, and three are orphans whom we take through charity. We have, also, seven slave boarders to teach and prepare for baptism and First Communion. Besides, we have a large number of day pupils and Negresses and Indians who come two hours every day to be instructed."[78]

The ranks of boarders swelled the following year, when the Ursulines took in girls orphaned by the Natchez Indian Rebellion. The educational mission of the Ursulines involved practical as well as religious education. In addition to catechism, the curriculum included reading, writing, French, English, geography, arithmetic, history, music, sewing, needlework, and housework. The nuns charged tuition only to those who could afford it, and their missionary goals toward "savages" and slaves (stated in their contract with the Company) created an exceptionally diverse female community and a relatively integrated educational experience. Social hierarchies may have been muted by a shared novice status. The Ursulines continued to educate the female population of New Orleans throughout the French period; the number of pupils and boarders grew significantly after they moved to a new complex built for them in 1734. Emily Clark credits the Ursulines for the unusually high literacy rate of New Orleans creole women by the 1760s.[79]

Although the colony had less success maintaining a school for boys, wealthier families hired tutors or itinerant teachers for their children. In addition, references to private schools set up by entrepreneurial teachers crop up in administrative documents. They do not tell how well attended these schools were or how long lived, but they do indicate that Louisiana residents valued education. The logistical difficulties—lukewarm financial support from the metropole and the bitter rivalry between the Jesuits and Capuchins—were similar to the obstacles faced in establishing other major public works and institutions in Louisiana. Colonists colored their frequent requests for educational aid with worry, emphasizing either the "wild" and uncivilized way in which children would grow up or the deleterious effects of luxury in a slave society. Marie Hachard was shocked at the ignorance of Louisiana's youth, who, she claimed, "[b]rought up on a plantation, at a distance of four or five leagues from the city . . . had never heard of God." Bienville lobbied for a colonial school, which would instill morality and practical skills such as geometry and piloting, while safeguarding creole loyalty to the colony. Both he and the Ursulines saw the need to provide education without charge to those who could not afford to pay, suggesting that learning was not necessarily a mark of distinction in the colony, but rather a moral necessity. The Ursulines' mission included a directive to educate Indian and slave women not only to be good Christians but also to be functional literates. No evidence exists to suggest that administrators or planters ever opposed this practice. Still, the missionary priorities of Louisiana's religious orders shifted by the 1720s from a focus on Native Americans to European and Canadian settlers who, through the influence of the natural and social environment, were becoming "savage" and Godless.[80]

The failure to permanently establish a boy's school during the French period caused many middling and wealthy Louisiana families to send their sons to France for an education. Ironically, this may have done more to sustain Louisiana's life of letters than any local institution could have done. Creole students who ended up staying in France helped maintain the lines of communication and intellectual influence between metropole and colony through the books and letters they sent home to their families. Jean Pradel, the active letter writer and merchant–planter, was among those who sent his children to France and struggled to get them to return, although he clearly enjoyed discussing the topics of their studies in his correspondence. Alexandre Viel was eager to have his son follow in his footsteps. His salary as a surgeon and botanist allowed him to send his son Etienne to the Juilly preparatory school at age seven in 1743. Even Madame Elizabeth Real Pascal Marin, who rose from obscure roots to become a respected businesswoman in New Orleans, sent her only son to France for his education, though she herself could not even sign a mark on the many business documents she registered with the Superior Council.[81]

The educational practices of creole New Orleanians demonstrate that, contrary to its reputation, the city did not fall into an ignorant "dark age" in the period of metropolitan abandonment after 1731. Enlightenment intellectual life continued and helped maintain connections across the Atlantic, and it fostered new connections within the Americas. Via these dialogues, participants on several shores imbibed ideas for experiments in economic forms and political organization.

✤   ✤   ✤

Although it shared a reputation for disorder with other colonies and other cities, the added burden of being written off as a failure so early in its development, and subsequently all but abandoned by the French state, gave an intensity to the dark image of New Orleans. It was as if its failure to develop according to metropolitan plans simply confirmed a deep flaw in character. At least some residents in the French period seem to have intentionally embraced this characterization. It became part of the city's self-image.

Two literary roles—roguish exile and Enlightened engineer—were key to the making of Louisiana. In their colonial careers and in their writings, men and women such as Le Page, Hachard, Dumont, and Bossu exemplify the many ways in which Louisiana participated in the Republic of Letters, and show how fiction could be as powerful as observation in the making of a colony. New Orleans, as the main site where observatories and libraries were built, played a special role in the colony's lettered life. It was the portal of a cross-Atlantic conversation carried on within personal and official correspondence. The city also played a prominent role in French imaginings of Louisiana, imaginings that in turn affected the colony's development.

Writing mattered. The careful mapmaking of Le Maire and the agricultural experimentation of Viel worked to make Louisiana a known and manageable quantity. The poor reputation of New Orleans, enhanced by the personal correspondence of Marie Hachard and the romance of Abbé Prévost, had a substantial impact on the flow of immigrants to Louisiana after 1730. Dumont and Bossu added luster to facets of the colony's wild reputation. Le Page's ethnographic descriptions and recommendations on the management of slaves attempted to make colonialism a moral science. Dumont's history of valor, misfortune, and villainy attempted to make colonialism an epic adventure. If writing on Louisiana had qualities of science fiction, living in Louisiana had qualities of fantasy. Despite the failure of absolutist experiments in economic and social engineering in New Orleans, many literate colonists carried on in a spirit of experimentation and observation. They also maintained a lively correspondence with the Republic of Letters. Parisian salons may have abandoned Louisiana after the 1730s, but colonists did not abandon the Enlightenment. New Orleanians made efforts to ensure that their creole children had the benefit of an education. As a result, some were well versed in a *philosophe* rhetoric of free trade, the "rights of citizens," and the horrors of despotism that seemed to fit the colonial situation even better than the metropolitan one. They were thus well equipped to justify rogue colonialism and, eventually, one of the first creole revolutions of the new world.

It is important to understand the meanings of the "order/disorder" discourse embedded in the literature on Louisiana, and its real impact upon the development of New Orleans. However, my main purpose in this chapter has been to unpack a burden—to free our understanding of New Orleans from this flat duality so that we can better see ethnographic complexities on the ground. Like most societies, New Orleans was in constant flux, simultaneously succeeding and failing on various fronts, being pulled between forces constructing structures of power and those trying to undermine them. It was simultaneously ordered and disorderly. Thus my goal in the rest of this book will be to give dimension to a rapidly changing landscape where *les grands* and *les petits* at first interacted in unsettled and unfamiliar circumstances, and then began to work out the fragile rules of a new creole society.

2

LA VILLE SAUVAGE
Nature and Urban Planning

In 1721 a French military engineer named Adrien de Pauger, freshly disembarked at Mobile from his transatlantic journey, transferred his instruments, papers, and personal goods into a small, shallow-draft boat. With a handful of other officers and soldiers on board, a Canadian guide took the boat out of Mobile Bay and westward, along the Gulf Coast and into wide-open brackish lakes, and finally, on the second day, into a sluggish, cypress-choked bayou. When the boat could no longer clear the muddy, snared bottom, the passengers got out, packed up their gear, and trekked another mile through a mixed hardwood forest that juxtaposed familiar-looking (though gigantic) oak trees and exotic, tropical palmetto fronds. Their eyes may have caught the evasive movement of snakes and large insects on the leafy ground fleeing from the noise of the travel party. One can imagine how their tripoint hats quickly became strewn with the ubiquitous and ticklish webs of the giant banana spider. The path they followed emerged from the shade of the forest into a marshy meadow dense with head-high rivercane and cattails. Finally, the air suddenly freshened and became lighter as they emerged into a small, muddy clearing on the site that was to become New Orleans.

Pauger's commission was to accelerate the clearing and building process that had begun three years earlier at the instigation of Governor Bienville. Bienville and the Company of the Indies, which had a proprietary charter for the development of the colony, had agreed that Louisiana needed a permanent settlement on the lower Mississippi. Well educated in the French tradition of the military architect Vauban, Pauger was a proud, proper, and religiously devout man who had great confidence in his own ability to discern what was best, and what was right. Upon his arrival at the chosen site, the widest swath of relatively dry land within one hundred miles of the Mississippi's mouth, he found a few huts scattered on the high bank of the river.

He immediately judged these to be temporary shelters rather than pioneering structures. Pauger was charged by the colony's chief engineer with the responsibility for designing a city in the wilderness and then overseeing its execution. He quickly got to work, using as inspiration designs he had brought with him in a stack of maps and his own handwritten copy of a treatise by Vauban, the artifactual badge of an engineer of his standing. The town plan he drew from these was a simple grid, with four rows of square blocks extending on either side of a central plaza. A church overlooked the plaza opposite the river, its cruciform footprint projected onto the streets behind, creating a second crucifix carved among the town's rear streets.[1]

The Jesuit traveler Father Charlevoix was prescient in his account of the scene he encountered when he arrived at the site in 1722: "[O]f the present conditions of New Orleans. The most correct idea that you could form of it is to imagine two hundred people sent to build a town and who are camped on the banks of a great river, where they have only dared to put themselves in shelter from the weather, while waiting to have a plan drawn for them so they might have some houses built. M. De Pauger, whom I still have the honor to accompany, just showed me a plan he has drawn. It is quite fine and quite regular but it will not be as easy to execute as it was to draw it on paper."[2] Charlevoix's depiction of a band of expectant habitants awaiting the engineer's plan is striking. The gridiron design was so important to the destiny of New Orleans as a great city that officials prevented settlers from establishing themselves until the royal engineer had completed his survey and assigned them perfectly measured lots, which he apportioned according to "the faculties of the inhabitants."[3] Concessionaires, company officials, and military officers received the best and the largest lots, situated on the high ground next to the river. This was not a free-for-all land grab of a frontier town.

Not everyone, however, recognized the orderly grid as a plan for the common good. Implementation was a conflicted and painful process. The first sign of trouble occurred in August 1721, when a squabble broke out between Pauger and a Sieur Dubuisson, who in Pauger's own testy words "wanted to build as he saw fit, without regularity and without plan . . . He wanted to erect a gaudy little shack in the axis of the Avenue where Monsieur de Bienville lives."[4] Soon thereafter Pauger nearly came to blows with Madame Bonnaud, Dubuisson's sister (and wife of the town cashier), because his grid cut off a corner of *her* lot: "She even would have struck me in the face if I had not stopped her. The devil is often in the malice of certain women. She began to cry that I was hitting her and . . . that I was a scoundrel and a mean cad . . . I responded to this attack on my character in kind, that she was a beggar and a loose woman and that she was not among the persons

I esteemed or honored." Only the intervention of the commandant-major Pailloux prevented a duel between Pauger and Madame Bonnaud's husband. Several members of the Superior Council complained about Pauger's manner and wrote letters to France requesting his recall. He accompanied his own letter with a neatly drawn map, marking the spots over which he had clashed with residents.[5]

The Bonnaud incident was not the only time Pauger got into a physical scuffle over his survey work. An unfortunate man with the ironic name of "Traverse" had a run-in with the city engineer when his house crossed the symmetry of the emerging grid. Diron D'Artaguette's journal contains the following account: "A man named Traverse, inhabitant of New Orleans, was released from prison today. Here is the cause for which he had been there: This man had built a house in New Orleans which was not in the alignment of the streets (having built it before the plan was proposed); Mr. Pauger had it pulled down. This man, not being very well pleased, presented a petition to the Council to request it to indemnify him and to give him the means of building another. Mr. Pauger sent to find him and, after having regaled him with a volley of blows with a stick, had him put in prison, with irons on his feet, from where the man got out today, almost blind."[6] Chief Engineer Le Blond de la Tour documented some of these disputed "misalignments" in his watercolor drawing of 1723, which also shows the extent of the clearing in that year (color plate 3).

In the Dubuisson-Bonnaud affair, Pauger had nearly crossed swords in order to settle things with his socially well-placed adversaries. With Traverse, who appears to be of a lower station, Pauger felt justified in enforcing the authority of his orders with a brutal and demeaning caning, in addition to the formal punishment of imprisonment. These incidents illustrate the contested nature of the city's genesis and the emerging conflict between *ancien régime* ideals and local interests.[7]

It seems entirely appropriate that the original architect of the city of New Orleans was one part idealist engineer and one part hot-tempered rogue. His imprint is still stamped upon the streets of the French Quarter that he originally measured and cleared. Poignantly, when he died in 1726 of a tropical fever, his was the first body to be buried below St. Louis Church, the symbolic heart of the town.

While crossing Lake Pontchartrain from the Gulf Coast settlements, Pierre Charlevoix had shared a boat with Pauger when he visited New Orleans in 1722. His impressions of the scene before him were framed by the reputation of the four-year-old town that preceded it, via promotional tracts John Law's Company had published in Paris newspapers. His impressions were also qualified by the engineer's pretty drawings, which Pauger had proudly shared with the traveling priest: "Here I am, in this famous town they call New Orleans . . . [T]he eight hundred fine houses and the five Parish Churches that *Le Mercure* gave it two years ago is today reduced to about a hundred huts placed without much order, a large warehouse built of wood, two or three houses that would not grace a French village and half a wretched warehouse they had been good enough to lend to the Lord [as a church] . . . [T]his wild and deserted place that canes and trees still cover almost entirely, will be one day, and perhaps that day is not far off, an opulent city and the metropolis of a great and rich colony."[8] Through his well-read travel account Charlevoix helped perpetuate a golden dream of New Orleans despite his apparent disappointment in its humble beginnings.

Charlevoix was not the only visitor to describe New Orleans as a wild, or *sauvage*, place. Decades later, in the 1750s, when a stuttering plantation economy had been established and the town did possess something close to eight hundred houses, another French visitor remarked, "The inhabitants, sailors, Indians, and slaves run around freely, inside as well as beyond the town. They meet in a multitude of negro cabarets frequented by slaves who have fled their plantations either due to laziness or want, and who survive by trading stolen goods. They meet in the thick and intruding woods that border the town almost all around. The woods trap humidity and provide a good cover for smuggling."[9]

The street grid that Pauger imposed upon the town had done little to control the social disorder that seemed to emanate from the dank woods and spill into the streets. Nor did the city's Enlightened planning mitigate the depths of French disappointment in New Orleans. By the 1750s the reputation of New Orleans as a disorderly backwater had been firmly established.

This chapter traces the old models and new visions of urban life that the French were importing to Louisiana and applying with experimental ambition in their designs for New Orleans. The idealized schemes that colonial planners devised demonstrate a conscious conviction that spatial control yielded political control, and that the success of an empire depended upon the aesthetics of its cities. Looking at their plans, it is virtually impossible to separate efforts to engineer nature from efforts to engineer society. Thus I offer a reconstruction of French approaches to nature (which had both rational/scientific and romantic/cavalier pretensions), the realities the planners encountered on the ground, and the ways in which they adjusted their plans based on practical experience, improvisation, and the knowledge and skills that Africans and Native Americans brought to the colonial endeavor. The character of the city in the French period owes much to the transformation of the environment that Native Americans had already wrought upon the site, as well as the urban lifeways that Africans and Native Americans themselves imported. Given all the competing ideas, habits, interests, and material constraints that factored into the construction of French New Orleans, it was bound to be a highly contested process. But it is one that helps us visualize in unusually vivid terms the tension between brash imperial planning and pragmatic colonial creativity.[10]

Experimenting with Cities

"The ideal of the city as the embodiment of social order corresponded to a moment in the development of Western civilization as a whole, but only the lands of the new continent afforded a propitious place for the dream of the 'ordered city' to become reality."[11] Indeed, at the beginning, Louisiana seemed to offer *ancien régime* officials in France an opportunity to create an "improved" society. The crown attempted to ban from the colony elements that caused trouble at home, such as lawyers and Protestants. Learning from experiments in Canada and problems at home, colonial policymakers decided to eliminate venality (the purchase of government offices) and to halt the practice of giving seigneurial titles with land grants to new settlers. These decisions severely limited growth in the recognized ranks of new nobles and upwardly mobile bureaucrats. The administration also saw in Louisiana an opportunity to try out new forms of managed agriculture and mercantile capitalism. And through its immigration policy, government officials hoped to help solve the problems of unwanted children, petty criminals, and blasphemous youth. Not only would the homeland be relieved of their burden, but a new life in the colonies offered the prospect for individual rehabilitation.[12]

Related to these experimental reforms, the chance to build a city from scratch presented an opportunity to engineer social space, give aesthetic expression to Enlightenment rationalism, and fine-tune the implements of absolutism. As the geographer Peirce Lewis notes, "New Orleans did not grow to become a city; it was decreed a city from the moment of its founding . . . The plan represented a perfected, purified Europe, ready to be stamped into the soil of the New World wherever Europeans willed it."[13]

The idealized design that Pauger created for New Orleans reflects both the Enlightenment ambitions of early eighteenth-century France and a deeper co-development between colonial policy and urban planning. Although the architectural strategies varied widely, urban planning and imperialism have been linked across the globe and throughout the millennia, from ancient China to prehistoric Peru and medieval Mali. Colonies present an experimental social and physical space where designers can play with ideas that the limitations of power or the inertia of the built landscape at home do not permit. The source of the design for New Orleans is thus rooted both in general conditions and in a particular genealogy.[14]

Studies of Greek and Roman cities have traced the early development of an orthogonal grid plan that seemed "especially suited to empires," suggesting a particularly self-conscious link between colonialism and urban planning in the Western tradition.[15] Greek and Roman builders viewed newly adopted territories as opportunities to create well-ordered and expressive landscapes. The designs of Vitruvius, the renowned classical architect and urban planner, were primarily realized in the new frontier zones of the Roman empire in the first century B.C.E.

During the Renaissance, the rediscovery of Vitruvius' *Ten Books on Architecture* had a profound influence on the architecture of Western Europe. The application of his mathematical principles and symmetrical aesthetics to whole urban spaces (rather than to individual buildings or complexes) took off with Spanish colonization efforts in the sixteenth century, but did not emerge in Europe until the onset of the Enlightenment in the late seventeenth century. Vitruvius-style grand designs took hold among the French at the very moment that the Bourbon monarchy was expanding its imperial domain on the Continent.

Part of what made the New World *new* was that it was a space where engineering experiments were tried out first. An extensive literature in Latin American history and archaeology documents a co-development between Spain's theories of urban planning and its overseas expansion in the Americas.[16] With their orderly rectangular grids and a single central plaza flanked by the seats of religious and political power, Spanish colonial towns were already quite distinct from European cities by the mid-sixteenth century. The genealogy from Vitruvius is not pure. Elements of their form closely resemble Mayan, Aztec, and Inca cities that impressed Spaniards during the early years of exploration and conquest. Several authors argue that indigenous architecture profoundly influenced development of the Spanish colonial model. Others point to a close study of Roman imperial design, or an inheritance of Arab town planning galvanized by the exigencies of absolutism and colonialism. While all of these sources probably contributed, Spanish theorists in the metropole redeployed these ideas as their own and began consciously experimenting with idealized urban forms, imposing them on a colonial landscape that, while not pristine, could be occupied with more total domination than politics allowed at home. Designers consciously wed this aesthetic and architectural order to emerging ideas of the desirable social order. In many Latin American towns, planners designated separate and segregated sections for colonial occupiers and indigenous laborers. A central plaza rooted these towns, flanked by monumental buildings of the two official powers—the church and the state. With its Place d'Armes overlooked by St. Louis Church, its rigid symmetry, and its segregated spaces, the original plan for New Orleans actually resembles Spanish colonial cities much more than it does old French towns of the eighteenth century.[17]

By the eighteenth century, European settler towns were cropping up across the eastern third of North America. Distinctions in their forms reflect the same variety of purposes that marked this checkerboard of colonial endeavors. Historians of Anglo-America often describe the colonial period as a time when the landscape expressed religious or political idealism before being "taken over" by the wild growth of capitalism and individualism in the nineteenth century.[18] Planned cities were not uncommon in English-speaking North America, although they may not have been dictated by metropolitan authorities to the same extent as in the French or Spanish colonies. In the seventeenth century Boston, Philadelphia, and Williamsburg were sketched and planned before they were realized on the ground. But these cities also reflected the oft-cited Anglo-American ambivalence about urban life in lieu of a pastoral, agrarian independence. Paradoxically, "the [British] colonial American city was designed to preserve values and a way of life ultimately rural in character."[19] Struggles over the course of their development often centered on obstacles to growth that had been purposely incorporated into the original designs for these cities.

Unlike British colonial planners, French designers did not seek to limit the urban character of New Orleans. In fact, they sought in any and all ways to accelerate it. France saw a "metropolis" as a necessity to this particular colonial endeavor. The success or failure of New Orleans was evaluated on the basis of its urbanity: how many houses, how well built, the appearance and design of public buildings and public spaces, the orderliness of the streets, the education and deportment of the citizens, the intensity of its commerce. While British colonial planners wanted to avoid replicating London, French planners admired London. They also wanted to re-create the best aspects of Paris. The nun Marie Hachard reported that she heard New Orleanians singing in the streets in 1728, "[T]his town has as fine an appearance as the City of Paris!" They were acknowledging the city's aspiration toward a standard of urbanity.[20] Whether their refrain was tinged with irony we may never know, but over time metropolitan Frenchmen and native creoles came to measure the city's success as a cosmopolis according to different standards.

In sixteenth- and seventeenth-century France, urban ideals were rapidly changing as the state dismantled elements of feudalism, and new forms of capitalist agriculture emerged. Theorists thought the city drove the economic development of the countryside rather than the other way around. Enlightenment writers used somatic metaphors to describe the relationship between the city and the country, as well as between the capital and the nation. The city represented the head of the rural body. As such, it needed to be well groomed and clear-thinking in order to direct the country on the proper course. By the turn of the eighteenth century, engineers and architects agreed about basic aspects of *la ville parfaite*, or the "perfect city." Its rationality should be expressed through a regular geometric design that separated and ordered the city's many functions—military, commercial, trades and services, political, and residential. The Enlightenment version of *la ville parfaite* was *la ville régulière*.[21]

Over the course of the eighteenth century, the language of the city/body intensified and became increasingly negative. Disease analogies were deployed in critiques of urban ills. Enlightenment texts such as Mercier's *Tableau de Paris* emphasized the oozing of putrid liquids, poisoned air, contaminated food, and courtyards covered in excrement. Mercier's obsession with the pollution and disorder of the city was increasingly shared by those responsible for planning and policing France's cities. Delamare's *Traité de la police* (1738) called for decrepit buildings to be torn down, streets to be straightened, and obscure corners to be well lit to prevent crime and facilitate surveillance. By the second half of the eighteenth century, the ideal city (*la cité idéale*) excluded cemeteries, hospitals, slaughterhouses, and fish markets. Its streets should be designed to let in light and allow the free circulation of fresh air and water. Planners thought this medical treatment of the city necessary not only to stave off the effects of the plague, cholera, and dysentery, but also to cure social pestilences arising from the miasma of squalidness, poverty, prostitution, and illegitimacy.[22]

Although the *cité idéale* was becoming more clearly defined at the time New Orleans was founded in 1718, the actual practice of urban planning was a nascent discipline in France.[23] In the previous century, Louis XIV had been an avid patron of architecture, and his courtiers had flattered him with the dedication of numerous *places royales* across the cities of France. These public works served the dual purpose of immortalizing the living king and spurring urban renewal. These new plazas carved out the center of dark and jumbled *vieux carrés* (or "old quarters," not coincidentally the local New Orleanian term for what tourists call the French Quarter), and quite literally allowed light to enter. In the words of architectural historian Richard Cleary, the *places* "replaced the local and the temporal with the immutable high culture of the crown, represented by ordered space and uniform architectural expression." The new public squares were "linked to comprehensive programs of street widenings and extensions that were intended to beautify, facilitate commerce, and make the city more readily knowable and predictable."[24]

The aesthetic of order, uniformity, and clarity seen in these new urban planning initiatives resonated with other Enlightenment projects that emphasized rationality and transparency in fields such as law, economics, and science. One of the first treatises on urban planning, Delamare's *Traité de la police* (1738), also advocated new methods for policing French subjects, underscoring the relationship between spatial and social control. He also tied urban order specifically to *imperial* success: "The Romans, like the Greeks, thought that public works were in the interest of the glory and security of the state. We have always regarded the embellishment and decoration of cities as an essential aspect of public order and our kings have always included this in the scope of government." The political court of Louis XIV consciously aspired to emulate the Roman empire, not only in terms of its monumental architecture, but in terms of its international hegemony in war and commerce. For strategists such as Colbert (Louis XIV's famous minister) and writers such as Delamare, the two were explicitly linked. They justified urban renewal projects in Paris because an empire must have an impressive and orderly capital. Architects throughout the eighteenth and nineteenth centuries attempted to make Paris worthy of its self-fashioned nickname, "the new Rome."[25]

When New Orleans was being worked out on paper, planning focused on public spaces and fell within the purview of the crown through the department of Les Bâtiments du Roi, the office of *le premier architecte du roi*, and a large corps of army engineers. Although the constraints of an existing cityscape often prevented engineers from giving full rein to their designs, four new types of cities built in the late seventeenth and early eighteenth centuries in France provide a genealogy for the plan of New Orleans: fortified towns, port cities, monumental cities, and garden cities.

Under the tutelage of Sébastien le Prestre de Vauban, named *commissaire général des fortifications* in 1678, France's soon-to-be-famous military engineers orchestrated profound changes in civic life, both in France and in its colonies. Although walled cities had been important in medieval times, Vauban's theories of defense and geometric aesthetics gave rise to a new genre of fortified towns and a reinvented profession of the architect-engineer as scientist. Fortified enclosures became the defining "sign of urbanity" in Bourbon France. The crown deployed engineers across France to map the countryside, build roads and bridges, and repair or redesign defenses. At the same time, the encroaching absolutism of Louis XIV and his many-fingered bureaucracy eroded the political autonomy of towns. One way of doing this was by relieving municipal governments of responsibility for town walls and making them instead a national project. Outside of Paris, the distinction between military and civic planning became difficult to draw. Scholars have interpreted the ring of fortifications that Vauban built for Louis XIV along France's borders as another genre in the display of absolutist power—in the same vein as equestrian statues of the king in Roman garb, monumental ministry buildings, and the *places royales*. As such, the fortifications were focused inward toward the French population as well as outward against France's foreign enemies.[26]

Historians have considered Vauban's fortified towns, such as Neufbrisach and Montlouis, as those "most faithful to the project of the perfect *ville*."[27] His designs placed more emphasis on defense than on civic or communal functions. He made streets narrow to funnel an invading force, and straight and gridded to move the town's regiment quickly. The soldiers' barracks were placed on the edge of town, close to the city's walls, to muster a quick defense. Vauban's designs often entailed a complex system of ramparts, palisades, moats, and bastions. The ideals for these military towns perforce limited their size, so that the populace could survive a siege. Although the walls thus prevented a *ville fortifiée* from becoming a true metropolis, in other ways they enhanced its urban character by creating a radical separation from the surrounding rural countryside. Retrofitting old medieval towns according to these ideals was often difficult and imperfect. But in the colonies, engineers "had greater freedom to do what they pleased" and "could give rein to their geometrical inspiration." As military men, "they wanted a city to be clear, broad, functional, cut out of whole cloth to a single pattern."[28] Notable differences distinguish France's "pre-Vauban" colonial cities like Québec and Montréal—with their winding streets and organic plans—and the post-Vauban cities, such as New Orleans and Louisbourg in Nova Scotia, that conform to the "imperial" orthogonal grid.

Another type of new city built in France during the *ancien régime* reflects the commercial and global aspirations of the monarchy. Beginning in the sixteenth century, the crown built five new port cities (Le Havre, Brest, Lorient, Rochefort, and Sète). Engineers designed these towns to facilitate and control the flow of goods and people. These cities necessarily had to be more open than fortified towns. Nevertheless, two characteristics they shared were essential to the ideal city: a regular grid that ordered social space hierarchically, and the separation of public and private areas. Historians have noted that this design facilitated the "policing" of the populace, desirable because the open walls of the port city allowed an influx of sailors and foreigners, whom authorities saw as sources of potential disorder. Nevertheless, ignoring royal edict and their own regulations, most of these towns rapidly grew away from their planned symmetry. Some historians attribute this failure to the individual initiative and private property rights allowed for a commercial city. The port cities are particularly significant for colonial history, as they were largely built to serve and expand France's imperial designs, including the slave trade. Lorient, as its name implies, was the home port of the Company of the Indies, the royal monopoly on colonial commerce (originally named La Compagnie des Indes de L'orient). A great number of the ships arriving in New Orleans throughout the eighteenth century originated from this small port in southern Brittany, including the majority of its slave ships.[29] Many colonial residents would have been familiar with the streets of Lorient; company employees bounced back and forth between the two ports.

The third manifestation of the ideal city in the *ancien régime* appears in the construction of the monumental cities of Richelieu and Versailles.[30] Cardinal Richelieu and Louis XIV constructed these towns to complement a château (and temporarily at Versailles, a government complex). According to French historian Roger Chartier, at Richelieu the strictly symmetrical street plan and homogenized façades were designed with three purposes in mind: (1) to express spatially the power of the cardinal by creating a binary relationship between himself and the king (for example, Richelieu's Place Cardinal was identical to and symmetrical to its Place Royale); (2) to quell political unrest in the region; and (3) to establish cultural institutions, such as a *collège royal* that would train the youth of the nobility to be better subjects. Richelieu is remarkable for its symmetry of paired elements and the controlled appearance of its identical façades. It represents the highest expression of urban aestheticism in a town plan in France.

Versailles was inspired by the town of Richelieu. However, the symmetrical duality at Versailles draws on a much larger scale, that between nature and city. Although French designers never intended for colonial cities to rival the glory of Richelieu and Versailles, the monumental elements of all French towns and cities were becoming increasingly important as incarnations of the royal presence in its territories. The proliferation of *places royales* in the seventeenth and eighteenth centuries throughout France's provincial cities was one way in which pieces of the visual power of Versailles were transplanted throughout the realm. Each regional center aspired to this new "sign of urbanity" by placing a statue of the king at the center of a landscaped square framed by identical monumental buildings.[31]

The "garden city" is another ideal that shaped New Orleans. The garden in many ways took precedence over the city at Versailles. This emphasis underscores Louis XIV's rejection of bickersome Paris for the tranquil countryside of Versailles, but also symbolized the expansion of absolute power outside of the capital and into the most remote rural corners of the realm. The focus of Versailles on gardens expressed a fascination with nature that was to grow throughout the Enlightenment. Many scholars have noted the influence of eighteenth-century garden design in city planning, both in the way in which gardens were increasingly incorporated into urban projects and residential design, and in the desired gestalt of cities themselves. In 1755 the French architect Laugier compared the city to a wild forest that needed to be transformed into a park by cutting roads and pathways to create separate sections with their own character.[32]

At the time that engineers went to work on the plan for New Orleans, an efflorescence in urban planning in France had produced competing ideals for the perfect city. Planners and colonials seem to have hoped that New Orleans would have elements of all: it would be a well-fortified frontier town, an orderly port city serving mercantilism, a symbolic metropolis representing the king in a vast new territory, and a garden city of simple pleasures. It is hard to imagine how any frontier town could satisfy all these expectations while its residents were struggling to clear tree stumps and keep their houses from being swept away by a formidable river.

Nature and Natives

When France's engineers arrived in the colony to lay out New Orleans, they did not find the *tabula rasa* they had imagined. The natural landscape of the lower Mississippi delta was no passive canvas. Rather, it gyrated, heaved, and entangled—constantly threatening to erase human traces from the ground. Even so, Native Americans had left their marks. The French encountered a landscape that had already been altered by human beings for thousands of years. And in other ways, too, the colonial environment did not present a clean slate. The new residents of New Orleans—Africans, Indians, Europeans, and Canadians—carried ideas of town life in their own minds, ones that did not necessarily derive from pen and ink.

Native Americans in the area belonged to diverse cultures with a complex history. They had already experienced over 150 years of the Columbian exchange, dating to De Soto's biologically disastrous trek through the region in 1540. European-introduced diseases had decimated their populations, causing political and cultural contraction. Friendlier European species had also preceded French colonization. The French noticed fig and peach trees, pigs, and chickens in Native American villages in the New Orleans and Mobile areas when they first began to explore lower Louisiana.[33]

But even before these European introductions, the "natural" environment of the New Orleans area had been modified by Native Americans confronting the same basic challenges that faced French settlers in New Orleans: sinking soils and endemic flooding. They responded by building up their sites with mounds of clamshells that provided flood protection, improved drainage, and enriched soil. This modification, in turn, encouraged the growth of trees in an otherwise flat marsh, stimulating the development of a diverse new ecosystem within the delta. Areas previously settled by Native Americans were thus especially attractive to French settlers. The land surface was elevated and better drained. Ancient settlement sites hosted useful hardwoods; recent ones were cleared and ready for cultivation.[34]

The terrestrial surface of southeastern Louisiana is geologically quite young, having been formed by the deposit of sediments from the Mississippi River over the course of the last 4,800 years. A process of sedimentary buildup and changes in the river's course gradually transformed the site of New Orleans from open Gulf waters to marsh, then swamp, and finally, a narrow strip of relatively dry hardwood forest stretching along the natural levee (or raised riverbank). Today, sediments are still in the process of settling and compacting following their recent deposition, and as a result, subsidence (or sinking) of ground surfaces is characteristic of the landscape. The river has been in its current channel only for the last thousand years, so that the land below most of colonial-era New Orleans is about the same age. In the colonial period, settlement concentrated on a "crescent" bend in the Mississippi, hugging the higher and drier land along the water (fig. 3). In town, elevations range from about 15 feet above sea level to 10 feet below. In profile view, the modern city forms a bowl, with the center of town being the lowest point and the edges along the river (more or less to the south) and Lake Pontchartrain (to the north) forming the high lip. Three bayous (St. John, Metairie, and Gentilly) cut through the central area, forming secondary dry land ridges along their natural levees. These bayous were important transportation routes and settlement areas in both the precontact and colonial periods, especially Bayou St. John which (with a short portage) connects the Mississippi to Lake Pontchartrain, an inland bay of the Gulf.[35]

Southeastern Louisiana lies in the subtropical zone characterized by a long hot season with high temperatures (mean high in July is 84 degrees F), high humidity (greater than 70 percent), and heavy rainfall (average annual rainfall of 64 inches). The hot season extends from late May to September. A cool season follows, characterized by lower humidity and a mean temperature of 64 degrees Fahrenheit. Occasional freezes do occur in the coldest months (December and January), preventing the area from having a truly

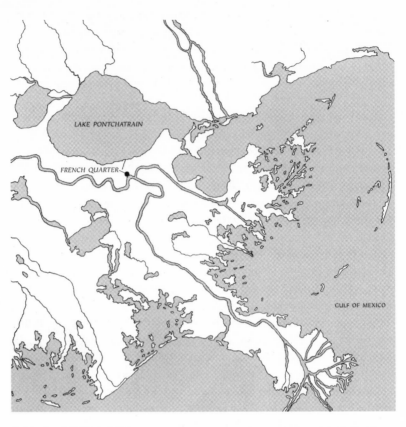

FIGURE 3. Location of New Orleans and the "Old Indian Portage." (Courtesy of Alicia Rogan Heard. Reproduced from Malcolm Heard, *French Quarter Manual: An Architectural Guide to New Orleans' Vieux Carré* [New Orleans: Tulane School of Architecture], 2, 5.)

tropical climate. The weather is influenced by conditions in the nearby Gulf of Mexico. Hurricanes pose a threat in the late summer and early fall.[36]

Before historic settlement, hardwoods such as sweet gum, hickory, cottonwood, magnolia, red maple, hackberry, pecan, and a variety of oak species dominated the natural levee areas, with palmetto plants occupying the lower story. Bald cypress, Spanish moss, swamp iris, and stands of native canes characterized low-lying regions back from the river and lakeshore. The riparian environment of New Orleans at the time of French settlement was quite rich, with a variety of species of native songbirds, waterfowl, snakes, and insects, as well as larger fauna such as opossums, muskrats, rabbits, raccoons, whitetail deer, foxes, and alligators. Fish, shellfish, and crustaceans were also quite abundant in the freshwater tributaries and nearby brackish lakes and marshes.[37]

Native American peoples have lived near New Orleans for at least 2,500 years, possibly as long as 4,000 years, from sites of the Poverty Point period (c. 1500–500 B.C.E.) to the protohistoric era. Sites become increasingly common for later cultural periods, as the geology and ecosystem of the New Orleans area stabilized. Precontact population levels peaked during the Coles Creek period (A.D. 700–1000), just after the river settled into its present course. Hundreds of small campsites and villages surrounding flat-topped ceremonial mounds have been identified in the New Orleans area. A developing dependence on agriculture probably spurred this settlement growth. Archaeologists have interpreted the architectural complexity and burial traditions evident on these sites to mean that Coles Creek society possessed a hierarchical social organization with an aristocratic ruling class and powerful religious leaders. In the subsequent Mississippi Period (1000–1700), this complexity remained the rule and in some cases became more elaborate. However, the peoples of the lower delta exhibited clear cultural differences from other groups in the valley. The Plaquemine people of the delta shared with the other contemporary Mississippian cultures maize-based agriculture, a ranked-class society, and the prominence of multi-mound ceremonial centers, but they differed in their lack of death cult religious motifs and in their use of lightweight, shell-tempered pottery. Given that this same pottery tradition is found on French and even Spanish colonial sites (perhaps as traded utilitarian wares or as containers for trade goods, such as bear fat), it has been assumed that most of the groups encountered in the New Orleans area when the French arrived at the end of the seventeenth century were immediate descendants of the Plaquemine people who had survived the demographic collapse of the 1500s. Linguistic complexity in the area, however, also suggests connections with Mississippian groups to the east.[38]

In the early French period, the peoples of the lower delta region comprised small ethnic groups the French referred to as *les petites nations*. They tended to live in smaller and more mobile villages than their upriver neighbors. Larger groups such as the Natchez and Tunica still dominated the Mississippi valley above Lake Pontchartrain. Their populations were concentrated in settlements clustered around a central ceremonial town.

In the eighteenth and early nineteenth centuries, several different *petites nations* lived in the New Orleans area. Within the boundaries of the modern city itself, Iberville had noted a "Quinipissa" village at the mouth of Bayou St. John in 1699. Twenty-five years later, Louisiana historian Le Page du Pratz said that a group of "Acolapissa" occupied this same spot and that one of the early settlers had bought this village from them for his plantation. Le Page stayed as a guest in one of the Indian houses included in the purchase.[39] In 1706 mapmakers placed a group of Ouma (modern "Houma") at the Bayou St. John village. The Ouma had fled their native territory in the north to take refuge at this long-established site following an attack by the neighboring Tunica.[40] Of the New Orleans–area *petites nations*, the Ouacha (pronounced *washa*) appear most frequently in documents. Up through the 1820s they moved about in the area between Bayou Lafourche and the Mississippi River to the southwest of New Orleans. Farther east, a closely related but smaller group, the Tchouacha, moved up and down the west (right) bank of the Mississippi River.[41] A group of Tchouacha lived near English Turn, at a bend in the river just below the city, in the early eighteenth century and had a settlement directly across the river in 1758.

Although engineers drawing up plans in France may have reduced Native Americans to features of the natural landscape, the Canadians who first explored Louisiana did not depict the country as an uninhabited, wild land. The foundation story of New Orleans credits Iberville's Native American guide as playing a key role during an exploratory trip in 1699. "The Indian I have with me pointed out the place through which the Indians make their portage to this river from the back of the bay where the ships are anchored. They drag their canoes over a rather good road where we found luggage belonging to people who were going or returning. He pointed out to me that the distance from one place to the other was quite short."[42] This portage at Bayou St. John linked the Mississippi to the large inland Gulf bay later named Lake Pontchartrain (fig. 3) and was a key factor in the selection of the site for New Orleans. It connected the main inland water routes to the Gulf of Mexico, obviating the need to navigate the arduous curves and shifting silts of the last hundred miles of the birdfoot delta. For the French, this meant that the settlements of Mobile and Biloxi were a one- or two-day trip away from the Mississippi, rather than weeks. This shortcut to the Mississippi "highway" strategically connected French posts in Canada, the Great Lakes, Illinois country, and Choctaw territory with the new Gulf Coast settlements. For Native Americans, as Iberville observed, it likewise served as a depot for trade and traffic between the river valley and the Gulf region. Archaeological remains at the mouth of Bayou St. John indicate that this portage had been used for hundreds of years by different Native American groups for purposes of trade or seasonal exploitation of Lake Pontchartrain.[43] Native Americans had already identified the advantages of the site for travel and trade, and the French followed their lead. In this and other ways, "Native Americans transformed the landscape of the colonial imagination," and helped the French envision a busy port city on the edge of a swamp.[44]

The French introduction of a metropolis was not as novel an imposition on the local landscape in the lower Mississippi Valley as it was in New France or the eastern seaboard. For 3,500 years, Louisiana groups had been constructing large towns that served as trading and ceremonial centers for thousands of part-year residents. Many of them had features of monumental architecture, such as large earthwork mounds, pyramids, and embankments. Some sites stretched over hundreds of acres, while mounds could rise to a height of 100 feet, making them the largest manmade features north of Mexico in the pre-Columbian era. Although many of these sites had been abandoned by the time of French colonization, due to post-Columbian depopulation, the "Grand Village" of the Natchez was still active at the time, serving as a political, economic, and religious center for approximately 5,000 people in the nearby area, a size that New Orleans only approached at the end of the French period.[45] In the first decades, many French traders settled at Natchez to take advantage of its role as a commercial hub in the Indian trade. After discovering that the surrounding soils were well suited to tobacco, other Frenchmen came to establish more permanent settlements, and a French "suburb" grew up around the Indian town of Natchez. Some officers proposed it as an alternative capital to waterlogged New Orleans. Natchez was certainly Louisiana's "second city" until French–Indian conflicts over land resulted in the 1729 Natchez Rebellion.

Among the men who settled at Natchez in 1720 was the future Louisiana historian and colonial *philosophe* Antoine Simon Le Page du Pratz. Le Page greatly admired the Natchez, whose manners he found "more civilized" than those of other Indian nations.[46] Part of what impressed him was their town life and the architectural formalities of the Grand Village. Impressions went both ways. New Orleans came to serve as an important site for Indian diplomacy in the French period. French administrators encouraged Choctaw and Chickasaw delegations to travel to the city, thinking they would be impressed by its size, sophistication, and undoubtedly its garrison. The centerpiece of town, a tall church facing an open plaza flanked by government buildings and housing for the military class, would have had direct parallels for people from southeastern chieftainships. Basic elements of town planning and symbolic architecture were mutually intelligible between the French and Native Louisianans. Mississippian towns characteristically possessed the elements of a central plaza framed by monumental architecture (mounds), and a boundary around the entire residential–ceremonial space, usually consisting of a fortified wall with gates.[47]

Another major segment of the colonial Louisiana population were Africans, who drew on their own experiences of town life. In the French period, a majority of Louisiana's imported slaves came from the west coast of Africa, specifically Senegambia and the Bight of Benin. Slave traders collected them at coastal port cities such as Saint-Louis, Gorée, Badagri, and Ouidah, and at inland river ports such as Juffure in Gambia. European forts and so-called "factories" dotted the entire western coastline of Africa by the late 1600s. Although the slave trade undoubtedly stimulated urban growth, African societies had been building large towns in the interior of the continent for over 3,000 years. The late precolonial period seems to have been a time of urban growth, particularly in the kingdoms of Mali, Niger, and Benin.[48]

Africans coming to Louisiana, even if they had grown up in a small village, probably had some firsthand experience with a nearby urban settlement. Some were predominantly African places with long histories, some were recent Euro-African creations, a few were European enclaves. Places such as Elmina, with a population of 15,000–20,000 in 1682, were significantly more urban (and perhaps more urbane) than New Orleans in the French period.[49] Although slaves may have seen little of African colonial cities from inside the walls of the fortresses where they were held before embarkation, those originating from areas near the coast or along major inland rivers would have been familiar with cosmopolitan port towns where peoples of many different colors, languages, and religions mingled to trade in an already global market. These towns, like New Orleans, had a reputation for "whoring, drinking, gambling, swearing, fighting, and shouting."[50]

In the early eighteenth century, the "Atlantic creoles" described by historian Ira Berlin played a significant role in West Africa. People of mixed European and African cultural (and sometimes biological) heritage often served as boatmen, merchants, and cultural brokers along the waterways of the slave trade in Africa. Their dress, eating, manners, and language showed the influences of European culture. Where Atlantic creoles constituted distinct settled communities, this syncretism extended to architecture and town layouts.[51] Often mistrusted and marginalized by both Europeans and

Africans, Atlantic creoles were not immune to enslavement. The records of Louisiana contain descriptions of light-skinned Africans who already spoke French and practiced Catholicism, suggesting that some slaves not only were sophisticated town dwellers before arrival, but also were familiar with French colonial towns. Both native African towns and Euro-African colonial ports were characterized by fortifications and large walled enclosures intended to keep slaves in and raiders out.

Although fortified walls featured prominently in early pen-and-ink plans for New Orleans, enclosing the town quickly became the least of the engineers' worries. The French did not anticipate just how difficult it would be to occupy the edge of a swamp and retain a respectable semblance of urbanity. Almost as soon as the first buildings were erected, the city was struck by a powerful hurricane on 11 September 1722. The royal engineer (Pauger's boss), Le Blond de la Tour, described the event in a letter: "This wind was followed an hour later [at 10 A.M.] by the most terrible tempest and hurricane that could ever be seen, that only ended this morning at four o'clock. It knocked down at least two thirds of the houses here and those that remain are so badly damaged that it will be necessary to dismantle them. The church, the *presbytère*, the hospital and a small barracks building where our workmen were staying, are among the number that were overthrown, without there being, thanks to the Lord, a single person killed." Actually, the engineer himself owed thanks to the Lord for destroying so many of the buildings. He continued, "All these buildings were old and provisionally built, and not a single one was in the alignment of the new city and thus would have had to be demolished."[52] If not for this fortuitous act of nature, there might have been even more conflict over implementation of the urban plan.

The hurricane of 1722 was one of the very few times that colonial planners found nature to be cooperative. Although reports from the colony raved about the fertility of the soils, the "warm" growing season, and abundant water that promised a prosperous agricultural colony, these same natural conditions were quite troublesome in an urban environment. Colonists wrote plaintively about flooding and dampness that not only caused great inconvenience to those caught in the quagmire of the streets, but also contributed to unhealthy conditions in the city.[53] Drouot de Valdeterre argued for the relocation of New Orleans, which, he said, "is established in muddy ground brought on by the waters that overflow twice a year . . . [T]he waters stagnate there from two to three months and render the air very unhealthy; there are only some wooden huts absolutely unlivable unless repaired after each overflow."[54] Claude Joseph Villars Dubreuil, one of early Louisiana's major concessionaires, recalled in 1740, "The establishment of New Orleans in its beginning was frightful, the river at its height spread out all over the land, and there were two feet of water in all the houses which caused general sickness and death."[55] Although it was not understood at the time that mosquitoes and contaminated water were germ vectors, the inhabitants of New Orleans were quick to make an association between stagnant water and disease. Historic accounts indicate that the city was hit with attacks of cholera, dysentery, malaria, and yellow fever throughout the eighteenth century.

Due to these baneful conditions, contemporaries and later historians have second-guessed Bienville for his selection of the site. Instead of bending to the recommendations of Drouot de Valdeterre and others to move the capital, he set about to engineer a cultural solution to the problems of nature. In 1722 work began on an extensive levee system to hold back the river. Soon thereafter, the Superior Council passed the first of several local regulations requiring residents to build canals, ditches, and levees through corvée labor of their slaves.[56] By the middle of the French period, the city was walled in from the river and the streets were scored with an intricate grid of ditches and canals crossed by little footbridges at intersections. It was a muddy compromise between Venice and Paris.

Environmental historian Christopher Morris describes the levee system as an attempt to "transcend" nature. This Sisyphean effort actually raised water levels along the riverbank and forced New Orleans to compete with upriver plantations in a spiraling building effort: "The river rose higher and higher because it was being contained within ever higher and longer artificial walls. In other words, longer, higher, wider levees necessitated still longer, higher, wider levees."[57] The first stage of levee building was completed in 1732, only to have the city struck again by a powerful hurricane. The levees proved woefully inadequate. After this calamity came three difficult years in which crops failed and famine threatened the population. Bienville temporarily despaired of his efforts to control nature and became pessimistic about the agricultural potential of the colony: "This country is subject to such great vicissitudes that one can almost not count on the crops at all. Now there is too much drought, now too much rain."[58]

Bienville's remarks reflect a clash between French impressions of American fecundity and the reality of a climate prone to extremes. Still, due to the diverse origins of the founding generation, it is difficult to generalize about a unified vision of the landscape and its potential. Actors viewed it with different experiences and aspirations. Canadian *coureurs de bois* may not have been as daunted by the density of vegetation and difficulty of travel as were French city dwellers, but they had a disparaging opinion of a land that could not produce profitable furs. Among those oriented toward agriculture two models competed. Some "had in mind the large estates of the

French countryside, with their wheatfields worked by a simple peasantry." The Marquise de Mézières wrote that she hoped her husband, who owned a concession in Pointe Coupée, would "select a beautiful site for a house, with enough land for three courtyards, a garden, a park, a wooded walkway, and a stream."[59] Others envisioned a profitable sugar economy based on the model of Saint Domingue, which had begun to bring spectacular profits by the time of Louisiana's founding. Those less optimistic about the natural climate of Louisiana saw it as more suitable to tobacco and looked toward Virginia as a model. The cultivation of both tobacco and sugar was attempted in the French colonial period. Sugar failed due to the shorter growing season in Louisiana, which kept most cane varieties from fully maturing.[60] Tobacco was slightly more successful, but only small soil zones around Pointe Coupée and Natchez were really suitable. After more failed experiments with silk and waxberry production, planters in the New Orleans area settled on indigo and rice as their main crops. These, though, rarely returned impressive profits.

Side by side with this struggling plantation economy, a *mētis* version of rural subsistence arose that readily combined French, African, and Native American practices. Due to its periodic wartime isolation and its lackluster export economy, Louisiana had difficulty obtaining provisions from Europe. The necessity of subsistence meant that most early agricultural efforts were devoted to livestock and food crops. Although a large influx of slaves entered the colony between 1719 and 1731, for the first several years those in the New Orleans area were put to work building levees, herding cattle, hunting, and tending gardens. Their labor tasks differed little from those of the idle soldiers in the city or the majority of free colonists, who were mainly concerned with feeding themselves. Louisiana colonists were forced to experiment with agricultural diversity to ensure their own survival.[61]

Agriculture was not limited to the plantation zone, but dominated concerns in New Orleans as well. French New Orleans was a city of gardens that combined subsistence and aesthetics. The engineer Pauger staked out long residential lots "of such a size that each and every one may have the houses on the street front and may still have some land in the rear to have a garden, which here is half of life."[62] Maps of the city from the 1720s and 1730s also show decorative parterre gardens current with aristocratic landscaping trends in France at the time (color plate 4). One example is the charming garden of the soldier-poet Dumont de Montigny, with whom we have already become acquainted, complete with a chicken ladder attached to the roof of his house (color plate 2). Early maps and contemporary descriptions indicate that Governor Bienville created a mini-Versailles for himself, placing his more decorative than functional "plantation" just outside the town center from where he administered the colony and entertained his favored guests (fig. 4, lower left). Dumont described the approach to the main house as a lane lined with orange trees.[63] These images and the pastoral musings of the Marquise de Mézières suggest that, for some, Louisiana represented an opportunity to play out a bucolic fantasy that the limits of land tenure and family resources did not allow in France.

Although they may have been persuaded to gamble with capital in a romantic foreign scheme (gambling was after all a genteel pastime), at least some of John Law's naive aristocratic investors retained a distaste for capitalist-style agriculture. *Coureurs de bois* and indentured servants who stayed in the territory and acquired land of their own also resisted official edicts to produce export commodities, reflecting what some have called a "lingering precapitalist mentality." As the self-invention of noble titles in Louisiana suggests, upwardly mobile immigrants may have modeled themselves more after the rural cavalier than the capitalist grain trader. Agriculture for surplus required a greater investment of capital and labor than many inhabitants had, as well as a somewhat quixotic effort to transform the land and make it into something it was not. Many realized that living in this environment required "working with and adapting to nature far more than they would have liked and in ways not unlike those of the indigenous people whom Europeans displaced."[64] While the founder generation may have initially resisted these adaptations, their creole children showed no such hesitation. Thus, if Louisiana's early experiments in agriculture and environmental engineering were characterized by blueprints and book learning, later efforts were characterized by improvisation and practical knowledge, or *mētis*.

This pattern can be seen in dietary changes in colonial Louisiana. Archaeological analysis of food remains from three colonial-period sites in New Orleans shows that residents incorporated a greater amount and variety of wild game into their diets in the creole generations than in the founder generation.[65] At the site of Madame John's Legacy, for example, the French-born Madame Real supported herself and her inn guests largely on a diet of beef cuts suitable for roasts and stews. But the creole households that followed her at the site widely expanded their diet to include duck, turkey, swamp rabbit, turtle, and a large variety of salt and freshwater fish. This evidence suggests that the urban diet actually became more "wild" and native in the creole period, even in comparison to the diet at two nearby plantations.

How this fish and wild game entered the New Orleans market is no mystery. Colonial censuses from the French period list a number of men with the occupation "hunter." Daniel Usner has also documented the common

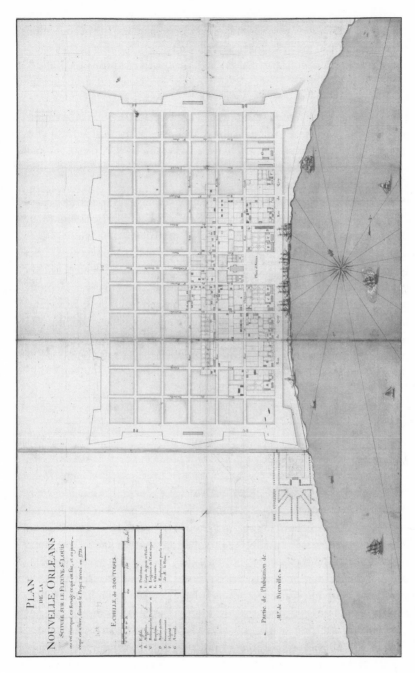

FIGURE 4. Plan of New Orleans, 1 September 1723. (Courtesy of Map Collection, Yale University Library.)

practice of plantation owners designating specific slaves as hunters. These hunters may have been provisioning their owners not only at the plantation great house, but at the townhouse as well. Convoys of hunting parties composed of Frenchmen, Indians, and slaves made seasonal trips to wildlife-rich areas such as the St. Francis Basin. In addition, Gwendolyn Midlo Hall has found evidence that by the late French period maroon slaves (or runaways) living in the woods south of the city were actively marketing lumber, handmade baskets, garden produce, and perhaps stray cattle through a maroon-slave-freeman trading network leading to New Orleans.[66] It is not much of a stretch to suggest that they were also marketing wild fish and game through these channels.

Not surprisingly, the archaeological data indicate that the charter generation in New Orleans attempted to replicate the diet they knew in France. In addition to beef, they raised sheep and/or goats primarily for dairy production. Scattered references to butter- and cheese-making experiments can be found in the documents, and archaeology suggests these practices may have been more widespread than previously thought. However, by mid-century references to dairy production become rare, and fewer farmers in the New Orleans area seem to have been intent on cattle ranching. The diet in New Orleans during this period turned more toward wild, native resources. While the town was growing, it was also becoming more *native American* through a process of creolization.[67]

The Plan

The French explorer Robert Cavelier de La Salle and his party passed through the site that would become New Orleans in 1682, in France's first bid to claim the lower Mississippi Valley. Other explorers and *coureurs de bois* likely visited the site between that time and Iberville's visit of 1699. In that year the real colonization of Louisiana began. Within a few years, a handful of Canadian and French settlers established themselves at an Indian village along Bayou St. Jean (present-day St. John) a mile or two inland from the future colonial town. Their holdings were confirmed by concessions in 1708. By 1715 French administrators recognized that a post located near the Indian portage would be a valuable asset. In 1717 the Company ordered that not only a post, but a "principal town" should be built on the site recommended by Bienville. The next year Company directors gave instructions for the design of the town to chief engineer Perrier. Company executives envisioned an Indian trading post similar to those in Canada and the Great Lakes region, which would evolve into a fortified town surrounded by cultivated

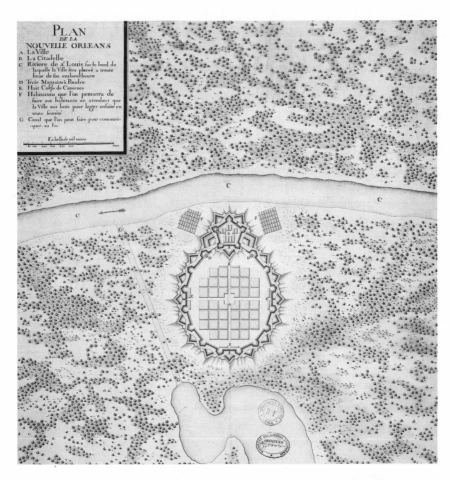

FIGURE 5. Earliest plan of New Orleans, attributed to Perrier, c. 1718. (Courtesy of Bibliothèque nationale de France, Cartes et Plans, IFN-6700307.)

lands.[68] This was the first of many calls made to enclose and fortify New Orleans. The drawing that Perrier or his subordinate drew up in Paris is remarkably idealized and strongly influenced by Vauban (fig. 5). A jewel-like enclosure frames a perfect cruciform street grid, hanging like a pendant from the river. However inaccurate the representation may be, perhaps no plan better captures the way in which French administrators aspired to impose an aesthetic and rational ideal on a colonial canvas.[69]

Toward the end of March 1718, Governor Bienville ceremonially cut the first cane at the chosen site for New Orleans. The city was christened with convict labor. Long-term resident Jonathas Darby recounts that thirty out of forty men sent to clear the dense canebrake were French convicts.[70] Within a year, a handful of buildings had been erected. The architecture in this early period consisted of impermanent structures exhibiting a combination of Native American and French techniques, with unpainted cypress posts and boards either hammered directly into the ground, or set on buried sills. Roofs of palmetto leaves substituted for thatch. Although New Orleans was not yet a sizable post, much less a town, Bienville succeeded in getting the capital of the colony moved from New Biloxi to New Orleans in 1722.

The impressive number of maps and plans drawn of New Orleans over its first twenty years (at least thirty-five original, and many more that are derivative) demonstrates how important planning and engineering were to the genesis of the town. Some of these documents were purely ideal projections; a few attempted to depict the city as it really was. The majority, however, were some combination of the two. For example, the 1723 Le Blond de la Tour map (color plate 3) accurately depicts the compound of Governor Bienville, but "erases" all the other extant buildings with the exception of the temporary church, because they did not conform to the new alignment. The map shows the areas that have been cleared of vegetation and projects the streets into the surrounding woods. Missing are the fortifications that French officials had ordered and that Pauger had sketched onto contemporary maps. In later maps draftsmen continued to draw these imagined walls around the city, detailed according to their fancy, although nothing like them was built until the very end of the French regime (fig. 6).[71]

Considering the small size of Louisiana's population in the early years, the number of architects, engineers, and draftsmen sent to the colony is remarkable. The crown or the Company sent at least fifteen to New Orleans in the first few years, though many of these (among them Perrier, Le Blond de la Tour, and Pauger) died within a few years of their arrival. Before he died, Pauger reported that despite continuing clashes with residents, progress was being made and conditions were improving, "At present everyone works, vying with one another. Workshops and buildings are seen to rise everywhere, so that New Orleans is growing before your eyes and there is no longer any doubt that it is going to become a great city."[72]

These were the hopes of engineers in the boom years of the 1720s. Before the end of the decade more permanent structures had indeed taken the place of the earlier crude cabins. The buildings, some of them two or three stories, were half-timbered, the walls filled with a local wattle and daub called *bousillage* that was made with native Spanish moss. Cypress shingles lined the roofs. Marie Hachard reported in 1728 that the houses were all whitewashed, suggested a Mediterranean-looking town rather than the more Caribbean pastels and Creole mustards that one sees in the Vieux

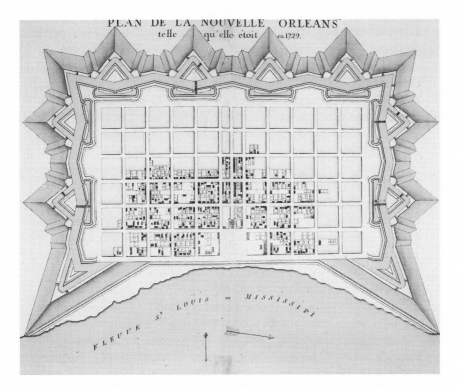

Carré today. Under the guidance of a long-lived engineer named Ignace François Broutin, residents built more substantial structures between the 1730s and 1750s. In the 1730s the architecture of New Orleans began to resemble "creole" forms (as they are known today) that responded better to local conditions. Brick structures, cooler and more resistant to rot, became more common than timber. Plaster covered the brick and timber to reduce exposure to the elements. Living spaces sat elevated over ground-level storage rooms so that damage from flooding would be minimized. Another creole innovation that transformed the appearance of New Orleans around this time was the addition of large "galleries," or overhanging porches on the front and rear of the buildings. These galleries provided ventilated spaces for living and sleeping during the long summer.[73]

The cityscape was changing not only in appearance, but also in size. By the 1750s the city had quadrupled from its 1720s charter phase. Creole-built buildings were more durable than the original half-timber structures, but still needed constant upkeep. Private property owners maintained appearances, but the French state neglected its own infrastructure. In the 1750s the decline of the architectural seats of government seemed to symbolize the state of political abandonment of the colony for one observer: "Almost all of these buildings must be rebuilt. The church and the presbytere are falling in ruin and are no longer susceptible of repair. The Government House collapsed several years ago. The Intendance has been uninhabitable for a long time. The two barracks buildings have collapsed, the hospital is not worth much more."[74]

This poor report may not have reached the ears of the king. Instead, Louis XV was treated to an artist's rendition of New Orleans in 1758 (fig. 7), showing the same buildings not only in pristine condition, but set within a scene of perfect order with neat rows of identical houses and gardens. The mapmaker had never traveled to New Orleans, but he may have been inspired by a spate of publications on Louisiana by former colonials, appearing in the 1750s.[75] Although Louisianans never knew it by that name, the artist designated the central square of New Orleans the "Place Royalle." This hyper-idealized plan incorporated some factual placements of the town's major buildings, but its main purpose was to imagine that New Orleans was a perfect expression of rational aesthetics flourishing under the patronage of the king. The author (a royal cartographer named Thierry) wrote in his dedication to the king, "I venture to offer this plan of New Orleans, this town built and established under your glorious reign in a place almost uninhabitable, but which today inspires the admiration of the world and demonstrates the vastness of your realm."[76] The Thierry plan shows that despite the city's reputation for disorder, the Enlightenment idealism that had given shape to New Orleans still rallied its boosters late in the French period.

Thierry's rendition imagines that the city unfolded according to Pauger's prescription, but in many ways the city had evolved away from the engineers' plans during the first creole generation. Walls are one example. While no enclosures of the city were ever built in the French period, it is not entirely accurate to say that New Orleans remained unfortified during the French period. Instead of one large wall enclosing the whole town, residents palisaded their individual lots by driving stakes close together in the ground. A visitor to town would have seen streets lined back-to-back with little forts created by high fences. Dumont's drawing shows a typical New Orleans lot during the French period (color plate 2). The Superior Council legislated these fences in the early years to make land claims clear and to control wandering livestock in the semi-rural town, but the palisades also gave each house lot a degree of private protection. The architectural

FIGURE 7. Thierry's *Plan de la ville de la Nouvelle Orleans capitale de la Province de la Louisiane. Dessine mis au net par le sieur Thierry Geographe Ancien dessinateur au Bureau des Fortifications et Batiments du Roy, 1758.* (Courtesy of Historic New Orleans Collection, Williams Research Center, Acc. No. 1939.8.)

independence of the private house lots mirrored a growing individualism in the social sphere.

The landscape of creole New Orleans also reflected a major demographic change. The rapid growth of urban slavery after the 1720s (discussed in chapter 4) meant that housing had to be added to accommodate a large group of residents whose presence the designers had not anticipated. Pauger originally created the town's large, long lots to provide for self-sufficient urban gardens, but as the creole generation came to dominance in the mid-1730s, large portions of these gardens were sacrificed to build slave quarters. Large lots of the wealthiest planters and merchants had additional service buildings, such as kitchens, smokehouses, and stables. A new, local model of urbanity arose that mimicked the plantation landscape.[77]

Comparisons between New Orleans and other colonial towns of the *ancien régime* help elucidate the relationship between urbanism and coloniality. The parallels to Mauritius, an island in the Indian Ocean, as described by historian Megan Vaughan, are stunning. She points to the literary tropes of "disorder" that dogged the colony, the economic importance of piracy and smuggling, a pronounced creole consciousness, political tensions within the colonial elite, the development of slavery, and difficulties maintaining *ancien régime* social boundaries. The main city of Port Louis was laid out with a grid template implemented by irascible engineers, but it failed to tame the roguish colony. Appropriately, Louisiana's last French *ordonnateur*, Denis-Nicolas Foucault, was sent to Mauritius after being pardoned for his part in that colony's revolt against the transfer to Spain. He must have found himself in a familiar element.[78]

The contrasts between two North American towns—Louisbourg and New Orleans—are as telling as the parallels between Port Louis and New Orleans. Although both towns were drafted by army engineers with the same training who came up with remarkably similar designs, the actual execution of the plans played out very differently, in ways that reflect the two colonies' distinct social histories. Four points of contrast are particularly striking. These have to do with churches, garrisons, monuments, and walls. The French selected the site for Louisbourg on Cape Breton Island (Île Royale to the French) in Nova Scotia in 1713, and royal engineers quickly went to work implementing a plan copied from Vauban's pattern book. Over the next several decades, Louisbourg grew rapidly as an Atlantic commercial and fishing port, until it was taken by the British in 1758. In a recent book on that city, A. J. B. Johnston emphasizes the strategic considerations of the town and the "desire for order" that dominated planning and politics. Although in Louisbourg engineers also tore down misaligned buildings, overall there appears to have been less conflict over the town's evolution than there was in New Orleans.[79] Johnston argues that the populace recognized the necessity of "maintaining order" in the frontier setting and cooperated with authorities. The contrast with New Orleans reflects different demographic and economic facts, as well as the much stronger influence of rogue colonialism in Louisiana.

In Louisbourg, the engineers' plans included a design for a church at a prominent spot in the center of the city in a layout paralleling that for St. Louis Church (later cathedral) in New Orleans. Johnston remarks that "in symbolic terms, this would emphasize the central role that Roman Catholicism played in contemporary society."[80] In this busy fishing port, however, the entrepreneurial populace never got around to building a permanent church, and the site set aside for it was commandeered for a marketplace. Louisbourg was a military and commercial town, and secular in its priorities. In New Orleans, in contrast, the church was completed within three years, despite the numerous hardships experienced by residents in the early 1720s. This is not to argue that New Orleans was a more religious place (its *curés* frequently complained about poor attendance at mass). However, it does show that those having influence over public works considered the church an important element in the town's administration and moral life.

Overall in New Orleans, the energy of public works focused either on nature or inward, toward the inhabitants, rather than on exterior enemies. This difference is also seen in how the two towns housed their soldiers. A basic principle of Vauban's defensive theory for fortified towns was that the garrison should be placed on the edge of town, along the walls, to be ready for quick action. The Louisbourg builders adhered to this principle. In New Orleans, the earliest plans also followed suit, but a few years later, when the time came to actually build permanent barracks, the structures were moved to the center of town, flanking the church and the Place d'Armes. The councilors' reasons were aesthetic. The barracks would help "embellish" the town.[81] The visual meaning of their placement overrode any functional consideration. In Louisiana, French soldiers doubled as the civic police force. The placement of their barracks at the center of town bespoke an effort to communicate the ready power of law enforcement. Ironically, this was one of the plans for New Orleans that went awry as the soldiers, who were desperately underpaid, underfed, and abused by superiors, became themselves a major source of social unrest.

Another contrast between Louisbourg and New Orleans lies in the former's emphasis on monuments, administrative architecture, and commemorative gestures. Île Royale administrators made a considerable effort to create physical symbols of a powerful and well-functioning state. They ordered medals, plaques, statues, and formal rituals to honor the king and affirm the town's connection to France.[82] These efforts re-presented and reinforced *ancien régime* hierarchies while proclaiming that Louisbourg (while no larger than New Orleans) was a civic center and an urbane place. "The overall effect of putting up so many urban landmarks with 'monumental' qualities was to reinforce the idea that Louisbourg was an ordered society that owed a great deal to the king, and, by extension, to royal officials in the colony . . . [A] town being built with such solidity and with so many adornments suggested strongly that this was a *ville fortifiée* striving for permanence."[83] Despite the dream of its destiny as a great metropolis, New Orleans lacked these symbolic structures and acts. Grand government buildings were planned but never built. Ramshackle residences doubled as offices. No statues or images of the king are recorded. Although the Ministry of the Marine sent letters ordering governors to have Te Deum sung in the church on important occasions, the only honorific ceremony for the monarchy that was celebrated on a large scale occurred in 1753, ostensibly in honor of the king's recovery from a recent illness, but also coinciding with the arrival of the new governor, Kerlérec, who was pleased to have gotten off on the right foot with the populace through his hospitality and fireworks display.[84] The closest approximation to a monumental space in New Orleans is the Place d'Armes, front and center of town. However, the plaza was left bare and empty throughout the French period, except when serving as a parade ground or place of execution. The plaza was originally ornamented by large garden areas along its borders and later cordoned off with a stockade fence. It did not focus on a statue of the king or the façade of a large government building, features that typified *places royales* in France.[85]

Overall, the absence of royal symbols suggests that in New Orleans the sentiments of loyalty attaching either *les grands* or *les petits* to the king were weak. New Orleans was becoming a place outside of what Arlette Farge calls "Royal Time," in which the rhythm of everyday life of *le peuple* was punctuated by events in the king's life through observances of birth, death, anniversaries, illness, recovery, wartime victory, and even assassination attempts.[86]

In the *ancien régime*, the walls "made" the town; they delineated urban space from rural space. New Orleans was a *ville* without walls. Vauban-inspired fortifications appeared as embellishments on many maps of early New Orleans, but nothing like them was actually built until the end of the French period, too late to convince the crown of the colony's fealty. In Louisbourg, fortified walls were a priority from the beginning and an almost non-stop building project throughout the city's life. They constituted "some of the most elaborate fortifications erected in North America in the first half of the eighteenth century."[87] From a strictly military point of view, this is somewhat understandable since Louisbourg was vulnerable to sea attacks (and indeed suffered a number of them by the British). New Orleans, however, was relatively protected by its difficult navigational approach. Still, the French had made enemies of powerful Native American groups such as the Natchez and Chickasaw, so administrators did periodically worry about the town's lack of defenses. After the Natchez revolt of 1729, they began work on a moat and palisade to surround the city, but the moat never reached a depth of more than a pathetic 12 inches and quickly silted up once the panic subsided.[88] A 1729 plan (fig. 6) illustrates these temporary ambitions for walls, but it also exposes the mistruths and exaggerations that colonial officials communicated back to the Ministry of Marine in France. The plan shows the town surrounded by massive and impermeable fortifications while its title reads "as it was in 1729."

The lack of walls certainly reflects the city's remoteness, its labor shortage, and lack of resources. But it also reflects social realities, for walls were meant as much to keep the populace in as to keep the enemy out. In France, sentries paced along the walls during the day and locked the gates at night. Movement both in and out of the city was restricted. The anonymous visitor to New Orleans in the 1750s quoted earlier was particularly alarmed that "the inhabitants, sailors, Indians, and slaves run around freely, inside as well as beyond the town."[89] The observer's language emphasized the disturbing permeability of the city's borders, or its outright lack of borders. No walls existed to control the flow of slaves, Indians, sailors, and vagrant rogues. Nor did a clear-cut boundary separate the city from the country, or culture from nature.

When local officials decided to revive plans to enclose New Orleans in 1760, they did so in an apparent response to exterior enemies. The French had just been defeated at Niagara in a major battle of the Seven Years' War (also known as the French and Indian War, 1756–63) and for the first time New Orleans now seemed vulnerable to the British from its upriver approach. In January Governor Kerlérec worked with one of the original (and now elderly) engineers, De Vergès, to draw up plans for a series of ditches, palisades, and bastions to surround the city. The fortifications were completed nine months later at the staggering estimated cost of 1 million livres (French pounds). Presented with this unexpected expenditure, metropolitan officials realized that Kerlérec's predecessors had never built the fortifications represented on the dozens of maps sent across the Atlantic in the 1720s and 1730s, and that the funds sent over for these projects had suspiciously evaporated. *Ordonnateur* Rochemore used the controversy of the walls to further his personal and political attacks against Governor Kerlérec. In 1763 Kerlérec was recalled to France, along with other leading citizens from both men's cabals. Several were thrown into the Bastille while police and judges investigated accusations of malfeasance and counteraccusations of defamation.

The story of the expensive but invisible walls of New Orleans became part of what was known in France as the "Louisiana Affair," a series of high-profile scandals and arrests of former Louisiana colonials (both French-born and creole) that took place between 1764 and 1769. The Louisiana Affair was playing out on the Continent at the same time that those back in New Orleans were plotting to tear down the new walls and welcome the British as trading partners in a new world of free trade.[90] Entrepreneurial rogues had always had their own plans for New Orleans.

⁕   ⁕   ⁕

New Orleans was an experiment in urban planning. In the early eighteenth century, the French thought it important to inaugurate their newest colony with the creation of a "metropolis." Accompanying the many structural changes initiated by Louis XIV was a new image of the ideal city as a rational head leading the agricultural body of the nation. While constraints at home prevented most architects and engineers from executing their perfect cities of the imagination, they hoped that the colonies would provide a clean slate for building. In some ways, the form of New Orleans reflects aspects of each of the four types of ideal cities in the *ancien régime*: the fortified town, the port city, the monumental city, and the garden. With the exception of Richelieu, New Orleans is more "perfect" in the dimensions and alignment of its grid according to early eighteenth-century building guidelines than any contemporary city in France. The only ones that come close are the other colonial cities the French built during the Enlightenment: Louisbourg, Mobile, St. Louis, Cap Français (Saint Domingue), Port-au-Prince (Saint Domingue), and Port Louis (Mauritius). Even these, however, do not match the rigid formal symmetry of New Orleans. As Gilles Langlois says of *les villes régulières*, "without a doubt, the most schematic of these are to be seen in the Americas . . . it must be admitted that New Orleans reflects the brilliant success of a model in execution."[91] The town never approached "metropolis" size in the French period, but by the 1750s it was larger than all these contemporary towns except Cap Français. Numbering between 4,000 and 4,500 inhabitants, it was a sizeable town in the context of what counted as "urban" in North America, comparable to New Haven or Salem at the time and second only to Charleston in the colonial South.[92] More striking, one-third of Louisiana's total colonial population lived in New Orleans.

The city's planners ensured that a social hierarchy would be inscribed in the landscape, by distributing lots on higher ground to "those with the means to develop them." In placing its main public square directly on the waterfront, the plan for New Orleans deviated from Vauban's defense ideals, but it reflects the fact that New Orleans was, despite its difficult approach, intended as a port city and built primarily to facilitate commerce and transportation. Planners also made sure that each lot had ample room for a garden. Though the gardens were intended to provide sustenance, there was also an aesthetic appeal, seen in the proliferation of "mini-Versailles" in the wealthier parts of town. Maintenance of these gardens against the exuberance of Louisiana's native plant life was another struggle that must have contributed to the town's disorderly appearance.

New Orleans did not go as far as it could have to realize its paper perfection. The defining feature of a Bourbon fortified town was missing: the city had no walls. This was perceived to be one of its principal failures, both as an experiment in urban planning and in social engineering. Beyond its aesthetic geometry and street names such as "St. Louis" and "Dauphin," the city did little to participate in the *ancien régime* movement toward architectural commemoration of the king. It had no *place royale*. By placing the church at the head of the Place d'Armes and the soldiers' barracks to the side, the city's builders seemed to put more faith in local instruments of social control. The king was too far away. Ironically, while the crown tried to write sectors of *ancien régime* society out of the colonial picture, in New Orleans the city seems to have erased the king. Architecture prefigured politics. The king's presence on the Louisiana Superior Council, which came to be run by a syndicate of local merchant-planters in the 1750s (as recounted in chapters 4 and 5), was also difficult to discern. The New Orleans example suggests that rogue colonialism may leave distinctive impressions on the colonial urban form.[93]

Some Frenchmen approached the lower Mississippi valley as a *bosquet sauvage*, or "wild woods," to be tamed by civilization through the building of roads, canals, and levees. Controlling the Mississippi River and its shifting silts was a more daunting task than they had imagined. Their mixed success meant that most New Orleans streets were ankle-deep in mud for much of the year, contributing to unhealthy vapors and miasmas that plagued the populace and bred disease. That a city built according to the latest ideas regarding transparency and circulation could be so unhealthy suggested a failure in the designs of modernity.[94] While in France the miasma of urban squalor was perceived to be endemic to the architecture of dense and tangled old cities, in New Orleans it emanated from the natural landscape. This unfriendly land caused some to despair of ever making the colony livable, while others attempted to tame nature in more modest ways through their garden fancies. Those who had the greatest success in their relationship with nature learned from local Native Americans. They recognized that colonial designs could not be cut from a pattern book, but had to be adjusted to the local terrain, which was *not* a *tabula rasa*. Creole modes of subsistence departed from both feudal and emerging capitalist models of settled agriculture.

Les grands—engineers, adventurous nobles, and Enlightened bureaucrats—viewed New Orleans as an experimental space in which to try out strategies of social control and fantasies of a privileged life. They did not anticipate that *les petits*—*engagés*, ex-convicts, sailors, slaves, and Indian traders—might also view this new urban landscape as a stage for reinvention outside the grid of absolutism. Despite having a street layout designed to communicate hierarchy and facilitate surveillance, New Orleans quickly became viewed as a place where social disorder reigned. Placing the garrison at the center of the town did little more than draw attention to the fact that its borders were unpoliced and its streets were full of rogues.

By the time the creole generation came of age in the 1730s, the streets of New Orleans still adhered to the grid irascibly carved out by Pauger. As I will discuss in the chapters that follow, creoles used the existing street grid to map a new social hierarchy. Native-born planters and merchants displaced French-born officials along the desirable riverfront. By the 1740s the latter were forced to rent small houses in the center of town. In other ways, the town strayed from the experimental order. Rather than being embraced in collective defense by a surrounding wall, the town was divided into hundreds of fenced lots. Rather than being a European metropolis of aristocratic gardens, New Orleans became a more African place, its gardens given over to slave quarters. Rather than serving as a major port for transatlantic trade, it became a hub for an intercolonial black market that defied mercantilist controls.

3

A BACKWATER ENTREPÔT

Today twenty-seventh of April one thousand seven hundred sixty nine, three o-clock in the afternoon, at the request of Dame Elizabeth Real, widow of the late Sr. Marin, living in this town in the Street of the Warehouses . . . being entered into the hall of the said House in which we have found the said Lady Widow Marin, seated between the two courtyard doors in the coolness, who seemed to us to be ill in body because of her great age, but sound in spirit, memory and understanding, it appeared to us that she was desirous of putting some order to her affairs and to dispose of the price of the Goods which it may please Divine Providence to grant to her, and to give her heirs all consideration.[1]

Thus begins the last will and testament of Madame Elizabeth Real Pascal Marin, whose life spans the experience of surviving and then thriving in French colonial New Orleans. Both documentary evidence and artifacts excavated from her courtyard in the French Quarter suggest that Madame Real's fortunes rose with those of the colony. During the charter period of John Law's Company of the Indies in the early 1720s, Elizabeth arrived in the stumptown that was New Orleans. She was then a teenager, from the Oleron district of Charente-Inférieur in the Bordeaux region. Though her exact arrival is uncertain, it is likely that she immigrated as an indentured servant transported to work for one of the concessions. From these humble beginnings, Madame Real transformed herself into a respectable colonial matron through two marriages and fifty years as a successful businesswoman.[2]

Archaeological artifacts from the later period of her household (1750s–1770s) include expensive, hand-painted Chinese porcelain, an ivory-handled fork, and etched wineglasses. A probate inventory enumerates her silver-plated fireplace irons, seven pictures in gilt frames, fourteen walnut chairs with straw seats, gilded coffee pots and tea services, fancy gaming tables for cadrille and piquet (popular French card games), a large mirror with gilt frame, and a mahogany bed with an embroidered cotton cover and silk mosquito curtains. Despite all the gilt, the Real house is not the estate of a large slaveowner; plantation slavery was not the source of Madame Real's wealth. Her will lists only one enslaved woman, named Mariana.

Despite her eventual wealth, Madame Real did not live an easy life. Her first husband was murdered, and she buried several children in the colony. Only one child survived to adulthood. Yet the documents show that in 1739 Madame Real had arranged an advantageous match for her only daughter to Chief Surgeon François Goudeau, a recent French arrival. By the 1760s two of her granddaughters by this union had married high-ranking French military officers with seigneurial titles. One of these was Paul Rastel de Rocheblave, a close ally of Louisiana's *ordonnateur* Rochemore. Over the course of her long life, Madame Real had worked her way into creole comfort and married her family into French nobility. Her family connections reached the top of the colonial power structure. She counted members of the Superior Council among her friends. Yet she was illiterate and could not even sign a mark for her name. Instead, she trusted her powerful, educated friends to execute the many documents of her professional and personal affairs that survive in the notarial archives.[3]

The author of Madame Real's will credited "Divine Providence" for her prosperity. But really she owed her success to "the devil's empire." Her fortune, like those of many of her New Orleans neighbors, was built on smuggling. Her first husband, Jean Pascal, was an Indian trader and boatman who circumvented the Company monopoly to conduct his own accounts. After he died in the Natchez uprising in 1729, she married another seaman, François Marin. Marin prospered as a shipowner who plied the waters of the Gulf of Mexico and the Caribbean; his itineraries included many officially banned ports. He and Elizabeth built a large house on a lot in New Orleans that she had inherited from her first husband. Although Marin is listed as an "innkeeper" in one document, the daily operations clearly fell to Elizabeth. The inn had a large storehouse that took up the entire bottom floor of the house, an amenity that appealed to business travelers. During his own frequent business trips, Marin granted his wife power of attorney to run their business and to manage his affairs. The Superior Council records contain dozens of similar arrangements between other husbands and wives in New Orleans. Because men were so busy traveling to the other entrepôts in the Mississippi-Caribbean sphere, the women who stayed behind played a prominent legal and economic role in New Orleans. Census snapshots of Madame Real's household also suggest that the resident population of New Orleans may be underestimated by as much as one-third due to the nature of its maritime economy, as her husbands were rarely at home to be counted.[4]

After Marin died in the early 1740s, Elizabeth continued to run the inn for another thirty years as an independent widow, using the contacts she had made through her husbands to sustain a business that catered to ship captains and traveling merchants. When she herself died in 1777, the property stayed within her circle of friends. It was sold first to the trader Santiago Lemelle and then to the family of René Beluche, a well-known smuggler and privateer who owned a corsair named *The Spy* that plied the waters of Barataria Bay below New Orleans. Her house, which was burned and rebuilt in 1788, stands in Dumaine Street today and is known to tourists as "Madame John's Legacy" after a fictional story by George Washington Cable about a creole woman of color who illicitly inherits her lover's property. The real Madame *Jean* Pascal built her legacy for herself. That legacy, as we will see, was not illicit, but it *was* built upon an illegal political economy.[5]

Planners designed New Orleans not just to realize the imperial aesthetics of Versailles, but also to serve the logistical and economic needs of a colonial monopoly. New Orleans began as a company town. Its establishment in 1718 was a symbolic groundbreaking for one of the boldest economic experiments undertaken in the eighteenth century—John Law's plan to integrate venture capital, banking, and the state treasury. The overnight appearance of a metropolis in the Louisiana wilderness would boost investor confidence, while the infrastructure of a well-designed port town would help protect the Company's monopoly privileges over both imports and exports. The entire city was intended as a laboratory for a new kind of colonial mercantilism. So important was New Orleans to Law's scheme that he rushed to meet his quota of immigrants, sending nearly 9,000 people in the space of five years (among whom was the young Elizabeth Real), though his charter allowed him twenty-five years. When the speculative Mississippi Bubble burst, most French investors gave up hopes of Louisiana ever bringing a profit. Soon thereafter the crown's interest in underwriting its imperial interests in the region flagged. As a result, hungry and impoverished Louisianans were left to their own devices, without the labor or capital to fully develop a plantation economy on the model of Saint Domingue or Virginia. This did not mean, however, that commerce came to a standstill.

The city did succeed as an entrepôt, but not exactly as planned. Although at times cut off from direct contact with France by wars and transatlantic shipping problems, New Orleans was far from isolated. Other suppliers and other trade routes took over. In 1753 newly arrived Governor Kerlérec reported to his French protector, "I must not, however, leave you in ignorance, my lord, of the fact that the commerce carried on by the agents at New Orleans has become very suspicious."[6] By the end of the French era, the material comfort of residents had improved to the point where luxuries such as silk, Bordeaux wine, gold jewelry, and fancy housewares were common.

Abused and abandoned by mercantilism, in the 1730s many New Orleanians turned away from the Atlantic world. Instead, they oriented themselves toward a world pioneered by Native Americans where trade had already created connections over a vast and diverse region. Africans and marginal Frenchmen were eager to explore this world and escape where they could the everyday despotism of the *ancien régime.* The business of New Orleans took its residents up and down the Mississippi and around the greater Caribbean. Because of the contacts they established, other members of the international circuit began reciprocating with frequent visits to New Orleans or its seaport at the mouth of the Mississippi.

In effect, New Orleans served as a major portal and marketplace not only for Louisiana's "frontier exchange economy," but also for an international network that I call the Mississippi-Caribbean World.[7] This circuit linked tiny New Orleans to the major ports of Veracruz, Havana, and Cap Français, as well as to sister cities such as St. Pierre, Martinique, and smuggling coasts such as Cartagena. Water-borne commerce flourished in a flotilla of pirogues, flatboats, coasting crafts, and small brigs that connected the Great Lakes to the South American mainland. This network became at least as important as the Atlantic in shaping everyday life in eighteenth-century New Orleans. Louisianans realized early on that their interests, if not their survival, depended more on local than on metropolitan economic ties. The maritime economy of the Mississippi-Caribbean appears only in the margins of official documentation of the custom houses and charter companies. Historians have often noted that relatively few of the "king's ships" docked in New Orleans on an annual basis. But the cargo of these ships represented only a small fraction of the goods moving through the port. Likewise, official censuses probably record only a fraction of the itinerant traders and sailors who made New Orleans their base of operations. Native Americans, Africans, Canadians, Spanish colonials, and seasoned French boatmen— and boatwomen—plied the waters as pilots, captains, coworkers, business partners, employees, and bound servants.

Archaeology suggests that colonial traders were taking advantage of land and water routes established in the prehistoric period. Eighteenth-century Louisianans reinvigorated an ancient international trade route between the Mississippi Valley and peoples living along the southern rim of the Gulf of Mexico. Although a work of the imagination, a painted poster created in 1720 to advertise the Louisiana enterprise captures the importance of the trade with Mexico, and the social interaction invited by a diverse regional economy (color plate 5). Not only did this non-Eurocentric commerce conflict with designs for Louisiana's dependence on the metropole, but most of this boat traffic was in fact illegal. In other words, New Orleans was a smuggling capital, one of many in the greater Caribbean. Although founded by mercantilism in the 1710s, by the 1730s the city was flourishing by undermining it. This fact has been overlooked in previous accounts of colonial New Orleans: it is easy to be taken in by John Law's blueprints and the red ink of Louisiana's official ledger.[8]

Smuggling not only helped fill the gaps of collapsed mercantilism and a disappointing plantation economy, it was the basis of the local *political* economy. In French New Orleans smuggling was the economic partner in rogue colonialism. A string of governors and Louisiana Superior Council members, from the inception of the colony until its ignoble end, were major investors in banned intercolonial trade. This served their interests, of course, but it also served those of the *petits gens* and the colony as a whole. Smuggling was licit, meaning socially acceptable, though clearly illegal. Where rogue colonialism is at work, the lines between the licit and illicit, or between law and disorder, become blurred.

Mercantilism and Alternative Economies

The specific rules of France's mercantilism fluctuated almost from year to year during the eighteenth century. The capricious nature of French policy may have encouraged a disregard for the rules altogether. In general principles, France's policies toward its colonies were more restrictive than those of Great Britain, but less restrictive than those of Spain.[9] Between 1712 and 1731 Louisiana colonists endured onerous terms under a series of proprietary companies collectively referred to as "the Company." The Company held exclusive control over all imports and exports. All nonlocal goods and necessities had to be purchased from Company stores at preset prices. Imported slaves could legally be obtained only from Company ships. All native exports, from tobacco and indigo to deerskins, had to be sold, commissioned, and/or shipped via the Company. After the crown took the colony back from the Company in 1731, independent French merchants gained the right to trade in Louisiana, but only if they operated out of a French port authorized for that destination, and only if they obtained a proper license. Though the particulars changed, the basic principles of official policy remained much the same: ships coming in and out of New Orleans had to be French-owned and carry French cargoes. Direct exporting to foreign markets by individual colonial traders was prohibited. Any violation of these economic restrictions—from the marketing of contraband to the use of prohibited trade routes—constituted a form of smuggling.

French officials found it difficult to enforce these laws on a distant frontier where sympathetic governors let local needs prevail. Still, Law's vision that New Orleans would play a key role in the colonial economy did eventually materialize.[10] Louisiana's commerce flowed along the internal waterways and overland paths established by prehistoric trade routes.[11] If this vast system had a center, it was New Orleans. Blankets and beads for the Indian trade flowed in and deerskins flowed out. New Orleans served as the central agricultural market where small farmers sold or bartered rice, greens, figs, sweet potatoes, eggs, and hams in exchange for imports such as sugar, coffee, wine, cloth, and furnishings. In New Orleans, plantation owners found buyers or commission agents for their cash crops of tobacco, indigo, and rice. Plantation slaves came to New Orleans on Sundays to sell the surplus of their provision plots, an activity protected by the Code Noir of 1724.[12] Records show they came on other days as well, either on their master's account or their own, to peddle produce and street food. Native Americans of lower Louisiana—the Ouacha, Tchouacha, Chitimacha, Choctaw, and others—frequented town, peddling fresh fish and game, bear oil, corn, herbs, and persimmon bread, in addition to deerskins. Dealers in lumber, pitch, and tar from the north shore of Lake Pontchartrain loaded their cargoes at New Orleans. The "frontier hinterland" of New Orleans was immense. Beaver pelts from the Great Lakes and wheat from French settlements in Illinois came regularly down the Mississippi, cattle drifted down on barges from as far away as present-day Texas, and deerskins from as far away as the Carolina border made their way to the wharves of New Orleans.[13]

New Orleans served as an entrepôt for four tiers of Louisiana's trade (fig. 8). The first tier corresponds to the local urban-rural exchange network involving what economic historian John Clark calls the "artificial hinterland," meaning the area of lower Louisiana below Natchez where settled agriculture dominated. In this circuit, nearby farmers along the lower river would sell foodstuffs and purchase supplies and sundries in the New Orleans market. Euro-Louisiana produce farmers (many of them German settlers), local Native Americans, slaves, and others traveled to the city once or twice a week to sell their goods at market. They also came to make purchases themselves and to attend to legal matters and business arrangements. For example, in 1737 François Calimache went to see the royal notary to sign a contract to deliver rice for the troops. In 1739 a free woman of color named Isabelle came to town to buy fifteen herd of cattle for her ranch and tar factory on the north shore of Lake Pontchartrain.[14]

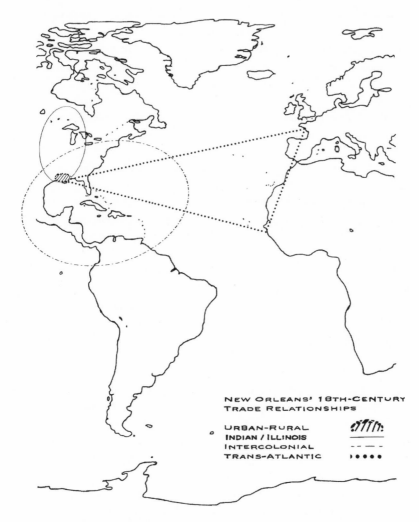

FIGURE 8. Tiers of New Orleans trade relationships in the eighteenth century. (Megan E. Edwards and Shannon Lee Dawdy.)

    Louisiana's second economic tier encompassed the Indian trade and Illinois farm country, a productive area and network of diplomatic relations cast over thousands of miles of the North American continent. *Voyageurs* would journey to the city to find buyers for their pelts and deerskins, and to acquire trade items such as arms, metal tools, beads, vermilion (valued as body paint), cloth, and liquor that had value in Native American markets. French and *métis* farmers in the Illinois country traded flour, hams, and bison tongues for imported luxuries such as sugar, wine, and cloth. Some of this trade was organized by the post commanders in the Illinois country; much of it was practiced outside the licenses and policies that were supposed to govern the economic interactions of colonists and natives. The convoys leaving New Orleans in flatboats and pirogues were manned by Africans, Indians, Canadians, and even a few Englishmen and Spaniards. Women and free people of color in Louisiana played a prominent role in this second tier of the Louisiana economy. While some operated storehouses, others owned or piloted boats. For example, Madame Labuissonnière operated her own boat that transported goods from the Illinois country to New Orleans. On one trip she hired a free man of color named Scipion who appears frequently in the records as a boatman working for various inland traders.[15] Throughout the French period New Orleans attracted delegations from Indian nations near and far that came to negotiate the terms of trade and conduct diplomacy—the two went hand-in-hand. A watercolor drawing by the draftsman De Batz depicts a Fox female slave, an enslaved African boy, an Attakapas hunter, and Chitimacha Indians in ceremonial paint mingling on the levee of New Orleans in 1735 among barrels of liquor and bundles of deerskins (color plate 6).[16]

The third tier of trade represents intercolonial commerce, most of which involved crossing the waters of the greater Caribbean (encompassing the Gulf of Mexico and the Caribbean proper). Louisiana consumers desired the sugar, coffee, flour, cloth, tools, liquor, Indian trade items, and household sundries available in island markets. Some of these items were local products, such as sugar, coffee, and rum, while others were European imports. After the Company period, slavers rarely entered Louisiana waters due to poorer payment terms and the greater distance, so the islands were practically the only source of new enslaved laborers for Louisiana after the 1730s. In official trade dockets, the French West Indies was the only legitimate destination for Louisiana exports such as pitch, tar, lumber, and rice. This third tier of intercolonial trade, however, included a brisk business with the Spanish, English, and Dutch colonies. Louisianans conducted this trade under various terms of legitimacy and illegitimacy in the eighteenth century. Most of these exchanges involved the acquisition of coin, flour, and livestock from the Spanish and the delivery of French cloth, wine, fine goods, and foodstuffs considered contraband by Spanish mercantile law.

This trade, which extended from nearby Pensacola to the coast of Cartagena in present-day Colombia, had its romantic side. A military officer named St. Denis became a legendary figure in eighteenth-century Louisiana for his smuggling escapades in Mexico, smooth-talking his way out of jail and wooing away a governor's daughter as his wife.[17] Nationless pirates and smugglers, such as Michel Fitzgerald and Jacques de Meyère (characters about whom we will hear more, below), found New Orleans a useful base of operations from which to reach Veracruz, Havana, Jamaica, and Portobello. Their visits had become routine in New Orleans by the late 1730s. Pirate Jean Béranger had scoped the scene in the 1720s, reporting: "Though the Spaniards have expressly forbidden their colonies to trade with the French, especially the Louisiana settlers, nevertheless when we learn how to carry out this commerce, we will profit from it because the Spaniards want our goods as much as we want their money. The proximity of Louisiana to the Spanish Indies assures us of good trade."[18]

The fourth tier, equivalent to the transatlantic trade, has traditionally dominated thinking about colonial economies. As many scholars have observed, in Louisiana this economic sector was governed by mercantilist policies, plagued by logistical nightmares, and crippled by shortages of labor and capital. In this sphere French Louisiana may, indeed, be measured largely a failure. Still, by the 1740s New Orleans employed a number of commission agents, transatlantic merchants, and longshoremen who handled hogsheads of tobacco and indigo destined for French ports. Planters delivering their crops to the city could attend a slave auction, purchase French imports stocked in city shops, or browse for delicacies in the bustling, open-air market. Transatlantic exchange was an underdeveloped, though not inactive, sector of Louisiana's economy in the French period.

This four-tier schematic represents interconnected fields of relationships, not separate spheres. For example, the Indian trade depended upon transatlantic shipments of beads and cloth. The colonial trade introduced European and Caribbean luxury items into the hand-to-hand bartering system of the local urban-rural trade. Local boatmen kept busy transporting pitch, tar, and lumber from Mobile and the north shore of Lake Pontchartrain to the city's quays; the busy Spanish colonial ports needed these products for shipbuilding and repair. Thus, Louisiana's most valued native exports in the intercolonial trade indirectly facilitated the transatlantic trade.[19] Temporarily separating these domains of the colonial economy helps us see the regional relationships they engendered and envision the circuits along which goods, peoples, and ideas flowed. It also reveals the centrality of New Orleans within three regional networks—the urban-rural, Indian-Illinois, and intercolonial—despite its small size and its marginal position in the fourth tier of transatlantic trade.

The Mississippi-Caribbean World

Jonathas Darby wrote in 1753, "We are excellently situated for the commerce with Spain. Communications exist between Pensacola and Mobile;

between Natchitoches, through the Adayes and Mexico, between New Orleans and Mexico by vessels from Veracruz, Campeche and Havana."[20] Darby's economic optimism shows how New Orleanians expanded their horizons well beyond the limits of mercantilism. Mercantilism entailed the engineered control not only of goods, but also of geography. Goods and people were supposed to move in a relatively straight line from metropole to colony and back again. This order envisioned for New Orleans, however, soon gave way to local "disorder," in which people, goods, and even ideas moved in circuits outside of metropolitan control. The French may have had some success in imposing their civilization upon the landscape through the street grid of New Orleans, but the course of Louisiana's economic development rested upon older and larger geohistorical structures that were more powerful than imperial resolve.

Although metropolitan planners may have imagined themselves as engineers at play in a virgin land, colonists on the ground soon looked to experienced Native Americans for guidance in how to contend with the forces of nature and the special geography of the lower Mississippi delta. The economic development of New Orleans in the French era shows how colonialism fit into long-term continuities at the same time that it introduced breaks within the smaller scale of social history.[21]

New Orleans as a port city presents something of a paradox. On the one hand, the site was selected because of its ideal position as a transportation hub, situated at an intersection of the continent's largest north-south river, an ancient east-west overland trade route, and a protected outlet into the waters of the Gulf of Mexico. On the other hand, for deep-keeled European vessels, the city's "front door" consisted of a dangerous, 100-mile-long stretch of winding, shifting water and silt that even knowledgeable pilots could not easily predict. With unloading time and adverse winds, the journey from the mouth of the river to New Orleans for an ocean-going ship could take up to six weeks, as long as a favorable voyage from France to the Caribbean. The city's "back door," through Lake Pontchartrain and Bayou St. John, provided a quicker passage to the Gulf of Mexico (the journey could be done in twenty hours), but only small coastal and riverine craft dared brave those shallow waters. And these small boats could be lost when the usually placid inland bay kicked up 15-foot swells during sudden storms.

Bienville selected the site for New Orleans on the advice of Native Americans who had found it a useful crossroads of land and water routes. He may have failed to fully consider the logistical differences between travel by canoe and brigantine. Still, the bustling Indian entrepôt that his brother Iberville described in 1699 has always been a bit of a mystery, since the area below the city was sparsely populated in the contact period. Who was going

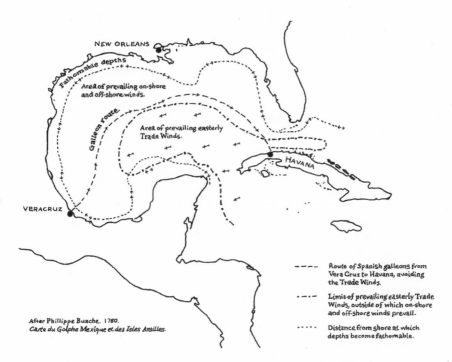

Route of Spanish galleons from Vera Cruz to Havana, avoiding the Trade Winds.

Limit of prevailing easterly Trade Winds, outside of which on-shore and off-shore winds prevail.

Distance from shore at which depths become fathomable.

FIGURE 9. Sailing routes in the Gulf of Mexico. (Megan E. Edwards and Shannon Lee Dawdy.)

where, and why? While it is possible that most traffic through the site moved east-west and from the north (traffic going to/from the Mobile area or down the river), another portage farther upriver, near present-day Manchac, would have been an easier transfer point. The portage at New Orleans makes more sense for traffic coming from the south, either up the Mississippi or through the flooded marshlands of the adjacent Barataria basin. While large ships in historic times struggled for weeks against the currents to reach New Orleans, *pirogues* (the local term for dugout canoes) working the shoreline eddies or navigating the slow waters of Barataria could arrive in just a couple of days.

From the perspective of the greater Caribbean, the foot of the Mississippi delta was ideally situated. By the early eighteenth century British and French mariners had learned what Native American and Spanish sailors knew centuries earlier: that winds and currents within the Gulf of Mexico create opposing spirals of force just a few leagues apart (fig. 9). Trade winds moving from the northeast to the southwest facilitate movement from the Florida straits to Yucatán. For the return voyage, tracking close to the coast in a counter-clockwise arc allows boats to avoid these headwinds and pick up the gathering swirl of the Gulf Stream before it spits out into the Atlantic between Cuba and the tip of Florida. Taking advantage of the wind and currents, the Spanish flotilla from Veracruz to Havana traced an inverted U-shaped route, the high point of which lies just below the mouth of the Mississippi. The site of New Orleans thus had the advantages of being the last stop along North American's greatest river, and being situated navigationally at the halfway point between two of Spain's most important colonial ports. The trip from New Orleans to Veracruz took about two weeks; the time to Havana was shorter. French colonials may have learned from native Louisianans how to navigate this ancient, trans-Gulf route in small craft that hugged the shallow coastline. Archaeologists have long noted apparent cultural connections between the Mississippi Valley and the east coast of Mexico, seen in ceramic technologies, religious ideas, and trade goods, as well as the distribution of maize and its cultivation. Archaeological evidence from colonial New Orleans sites demonstrates a continuation of this ancient trading network with historic-period importation of Mexican pottery and a distinctive variety of corn.[22] French settlers entered into an Indian-dominated area characterized by extensive international trade and diplomatic contacts. That their own developing colonial culture soon came to resemble this reflects the unique geographical position of New Orleans, but it also underscores the role of Native Americans in the making of colonial Louisiana.

New Orleans was a busy port with far-reaching New World connections, but it was a port mainly of pirogues, barges, and small single- or two-masted coasting vessels. The few large vessels that ventured to town moored just downriver from the Place d'Armes, while smaller craft pulled up to the levee opposite the city's upriver market area. Small vessels approached from three main directions: west-northwest (upriver) via the Mississippi, north-northeast through Lake Pontchartrain and Bayou St. John, or south from the mouth of the river or the Barataria marshes (see figure 3 in chapter 2).

Trade between upper and lower Louisiana moved to an annual rhythm. Joining the regular traffic by Indian traders in pirogues, convoys of rafts and flat-bottom riverboats left New Orleans with supplies of imports, such as coffee, sugar, and cloth, for the more remote French settlements. They brought back flour and cured hams for city residents. The expeditions numbered up to twenty boats, leaving New Orleans in the early autumn and reaching Fort Chartres in Illinois three to four months later. They returned in the early spring, floating rapidly downriver in as few as twelve days. Small solo craft also made weekly trips to the east Gulf ports. The journey to Mobile took four to five days, to Pensacola a day or two more.[23]

The lower Mississippi presented serious problems for tall sailing vessels. Besides the dangerous and unpredictable nature of the riverbed, a sandbar

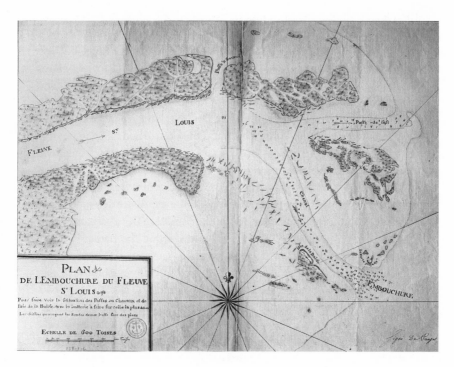

FIGURE 10. *Plan de L'Embouchure du Fleuve St. Louis,* Adrien de Pauger, 29 May 1724. Fort La Balize was located on the large island at lower center. (Courtesy of The Newberry Library, Chicago.)

in the main pass of the river often had a sounding of only 10–12 feet, while most large ships laden with cargo drew 15–20 feet. To address these problems, the French built La Balize ("the beacon"), a fort at the mouth of the river's birdfoot delta (fig. 10). There incoming ships could hire resident pilots or transfer their cargo to barges and smaller craft (called lighters) that would complete the journey to New Orleans. In 1727 fifty-five Company-owned slaves lived at what the census-taker referred to as the "port" of La Balize. After the fort was built, these men were mainly employed in transferring cargoes.[24] Although located 100 nautical miles downstream, La Balize served as the primary harbor for New Orleans. The majority of goods loaded and unloaded there still passed through the city, but they arrived on small, local transports.

Bienville made no effort to conceal another advantage of La Balize: "We cannot count on any commerce with the Spaniards of Campeche, Veracruz and Havana if they are obliged to go up to New Orleans to carry on their trade with us . . . in four days' time they would transact their business at

The Balize and they could in this way easily hide from their governor the secret commerce they might carry on with us."[25] In other words, not only was it unnecessary for large ships to struggle up to New Orleans, but also such an exposed move might inhibit free trade. Officers and soldiers in the garrison at La Balize facilitated smuggling sanctioned by the governor and engaged in exchanges on their own account. The agents controlling access to the river were among those most invested in smuggling (Bienville's posse of cavaliers, freebooters, and privateers), and the French had failed to provide the colony with either a police force or a customs house to enforce their own designs of mercantile returns.

The multiple mouths of the Mississippi delta create at least four separate passes into the main channel of the river, but even Bienville's men never attempted to control more than one of these passes. The alternate entries into the river, as well as nearby marshy inlets within the Barataria basin, provided countless spots for clandestine trade. The term "Barataria" itself refers to an act of maritime fraud, a faked or intentional shipwreck that allows the captain or crew to make off with the cargo.[26]

The rear entrance to New Orleans was also well suited to smuggling activity. Cargo transfers could easily be concealed along the stretches of Lake Ponchartrain's beachline or within the dense cypress swamps bordering parts of the Bayou St. John and its tributaries. In 1766 a British captain, Harry Gordon, described the scene at the mouth of Bayou St. John: "To this place the Trade from Mobile comes, & all manner of Smuggling: There are three Schooners, [that] constantly ply betwen the East side of Lake Pontchartrain." He noted that local residents profited from this busy trade by charging an exorbitant 20 "dollars" per boatload for the two-mile portage between the bayou and the Mississippi.[27]

Although few made the journey up to New Orleans, tall ships from major European and colonial ports did frequent La Balize. The delightful watercolors of Louisiana visitor Caillot show some of the larger vessels that made the transatlantic voyage with relative ease, but then struggled to make their way up to the docks of New Orleans (color plate 7). Independent French ships found Louisiana a convenient base from which to ply the Gulf searching for an entry into the Spanish market. By 1726 Spanish ships were arriving at the Mississippi looking for cargoes; three at a time were stacked up at La Balize during the War of Jenkins Ear (1739–48). The Louisiana Superior Council actively encouraged this practice and preferred that Spanish customers come to La Balize to avoid the vigilance of Spanish officials.[28] Bienville and Salmon wrote in 1733: "Although the royal officers of Havana and of the different ports of Mexico are extremely rigid about this commerce it will not be impossible to induce some private persons from these ports to come to ours." By this means they also guaranteed a flow of specie into town and ensured outbound shipping for Louisiana's exports.[29] Although New Orleanians made special efforts to welcome Spanish vessels, most of the smuggling ships that tied together the international community of the greater Caribbean sported intentionally ambiguous nationalities. Their sea chests contained assorted flags that could be hoisted as the occasion required.

Winds, currents, and profits propelled the ties between New Orleans and Veracruz and Havana. Havana was not just a port, but a portal, positioned at the gateway of Spain and New Spain in the transatlantic journey. Spanish ships going both directions stopped there, as did many non-Spanish ships looking for provisions, repair, or trade opportunities. Like Louisiana, Cuba had an agricultural economy that grew slowly until the late eighteenth century, but the city of Havana rightly deserved the title of metropolis as one of the largest and busiest cities in the Antilles. Havana's harbor was relatively well fortified (although the British did invade it in 1762), making it easier for motivated officials to detect illicit trade. Contraband commerce, however, flourished in small coves and beachheads outside Havana, along Cuba's southern coast, and in the eastern town of Santiago de Cuba. In the eighteenth century Cubans eagerly traded for dry goods from Europe; they also paid well for slaves from Jamaica and the French West Indies. In the early period Louisianans offered mainly provisions and ship stores in exchange for Spanish silver. After 1748 this trade was expanded to include "the re-export of French manufactured goods and luxuries . . . [that] substantially broadened the town's economic base, and therefore its communications network, despite Spanish officials' view that New Orleans existed merely as a haven for smugglers."[30]

Veracruz, at the opposite end of the Spanish galleon route, served a large and rich hinterland. Founded in 1600, the city quickly became the most important port of entry into Mexico and the "principal western terminus of the trade between Spain and New Spain." Veracruz merchants described it as "the neck" through which all Mexican imports and exports must pass. Spanish manufactures represented only a fraction of the European goods entering into Mexico via Veracruz. If this demand market were not attractive enough, the city was also a major point of egress for Spain's colonial silver. Both pirates and smugglers found the port irresistible and access easy due to its low, marshy approach. Cargoes moving through New Orleans destined for Veracruz comprised primarily French wine and brandy, textiles and hats, and Louisiana pitch and tar.[31]

Different considerations motivated the ties between New Orleans and other ports. A degree of economic and administrative dependency defined the legitimate relationship of New Orleans to Cap Français in Saint Domingue. The centripetal force of Saint Domingue's sugar boom quickly made it the most important stop of the French transatlantic trade by the early eighteenth century. It became a transfer point for the rest of France's American colonies. The island even played middleman to Canadian trade. In Saint Domingue, prices were high and officials vigilant. To circumvent both factors, New Orleans formed trading relationships not only with easily accessed "natural" destinations, such as Veracruz and Havana, but also with culturally similar ports, such as St. Pierre in Martinique and Portobello on the Panamanian isthmus. These were two of the most active smuggling entrepôts in the New World.

New Orleans was one among dozens of small port cities in the greater Caribbean that largely abandoned the transatlantic trade to the "megaports," such as Cap Français or Havana, and instead turned their attention "inward toward the Caribbean," and established a "thriving coastal and short-distance regional trade of small locally-built vessels." As early as 1713 Duclos reported that small ships from Louisiana were making regular trips to Veracruz. Governor Bienville's ambitions for New Orleans as an international entrepôt materialized after the Company gave up its Louisiana monopoly in 1731, allowing a group of naturalized, creole, and nationless traders to push more confidently into the waters they had come to know on their small, spry vessels.[32] Caillot's *mémoire* reports that in 1730 two brigantines, a sloop, four boats, three flatboats, and fifty pirogues were already serving the trade. Two damaged tall ships sat along the quay awaiting repairs.[33]

Though not a systematic or complete list, Louisiana Superior Council records identify twenty-five ships based in New Orleans in the French period, and list several more unnamed vessels. One that plied a trade between La Balize and Havana in 1748 was christened *La Nouvelle Orleans*. *Le François* was a 50-ton ship owned by François Marin (husband of Elizabeth Real) and his partner Fillart that traveled to Pensacola, Havana, and Martinique in the late 1730s. A 50-ton brigantine named the *St. Jean Baptiste* provided a particularly active link between New Orleans and its colonial neighbors, making numerous voyages to Havana, St. Pierre, Pensacola, and Veracruz between 1737 and 1745. New Orleans merchant and Superior Council member Gerard Pery was part-owner of several boats between 1736 and 1743, including the brigantine *Marie Elizabeth*, *Les Deux Amis*, and the 50-ton *St. Louis*. A 130-ton snow called *The Nymph*, purchased by innkeeper Ignace Petit in 1743, was one of the largest New Orleans vessels. A pirate and sometimes privateer named Michel Fitzgerald did much to keep the New Orleans fleet replenished. In 1735 he purchased a 30-ton boat named *La Guyonnette*, and the following year bought a bark (a large three-masted ship) called the *St. Anne* that was large enough to handle shipments of lumber and tar. Fitzgerald sold *The Mary*, a prize from Carolina he had captured, to a local captain who renamed it *L'Hirondelle* and plied a trade along the Florida and, ironically, Carolina coasts. Fitzgerald later acquired the frigate *La Fortune* as a prize from the English (its former name was *L'Avare*, or *The Miser* in English) and sailed it between New Orleans, Jamaica, and the West Indies in the mid-1740s before selling it to another local man.[34]

Smuggling Empire

The Louisiana colony was nurtured by piracy and smuggling from its beginnings in a way that clouds any easy distinction between legal and illicit enterprises. In 1698 Iberville hired a well-known Dutch pirate named Laurens de Graaf to act as his pilot in Gulf waters. The first Louisiana census names thirteen men with the occupation of "freebooters" (*flibustiers*, or men who worked for booty) living at Fort Maurepas in December 1699. A pirate and smuggler named Béranger described how he helped settlers survive by running a corsair between Martinique and the Gulf coast in the early years, preying upon New England ships when not docked at Tortuga, the legendary port of the Caribbean underworld. He provided Louisianans with wine, eau de vie (brandy or crude rum), flour, and dry goods plundered from New England ships in exchange for Native American slaves and lumber. He gave them a "good deal" on munitions they needed due to the Spanish threat at nearby Pensacola. Béranger also lavished praise on Commandant Bienville, who had encouraged his services.[35]

By 1706 Bienville and his brother Iberville themselves had gained a reputation for smuggling and profiteering. A contemporary reported that Bienville "has employed for his private service all the people maintained by his Majesty and that the crews of the small vessels that are in Louisiana were almost always employed for the account of the late Sieur d'Iberville and his brothers to transport their goods to Veracruz." By 1718 Bienville was also supporting regular runs to Havana, although statistics are scant. Not all Louisiana officials cooperated in the trade. Long-time Mobile post commander Diron D'Artaguette warned French ministers in 1712 that the colony was becoming a "pirate settlement." In the course of his career, the Ministry of the Marine twice recalled Bienville to France, largely over his suspicious commerce and a lack of zeal in enforcing the Company's trade monopoly.[36]

Bienville's troubles do not reflect a violation of principle so much as the occasional conflict between a state and its agents when both are in pursuit of the same reward. With its patent to the first Louisiana Company in 1712, the French crown had actually endorsed smuggling as a colonial venture. The proprietor, Antoine Crozat, made the Spanish trade a priority. Through its share in Company profits, the French crown sought Mexican silver and South American gold to stabilize its treasury. Discouraged by efforts to gain direct access to Spain's colonial wealth through expansionist campaigns or outright piracy, the French turned to gentler means—by offering Spanish colonists stylish goods for purchase. Nevertheless, the state wanted this to be *controlled* smuggling, as made clear by a document entitled "Project for the Royal Company of the Indies on the Subject of Trade with Mexico." The crown still frowned upon small-time smuggling by independent colonists, be they military officers or marooned slaves. Both the Crozat and Law company charters barred individual colonists from direct foreign trade. A royal decree of 1727 reinforced this by banning *pacotilles*, or "ventures," the small cargoes that sailors and passengers were customarily allowed to trade on their own account. The decree also outlawed hand-to-hand trade between sailors and colonists. It made clear for the first time that colonial smuggling was a treasonous activity. The decree remained in effect throughout the French period, although in Louisiana enforcement was irregular at first and by the 1740s nonexistent.[37]

That smuggling by individual colonists not only continued after the decree of 1727, but soon outstripped state-controlled smuggling was one of the reasons the king and his advisers fretted over the "disorders" of New Orleans. Another reason was that uncontrolled smuggling could damage the imperial political balance by angering Spanish officials or allowing English "spies" to enter Louisiana. Despite these worries, France did little to enforce its own policies.

Since the mid-sixteenth century, roving pirates and rogue smugglers had been a fact of life in the Caribbean. Although outright piracy declined in the eighteenth century due to coordinated actions of the European powers, smuggling actually increased during this period, becoming more organized, more predictable, and more political. A large body of literature considers the two main players in this high-stakes game, the British and the Spanish. But French, Dutch, and Portuguese nationals carried on a lively trade with both sides, as did a motley crew of "masterless" seamen of ambiguous nationality and shifting allegiance.[38]

The smuggling basis of the New Orleans economy in the French period has been understated in the historical literature.[39] One reason may be the problem of evidence. Smugglers of course strive *not* to leave a paper trail. This presents difficulties for the historical study of illegal trading and informal economies throughout the world, not just in colonial Louisiana. Lance Grahn, in his study of smuggling on the coast of eighteenth-century Nueva Granada, acknowledges that "the history of illegal activity will always be an incomplete narrative. After all, the secrecy of an illicit act is one of its principal measures of success." He goes on to describe how smugglers of many nationalities employed strategies from the same "bag of tricks," depending upon the local physical and political environment. The offloading of cargo along remote shorelines, conducting open-water transfers to smaller craft, sending disguised cargo to upstanding merchants in port, and paying bribes to the right officials were among the techniques used by smugglers in Nueva Granada, as well as by France's own domestic tobacco smugglers. In an indulgent political climate, they deployed more subtle means, such as inventing a legitimate pretext to enter an off-limits port or unload a banned cargo. Ships were forced off course by "bad weather" or claimed a need for emergency repairs or provisions. Wartime invited faked seizures and the liberal use of "flags of truce." All of these strategies crop up in Louisiana's Superior Council records. In 1724 Jean Béranger recommended befriending the port captain at Veracruz, as "he comes to Louisiana with cash and fears no confiscation upon his return since the very ones who could confiscate benefit from this trade."[40]

Although relatively few smuggling cases were prosecuted in eighteenth-century New Orleans, evidence suggests that tactics such as those described by Béranger were constantly used. Thus, the lack of a regulatory record probably results more from a pervasive complicity by officials than from lack of activity. Notarial documents in the Superior Council records show people going where they are not supposed to go. Archaeology shows them having goods they are not supposed to have. The behavior of colonials suggests a conspiring elite and a highly mobile and insubordinate underclass. When these multiple lines of evidence are made to converge, the economy of colonial New Orleans appears considerably more complex than it does on official balance sheets.

The city's greatest economic advantage was that it operated as a port of free trade throughout much of the eighteenth century—sometimes officially, often unofficially. The court relaxed mercantilist restrictions during times of war when hazardous shipping conditions cut off the colonies from the metropole. During these "hard times," Louisiana governors had permission to make exceptions and allow supply runs to Spanish colonial ports such as Pensacola, Havana, and Veracruz. As France was at war almost continuously during Louisiana's first twenty years, these trading "exceptions" became a habit hard to break. Periods of war affected Louisiana's trade balance, but the results were not always negative, as has often been assumed.

When we plot 823 documented ship arrivals in Louisiana (about 90 percent of them at La Balize or New Orleans) against periods of war and peace, a flickering image of Louisiana's shipping links to the outside world emerges. The first spike corresponds to the dramatic influx of people and materials that occurred during the John Law period (1717–21). Just before the bubble popped, Louisiana experienced a high of 29 official ship arrivals in 1720. A few years later, the colony was "abandoned"—an annual average of only 6.6 French ships were recorded between 1723 and 1734. But beginning in the mid-1730s Louisiana's maritime activity began to take off dramatically. Recorded ship arrivals (based on incidental reports of the number of ships in port at any one time) jumped to 18 in 1735 and reached a high of 49 in 1745, at a time when France and England were at war. Theoretically, navy blockades and privateering should have made this a time of hardship for Louisiana. Although official ship arrivals may have leveled off in the 1750s, judging from years for which records are more complete, they still hovered around 28 ships per year, the overall average from 1737 to 1764. It is estimated that these recorded ship arrivals represent a 20–30 percent sample of *actual* (and largely unrecorded) shipping, meaning that by the first creole generation, New Orleans was averaging over 100 ships per year. If they stayed in port for a typical two-week period for repairs, trade, and provisioning, then historical descriptions of 10–30 tall ships resting in port at any one time seem quite plausible. New Orleans might have been a navigational backwater, but it was not sleepy.[41]

In the 1730s Louisiana's maritime trade began to boom just as the creole generation began to come into inheritances and positions of influence. When the Company of the Indies gave up its monopoly of Louisiana in 1731, French ministers relaxed prohibitions against direct trade with other French colonial ports. While the policy eventually resulted in more traffic to Saint Domingue and Martinique, the effects were not immediate. An average of only 3 ships per year was recorded arriving from or departing for the French West Indies in the 1730s. Rather, much of the growth relates to increased Spanish colonial traffic encouraged by local, not metropolitan, policies. Governor Bienville, who had long advocated the Spanish trade, returned to the colony for his fourth and final term in this office in 1733. In the 1740s the West Indies and the Spanish colonial trade got a further boost from Bienville's successor, Vaudreuil, who promoted an open-port policy from 1743 to 1744 during King George's War.

Vaudreuil estimated that the trade between New Orleans and the Spanish colonial ports in these years totaled 750,000 livres (French pounds) per year. Although the crown declined to extend his policy during peacetime, Vaudreuil appears to have unofficially encouraged free trade throughout his prosperous tenure (1743–53). Vaudreuil reported that the value of the Spanish trade had grown to 1 million livres by 1752. This amount is staggering when compared to the value of Louisiana's raw exports, estimated at 300,000 livres per year for the same period. Vaudreuil's figures reinforce the impression of strong and steady growth in the intercolonial trade through the 1740s and 1750s, much of it technically illegal. Darby, an Englishman who had worked for the Company in Louisiana before striking out on his own as a planter, remarked that from 1745 to 1750 "our commerce had prospered by the circulation of Spanish money. Our people lived contented and the colony was in honor abroad. Many vessels came in from various ports to share in the benefits of commerce."[42]

The same Superior Council Records that mention ships in port often indicate the ship's origin or destination. Although this fragmentary record is biased toward legitimate trade with the West Indies and France, significant patterns in the relationship between New Orleans and other ports in the greater Caribbean emerge when these voyages are tallied. The percentage of banned "foreign" ports and the number of intercoastal voyages to other small, secondary ports stand out. Between 1735 and 1763, the origin or destination of 229 intercoastal voyages can be determined. As seen in table 1, the "megaports" of Havana, Veracruz, and Cap Français (Saint Domingue/Haiti) play a large role in New Orleans trade, as expected. The surplus of Spanish silver in Havana and Veracruz made those ports worth the risk of detection or rejection by officials. Although a longer journey by sea than the Spanish cities, Cap Français was a necessary stop, if not for goods, then for regular postal service to France, because of its official role as the primary port of transfer for French transatlantic naval and commercial shipping. But combined, these three mega-ports make up only 27 percent of the known coastal trade. Over half of the recorded voyages (51 percent) involve foreign (and usually banned) Spanish, British, or Dutch colonial ports. Most shipping connections of New Orleans in the greater Caribbean were with other secondary ports and small coastal transfer points. Many of these, such as Cartagena, Portobello, and Jamaica, were notorious smuggling harbors. Table 1 also provides evidence of a previously unrecognized shipping link to Martinique. Although trading to this sister colony of the French empire was legal for licensed ships, it was a long and dangerous journey to the Windward Islands. But the bustling black market of the town of

TABLE 1. Origin or Destination of Recorded Intercoastal Ships through New Orleans or La Balize, 1735–63

Spanish colonies (unspecified)	9
"Côte d'Espagne" (Spanish Main)	3
Cartagena	5
Portobello, Panama	2
Mexico	2
Campeche	10
Veracruz	20
Cuban coast	2
Havana	16
Florida	2
Pensacola	16
St. Augustine, Florida	3
St. Marc des Apalache	2
SPANISH COLONIES TOTAL	92 (40%)
French West Indies (unspecified)	35
Saint Domingue	10
Cap Français	24
Leogane/Petit Goave/Port-de-Paix/Cayes St. Louis, Saint Domingue	6
Port-au-Prince, Saint Domingue	7
Martinique	18
St. Pierre, Martinique	11
Guadeloupe	1
FRENCH WEST INDIES TOTAL	112 (49%)
Curaçao	7
English colonies (unspecified)	2
Carolina	3
New York	1
Jamaica	6
Londonderry, Ireland	1
Philadelphia	3
Rhode Island	2
OTHER COLONIES TOTAL	25 (11%)
TOTAL	229 (100%)

St. Pierre probably made it an attractive alternative to officious Cap Français in Saint Domingue.[43]

Patterns in the local shipping connections of New Orleans shifted somewhat over time, but smuggling activity was a constant. Vaudreuil's free-trade experiment appears as a dramatic spike in recorded voyages in the mid-1740s. Over the entire period, Spanish and West Indian trade usually rose and fell in tandem, although in the late 1740s the Spanish colonies for a while surpassed the French Indies in importance. The British colonial and Curaçao trade really only became significant during the last dozen years of the French period. This international commerce, however, was growing rapidly by the mid-1760s and becoming nearly as important as the Spanish colonial trade. Spanish officials were not pleased to inherit yet another port whose populace collaborated with aggressive British traders.

Table 1 excludes transatlantic French ships but they, too, had a hand in the smuggling trade. Ship's crews (even on naval "king's ships") dealt in *pacotilles* and contraband goods in violation of regulations. After 1731 most French commercial ships could legally enter New Orleans or La Balize with the appropriate paperwork. They often used La Balize as a base from which to reach less legitimate destinations in the Spanish colonies.

One prominent example of the collusion between approved transatlantic commerce and local smuggling is provided by the Rasteau family trading house, based in the city of La Rochelle, France. They sent son Paul Rasteau to New Orleans, ostensibly to take care of its Mississippi trade, but what Paul largely did was to use New Orleans as an entrepôt and transshipment point for illegal trade with the Spanish colonies. In a letter of instructions, elder family members advised Paul to consider the destinations of Veracruz and the coast of Campeche. At the same time, they advised him to reassure Louisiana's *ordonnateur* Salmon that their object was to attract trade to Louisiana. The family's orders to the captain of the Rasteaus' ship *Lion d'Or* advised a cautious approach in Mexico, leaving much up to his "discretion." They were obviously aware that they were engaging in legally questionable traffic. The *Lion d'Or* made several journeys between France, Louisiana, Pensacola, and Veracruz. The Superior Council records even contain a bill for "gifts" made by its captain to the master gunner and harbor master of Veracruz. The Rasteaus received gold and silver coin in exchange for luxury items, such as gilt mirrors and beaver hats. Paul Rasteau, a Protestant, became one of the most prominent merchants in New Orleans and himself made many trips to Veracruz before perishing in a shipwreck during a smuggling journey to Florida and Carolina around 1747.[44]

Another glimpse of how smuggling operations worked comes from a written set of instructions that New Orleans merchant Barthelemy Milhet prepared for a ship captain in 1751. Milhet told him to stop first at Veracruz and then on the Campeche coast. He advised that the crew should be composed mostly of Frenchmen and disguised as navy sailors in case they should meet with the Spanish Costa Guardia or be taken by an English corsair.[45]

In New Orleans, enforcement of mercantilist restrictions and contraband laws appears to have been lax at best, with the exception of a brief period under the Company of the Indies between 1718 and 1731. During this time, when trade restrictions were tightest and the Company had vigilant agents on the ground willing to look out for its interests, the Superior Council investigated a number of smuggling and profiteering cases. Most of these cases remained unresolved, perhaps because the trail of evidence led to the top of the colonial power structure. Although few in number, they shed light on local operations. Prosecutions became rarer between 1731 and 1769, but a stack of circumstantial evidence from the civil and notarial records (which even includes civil suits between identified smugglers and pirates) strongly suggests that the colony's creole elite and its French- and Canadian-born governors had institutionalized illegal foreign trade. This commerce, however, was notoriously difficult to control from the top.

The evidence of smuggling, garnered from Louisiana's notarial archives and official correspondence, demonstrates how colonial elites were less oriented toward fulfilling metropolitan plans than toward consolidating their own wealth and power. Whether politicians, smugglers, or both, these were rogue agents who created a colonial political economy disjointed from imperial plans.

In 1723 the Superior Council conducted an inconclusive investigation into 500 gallons of brandy missing from the slave ship *Courier de Bourbon*, docked at La Balize. The cargo had been offloaded onto a small boat that then worked its way upstream. In depositions, residents caught with the contraband liquor claimed not to remember who had sold it to them. In September 1724 Thomas Desarsy was likewise accused of illegally selling wine he had bought off the French ship *La Bellonne*. A few months later this same ship sank in the harbor of Isle Dauphin with an illegal shipment of Spanish colonial tobacco, as well as Louisiana exports, such as skins and barrels of tar. The lengthy investigation into the wreck cast suspicion on the captain and mate because they were "reluctant to return to France" and apparently had been lingering along shore waiting for more contraband to make their trip worthwhile. In 1724 the Louisiana attorney general also attempted to prosecute a "treasonable plot in connection with an expedition in search of salt, very scarce in the Colony, but obtainable, it was believed, at the 'Salt Keys.' Mr. Causse, commanding the enterprise, was ordered not to enter Havana; but it appears that he not only disobeyed, but engaged in a plot there, shared by some parties at New Orleans." The latter included a Superior Council member named Fazende.[46]

That same year, Attorney General Fleuriau ordered an inspection of the ship *Chameau* in port at New Orleans because he was advised by unnamed sources that "the officers and crew of the *Chameau* are plying a trade of their own, infringing thereby on the rights of the Company of the Indies, nay more, will accept no currency but Spanish dollars at four francs." In an amusing exchange, the sheriff and two councilors went to inspect the ship, which was curiously devoid of any cargo (perhaps the crew had been forewarned), except for a trunk full of hats belong to one Monsieur Delaplace, which they seized. Upon Delaplace's protest that the hats were intended for his friends, the Council returned them. They noted weakly, "[T]his does not as a result lift the rules on pacotilling and selling any merchandise on arrival, nor on going to meet vessels coming to New Orleans." The implication was that the inspectors had arrived too long after the buyers.[47]

In 1729 certain members of the Superior Council went much further in the case of the *St. Michel.* This, the best documented case of smuggling in French Louisiana, illustrates the ways in which colonial officials were becoming entangled in illegal trade through ties of family, friendship, and debt. The surprising epilogue to the case marks a turning point for the place of smuggling in the political economy of New Orleans.[48]

In August 1729 a French ship outfitted in Nantes arrived at La Balize with a merchant on board named Laurent Macmahon who soon proceeded to town. On the morning of 3 September he was awakened by a visit from the *ordonnateur* Delachaise and a clerk from the Superior Council to answer whether he and the ship's crew had been selling cloth and brandy to plantation residents between La Balize and New Orleans, as well as to some dealers in town. He answered yes, he had sold two bales of French linens and two casks of brandy to a merchant on Chartres Street for 2,136 livres (a considerable sum). He offered this information freely, but demanded to know why they were asking him all these questions. They answered, to his chagrin, that according to the king's letters patent of 1717, "it is prohibited to all subjects of His Majesty to sell or to trade in any merchandise throughout the extent of the Government of Louisiana during the existence of the privilege of the Company of the Indies under penalty of confiscation." The *ordonnateur* then proceeded to send another councilor, his son-in-law Prat, down to La Balize without the knowledge of the rest of the Superior Council members. He ordered Prat to seize the ship and its cargo and to find out what he could about guilty buyers on the downriver plantations.[49]

In the procedures that followed, Macmahon declared that his vessel had been bound for Mexico when a leak in the ship's hull forced them to come in at La Balize. He had sold the goods to merchants in town in order to pay for repairs. He understood these actions to be legitimate and approved by Governor Périer. The Council's investigations identified at least five buyers, by the names of Dumanoir, Voisin, Bunel, Abbé Bertelon, and de Coustilhas. When questioned, they offered various excuses. Meanwhile, the delegation sent to La Balize had surprised the captain of the *St. Michel.* He explained that they had stopped to take on water and wood, making no mention of a leak. Prat sealed the ship's hatch and ordered the captain to sail up to New Orleans. There, following protocol, Attorney General Fleuriau ordered an inspection of the ship, "to find out where the leak is, if it is real or supposed, or done expressly and simulated." The Council took several depositions, wherein it became clear that a shallop and a "*flotille*" of small boats had weeks earlier offloaded much of the *St. Michel*'s cargo and dispersed into the waterways of lower Louisiana. The *St. Michel*'s pilot took the shallop up and down the Mississippi, visiting plantations with the aid and company of the Fort Balize storekeeper. They claimed to have just been paying social visits to planters and that the several casks of brandy and wine still on board the shallop were for their personal consumption.[50]

As the investigation proceeded, the righteous fervor of the *ordonnateur* attacked established relations and accepted practices. In an attempt to thwart his prosecution of the smuggler, three Superior Council members asked to be recused from the case on grounds of their close ties to either Macmahon or the *St. Michel*'s captain. Attorney General Fleuriau claimed that his wife was second cousin to Captain Lobry and he did not want them to think that "it was the wish to serve his relative that made him so clear-sighted" in this "senseless affair." Councilor St. Bruslé claimed exactly the same degree of relation. Governor Périer stated that "being an intimate friend of Sr. Marc Mahon a long time, he has not been able to refuse giving him valuable and certain advice, since his arrival in this city up to date, on this affair and this is why he requests to be excused." Perhaps Périer was the one who advised Macmahon to claim that the ship had a leak, knowing that as governor he had the power to make exceptions to trade bans in such a case. Further entanglements are suggested by the fact that Macmahon was staying at the house of the Superior Council's principal clerk, Rossard, while one of his major buyers, Abbé Bertelon, was the governor's personal chaplain. The remaining four Council members voted to approve the seizure of both ship and cargo, taking the proceeds for the Company of the Indies.[51]

The winds of fate then shifted. The zealous *ordonnateur* Jacques Delachaise died suddenly on 6 February 1730. On 17 April 1730 the colony's remaining leaders nominated none other than his former opponent, convicted smuggler Laurent Macmahon, to take his place on the Superior Council. To cement his position, Macmahon also replaced his nemesis in the role of agent of the Company of the Indies. Rumors flew around town that Delachaise's sudden death looked suspiciously like poisoning. Not surprisingly, no smuggling cases were prosecuted during Macmahon's tenure. The pro-smuggling faction on the Council continued to make strategic appointments. After Macmahon departed in 1732, one of his best customers, a contraband dealer named Jean Baptiste Dumanoir, replaced him as the locally nominated agent of the Company of the Indies. One way to make sure that strident administrators appointed in France did not prosecute friends or put a damper on local commerce was to load the Superior Council with sympathizers. Complaints about the smuggling and profiteering syndicate of New Orleans did eventually reach France. A critic wrote to Governor Périer that this shady business "is in the hands of the Councillors and principal employees of the Company and of people protected by you such as the Abbe Berthlen."[52]

Criminals or not, international traders and merchant-planters became the most powerful group in New Orleans from the 1730s to the 1760s through their influence over the Superior Council and their political alignment with Louisiana's pragmatic governors. In 1728 Governor Périer had given his official blessing to a "syndicate" elected from New Orleans *négociants* (or merchants) that probably helped orchestrate these political appointments. Although its official responsibilities remain hazy, the syndicate did author petitions and open letters to the government promoting its interests. A version of this group remained active up through the revolt of 1768. Long-serving councilors Gerard Pery, François Fleuriau, Bobé Descloseaux, Jean Baptiste Raguet, and Augustin Chantalou were among the most prominent merchants in New Orleans after the mid-1730s; each of them appears to have run both legitimate and illegitimate accounts in their affairs. Their control of the main recordkeeping arm of the colonial government, the Superior Council, meant that activities they did not want documented could be kept off the books. The extent of smuggling operations in New Orleans, however, can be discerned in between the lines of civil cases from the post-monopoly period.[53]

A shipowner and known smuggler from St. Pierre named Jacques de Meyère made New Orleans his second home for a while in the 1740s, where he got into legal scrapes that appear in the Superior Council records. In 1741 he arrived on his ship, a two-masted snow called *La Chevallière*, under the pretext of repairs. While in port, the ship's captain and de Meyère got into a fracas over who should give orders to the ship's carpenter. The Superior Council took the captain's side over the owner's, apparently because de Meyère had outstanding debts to merchants in town. The councilors ordered the ship and its cargo seized and distributed as "legitimate" spoils.[54]

De Meyère had also allegedly attempted to cover his debts by "overcharging" local smugglers Michel F. Gerald (alias Fitzgerald) and Jacques Lorrain *dit* Tarascon. They had purchased beer, rum, cloth, syrup, and soap they intended to sell at the Pensacola post in Spanish Florida. Governor Bienville supported Gerald in his suit against de Meyère. De Meyère countered that

Gerald had tried to "extort" a price break by causing unnecessary delays while piloting *Le Chevallière* to port. De Meyère brought up Gerald's past imprisonment in Mobile for suspected piracy and his flight from Saint Domingue, where he was known under the name Fitzgerald. Gerald countered with an accusation of slander.[55]

In 1743 de Meyère became involved in another case over a business trip to Veracruz. A New Orleans *pacotille* partner on that venture was merchant and Council member Gerard Pery, who sued him over an unexpectedly low return. In his defense, de Meyère said that costs were high at the time in Veracruz due to a crackdown on smuggling. He had had to pay large "favors" to officials and act with "discretion" by biding his time. De Meyère produced a letter and receipt from a Veracruz client who asked that they keep the affair out of the Mexican tribunals, as he did not want to divulge any evidence of "illicit commerce." The case dragged on for six months. In one of his last appeals, de Meyère complained that the arbitrator who had ruled against him had no knowledge of the "interlope" commerce. He then produced testimony from five ship captains then in port who supported de Meyère's claims. Among them was Juan Pérez, who matter-of-factly described himself as a "contraband trader between the Spanish and French coasts."[56]

The governors, as well as members of the Superior Council, were deeply implicated in smuggling and even piracy. Bienville's relationship to Michel Gerald/Fitzgerald went back at least to 1736, years before he offered his backing in the 1741 de Meyère suit. Gerald was among "fourteen men, Englishmen, Frenchmen, Spaniards and Italians, who had taken refuge at the Perdido River along the seacoast . . . [who] were looking for an opportunity to capture several prizes in order to become pirates." The Mobile post commander Diron d'Artaguette sent a detachment after them, capturing an Italian man and Gerald. The Italian told D'Artaguette they had "planned to take New Orleans by surprise," so he imprisoned them. Governor Bienville ordered the men released with little explanation, so that Gerald was "at liberty to travel in his own interests from New Orleans here and wherever he likes."[57]

In 1737 Governor Bienville attempted to protect a local contraband dealer named Olivier against the vigilance of D'Artaguette. Olivier had several times arranged rendezvous with ships arriving along the Gulf Coast from Carolina and New York. The ships arrived "full of all sorts of trading goods which must be hidden away in places among our islands." These meetings, which D'Artaguette refers to as "*commerce de contrebande*," were clearly illegal under the 1727 decree banning direct foreign trade by inhabitants, but both Bienville and Attorney General Fleuriau wrote letters to D'Artaguette urging him to look the other way. To add a further wrinkle, Olivier had been arrested by the "pirate" Gerald while on board a visiting ship. Acting as a mercenary of the Louisiana government, Gerald seized the English ship and its cargo as a prize, killing at least one enslaved man on board. Bienville and D'Artaguette proceeded to struggle over who had rights to the proceeds of the prize, which D'Artaguette said came from "knavery" (*fourberie*). Bienville claimed to have given Gerald privateer orders to seize the ship, which would give him a one-third share. Fleuriau's letter to D'Artaguette described how the Council had gone through the obligatory legal motions to consider Olivier's case, but did not feel it should be pushed further. Fleuriau's language suggested that he upheld the appearance of legal propriety, but did not enforce the spirit of mercantile law.[58]

The pirate and privateer Gerald may have operated under yet another alias as "Gerard Fitzmaurice" in 1743. A man by this name served as a pilot on board the schooner *Elizabeth*. When the ship came back to New Orleans after a long expedition, Prevost, a prominent merchant and representative of the Company of the Indies, sued the captain and the absent "Fitzmaurice" for a friend in Saint Domingue who had been swindled out of 40,000 livres. The captain defended himself by saying that he had diverted the ship to Havana on the advice of Fitzmaurice who, as the only one who spoke any Spanish, was in charge of any deals made there. The Louisiana Superior Council seized the *Elizabeth* and her cargo. Probably the same culprit, "Gerald F. Maurice," appeared in the Superior Council a few months later as captain of *La Fortune*. A passenger entered a complaint into the registry that Gerald had "arranged" for their ship to be abducted by the English and taken to Jamaica (where he probably met with good trading terms).[59]

Not everything went smoothly between water-based smugglers and land-based contraband dealers. In 1741 Bienville ran into trouble with some New Orleans merchants and the *ordonnateur* Salmon over his continued protection of Gerald, whom Salmon described as a "pirate" (*forban*). The members of the merchant syndicate, however, were not so much miffed that the governor had failed to stop Gerald's activities; rather, they were angered that the governor had allowed him to skip town without making good on his debts. Apparently local merchants supplied Gerald in his outbound smuggling trade to the Spanish colonies. The real purpose of the merchant syndicate appears to have been to politically and fiscally manage smuggling operations. Ironically, it attempted to make smuggling a controlled and protected privilege. But the syndicate struggled to control "masterless" men such as Gerald whose skills and contacts it needed.[60]

Bienville's successors in the 1750s and 1760s kept their hands no cleaner. Governor Vaudreuil engaged in private deals that aroused suspicion, although his wife appears to have been the real entrepreneur in the family.[61] In 1761 Governor Kerlérec was accused of sending a pilot to guide an English ship through the southwest pass (thus evading La Balize); "two days later the governor had it proclaimed to the sound of the drum throughout the entire town that this Englishman had arrived and that he was going to begin his sale." In the middle of the Seven Years War, this act constituted not just smuggling, but trading with the enemy. When he had first arrived in Louisiana eight years earlier, Kerlérec had dutifully reported the "suspicious" and "unfaithful" actions of officials and merchants in New Orleans. He promised his superiors he would soon "put it in good order." Instead, it appears that the "disorder" of the New Orleans smuggling economy had soon seduced him.[62]

Complaints by officials that New Orleans was "cut off" from contact with France and suffered want of provisions during wartime have been misinterpreted to mean the entire colony suffered isolation and duress. After the 1730s most of these complaints turn out to be statements of problems specific to the colony's military establishment. Louisiana's civilians were exempted from quartering troops, so colonial soldiers and officers depended upon the king's ships to deliver supplies and treasury notes. This did not mean that provisions were unavailable in private stores in the colony, but that the governor had exhausted his credit lines. Governor Kerlérec complained during the Seven Years' War that the Louisiana coast had been blockaded by Jamaican privateers, and no French naval ship had responded to his pleas, though he claimed to have sent no fewer than 160 letters by private ships requesting aid from France. The privateers enforcing the "blockade" evidently permitted a large number of private ships to come and go (those carrying the letters), while scaring off the king's ships. Documents indicate that local shippers made several supply runs to Veracruz during the war and made large profits off their returns. One New Orleanian described the Treaty of Paris that ended the war as "bad news" that precipitated a slump in prices.[63]

The lines between entrepreneurial smuggling, criminal piracy, and legitimate privateering were hazy.[64] During the Seven Years' War French privateers seized British ships as a way of provisioning Louisiana, but indications are that many of these "seizures" were friendly arrangements made to look like a military act and provide a means for British traders to safely enter a banned port. Privateering by both French and foreign ships during France's wars boosted the colonial economy. At least five corsairs operated out of New Orleans during the French period. New Orleans merchant Nicolas Judice outfitted one in 1745. During the Seven Years' War, the corsair schooner *Le Petit St. Antoine* ran back and forth between Port-au-Prince and New Orleans under Captain Gerome Matuticte, bringing in at least three prizes during the final years of the war. *Le Petit St. Antoine* may have been one of two corsairs that brought in four prizes from Philadelphia, Rhode Island, and Jamaica between 1758 and 1759. Local contraband dealer Antoine Olivier outfitted the brig *Le Franc Masson* in 1762 as a corsair, though he subsequently sued the captain for engaging in peaceful smuggling at Campeche rather than actively pursuing English prizes, which would have been more profitable.[65]

The governor of Martinique wrote to Louisiana Governor Kerlérec in 1759 that cartel ships "are today our only means of subsistence . . . [it is] important that we encourage them." Anglo-American sailor William Perry reported that friendly smuggling continued in and around the city during the war. Perry was seized as a prisoner of war, along with the rest of the crew and cargo of the *Sea Flower*, which had left Rhode Island bound for Honduras. Their French captor steered them to La Balize, where they met another British prize (the *Lancaster*). Perry reports that a third prize, a brig from Philadelphia, had already docked in the city. Its cargo of flour was especially welcome and sold at high prices. He was told that three New Orleans ships had departed just days before his arrival, destined for St. Augustine and then Philadelphia. Perry observed that the city also received many types of goods from Jamaica on board British ships flying "flags of truce." Flags of truce (*parlementaires* in French) were another mechanism that smugglers used to cloak their activities. Ship captains obtained permits to travel to enemy ports under the pretext of returning prisoners of war. The prisoners (who could simply be willing passengers of the appropriate nationality) usually accounted for only a fraction of the cargo unloaded. Perry himself returned via a French flag of truce with three other prisoners to the busy smuggling port of Philadelphia. Perry reported that the Jamaican ships arrived in New Orleans "laden with Bales of Goods and Flower, and above a hundred Negroes to trade with, with a few Prisoners, and that they took back only Twelve Prisoners, and a Lading of Indigo, Beaver, Deer Skins, Parchment and Logwood."[66]

A Jamaican ship that arrived in 1759 named the *Texel* caused an uproar in New Orleans and, eventually, in Paris. Governor Kerlérec, a seasoned sailor and ship captain himself, welcomed the *Texel* as a friendly supplier of much-needed flour. The newly arrived *ordonnateur* Rochemore and a small cabal of mostly French-born officers (already at odds with Kerlérec over other matters), impounded it as an illegal smuggling ship and imprisoned its captain as a spy. Rochemore repeated the drama a few months later when another English ship, the *Trois Frères* (probably the same ship that bore the English name *Three Brothers*) arrived. Kerlérec put a stop to this "*insubordinance*" by throwing several Rochemore allies into prison, where some remained as long as three years until Kerlérec was recalled to France under his own cloud of suspicion. The governor's encouragement of foreign trade became one of the major issues in the "Louisiana Affair," a convoluted scandal that became the talk of Paris in the early 1760s. Court officials took the evidence seriously enough to exile Kerlérec from Paris upon his return.[67]

Smuggling was at the root of one of the last political "disorders" of French Louisiana. The composition of Kerlérec's cabal only reinforces his guilt in what had become business as usual in New Orleans. In 1763 a self-described group of New Orleans *négociants* signed a letter of support for Kerlérec, the majority of them Louisiana creoles or natives of the greater Caribbean. Among the signatories were known or suspected smugglers Olivier, Cádiz, Milhet, Monsanto, and Braud.[68]

As these clues about smuggling activities in New Orleans mount, it becomes difficult to avoid the conclusion that smuggling was not just the basis of the local urban economy, it was a major partner in the local *political* economy. Governors and Superior Council members from the beginning of the French colony until its final days were deeply implicated in the illegal trade. They used their local power, greater Caribbean contacts, and metropolitan patrons to defend, expand, or cover up their business dealings. Their activities greatly benefited a colony chronically short of approved supplies and unable to find a profitable plantation crop. Smuggling was the most "roguish" of French Louisiana's economic sectors. It was also its most successful.

A "Masterless" Community

By the time of the Spanish takeover in 1769, smuggling involved the highest officials and wealthiest citizens. Historians have made the argument that the 1768 New Orleans revolt grew from a fear that Spain's restrictive policies would devastate the Louisiana economy. I would add that it was not so much a fear of Spain's mercantilism that drove the rebels—for on paper this already existed under the French—but a fear of *enforcement* by the Spanish. In the early 1760s the Spanish had commenced a renewed and vigorous campaign to clamp down on smuggling throughout their New World possessions. Integration into the Spanish empire would mean Louisiana traders could be cut off from their French, British, and Dutch suppliers. When the Spanish government arrived in the form of strongman Alejandro O'Reilly, ship owners were required for the first time to obtain local licenses for their voyages. Although O'Reilly calmed some fears by permitting traffic to Saint Domingue, captains had to submit a detailed list of all the cargo they intended to bring back. Anything not on the preapproved list would be seized as contraband.[69]

Spain's new restrictions threatened to sever not just trade relations, but also social relations. In the eighteenth century merchants and port dwellers developed communities that spanned large stretches of water and increasingly crisscrossed imperial boundaries. Historians of the Atlantic world have begun to map out these communities, particularly among English-speaking merchants and a "hydrarchy" of peg-legged sailors who plied east to west across the Atlantic.[70] Similar patterns obtained in the French- and Spanish-speaking Atlantic, and in circulations that tracked comparable distances in a north-south direction within the Americas.

In the New Orleans records we see a network of social and affective ties interwoven with the (illegal) economic infrastructure. New Orleans merchant Nicolas Forstall regularly sent money and letters to his son, who operated a branch of the family business in Veracruz. Paul Rasteau, the New Orleans–based trader in French imports and smuggled exports, caught a ride home on a Spanish brigantine bound from Veracruz where he had been catching up with old friends and negotiating new deals. In New Orleans he often had the opportunity to see his two brothers, Pierre and Eli Rasteau, both ship captains who made several voyages along the La Rochelle–New Orleans–Veracruz route. He also communicated often with his uncle Jean Benjamin Rasteau, who oversaw operations in Saint Domingue. New Orleans merchants such as Bancio Piemont and Jean Pradel maintained an active correspondence with friends and partners in barred ports.[71]

The social and cultural connections formed by smuggling were carried not only by merchants and cargo agents, but by the people manning the helm and the rigging. Daniel Usner documents how motley crews of French *petits gens*, Indians, slaves, and free people of color traveled the rivers and overland paths for the Indian trade. The Company of the Indies for a while encouraged the importation of skilled "Atlantic creole" and Senegalese sailors, and trained others as pilots and boatmen. They had a labor need to fill, but they also wanted to circumvent the tendency of French boatmen to conduct business on their own account. The Louisiana Superior Council documents record an increasing number of slaves hired out as pilots and boatmen through the French period. Other sailors of color drifted in and out of port in the regular tide of sea traffic. Etienne La Rue, a mulatto pilot originally from Senegal, was in town in 1747. While his ship was undergoing repairs, he got into a scuffle with three French soldiers in a scene that authorities complained was all too common in the streets of New Orleans.[72]

While it may be a cliché to say that maritime society was diverse and multilingual, this was even more true in the smuggling circuits of the greater Caribbean. The crew of the New Orleans–based smuggler *La Superbe* consisted of French creoles, seventeen Spaniards or Spanish colonials, and at least fourteen "blacks and mulattoes." Documents identify only one crew member from France, Montel de Bordeaux. In the year before it sank off the coast of Texas, *La Superbe* had traveled to Portobello (in modern Panamá), Martinique, New Orleans, and Veracruz.[73]

Innkeepers played an important role in providing shelter, information, and local assistance to this roving community. They were often former ship captains or traders themselves with worldly experience and language skills. New Orleans innkeeper Juan Gonzales acted as a translator for Spanish-speaking traders, while François Marin (the husband of Elizabeth Real, whose story opened this chapter) acted with power of attorney for his guests, nursed them when ill, and helped settle their estates.[74]

Given Marin's maritime activity, it is tempting to interpret the artifactual evidence from the Marin-Real inn in terms of smuggling, although the evidence is no more direct than the obfuscating paper trail. Unlike the situation in the Spanish colonies, most smuggled items would not have been identifiable by their foreign origin. French goods (particularly wine, liquors, and cloth) were the most sought-after commodities on the black market. The New Orleans economy thrived on transshipment and middleman trade. Cloth and wheat flour, two of the most desirable imports, rarely leave an archaeological record. The most sought-after Spanish commodity—gold and silver coin—was less likely to be lost, abandoned, or discarded.[75] Still, colonial artifact assemblages from New Orleans contain a small but consistent percentage of objects originating from Spain or its colonies.[76] Archaeological evidence also proves that New Orleanians were able to acquire fashionable new British ceramics almost as soon as they hit the worldwide market, supplied by contacts from Philadelphia, Rhode Island, and Jamaica. The archaeological evidence from French colonial New Orleans echoes what has been found at the Alabama coast settlements, which "does not suggest an impoverished colony teetering on the brink of financial ruin."[77] As early as 1730 (a year after the Natchez Rebellion) a visitor to New Orleans, Sieur Caillot, described, not a town suffering privation, but rather a place with "many inns and cabarets where you are not only well served, but also catered to. You will also see there many dry goods shops of various merchandise that they buy off ships, although this is against the orders of the Company. They buy from women that sell in the streets."[78]

Another very significant part of the smuggling trade that neither the archaeological nor the textual record can adequately account for is the black market in human beings. Slaves were both a measure and a means of wealth, among those possessions most sought after by socially ambitious colonials. Historian Ibrahima Seck rightly cautions that "the reported insolvency of Louisianans must also be put into perspective," as they paid cash, not credit, for slave purchases in the 1750s and 1760s. Transshipments were diverted from Martinique and other islands because New Orleans had a reputation of paying top prices. English smugglers from Jamaica also made regular appearances in the port from the 1740s onward. This is not the portrait of a sleepy backwater town left behind by the Atlantic system.[79]

From a metropolitan perspective, intercolonial smuggling was a disorder bordering on treason. From a local perspective, smuggling meant survival and prosperity, but it did more than supply demand. It helped knit together a colonial world where ideas and identities were forming outside the confines of the mercantilist Atlantic. While captains and marine officers enforced class and racial hierarchies on board ship, water travel and the illicit nature of smuggling voyages contributed to a dream of what Julius Scott calls a "masterless existence" and what Linebaugh and Rediker call "hydrarchy."[80] A masterless existence meant different things to people of different stations—for one "free trade," for another freedom from physical and psychological bondage. The same water currents that made trading expeditions to other Gulf ports easy also made escape from slavery and military service possible. Slaves and deserters with access to a large pirogue could reasonably aim for Havana, as did one interracial group in 1739 that then established a community of Louisiana exiles in the Spanish port. News of their new life enticed other runaways to head in that direction.[81] Whether escaping imperial or personal despotism, citizens of the greater Caribbean transformed port cities into the terrestrial equivalent of smuggling ships. While not "masterless" spaces, they thrived on a freedom of movement and a jumbling of people that meant liberation for many in the streets and disorder to a few on the balconies. "Slaves deserted plantations in large numbers; urban workers ducked their owners; seamen jumped ship to avoid floggings and the press-gang; militiamen and regular troops grumbled, ignored orders, and deserted their watch; higglers left workplaces to peddle their wares in the black market; and smugglers and shady foreigners moved about on mysterious missions from island to island. Furthermore, the very commercial growth which planters and merchants welcomed opened new avenues of mobility. Cities grew and matured, attracting runaway slaves and sheltering a teeming underground with surprising regional connections."[82]

As merchants, planters, and political officials in New Orleans became more deeply involved in the intercoastal smuggling circuit, they inadvertently supported the growth of a terrestrial smuggling network between New Orleans and its agricultural hinterland—a local "disorder" that increasingly worried Superior Council members. Slaves, maroons, sailors, soldiers, and other poor free people conducted an active hand-to-hand trade that benefited from the flow of illegal imports into the city. Runaways, in particular, found peddling smuggled goods a viable employment. By supplying their contacts with clothing items, liquor, and small luxuries difficult to get in rural areas, runaways played a key role in the distribution system to plantations that tied the internal economy of slaves to international smuggling rings. Race was no barrier to illegal trade, nor were black traders excluded from the black market. In town, buyers and sellers favored taverns and cabarets as meeting spots where business transactions could be made under the cover of sociability. Authorities made repeated attempts to crack down on the exchanges (both social and material) taking place at the taverns, inns, and cabarets of colonial New Orleans. In 1746 the Superior Council attempted to segregate establishments into those serving soldiers and those serving "travelers, sick people, the inhabitants, and seafaring men," limiting the former to two canteens and the latter to six taverns. The ordinance also banned these businesses from selling alcohol to Indians or slaves. As Edwin Davis notes, "the new regulations, however, were generally ignored, and New Orleans remained a wide-open town throughout the French period."[83]

✤　✤　✤

Some historians have dismissed the international trade of New Orleans in the French period because of its problems with large-vessel shipping and the small number of official ship arrivals. Yet this conclusion presumes that merchants were oriented toward the Atlantic world. The founding generation of Louisiana lived on intimate terms with Native Americans who were oriented toward a quite different Mississippi-Caribbean world. Their knowledge informed the selection of the site of New Orleans which, though soggy, had the advantage of being a major crossroads of the New World. Focusing too much on the Atlantic ignores the potential importance of smuggling to a backwater entrepôt like New Orleans. Factors that could be a disadvantage in transatlantic trade could be an advantage in intercolonial trade. The shallow, dendritic waterways surrounding New Orleans created havens and highways for smuggling by small vessels.

Smuggling and piracy nurtured Louisiana in the early years and colored its reputation in France. Smuggling controversies stalked two of Louisiana's governors—Bienville in 1708 and Kerlérec in 1759—whose tenures frame the history of the French period. These economic "disorders" were taken seriously by France's ministers and perhaps bemusedly by the gossipy French public. In 1764 satirical songs about Kerlérec could be heard in the cabarets of Paris, and several pamphlets circulated depicting him as a criminal despot.[84] At the end of the French period public opinion also held that New

Orleans was an economic backwater because it failed to return any significant profits to the metropole. From the local perspective, however, New Orleans did not so much fail at mercantilism as triumph over it, through everyday acts of resistance and a few spectacular acts of defiance and revolt.

Intercoastal trade began to drive the New Orleans economy in earnest by the late 1730s. The first generation of creoles embraced smuggling, while the town became a truly international community. The rise of these "non-French" to local power, both on the Superior Council and in the merchant syndicate, marked a significant step away from the failed experiment of Law's mercantilism. The rise of certain creole families into an increasingly endogamous elite paralleled the formalization of a new economic order based on free, if illegal, trade. The difficulty for creole merchants, planters, and officials was that although business was brisk, smuggling attracted to their capital city a highly transient and masterless population. While they institutionalized one kind of disorder for their own profit, they created another that threatened their power.

The smell of money brings out the "rogues," or self-interested agents working within the crevices and border zones of the colonies, perhaps more than any other facet of imperial experimentation. It is easy to see how the smuggling economy of New Orleans undercut the blueprint of John Law's monopoly. It is also easy to equate rogue colonialism with simple criminality and corruption on the part of Louisiana's piratical governors and contrabandist councilors. These characterizations, however, would oversimplify both the facts of the colonial economy and what I mean by "rogue colonialism." The New Orleans example underscores the difficulty of disentangling the illegal from the licit, or the formal from the informal in the economic sphere. Nor is it a simple matter to separate out individual agents acting in their own self-interest from the collective policies and practices that govern a community, or even a colonial state.

The French crown acted to create its own monopoly on smuggling with the Spanish colonies while outlawing free trade among its colonists. Governors such as Bienville and Vaudrueil who violated the royal monopoly by aiding and abetting small-time smugglers were acting to keep Louisiana politically stable in the absence of French subsidies after the political divestment of the 1730s. In doing so, they not only held onto the territory for France's imperial contest with England, but also attracted immigrants and traders to the area. Louisiana evolved over time from a buccaneer outpost to the base of a sophisticated creole syndicate, but neither incarnation was ever divorced from the political operations of the colony. This was not a "shadow" or underground economy. It was fully and openly integrated in the day-to-day governing of the colony. New Orleans was not only a backwater entrepôt, it was what Janet Roitman calls a "garrison entrepôt," where military and commercial functions were blended in a context of high social mobility and inventive economic practice defended by violence.[85]

Social scientists who study smuggling and informal economies in the context of present-day globalization draw a distinction between two different kinds of legitimacy—the legal-political and the licit-social. The first refers to state-sponsored laws, the second to social norms and values.[86] This is a helpful distinction for thinking about the interplay between metropolitan plans and colonial practices. In the Louisiana case, although actors both big and small probably knew that smuggling was a technically illegal activity, most of them also agreed that it was socially acceptable and pragmatically necessary. Thus we can say that the exchange economy of French New Orleans was both illegal and licit. Other combinations are possible. Strident metropolitan defenders such as Delachaise and Rochemore undoubtedly viewed smuggling as both illegal and illicit. At the same time, Louisiana colonists and many eighteenth-century critics of absolutism considered mercantilism to be legal but illicit, in that it brought starvation and hardship for French subjects both at home and abroad.

An illegal but licit political economy, such as that which operated in French New Orleans, is not an uncommon development. The mutual attraction between political power and economic crime seems hard to resist; it is an affair that leads either to scandal or to enduring interdependency. Willem van Schendel notes, "Transnational entrepreneurs and state elites can form alliances that simultaneously prop up state structures and allow these to serve the interests of 'unauthorized' transnational flows . . . those who routinely undermine the state's territoriality emerge as its kingmakers and office bearers."[87] Although this evaluation derives from our own period of globalization, I would argue that early modern colonies, with their poorly defined (and even more poorly policed) borders, were especially prone to such alliances. The porous geography of southeast Louisiana made smuggling not only a pragmatic economic option, but a natural adaptation.

The reputation of New Orleans as a place of disorder acted as a form of advertising. Smuggling was a public enterprise. The story of the city's economy, from the smuggling of the French period down to the party-town tourism of the present, proves that there are real, "material effects of representations."[88]

There is both a romantic and a tragicomic side to this story. The romantic view would be that smuggling represents a form of "creole economics," as identified by anthropologist Katherine Browne in contemporary Martinique. She describes the working of informal trade and labor networks underlain by a strong local identity that values clever circumventions of metropolitan policy.[89] In French Louisiana one can easily imagine that in addition to its survival value, smuggling represented ideological resistance to the imperial impositions of mercantilism and chattel slavery. This romantic version of the story idealizes free trade and informal economics as revolution from below. Undoubtedly, many actors on the ground in New Orleans consciously acted against the rules, both imperial and local, in defiant pursuit of their own interests. The slaves, higglers, sailors, tavern keepers, and small-time contrabandists who kept the city's unofficial economy bubbling along quite likely viewed their activities as a matter of pride, skill, and independence.

The tragicomic side of the story reveals the hypocrisy of colonial officials who issued injunctions to control fencing and hand-to-hand trade in the multi-hued taverns of New Orleans, yet themselves acted as underwriters for pirates, privateers, and large smuggling operations. One might well label smuggling at the merchant syndicate level in New Orleans a form of "creole economics," but by the second half of the eighteenth century, it was the economics of an elite creole oligarchy, not a group of romantic revolutionaries resisting slavery and petty imperialism. As a group invested in establishing a monopoly over free trade, syndicate members were more committed to establishing control and political power than in overthrowing it. But it was control and political power wielded in their own interests, not necessarily in the interests of the French state. As we shall see in a later chapter, they were even more likely than petty traders to advocate political independence from France.[90] Thus, although the New Orleans political economy of smuggling united the highest and the lowest colonial subjects in the same activities, it did not create a unified revolutionary front in the face of imperialism. Locally, it was simply an illegal but licit basis for a new social hierarchy rife with its own class tensions. But regionally, the smuggling basis of the city's colonial economy did link its residents to a vast and intricate network of mutinous sailors, runaway slaves, and nationless traders who in the second half of the eighteenth century sparked revolutions against both local and global empires around the Atlantic world.

PLATE 1. Drawing by Dumont de Montigny, *Crocodille ou cayment fixant ses œufs*. (Courtesy of Edward E. Ayer Collection. The Newberry Library, Chicago.)

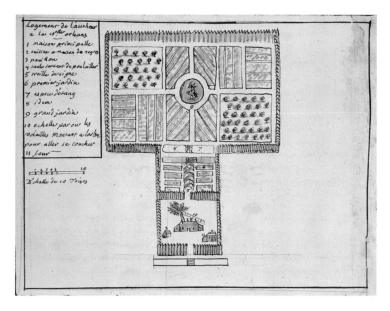

PLATE 2. Dumont de Montigny's house and garden. (Courtesy of Edward E. Ayer Collection. The Newberry Library, Chicago.)

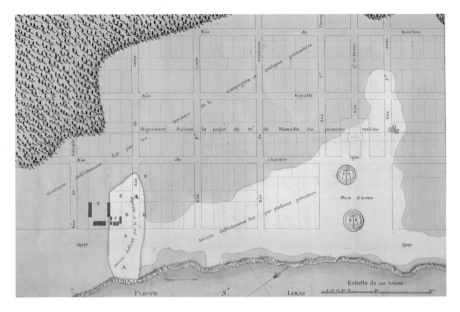

PLATE 3. Le Blond de la Tour map showing "Misalignments," 12 January 1723. (FR.ANOM. Aix-en-Provence. 04DFC68B. All rights reserved.)

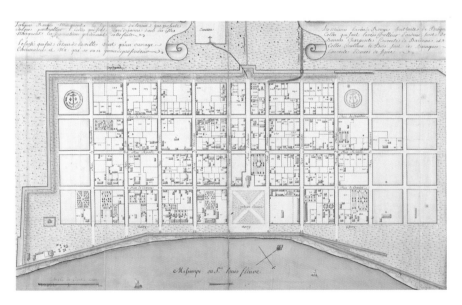

PLATE 4. *Plan de la Nouvelle Orleans* by Gonichon, December 1731. (FR.ANOM. Aix-en-Provence. 04DFC89B. All rights reserved.)

PLATE 5. *Le Commerce que les Indiens du Mexique Font avec les François au Port de Missipi,* c. 1720. (Courtesy of Historic New Orleans Collection, Williams Research Center, Acc. No. 1952.3.)

PLATE 6. *The Savages of Several Nations, New Orleans, 1735,* by Alexandre de Batz. (©2007 Harvard University, Peabody Museum, Photo 41–72–10/20 T2377.)

PLATE 7. *Ships Making a Voyage to New Orleans in 1730*, frontispiece to Caillot, "Relation du Voyage de la Louisiane ou Nouv.lle France fait par le Sr. Caillot en l'année 1730." (Courtesy of Historic New Orleans Collection, Williams Research Center, Acc. No. 2005.11.)

4

LA RENOMMÉE
From Colonial Experiment to Creole Society

In 1984 archaeologists had a chance to examine burials from the first cemetery of New Orleans as it was being destroyed to make way for a condominium development. They caught a glimmer of a colonial society frozen in the ground. It was not exactly the one they were expecting—the majority of the interred were African males whose muscle-scarred bones had become jumbled with those of Europeans, Afro-Europeans, and children of mixed European and Indian ancestry. People whom we have come to think of as racially distinct lay side by side. Their ages indicated that the environment was a great social leveler, at least when it came to who would live and who would die. Any class differences their clothes and coffins had once expressed had been dissolved by microbes. Death provided the illusion of a classless, color-blind society. French New Orleans was no such place, but the ways in which it created a social order are unfamiliar and at first difficult to see.[1]

In the St. Peter Cemetery (c. 1725–88), one person was distinguished by the care taken over his funerary arrangements. "Burial 11" was that of a man we will nickname "St. Antoine." His was the only coffin of the salvaged sample to contain burial objects: a complete, jewel-set rosary with two saint's medals attached and a separate medallion of silver and gold with an image of the Virgin Mary encased in glass. One of the double-sided rosary medals depicts St. Anthony of Padua, while the other is an unidentified saint holding a book, possibly St. James or St. Peter. If these objects were placed following Catholic custom, the rosary would have been wrapped around his hands, the medallion perhaps on a string around his neck.[2] He seems to have been buried by people who loved or esteemed him, for a concentration of pollen from a bouquet of flowers was found within the coffin. Because the cemetery was consecrated ground, all of the people buried in St. Peter Cemetery had probably been baptized.[3]

Most likely, "St. Antoine" had been born in Africa and sent to Louisiana as a slave in his youth; he died in New Orleans sometime in his forties. Two of his teeth (lower incisors) bear decorative notching similar to patterns documented from Congo. But unlike most of the other African-descended men in the cemetery, his bones did not show signs of a life of hard labor. Whatever he did, as a slave or freeman, it was not the heavy work of ditch-digging, logging, or indigo cultivation. "St. Antoine" may have been one of Ira Berlin's "Atlantic Creoles" who arrived in Louisiana already Catholic, with skills (sailing? translating? medicine?) that excused him from harsh menial tasks.[4] African or already creole, he found ways to negotiate life in a new cultural crossroads. Appropriately, St. Anthony, whose image he gathered to his chest, is the patron saint of travelers and sailors, oppressed people, and the hungry.

The section of the cemetery in which "St. Antoine" was found seems to have served as a burial area for slaves and poor free people of any color. Archaeologists were able to examine four small clusters of coffins within the site. Analysis of the skeletons allowed them to estimate the geographic origin of the individuals or their recent ancestors. One was a grouping of an Afro-European woman in her twenties, a European man the same age, an Afro-European man in his forties, and an infant. Another cluster comprised a mixed Euro-Indian child between the ages of five and nine, a woman in her twenties of indeterminate ancestry, and an African male teenager. Identifiable individuals in the next cluster were two African women in their twenties and an African man in his forties. The last and largest group included two African men in their forties and fifties, a European man in his forties, an African teenage girl, and an African woman in her forties.[5]

Assigning areas of a cemetery to particular families or households was a common practice by the eighteenth century, even among the poor. It is likely that some of the individuals buried adjacent to one another in these clusters were related by blood or marriage. The placement of the coffins suggests spaces left to be filled in later, rather than regular rows of sequentially filled plots where strangers were made neighbors in death. If the groupings do represent a relationship among the interred, then the presence of two European males surrounded by people of African and mixed ancestry suggests that *métissage* (race-crossing) may have been occurring consensually within the poor population, as well as through coercive concubinage and/or rape in the context of slavery. Jennifer Spear notes that while documentary evidence of attempts to regulate cross-racial unions in the early decades of the colony is plentiful, tracking the extent and patterns of actual practice in the French period is difficult.[6] This small physical sample, however, does support the impression of shocked visitors to eighteenth-century

New Orleans. *Les petits* of the city were a multihued lot who mingled in casual, intimate, and sometimes profound ways. The metropolitan strategy of segregation did not succeed, even in death.

We might be tempted to approach the boxes that appear on a census form as a metaphorical coffin—a rather permanent, modular container that represents the customs of the country, a legible unit of social classification. Individuals placed in a colonial census box reading "free French woman" or "Negro slave" might be expected to stay for a lifetime. Pursuing this metaphor, though, one might say that a census box is more like the backless coffin of a stage magician: it only appears to trap and contain, and one can never be sure of the actual location of the occupant. In Louisiana, some boxes, or census categories, arrived as imports from the *ancien régime*, some were experimental hybrids custom-made for the colonial experiment, and others were purely local inventions. Census categories were (and are) always in a stage of research and development. In New Orleans the mobility, clutter, and noise of a port town facilitated escape from social containment. Sailors, runaways, and vagabonds inspired others to jump the bounds of their world. Throughout the period, many official complaints of disorder focused on *les petits* (in eighteenth-century French, also called *le menu peuple*, literally, "the little people" or simply *le peuple*), who mixed with and corrupted one another. Toward the end of the French regime, however, ministers increasingly worried about the creole elite, who were implementing their own version of order, foreign to metropolitan designs.

The subject of this chapter is social organization. As in the realms of urban planning and economics discussed in earlier chapters, we find once again the three key elements to understanding French colonial New Orleans and places like it: experimentation (evident in attempts at social engineering), major transformations in the creole generation (a move toward a new form of social hierarchy), and rogue colonialism (in the form of heightened social mobility, rampant self-fashioning, and emerging individualism). Beyond investigating the ways in which French ministers attempted to engineer a new kind of society in Louisiana, my aim is to develop a picture of the social order in early New Orleans as it looked "on the ground": who populated the town, where they lived within it, how they related to one another, and how this changed over time. I argue that in the charter phase, metropolitan plans contained overt intentions to socially engineer New Orleans along new lines of class and color, but that these plans never got much traction.

One of the original ideas was to halt what in France had become a steady stream of promotion into the titled nobility. Instead, colonial conditions simply redefined the terms of elite membership by equating it with wealth (particularly slave and trade wealth); these same conditions gave the free laboring classes expanded opportunities to acquire property, and thus greater possibilities of movement through the social ranks. While this process was taking place gradually within Europe as a result of the intensification of capitalism, the transition in the settler colonies to this new type of social order was early and abrupt. The resulting opportunities for social advancement created intense competition and inventive possibilities for entrepreneurial free subjects.

Another element of the social design that did not take off as planned was the imposition of a black/white racial code and elaborate segregationist policies governing public space. What took hold instead in the charter period was a hierarchy based upon legal status, particularly sensitive to degrees of servitude, such as convict laborer, soldier, indentured servant, and slave. As the more unusual legal statuses became obsolete with the decline of immigration, the distinctions between free, freedman, and slave became clearer.

By the second creole generation, one could characterize New Orleans as a society with four basic social strata: large slaveholders and merchants, small slaveholders, non-slaveholders, and slaves. Mobility into the top tier had become circumscribed by marriage and inheritance, but considerable fluidity remained among the other social classes. Individuals could transform themselves from slaves to small slaveholders and, under legal duress, back again. In face-to-face interactions, racial features were probably noted as an approximation of legal status and clan pedigree, but there was no enforced calculus of skin color and social rank. Although observers at both the beginning and the end of the French period remarked upon the diversity and confusion of the New Orleans social scene, by the 1750s slavery and trading wealth had begun to harden into caste-like distinctions. These were just not the same distinctions that French planners and later Spanish administrators accounted for in their bureaucratic visions.

Social organization is sometimes difficult to separate from economic organization. In chapter 3 I presented the case for the pervasiveness of smuggling and its connections to the far-flung Mississippi-Caribbean world. In this chapter my focus will be internal, on the divisions within the local population that reflect a developing social structure based on entrepreneurial wealth, and on the social facts of smuggling. Previously convicted salt and tobacco smugglers made up a surprisingly large fraction of the French immigrant population. To understand their background in France and their role in Louisiana, some accounting of their legal and social history is required.

Social organization is also difficult to separate from spatial organization. While in chapter 2 I focused on Enlightenment aesthetics and relationships to the environment as expressed in the urban plan, here the built environment comes into play as an expression of the social order, both as dreamed and as lived. With the founding of New Orleans, metropolitan planners attempted to implement their designs for an improved society through urban planning and physical segregation of different sectors of the colonial population. But spatial facts larger than streets and walls challenged them. The town's serpentine, swampy physical setting and seaport nature worked against clear delineations. Michel Foucault observed that the port town of Rochefort (from where the majority of Louisiana-bound naval ships departed) acted as an "experiment and model" in the first movements toward enclosure and disciplined society in the early eighteenth century. If Rochefort was the domestic experiment, New Orleans was the colonial experiment. What was true of Rochefort was more true of New Orleans: "A port, and a military port is—with its circulation of goods, men signed up willingly or by force, sailors embarking and disembarking, diseases and epidemics—a place of desertion, smuggling, contagion: it is a crossroads for dangerous mixtures, a meeting-place for forbidden circulations . . . Hence the need to distribute and partition off space in a rigorous manner."[7]

In New Orleans the mixture was more dangerous, involving an underclass with origins in three continents representing at least seven different types of legal status—free French subject, freeborn person of color, *affranchit* (freedman), *engagé* (indentured servant), soldier, *forçat* (forced exile or convict laborer), and slave. Among themselves, free Frenchmen experienced a jumbling of the *ancien régime* classes in a new and unsettled order. To those newly arrived from Europe, New Orleans looked like a carnival town, always threatening to turn upside-down.

In this chapter I examine the ways in which New Orleans was shaped by social engineering efforts and the consequences of these designs for the founder and creole generations. I discuss the intended blueprint for Louisiana society according to French policy-makers, expanding upon the example of *forçats* sent to Louisiana with the hope of reform. I then look at census-taking and mapmaking as methods used to control the colonial experiment. Departures from the plan and the character of the developing creole social order of New Orleans are illustrated through self-fashioning and nicknames, biographies of social mobility, and the shifting boundaries of color and class. The tension between metropolitan designs and colonial *mētis* comes out in the failure of experimental new census categories, such as those designating skin color or ethnic origin, to stick. This pattern was echoed in the failure of segregation strategies on the ground—in residential neighborhoods, taverns, bedrooms, or even cemeteries.

The overriding principle of social classification as actually practiced in the founder generation was that of legal status. As noted above, there were no less than seven possible legal statuses on a spectrum from enslaved to free, most of these measuring a degree of limited rights and servitude.[8] If we add the dimensions of gender and age for women and minors, then we can count at least twenty-one different types of legal person populating French colonial New Orleans, with frequent foreign visitors and visiting Native Americans expanding the possibilities further. Although the legal instruments of the state were spare in the colonial setting, when enforced, these statuses had profound implications for the bearer regarding their rights to property, relations to others in the social order (whom they could marry, socialize with, win a civil suit against, and so forth), as well as control over their own time, labor, and body. Legal status defined one's relationship to the colonial experiment itself, at minimum ordaining who was settled for the long term and who was free to move on. These legal classifications, though existent in France, took on new prominence as substitutes for more familiar contours of class and ethnicity. This shift was understandable in a context in which the origins of immigrants could be uncertain and the possibilities for social mobility through self-fashioning and entrepreneurship were extraordinary in comparison to the Old World.

The tensions produced by the unsettling of familiar social structures are evidenced in a significant number of insult and slander cases. These legal suits demonstrate that the social order in early Louisiana was anything but clear. But beginning with the rise of the first creole generation in the 1730s and 1740s, a wealth-based system began to appear. By the second creole generation, mobility into the top tier of large slaveowners and merchants was limited by practices of intermarriage and inheritance. Meanwhile, mobility and fraternization among the middling and lower orders continued to be the norm, captured best in the hurly-burly scenes of New Orleans drinking establishments, which officials attempted repeatedly, and unsuccessfully, to regulate. Unable to segregate others, the elite began to segregate themselves.

An Uncontrolled Experiment: Designing and Measuring Colonial Society

Due to its experimental nature, French immigration policy toward Louisiana was uncertain and inconsistent during the turbulent period from 1717 to 1732. Although they may have disagreed about strategies, the king's advisers sought to design a society that enforced some elements of *ancien régime* society while it eliminated others. Louisiana society was not to be just like French society. Ministers hoped in some ways it would be better. They wanted changes at both the top and bottom of the social hierarchy.[9]

The design for Louisiana society placed limits on the size, power, and privileges of both the nobility and the third estate (middle and lower classes) in the interest of the crown. Unlike in Canada, no new seigneurial titles were to be granted with land concessions. Nor was venality, or the purchase of offices and titles, to be permitted in Louisiana. This would theoretically limit the merchant and professional class's political influence, as well as their conversion into nobles.

Politically, the Louisiana Superior Council had some parliamentary functions, but within the small structure of the original council, the official representatives of the king could easily effect a veto against local interests. In their designs for Louisiana, policy-makers had identified lawyers as a troublesome element that should be banned from practicing their trade. This move was intended to curb litigious activity and forestall legal challenges to crown authority. Neither objective was realized. By the late 1730s New Orleanians had succeeded in expanding the number of officeholders on the Superior Council both to dilute the voting power of the king's representatives and to handle the huge number of civil cases submitted for its review. As early as 1729 locals were directly nominating some members of the Council. Under creole rule in the following decades, the Council was essentially transformed into a representative body of a local merchant-planter oligarchy that counted Protestants and those with non-French roots within its ranks. This was not what French ministers had intended.[10]

The design for Louisiana excluded Jews and outlawed Protestants. Saint Domingue's *Code Noir*, written the same year as the Revocation of the Edict of Nantes in 1685, had first asserted their exclusion from the colonial domain. The first several articles of the code, which formed the basis of Louisiana's own *Code Noir* of 1724, outline restrictions on religious minorities before turning to the control of slaves and slaveowners. Yet the crown gave officials of the Company of the Indies permission to recruit Louisiana settlers from heavily Protestant regions of Germany, Switzerland, and Alsace. It is estimated that Louisiana's early immigration wave included 1,300 Protestants, or at least 20 percent of the European population, and that these settlers were among those most likely to stay and make a go of it. Their contracts stipulated that in return for swearing to the Catholic faith, they would be given supplies to establish themselves as farmers. Some policy-makers may have hoped to reform Protestants into faithful Catholics by offering them landownership. But some of the clergy were suspicious of the "apostates," whom they claimed were another source of Louisiana's "disorder."[11]

Another major immigrant group targeted for reform in Louisiana was that of the forced exiles and convict laborers known as *forçats*. Beginning with its first charter under Antoine Crozat, the Company worked with the crown to collect and outfit thousands of deserters, petty criminals, and subjects of *lettres de cachet*, a legal instrument used to round up alleged moral delinquents. Metropolitan administrators flattered themselves that these emigrants would be grateful for the commutation of their galley sentences (according to mortality statistics, a slow but near-certain death sentence) and would undergo a personal reformation through the Louisiana experience. Shortly after their arrival, colonial administrators complained loudly and clearly that this particular aspect of the social experiment had gone utterly awry. Of all the many reasons that Louisiana and New Orleans were perceived as disorderly failures, the recruitment, transportation, and colonial careers of its forced immigrants merit top billing. Although historians have questioned the demographic impact of *forçats* on Louisiana society, their impact on the colony's reputation remains undisputed.[12]

Finally, the fourth group in the Louisiana experiment consisted of African slaves. Although France already had decades of experience in the slave trade and with plantation economies in the Caribbean, the ways in which slaves were to be ruled and integrated into the social system of *ancien régime* society were still very much in flux. Slaves, especially baptized slaves, were simultaneously property and protected persons under French law. Partially as a result of this contradiction, slave policy and conditions for slaves in Louisiana varied from year to year and from owner to owner. Council members amended Louisiana's *Code Noir* of 1724 with several local ordinances throughout the French period. The rules for running a slave society—even the rules for creating racial difference—were highly localized evolutions. Colonial administrators and Louisiana slaveholders experimented with different methods for controlling difference and enforcing inequality, from the extreme segregation of the early engineers to the "Enlightened" paternalism of Louisiana planter Le Page du Pratz.[13]

In the 1710s and 1720s New Orleans began as a relatively segregated space reserved for Frenchmen, ringed by an African-majority plantation zone that extended for dozens of miles upriver and downriver from town. This Africanized agricultural area was itself surrounded by a vast Indian-dominated territory. One of the early anxieties of Louisiana administrators arose from the struggle to maintain this separation of French/African/Indian spaces along the boundaries of city/plantation/wilderness.

In early plans and maps of New Orleans, it appears that African slaves were originally intended to be housed entirely outside the proposed walls of the city. In the first several years, the majority of slaves who worked in New

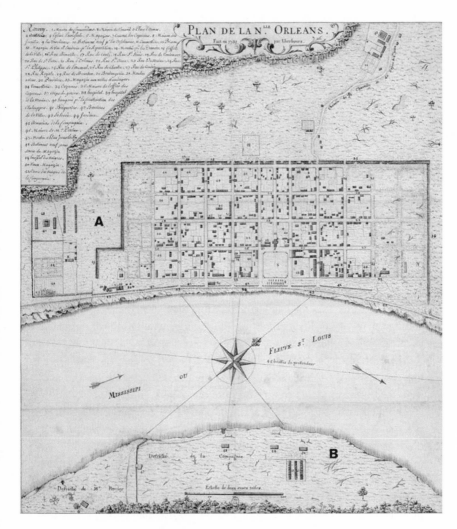

FIGURE 11. *Plan de la Nll. Orleans. Fait en 1731 par Lherbours.* A is slave quarters at the governor's plantation, B is slave quarters at Company plantation managed by Le Page du Pratz [letters added]. (Courtesy of Bibliothèque nationale de France, Estampes et Photographie, Vd 21, t.3 [P184 322].)

Orleans lived at one of two communities: at the Governor's plantation to the west, or at the Company plantation managed by Le Page du Pratz across the river (marked A and B, respectively, on figure 11). Thus, New Orleans began as a segregated space reserved for free whites. The segregation of white and black space was intentional and "prudent," in the words of Le Page du Pratz. Fancying himself an architect, Le Page set about designing slave quarters for the King's Plantation in the late 1720s.[14] During an inventory of the king's properties in 1732, a colonial draftsman drew a plan of the "Camp des Negres" that Le Page had built (fig. 12). Le Page wrote of his model: "The negro camp ought to be inclosed all round with palisades, and to have a door to shut with a lock and key. The huts ought to be detached from each other, for fear of fire, and to be built in direct lines, both for the sake of neatness, and in order to know easily the hut of each negro."[15] Le Page imagined that the separation of huts would help him observe and monitor workers he did not trust.

In attempting to control behavior through architectural design on the outskirts, Le Page du Pratz was in line with the French engineers who designed the perfect grid of New Orleans and assigned public and private space according to emerging ideals of the *ancien régime.* Clear, linear streets and public spaces overlooked by official buildings were thought to make surveillance of citizens easier. In this respect, Le Page was applying principles developed to control "free" Europeans under absolutism, to control enslaved Africans and Indians. Le Page and the engineers of New Orleans also applied the principles of segregation in their designs, aiming to discourage elements of the population from mixing, which in turn might lead to crime and insubordination.

These buildings segregated not only civilian and soldier, slave and free, but also Swiss, German, and French. In the city's first few years, the majority of European *petits gens* (a mixture of soldiers, indentured servants, condemned exiles, and a handful of voluntary farmers and artisans) lived in large barracks buildings in the town center. One motivation for isolating these groups may have been fear of the spread of Protestantism. Administrators also worried about the loyalty of foreigners. Swiss mercenaries like those sent to Louisiana were commonly used by the Bourbons for police functions against French subjects. Although the Swiss regiment reported directly to the Louisiana governor, governors resisted an effort to have the entire 150-man regiment housed at New Orleans, "fearing the capital might become hostage to a troop revolt by foreigners." Despite these worries, the Swiss troops gradually integrated into the French forces and New Orleans society, finding wives among the daughters of local settlers.[16]

Although ethnic, religious, and racial separation defined the original design for the town, segregation was not ultimately a successful strategy in New Orleans, particularly after the first creole generation became established in the 1730s. Still, France's social experimentation had a profound effect upon New Orleans. The town concentrated both the highest and lowest rungs of Euro-Louisianans under terms new to both, while the unintended

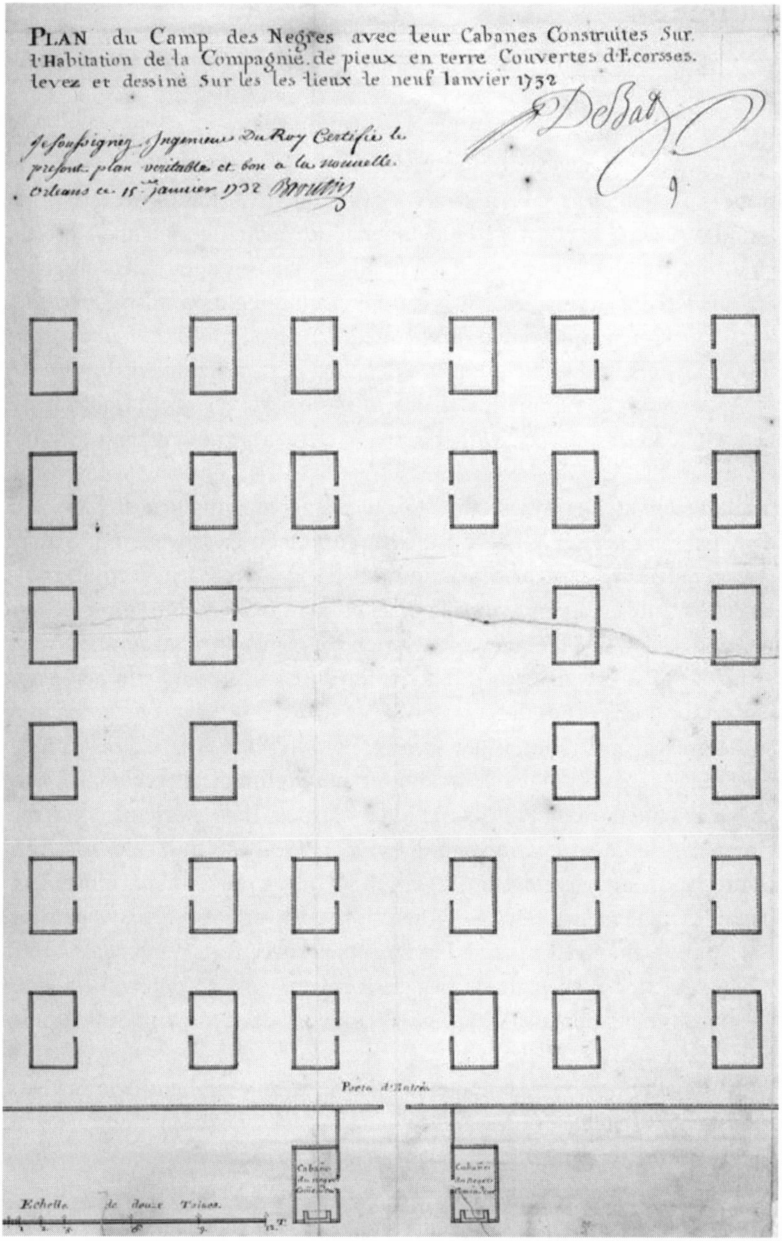

FIGURE 12. *Plan du Camp des Negres* . . . , Alexandre de Batz, 9 January 1732. Designed by Le Page du Pratz. (FR.ANOM. Aix-en-Provence. 04DFC91B. All rights reserved.)

growth of urban slavery strained the policies of segregation and difference the original planners had envisioned.

John Law's Company charter required him to deliver 6,000 European colonists and 3,000 enslaved Africans over the course of twenty-five years. He found it difficult to convince Frenchmen to leave their homes and start life anew in a far-off colony. To fulfill his obligations, Law appealed to foreigners, such as the German and Swiss farmers, and sought permission to redirect French men and women condemned to the galleys. The state was only too happy to be rid of these wards and potential troublemakers.[17]

Apparently the number or quality of these first recruits did not satisfy Law. He soon struck a deal with the crown to create a group of bounty hunters called the "*bandouliers du Mississippi*." These men were paid by the head to facilitate the crown's directive to cleanse the kingdom of idlers and drifters. Their brief reign of terror sparked riots in Paris while Louisiana's poor reputation caused prisoners awaiting transport to stage revolts. Louisiana's ill repute crystallized during this period of mass mobilization (1717–20), and fears flared up again a generation later when in 1750 another panic gripped the streets of Paris due to a rumor that children were being abducted for transport to the colony.[18]

Before leaving France, galley slaves (called *galériens*) and exiles destined for Louisiana endured harsh conditions and high mortality, but such suffering was the norm of pre-Revolutionary justice. The new element was the Company's large-scale campaign to transform convicts into colonists. This immigration strategy dovetailed with the "Great Confinement" movement begun by the regency in 1719, in which poverty and rootlessness became criminal. In the late 1710s and 1720s police sweeps throughout France's major cities collected vagrants, beggars, orphans, single women, the handicapped, and the mentally ill, along with military deserters, salt dealers, and tobacco smugglers.[19]

It was colonization by abduction. The high-profile publicity of John Law's resettlement scheme created an instant association between Louisiana and the "cleansing" program. The French public came to see the colony as a cause of misery at home as well as abroad. As if the logic that equated Louisiana with the galleys were not enough to cast a shadow on Louisiana's reputation, reports coming back to French seaports during the early years of hunger and hurricanes painted a dismal future for *forçats*. Already in 1718 popular songs heard in Paris advised choosing poverty at home over hope in Mississippi and warned husbands to control their anger at wayward wives, or "Mississippi will be your end."[20] Additional publicity about the conditions of galley slaves occurred when, instead of rotting out of sight in public jails, hospitals, and poorhouses, those destined for Louisiana were placed on forced marches to the seaports, with their misery displayed for all to see.

Not all Louisiana exiles came from the margins of French society. Some noble families sent their blasphemous and rebellious kin to Louisiana as an alternative to prison. Requests for *lettres de cachet* soared during the brief Law period. One rationale for exiling these elite convicts was that they would have a chance to reform and start over in a new society, leaving their bad reputation behind. In one of the first experimental steps toward modern notions of penal correction, proponents in France extended this ideal to Louisiana's lowliest *forçats*. Louisiana administrators, however, complained that this part of the experiment was an utter failure. In 1719 Bienville lamented that "it is most disagreeable for an officer in charge of a colony to have nothing more for its defense than a bunch of deserters, contraband salt dealers, and rogues who are always ready not only to desert you but also to turn against you."[21] Louisiana attorney general Raguet was so exasperated by the activities of French salt and tobacco smugglers that he wanted them to be "re-exiled" farther from the center of the colony. He complained of their demoralizing influence in New Orleans. Far from reforming in exile, they used the port to engage in "illicit commerce," and they "corrupted" the French servants, Indians, and slaves.[22]

Many historians have asserted that the harsh conditions of Louisiana's early years took a particularly heavy toll on Louisiana's *forçats*, concluding that though they had a tremendous impact on the colony's negative image, they had almost no demographic impact whatsoever. By one estimate, only sixty convicts out of "several thousand" designated for exile to Louisiana remained in 1721. Another author avers, "The exiles who arrived before 1731 were unwanted, unmotivated, and most of them soon dead . . . those who did survive the early years were mostly 'respectable' people." It is difficult to either confirm or refute this view using census information because *forçat* status simply stopped being systematically recorded after 1721 and *forçats* were prone to pick up nicknames that obscured their pasts. Death registries do sometimes note that an individual "arrived by force," but these references do not occur in large enough numbers to prove a higher mortality for this group. *Forçat* shipments were ordered halted by the crown in May 1720, but in late 1724 (four to seven years after their arrival in the colony) *forçats* were numerous enough in New Orleans to be of serious concern to the Superior Council.[23]

Within the founder generation, about one-quarter of Louisiana's European men came from the ranks of "illicit salt dealers, tobacco smugglers, army deserters, and other criminals taken from the streets and prisons of French cities." The proportion of smugglers among them appears to have been quite high, near 69 percent, meaning that over 1,100 Louisiana immigrants arrived as experienced smugglers. Louisiana recruiters strongly preferred smugglers over other galley slaves. Fittingly, their punishment entailed exile to a colony supposedly ruled by economic policies even more restrictive than those of *ancien régime* France, but where the economy quickly became oriented toward illegal trade, helped along, no doubt, by the skills of contrabandists.[24]

The monopolies, especially under Law's giant octopus of a corporation, ruled commercial life through mercantilism at home as well as in the colonies. Tobacco, salt, and silk were among those commodities tightly controlled within France's borders through a complex system of regional price-fixing, weights and measures, and the regulation of manufacturers, distributors, and importers. Operating almost any kind of business touching foreign commerce required a license and constituted a privilege. While smuggling certainly existed in France before the eighteenth century, organized contraband activity was exploding at the time of the founding of New Orleans, as a result of monopolistic expansion under Louis XIV and the hard economic times of the early eighteenth century. Law's recruiters cut out a sector of this smuggling subculture and transplanted it to Louisiana.[25]

Although Louisiana administrators complained about the moral qualities of forced emigrants, they reluctantly welcomed salt smugglers, a significant number of whom were *voituriers* (boatmen). The salt trade in France flowed along its rivers—the Loire, Mayenne, Oudon, Vienne, Creuse, and Allier, among others. Colonial officials early on recognized the importance of water transportation in Louisiana, both in the Gulf and along the Mississippi. They repeatedly stressed to French superiors their need for skilled pilots, shipmasters, and boatbuilders. Salt smugglers fit the bill cheaply. On the passenger list of the *Duque de Noailles* that sailed for Louisiana in 1719, the note "able seaman" was entered next to the names François Couttant and François Berthelot *dit* Marais (*dit* means "called," thus Marais was his nickname) in a list headed *contrebandiers du sel*. These men also came with an entrepreneurial disposition and a lack of respect for authority likely to be in conflict with colonial designs.

In France, *contrebandiers* had a reputation for defying authority while enjoying popular support. They sometimes resisted apprehension with force of arms, and were implicated in several incidents of rebellion in the provinces. While Louisiana officials were in desperate need of sailors and boatmen, these same men had been sources of disorder in France. In Louisiana officials complained that long after the ban on *forçats* announced in

1720, the flow of these troublesome immigrants continued into the 1750s, though now disguised with the label "soldier." The ministers "have satisfied themselves with sending here every year a certain number of recruits, most of them bandits and vagabonds . . . They breathe here nothing but desertion and revolt . . . can one expect solid establishments from such petulant and unstable characters?" This included the officer corps. Cadet Dutertre was sent to the colony—unfairly, he claimed—by a *lettre de cachet.*[26]

Like salt, tobacco was also taxed and controlled by a monopoly in France. It became a "necessity" in Europe in the late seventeenth century, and its popularity both in snuff and smoked forms grew exponentially in the eighteenth. Tobacco consumption in France had a direct impact on Louisiana. In 1718 Law succeeded in convincing the crown to grant his Company of the Indies exclusive rights to control the import and sale of tobacco in France. He argued that this would be the only way to protect French colonial growers from foreign suppliers and to ensure that the royal treasury received its share of tax revenue. As a result of his efforts, all non-Company tobacco became contraband. Louisiana tobacco sent to France without the oversight of the Company was also contraband. As with the salt policies, tightened restrictions produced a counter-reaction of fraud and smuggling.[27]

While France's salt trade traveled on freshwater routes, its tobacco trade depended upon international saltwater routes. Many tobacco smugglers were sailors and port dwellers. International networks involving sailors, merchants, and ship captains facilitated the transfer of contraband tobacco from sea to land. Tobacco smugglers, like salt smugglers, were valued by Louisiana administrators for their sailing abilities. Often multilingual, tobacco smugglers excelled in clandestine communication and commercial networking across long distances. Ironically, tobacco smugglers exiled to Louisiana were brought closer to their source, if not put to work growing it themselves. Unfortunately for their superiors, conditions in the colony provided these able dealers with opportunities to establish new international networks outside the confines of *ancien régime* privilege. While deliberately sent to Louisiana as part of the plan, they quickly adapted their own designs. They were experts at evading monopolies and bureaucracies, and as a result these imported smugglers have been undercounted in the archive of New Orleans.

CENSUS-TAKING

The crown had decided to conduct a social experiment on Louisiana's undeveloped shores. Census-taking represented an effort to record and control the experiment. As with the hundreds of maps made of Louisiana and New Orleans in the first few decades of the colony, the hundreds of pages of tally sheets created for the colonial censuses reflect the French administration's initial passion for information-gathering and planning. Beginning with the first year of Louisiana's official colonization in 1699, door-to-door censuses collected the name, age, origin, and legal status of household members in the settlements. Officials undertook censuses of New Orleans and/or its immediate environs in 1721, 1724, 1726, 1727, and 1731–32. A second phase of census-taking occurred three decades later, just before the transfer to Spanish rule, with the censuses of 1763 and 1766.[28] These sets of documents provide an unusual diptych of a colonial founding generation and the succeeding creole generation in its maturity.

The colonial Louisiana censuses were a product of French absolutism in which urban planning, police surveillance, and the bureaucratic creation and control of information were openly embraced as tools of social control. Methods were in rapid development at the time of Louisiana's founding under the policies of the regency and Louis XV. The colony could be a proving ground for new technologies. During the "Great Confinement," the crown attempted to purge France of *inconnus* and *gens sans aveu*—the "unknowns" and those without a home, a position, a patron, or a verifiable identity.[29] Many were sent to Louisiana. Through their obsessive census-taking of Louisiana, administrators attempted to make this colonial population "known" and to place limits on its indigenous and imported tendencies toward wandering. But the colonial censuses also represented an extreme, unlike anything attempted up to that time on the mainland, even within the context of the colossal Bourbon bureaucracy.[30]

Although Louisiana historians have availed themselves of the rich data contained in the colonial censuses, the act of census-taking itself has rarely been a subject of study. The way administrators framed the censuses through categories, terminology, and organization gives us insight into the changing mentality of colonial rule and the transition to a creole sense of order. What census-takers decided to leave out of the picture is as important as what they put in.

Census-takers had noted the presence of slaves since the first official importation of African laborers in 1719, but subsequent censuses of early Louisiana reflect a set of changing priorities in how status, origin, and appearance were marked. Talking about race in French Louisiana is difficult for at least two reasons. First, "race" as a category of human classification was not yet clearly articulated. Second, the terminology that Louisiana administrators did use to describe origin, color, and legal status varied widely from census to census and enumerator to enumerator. In the early eighteenth century, French travel-writing and philosophical texts still tended to discuss human groups as "nations," a category closer to the modern idea of ethnicity than race.[31]

The more mundane documents of colonial administrations, however, had begun to erase national differences and move toward a new classification based on a combination of color and legal status. Saint Domingue's *Code Noir* of 1685 already used the terms *blancs* and *noirs*. Louisiana's version of this code, created by French ministers in 1724, reiterated this color binary, corresponding to the directions given to colonial engineers, to separate white and black spaces. On the colonial ground, however, these terms appear to have been little used. One Louisianan explicitly challenged the idea that skin color was the most important difference between *nègres* and Europeans; rather, the difference lay in culture. Le Page du Pratz remarked in 1758, "[t]he negroes must be governed differently from the Europeans; not because they are black, nor because they are slaves; but because they think differently from the white men."[32] One implication is that creole slaves who were acculturated to French colonial "thinking" would have been little different from French subjects. Le Page seems to have been expressing a view that was common in Louisiana. The early Louisiana censuses are most concerned with legal status, and secondarily with origin and color. Within the ranks of slaves, an emerging distinction between *nègre* and *mulâtre* corresponded to color, while *sauvage* described Native American origin. The engineers and military officers who acted as enumerators identified the color of free people only sporadically and inconsistently; they never used the term *blanc*. Religious administrators making entries in baptismal or death registers seemed more interested than their secular counterparts in the issue of color, but even their methods were "haphazard" and their conception of race "inchoate."[33]

Although early Louisiana censuses were especially haphazard in regard to color, with the first census of New Orleans in 1721 administrators began to record legal status and origin more consistently—underscoring the role of New Orleans in French schemes to experiment with social hierarchy in the new world.[34] There were several categories for each household: men, women, children, French domestics (probably indentured), Negro slaves, and Indian slaves (*hommes, femmes, enfants, domestiques français, esclaves negres*, and *esclaves sauvages*). In addition, forty-two male and thirteen female *forçats* were labeled individually, although the original census was not designed with this category.[35] Census-takers entered free people in one of the first three generic categories (men, women, and children), which were unmarked for race or ethnicity. While the majority of this group were Europeans, Canadians, and young creole children, the lack of a distinct category for free people of color of African or Native American descent makes it conceivable that they, too, were included in this group. In addition, some common-law wives may have been listed incorrectly as slaves.[36]

The colonial census of 1731–32 marks a change in methodology, as well as the changing social structure of New Orleans.[37] The timing of this census coincided with the end of a large wave of forced African immigration to Louisiana, involving approximately 5,700 people, of whom approximately 4,000 had survived to be counted in the 1732 census. It also corresponded with retrocession from the Company back to crown rule.[38] While the categories used in Louisiana's rural areas were much the same as those in previous censuses, in New Orleans census-takers attempted to develop a more nuanced categorization of residents. They added five new categories (for a total of seventeen). Race and gender became more finely tuned than in any previous colonial census.[39] Within New Orleans, major status distinctions within the ranks of Euro-Louisianans dropped out as those with the "semi-free" status of *engagé* (French domestics) and *forçat* were manumitted or left the colony. The 1732 New Orleans census represents the first time mixed-race individuals were delineated, but census-takers were only interested in color differences among slaves. Free people of color continued to be grouped in the generic "free person" category, although census workers occasionally noted "*nègre libre*" (free black) or "*mulâtre*" (mulatto) in the same way they infrequently jotted the descriptive tags "Canadian," "German," or "Swiss" next to names. The incidental manner of these notes leaves the strong impression that the censuses in no way account for all the individuals from these backgrounds, nor were they designed to. Sometimes the same free person was in one census marked for color/origin, and in another unmarked. For example, in the 1726 census Nicolas Xavier was listed as a free head of household on Bourbon Street without any indication of his color. In the 1732 census he was again listed as a head of household, with the parenthetical remark "free mulatto." By this time, administrators had begun to concentrate on color difference within the slave undercaste, but never in the French period did they enforce stark racial differences among the free.

Soon after its founding, New Orleans emerged as an urban place characterized by a wide variety of nonagricultural activities and professions. Demographically, New Orleans was set apart. Compared to the rest of the colony, it had twice the proportion of military personnel and six times the number of "free" European workers (those exempt from forced labor or contracts). The town's free population can be divided into five main sectors, listed in order of their proportion of the whole, from largest to smallest: (1) skilled artisans; (2) those involved in transportation and commerce; (3) low-skilled laborers; (4) public servants and soldiers; and (5) those involved in food, agriculture or hospitality, including many wealthy planters who kept second homes in town. In town, enslaved people were most likely to work in the first three sectors. The census of 1727 recorded the occupation of 313 household heads. Artisans such as carpenters, blacksmiths, coopers, candlemakers, and tailors made up the largest group (29 percent). New Orleans concentrated the colony's poor freemen whose trades benefited from an urban setting or who simply lacked the skills and resources to live off the land.[40]

New Orleans also concentrated the colonial elite. Nearly all Superior Council members, Company representatives, wholesale merchants, and major plantation owners kept a New Orleans townhouse, as did most commissioned military officers with posts in town or nearby. Yet this class made up less than a quarter of the town's free population. Artisans, laborers, and sailors far outnumbered large slaveholders in French colonial New Orleans.

New Orleans was also a port town of itinerants and part-time residents. The census data show a significant number of *voyageurs*, or Indian traders, who kept houses in New Orleans. Some of these traders were identified with posts in upper Louisiana, suggesting they kept more than one residence. Others were associated with specific Indian villages. Pierre Ferand on Bourbon Street was identified as a "trader with the Houmas," while Barbier was "of the Tonicas Indian village." Pierre La Houx "of the Akansas" lived on Orleans Street with his wife and child.[41] Whether these men were ethnically European, Indian, or *métis* is unknown and, more important for understanding the social system of colonial New Orleans, unmarked in the censuses.

Some aspects of the city's occupational profile changed over time. European domestic servants constituted the largest single subgroup in the 1727 census (forty-five households) but by 1732 they had been replaced by slaves, as indentured contracts had expired and African immigration had intensified.[42] A significant number of the colony's *engagés* appear to have moved to town and entered the ranks of skilled artisans at the end of their contracts, as this category jumped from 29 percent to 38 percent in 1732.[43] *Forçats* also contributed significantly to the city's lower socioeconomic strata. Most had been exiled for life and did not have the option of returning to France, though the censuses suggest they were granted freedom from forced labor when the Company turned over the colony to the crown in 1731.

When the metropole pulled back the scale of its investment in Louisiana in the 1730s, the census-taking fever died down, although officials continued to offer rough estimates of the colonial population in their reports. Official European and African immigration came to a near standstill, but the population was far from stagnant. Censuses taken at the end of the French period (1763, 1766, and 1770) demonstrate a remarkable demographic recovery and growth among first- and second-generation creoles. Between 1721 and 1763 New Orleans had grown from a large village of 519 to a respectable town of 2,524.[44] In 1721, during the land clearing phase, enslaved workers played a significant role in building the town, temporarily comprising 33 percent of the population. About half of these slaves were impressed from planters and concession owners in nearby areas to contribute to the public work of building the town, while the other half were owned by the Company of the Indies itself. After reaching a low in 1726 due to an influx of European immigrants, the proportion of people of color in the city tripled, comprising 35 percent of the population by the end of the regime. Still, the city maintained a free (and largely French) majority throughout the period, ranging from 88 percent to 67 percent of the town's population.[45]

Whether New Orleans had actual or imaginary walls, the town's limits were clearly marked by the perimeter of its street grid and by the notations of census-takers. They separated the in-town census from that of the surrounding area in different sections of all the censuses, and even changed their methods for identifying households once within the town limits. The *Code Noir* and other ordinances specifically limited slaves' access to town and attempted to legislate a boundary between the rural plantation zone and the city. While in the country the census-takers were mainly interested in the total headcount of widely spaced settlements, in town they were concerned with creating a complete map of property ownership and social status. Only in New Orleans did they regularly note the trade or employment of the heads of households and male boarders. Small as New Orleans was, in the minds of Louisianans it was a social and economic space set apart from the rest of the colony.

These frequent adjustments in census categories and forms, as well as the mismatch between census terminology and that used in the court records of colonial Louisiana, show that census-taking was an attempt not to record the social order, but to create it. As administrators worked to collect knowledge on the colony's diverse population, they invented the social categories they wished to see.

MAPPING STATUS

Mapmaking was another way in which administrators expressed their desire to know and engineer the social space of New Orleans. Concurrent with the censuses, the Superior Council in 1728 and 1731 ordered the city's engineers to create maps that identified all the property owners and major tenants (fig. 13). These maps plot a social hierarchy within the small space

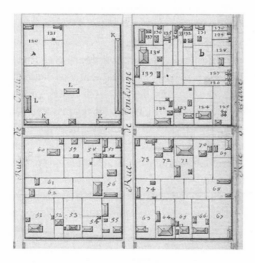

FIGURE 13. Detail of *Plan de la Nouvelle Orleans* by Gonichon, December 1731 (*see color plate 4*). Shows numbered properties tied to a key of owners' names. (FR.ANOM. Aix-en-Provence. 04DFC89B. All rights reserved.)

of the town grid. Their numbered keys correspond to notes on the identities of owners and residents. The engineer de Pauger assigned lots according to the resident's "means to develop" them. The plots varied by size and quality. The most desirable lots were those close to the natural levee of the river—the high ground—while those farthest from the river, facing the woods, were less desirable and prone to flooding. A list of 300 property owners drawn from these maps captures members of the founding generation who had survived "seasoning," as well as their growing creole families. When the maps were made, they had lived in the colony at least seven years, and in one case as long as thirty-two years. If we cross-reference these 300 individuals with their appearances in other documents, the character of the town and its bit players emerges more clearly.[46]

While using a list of property owners as a baseline for the community might be expected to bias the sample toward the wealthy, in fact the varied backgrounds and occupations of these individuals suggest the full range of free people, from day laborers to plantation owners. That property ownership was so generalized speaks to how the colonial situation, despite its hardships, allowed for a greater degree of socioeconomic mobility than in France.[47] Yet this mobility could still be circumscribed by the street grid of New Orleans.

In 1731 the first row of blocks along the river flanked the symbolic center of town, the Place d'Armes (see color plate 4, and figure 6 in chapter 2). The largest private lots were concentrated in this row, where the town's elite could monitor comings and goings along the river. Parterre gardens and orangeries in the Versailles style lent aristocratic pretensions to the neighborhood. The first square along the levee (or quay), on the upriver side, belonged entirely to Governor Bienville for his private residence. Moving downriver, the next square was occupied by the *ordonnateur* Delachaise, and the owners or officers of major concessions. The square bounded by St. Louis and Conti held the townhouses of major planters, such as Sieur Tixerant and the Canadian Chauvin brothers, as well as prominent military officers. This mixture of high-status residents—large plantation and concession owners, company employees, government officials, and military officers (or the recent widows of these men)—characterizes the remainder of the squares in this row. Close to the Place d'Armes, their private residences shared squares with public buildings and warehouses.

The draftsmen of these maps marked social status through the use of abbreviations before the owners' surnames. The simple "Sr." for "Le Sieur" indicated reliably that the occupant held a prominent public position or was the owner of a large plantation (more than ten slaves). Every one of the male property holders in the riverfront squares was granted this honorific. In contrast, in the first block of the next row away from the river, half of the occupants are *sieurs* while the names of the other half are preceded by the abbreviation "Né." for *nommé* or "the one so named." The mapmaker's method of differentiation emphasized the difference between a known and respected identity and a "supposed," unverifiable identity, consistent with social ordering in the *ancien régime*. Those who traveled outside familiar circuits were suspicious. The terminology used in New Orleans underscores that immigration and/or intentional self-fashioning obscured the origin and identity of many residents.[48]

The character of the second row of blocks behind the river was mixed, as indicated by the combination of "Sr." and "Né." tags. Thus the blacksmith Né. Joseph Daublin and the former soldier Né. Nicolas Pierrot *dit* Vendome were neighbors of Sr. de Morand, "inspector of workers" for the company, and of Sr. Morriset, another company employee. The properties belonging to higher status individuals tended to front Chartres Street, closer to the river and facing the houses of the prominent residents along the riverfront block. Interspersed among mid-level company officials, military officers, and plantation owners were *les nommés*, such as the carpenter St. Hilaire, the turner and sometime poultry dealer Vallerant, baker Jean Caron, the Indian scout and trader du Sablon, and the widow Sarrazin (her husband had been a warehouse guard). While some families lived along this row of blocks, other houses belonged to prominent bachelors, or were the part-time residences of planters and traders.

In the third row back from the river, another transition occurs. The outer squares (the ones farthest downriver or upriver) have "respectable" larger residences, such as those of Dr. Alexandre and planter Sr. Joseph Chaperon, but the interior squares belong almost exclusively to *les nommés*. The lots become smaller and houses more crowded. One neighborhood comprised a dense row of houses along Bourbon between Toulouse and St. Peter Streets. This area was home to the following small property owners: Paul Vitre, a woodcutter who worked part time at the port of La Balize; Marie Françoise, a free woman of color who had been baptized as an adult in 1729 and was probably an ex-slave; the cutler Commercy; former *engagé* and dayworker Christophle Thomas; and baker Nicolas Francoeur. The neighborhood im-mediately behind the church between Toulouse and Dumaine Streets was also a diverse and lively one. It concentrated small, non-slaveowning fami-lies and year-round residents.

The fourth and final row of city squares lay farthest from the river, run-ning between the north side of Bourbon Street and the ditch where the fortified wall should have been. Lots here belonged almost entirely to *les nommés*, consisting of the poor and the itinerant, as well as aspiring new-comers without the means to purchase lots in the dryer parts of town. Some long-term residents included charcoal-maker Allain Gardela and gardener Adrian Flamand. Their neighbors were soldiers and ex-soldiers known pri-marily by their nicknames, such as Moin, Belleroze, and Marche-à-terre. This "back of town" area (as the swampy portions of mid–New Orleans later became known) also accommodated those in the maritime trades. Sailor Sarrot lived with two enslaved sailors he had trained, while sailor Chupé lived around the corner from ship captain François Chereau. Some for-mer *engagés* living in this row had established themselves as tradesmen — ship carpenters and metalworkers, such as Pierre Gautier, Phillip Le Duc, and François Castel La Roche. Households of single men cohabiting were common, and the neighborhood boasted most of the city's troublesome cabarets.

Not surprisingly, the residences of enslaved people tended to closely fol-low the tiered hierarchy of *sieurs* and *nommés* from the river to the back swamp. Almost all the households with a view of the water had enslaved members, and those with the largest domestic staffs were located here. To-ward the back of town only a handful of residents cohabited with slaves in small cabins. Some of these enslaved residents had probably been hired out by their owners to man the Illinois rafts or to learn a craft.

Censuses and maps from French New Orleans provide evidence for the designs and deviations of the colonial social plan. They are imperfect instruments of measurement and control, but between the lines we can discern a new social order emerging in the creole period. It is characterized by organizing principles held in high tension—a hierarchy of wealth and a climate of social mobility, the inequalities of slavery and the intimacies of urban living.

Creoles and Insubordinates

Slavery became a major basis and symbol of wealth in colonial Louisiana. Under Company rules, Africans were sold on credit to those with social capital. Noble officers and bourgeois bureaucrats often had only reputation and inherited status to offer as collateral. In this way, Old World status begat New World wealth in an exclusionary manner. But credit loans for the first shipments of slaves and access to the Superior Council were about the only vestiges left of traditional *ancien régime* privileges for the nobility and upper bourgeoisie. Even these privileges could be threatened by pretenders who used the colonial disjuncture to exaggerate a reputation or invent a past. As a result, social status was more malleable in Louisiana than in France, even among the first generation of French natives. Clever entrepreneurs or social climbers could acquire a sort of colonial noble status much more rapidly than could their counterparts in France whose identities were more verifiable, and who depended upon venality and patronage for advancement. As colonials had little recourse to these latter avenues, status came to rest on the simple privilege of wealth by the late 1730s, and on the more provincial privilege of family connections by the 1760s.

From the beginning, the crown had attempted to lay down entirely new laws regarding social status and mobility that were remarkably different from the realities of *ancien régime* France. Advisers had hoped to limit noble privileges that chafed against the king's power, as well as the social mobility of a rapidly growing bourgeoisie. The crown's own policies legislated the extinction of the three-estate system in Louisiana. The new system meant that old group loyalties brought few advantages; this had an individualizing effect upon New Orleans society. The unintended consequences of this experiment created new types of "disorder": the heightened social mobility of *les petits gens*, the growth of urban slavery, a persistent and often intimate social mingling across old status categories, and a decline in the power and influence of the crown itself, which by the end of the regime faced challenges from a new interest group—a wealthy creole oligarchy.

La Renommée (The Renowned or The Renamed) was the personal ship of Pierre Le Moyne d'Iberville used during the early exploration and settlement of French Louisiana.[49] It provides a fitting symbol of the invented identities and notorious reputation of many of Louisiana's founder generation. If they survived the long seasoning period of disease, hunger, and coerced labor, immigrants found themselves in a place where they could experience a great range of physical and social mobility. In their movements, they picked up nicknames like souvenirs. And enslaved immigrants used alternate names to facilitate psychological, if not physical, distance from their enslavers.

Iberville's brother, Jean-Baptiste LeMoyne de Bienville, is the first local resident known to have used the term *creole*.[50] This, too, was an act of renaming that created a break with the French past. The "disorders" that New Orleans became known for had much to do with the slippery identities of its founders and the independence of its creoles. In France, both had a reputation for insubordination.

In 1719 a low-ranking officer named Dumont de Montigny watched over 500 *forçats* imprisoned in the tower of Saint Nicolas in La Rochelle, waiting to embark for Louisiana. Three hundred were deserters. The rest were "young people whom their relatives wanted to be rid of, whom they were sending, it was said, to seek their fortune. Without a doubt I was one of this number, although honored with the commission of an officer."[51] These young people were the subjects of *lettres de cachet* whose families had requested their imprisonment or banishment for leading a dissolute life or having a rebellious disposition. Dumont's *mémoire* suggests he was sent to Louisiana for similar faults. Due to some undisclosed indiscretions in his youth, his family sought and found an assignment for him far from France.

As they crossed over the Tropic of Cancer during the sea voyage, the passengers and crew assembled on the deck for a mass baptism of all those traveling to the New World for the first time. A sailor, dressed up as "the Old Gentleman of the Tropics," greeted his "children," brandishing a trident of Neptune and splashing them with water. He then gave them new names by which they were to be known in his world. Dumont does not say whether he also received a new name at this time, but he did have two nicknames during his colonial service. The first was "de Montigny," a family nickname with seigneurial connotations that he adopted more officially in Louisiana.[52] The second nickname, "Chevalier Le Blanc," was given to him by friends who appear to have been poking fun at the frequent name-dropping of his high-placed protector, the minister of war, Claude Le Blanc. Like many French immigrants to Louisiana, Dumont adopted a new name in an attempt to refashion himself and gloss over a troubling past. Others gave him another nickname in an attempt to put him back in his place.

Natalie Zemon Davis explains the now famous case of Martin Guerre as occurring within a context where nicknaming, carnival masking, and forging false identities were common practices in early modern popular culture.[53] By the eighteenth century nicknaming appears to have been widespread among France's urban poor and even among salon sophisticates in the form of pen names and allegorical libels. These practices carried over into Louisiana, where they added to the confusion and the possibilities of colonial life. Historian Carl Brasseaux notes that nicknames were "extensively" used by Louisiana's noncommissioned officers and enlisted men, to the point that they could appear in important official records under nicknames such as "Francoeur" (Braveheart), "Sans Regret" (Without Regret), or "San Façon" (Without Ceremony). Many of these were *noms de guerre* that marked a right of passage among the soldiery.[54]

My examination of the Superior Council records found that at least 18 percent of property owners in New Orleans between 1728 and 1731 possessed aliases used in legal proceedings. The same sources indicate that nicknaming was probably even more common among those less likely to own property. It was rare for Canadian settlers, soldiers, craftsmen, and those in the traveling trades, such as *voyageurs* and merchant sailors, *not* to have a nickname.[55] An examination of nicknaming practices is important as an example of the means immigrants used to remake themselves in the colonial setting, and of the challenges administrators faced in trying to control their social experiments.

The sources of nicknames varied. Many were unimaginative adoptions of patron saint names or place of origin. Sailors called to testify in a 1723 desertion plot were identified as Jean Daniel *dit* (called) St. Jean and Pierre Chauvin *dit* St. Pierre. Jean Baptiste *dit* Lyonnais and Thomas Asselin *dit* Orleans were small property owners in New Orleans in the 1720s. Notorious tavern keeper Jan Lamesse was known as "Le Flamand" (the Fleming). The *procureur général* Raguet complained about Flamand's tavern as a center of criminal activity in his 1724 campaign against *forçats* in New Orleans. Significantly, he added about the patrons, there are "thoses whose [real] names are not known, but who are certainly familiar to all."[56]

Canadian trader Larche Lainé (L'Arche the Elder) more often appeared under his nickname "Larchevesque," a play on words meaning "the Archbishop." He even signed his name as "Larchevesque" in a legal document related to his appeal of a gambling debt on the grounds that he was drunk, did not remember the transaction, and in any case, gambling was outlawed by the Council so the loser was out of luck. A similar play on words transformed the New Orleans blacksmith François Durocher Castillon into "La Roche Castel" (Castle Rock). Most nicknames were probably invented or imposed by associates, but some expressed a self-fashioning ambition. Bertrand Joffre *dit* La Liberté appeared frequently in the Superior Council records from 1721 to his death in 1741. The documents track his rising fortune from a modest New Orleans householder to a proprietor of a major tar-making plant. The "liberty" he found in Louisiana ironically meant the enslavement of seventeen other people by the end of his life.[57] Poor Jean Foutre from Switzerland, the census-taker remarked with obvious amusement, "wished to be called 'Renard'" (figuratively, Sly Fox). Renard's German-speaking parents had bestowed a name upon him that translated into French as "bugger," meaning either "jackass" or, more literally, "sodomite." Perhaps that was reason enough to emigrate and change one's name. Other New Orleans residents, such as the pirate Michel Fitzgerald, clearly played with naming and identity to suit more underhanded purposes. He appears in the greater Caribbean area under at least a half-dozen aliases.

Adopted names could be significant instruments of self-fashioning. They could even become permanent and legitimate through the workings of memory and legal notation. Wives and widows were often known by their husband's nicknames. More significantly, creole children could inherit their father's nickname as their proper surname. By entering the new name in church records, successions, and property transfers, the family lineage became transformed and the father's past obscured. Claude Renaud *dit* Avignon, a trader and New Orleans smallholder, passed "Avignon" on to his wife Marianne, as well as his daughter Marie. A grandson named Louis Avignon made claims against his estate in 1774. An old Canadian pioneer who had started at Biloxi in 1700 had an illegitimate son who inherited his complete name intact—Christian name, surname, and nickname. His son appears as Jean Baptiste Baudreau *dit* Graveline, *fils* (or Jr.) in a number of legal scrapes in the 1740s and 1750s.[58]

Nicknaming practices caused headaches for colonial administrators who were in charge of keeping immigrants within their different legal stations—as *engagés*, soldiers, *forçats*, apostates, concessionaires, and, of course, slaves. Although censuses rarely mention the names of enslaved household members, other documents, such as acts of sale, successions, and criminal proceedings, indicate that slaves also maintained aliases and played with nicknaming. Alternate names appear most frequently in cases involving runaways, suggesting the use of aliases to evade authority. "Sans Peur" (Fearless), "La Richer" (Moneybags), and L'Eveillé (Spunky) were among a group of Bambara and Samba runaways who lived on raccoons and muskrats in the woods for several months. Pierrot *dit* Jasmin was a slave "of the Sango nation" who ran away from his mistress in Arkansas on a trip to the market in New Orleans. Many founder-generation slaves maintained African names by which they were more commonly known in their communities, such as Charlot *dit* Kakaracou of the Coneda nation and François *dit* Baraca of the Poulav nation.[59]

Officers compiling passenger lists of ships headed for Louisiana during the large French immigration wave of 1718–23 carefully noted both the given names and the nicknames of *forçats*, perhaps hoping to prevent these immigrants from escaping their past upon arrival in the colony. These recording efforts were not entirely successful. By 1721 about half of those listed as *forçats*, sent to help clear the land at New Orleans, were known only by nicknames such as "La Roquette" (The Rocket) or "La Terreur" (The Terror).[60]

Louisiana was a dangerous mixture and *forçats* a volatile additive. Nowhere in the colony was the mixture more intimate than in New Orleans. Although *forçats*—so marked—disappear from the censuses by the late 1720s, evidence suggests that survivors gravitated toward New Orleans. The careers of many can be traced in the mundane paperwork of town life—church registries, mortgages, and civil spats. Most *forçats* came from France's cities and would have been at a loss to feed themselves in the woods and fields of the hinterland. Crude and muddy as they may have been, the streets of New Orleans were as close as the *forçats* could get to something familiar.

The case of emancipated *forçats* exemplifies how microhistory can correct the dubious reality of official records. The life stories of former convicts show the ways in which New Orleans society was structured along class lines, yet also was flexible enough to allow individuals to jump the lines and overcome their history. *Forçats* used the ambiguities and opportunities of frontier life to transform themselves into successful entrepreneurs, and in some cases upstanding citizens.

The *forçats* who became members of the New Orleans community represented the full spectrum of free French society in the colony—from lowly soldier to public official. Of the New Orleans property owners whose names appear on passenger lists from the 1710s and 1720s, 20 percent were *forçats*, proportionate to (or even a little higher than) their original numbers within the John Law immigration stream.[61] Not only did these men and women survive the seasoning period, they were playing active roles in the local economy and establishing families. They founded several creole lineages.

Pierre Bideau *dit* St. Jacques helped found New Orleans. He appears on the 1721 census as one of the *forçats* sent to help the engineer Pauger clear trees for the new settlement. A twenty-eight-year-old native of St. Gaultier and son of a wagonmaker, Bideau had been placed on a ship departing for Louisiana in 1719 for the crime of desertion. He was killed at Natchez during the uprising of 1729, as was his wife. Another man, François Jouteur of Lyon, was one of a handful of *forçats* sent with family members, although his only crime was being a "vagabond." His wife Marguerite Michon embarked with him in 1719. She may have been the same woman living with him on Orleans Street in 1727. They buried a son in 1729.[62]

Mathurin Roger was among the large number of salt smugglers sent to Louisiana. He had embarked on one of the first ships loaded with *forçats*, arriving on the *Neptune* in 1717. By June 1721 he had a wife and child living with him at Mobile, where he worked as a shoemaker. The Roger family relocated to New Orleans soon after it became the capital in 1722. In January 1724 he and his wife Catherine Blanchart buried their son Jean François in the town cemetery. A shipmate of Roger's, Pierre Masson *dit* Chevallier, also an illegal salt dealer, came from Mans in Champagne. He was listed as the owner of a "small boat" in 1723, apparently attempting to generate income to supplement his post as a soldier in the city regiment. He died nine years after arrival, in 1726, with the epigraph *"homme de force"* (or *forçat*), in the church registry. A third salt smuggler, Joseph Le Champ (or Deschamps) *dit* La Rose from Lambray was forty years old when sent to Louisiana in 1719 on the *Duc de Noailles*. La Rose found a companion in the New World and started a family; he was living on Bourbon Street with his wife and child in 1726.

Jean François Herisse (or Housset) *dit* Ringal was a thirty-five-year-old native of Chambly listed among the deserters and exiles embarked on the *Marie* in May 1719. Although he died at the hospital in New Orleans, this was not until September 1728 (probably of yellow fever), as an "old" man of forty-four. At the time of his death he was listed as a soldier, suggesting a continuation of enforced service for male *forçats*, but also a means of subsistence. The death registry of another *forçat* who died the same year, Jean Randon, notes that this native of Berlin had been "brought to this colony as a prisoner." Although conditions in New Orleans had allowed him to become a modest property owner, in death he could not escape the stigma of his past.

Marie Michel was among the approximately 250 female *forçats* sent to Louisiana. She appears as one of the "women and girls exiled for fraud" on the *Deux Frères* in 1719. Nine years later she had become sole proprietor of a lot and house in New Orleans. Marie Baron was put upon the *Mutine* in 1719 and shipped with several other women "under orders of the king." A young woman of eighteen or nineteen, it appears she had become pregnant out of wedlock. After burying a little girl at Biloxi, she married and settled at

Natchez. There she lost her first husband and another child in the Natchez uprising and was herself taken captive. When she escaped to New Orleans, she met up with the picaresque historian Dumont de Montigny, whom she soon after married. They settled into a house on Dauphine Street. They had two children in the colony, who returned with them to France in 1737.[63]

Louis Manseau (or Marsseau), a tobacco smuggler, also arrived on the *Deux Frères* in 1719. He was perhaps one of the most entrepreneurial of the exiles, forming a partnership with a man named Louis Louer (or Louet) to cultivate indigo at Natchez. He petitioned the council for credit to purchase slaves in 1725 and appears in the Natchez census in 1725. He apparently survived the Natchez Rebellion of 1729 and moved to New Orleans, where he had a house in 1731. Another exile who did well for himself was François le Clef, who appears on the 1721 list of New Orleans *forçats*. He married Christine de la Vallie with whom he lived on L'Arsenal Street in 1726 at the edge of the woods. His occupation was listed as sailor. The couple buried an infant son in 1728. Despite personal losses, his social and economic status had risen by 1732 to that of "boat captain," and he had moved to a more respectable address on Bourbon Street.

Other *forçats* did even better for themselves. "Sieur" Soubagnier (Sabannier, other spellings), was a tobacco smuggler from Dax near Bayonne who was exiled in 1719 along with his wife Catherine Detrouillet and two daughters. Soubagnier came from the noble ranks of smugglers who continued their trade in Louisiana. In a report of 1723 he was described as a "speculator in private merchandise" as well as a plantation owner at Gentilly, just outside the city. A few years later census-takers found him in residence at Natchez. The couple had at least two more children after arrival in the colony. One of them was killed, along with her parents, during the Natchez Rebellion.

Finally, one of the most fascinating *forçat* biographies from early New Orleans underscores the ways in which colonial conditions encouraged new beginnings, although there were limits to social mobility on the frontier even for those with friends in high places. Le Sieur de Chavannes (or Chavanne) was a thirty-five-year-old Parisian of apparently noble background listed on board the *Marie* in 1719 *"par Lettre de Cachet."* As Chavannes explained it years later to Louisiana's *ordonnateur*, he had killed a friend in self-defense during a drunken fracas. When he first arrived in Louisiana, Chavannes tried his hand at planting, living in the mixed Indian-French village of Petit Colas upriver, where he resided with three other French men and four free women in 1723, probably *engagés* paid for by his family or protectors. When their terms ended, Chavannes had the means to replace them with two African and one Indian slave in 1726. He had also by this time curried favor with the administrative elite, where his noble title, manners, and education impressed Superior Council members. They appointed him secretary to the Council in April 1725, and he began to keep a residence in town, living alone on Bienville Street after he buried his baptized slave Pierre in September of that year.[64] He requested credit for more slaves in 1726. The next year, he added two African slaves to his household, which he had moved to a larger structure on Conti Street. Chavannes's resources thereafter grew rapidly, suggesting the possibilities of converting social and cultural capital into economic capital. By 1731 his plantation upriver had twenty-six African slaves, nine Afro-creole enslaved children, and one Indian slave. He was speculating in real estate by buying, selling, and leasing property in town and in the plantation areas. Chavannes's bureaucratic career also went well even though Governor Bienville had taken a dislike to him. The new *ordonnateur* Delachaise, however, said he was an "honorable" man. Several years later, after Delachaise had died, the political tide turned against Chavannes; the new governor called him an "indiscreet and ill intentioned" person in 1729. The story of the homicide resurfaced, and he was removed from his post in a loud scandal. Nonetheless, Chavannes remained in Louisiana for the rest of his long life as a successful planter and merchant, sliding down a notch perhaps on the scale of local nobility, but still wealthy. Not yet ready to retire at the age of fifty-five, he contracted in 1739 to have a 44-foot boat built to expand his business ventures, probably to try his hand at smuggling or privateering.[65]

These *forçats* who survived to 1731 were spread across the town's residential hierarchy. Chavannes owned a townhouse on the mixed "second row," appropriate to his role as secretary to the Council. The others were scattered among the artisans, traders, and working poor of the third and fourth rows. As they improved their lot, they moved closer to the river. Some became wealthy slaveowners, some did not. Most were in between, such as the salt and tobacco smugglers who used their nautical skills for profit in the hustling sector of the colony's economy. Unfortunately for them, this meant that many were upriver near Natchez at the time of the rebellion in 1729 and they lost their lives. This occupational hazard, however, is the only indication of a higher mortality rate for *forçats*. Of those whose ages are known, the average age of death was forty-six, consistent with life expectancies of the period.[66]

CONTESTED REPUTATIONS

"These hideous calumnies . . . interest the colony in general, if one suffers defamation as soon as one arrives, this is not the way to convince people to come here in the hope of establishing themselves," declared slandered party

Charlotte Milon in New Orleans in 1730. That same year Jonathas Darby brought his case to the Superior Council, saying that before the slurs spread by his enemy regarding a tobacco transaction, he had "enjoyed a good reputation, and would not now pass for a thief, knave or forger."[67]

The records of the Louisiana Superior Council contain a prodigious number of slander and insult suits that present convincing evidence of how self-fashioning was rampant and social status very much in flux within the founder generation.[68] Louisiana, as viewed through civil suits for insult and defamation, looks like an anxious, contentious place, with evidence both of privileges imported from the Old World and a spirit of independence fostered by conditions in the New. In its charter phase, French Louisiana was an experimental colony that involved reengineering *ancien régime* society and reinventing the individual.

Certain patterns in the defamation cases outline the evolution from colonial experiment to creole society. Most important of these is that a significant number of slander cases involved false accusations of a crime. Second, verbal violence often announced challenges to status within and across class lines, but race did not appear at all until the 1740s. In terms of frequency, verbal violence cases peaked in 1728–29, tapering off until the end of the French period, when they rose again. Insults and slander occasionally marked gender, but it seems as if the disproportionate ratio among the sexes meant that women were more valued than feared in the colony. Similarly, early Louisiana's racial vocabulary was too undeveloped to form a powerful slur, and thus racial overtones are conspicuously absent from charter-generation defamation cases. However, by the mid-eighteenth century occasional racial epithets began to be heard, from Frenchmen and creoles alike.

The ambiguous pasts of immigrants and a propensity among Louisianans of both high and low rank for self-fashioning contributed to open conflicts over status and reputation. Once in Louisiana, immigrants struggled for position in a new society. Most immigrants had little more than reputation on which to stake a claim. While arriving Frenchmen of the petty nobility and members of the aspiring merchant-bureaucrat class looked down on Canadians and challenged their pretensions, they had their own aspirations. Many French concessionaires and military officers were younger sons of the old nobility or newer officeholders. Many of them saw plantation agriculture as an opportunity to adopt the lifestyle of a feudal lord, a possibility their birth-order or bourgeois origins made unlikely in France. Some had a past to escape. In *ancien régime* France, social esteem was not a fixed quality, even among the nobility. It could be ruined by a stain upon the family's reputation or honor. Indiscreet affairs, a rebellious youth, or serious crimes could merit exile to the colonies through a *lettre de cachet*. Families hoped that their sons and daughters would welcome Louisiana as an alternative to the Bastille and do better in a new society than their infamy allowed in the old.

French reformers had hopes that the colonial experience would also reform the lowest ranks of French immigrants—those condemned to the galleys for desertion, vagabondage, salt and tobacco smuggling, prostitution, and other petty crimes. *Forçats* had strong motivations for obscuring their past and reinventing themselves in the New World. They were also individuals prone to challenge authority.

When knowledge of an immigrant's origins was hazy, a shadow of suspicion could trail his or her new life. As a result, Louisianans may have reacted more defensively to the casual remark than their counterparts in France or the other French colonies. Someone might just believe they really *were* a former thief, bugger, or slut. Whether simply trying to nudge their way up into the ranks of petty nobles or trying to cover up a dark secret, many Louisianans had both motive and opportunity to improve their lot by fashioning themselves anew. It is no coincidence that the same royal edict that prohibited residents from filing claims to noble titles in the colony also banned colonists from filing pardons for crimes without special permission of the king.[69] Slander provided another check-and-balance system against feigned identity and exaggerated claims.

In the eighteenth century as today, the legal system drew distinctions between slander, libel, and simple insult. Insults were considered "minor acts of violence."[70] They often drew on a common vocabulary of obscenity. In Louisiana cases where the testimony is detailed, the favored insults were, in order of popularity: Jean Foutre (and conjugations of *foutre*, "to fuck"), *coquin* (rogue/scoundrel), *bougre* (bugger), and *fripon* (cheat). We find *putain* (whore) and *cocu* (cuckold) in a few instances as well.[71]

Louisiana's pattern was unusual in comparison to eighteenth-century defamation in France and Canada in that calumny made up the majority of slander cases from 1726 to 1731. The accusation was usually for theft or fraud. Allegations were equally likely to be confined within the ranks of the elite or to cross class lines, but those of the lower orders rarely accused one another of property crime, or at least made a public case out of such "false" accusations. Although the presence of a small number of prostitutes and condemned adulteresses among Louisiana *forçats* led to a public-image problem for colonial women back in France, in calumny cases accusations of a sexual or moral character were surprisingly infrequent, even compared to French Canada. I could find only seven cases that dealt solely with sexual conduct or moral character.[72] Five questioned the sexual morality of women. Two cases involved accusations against men, one for sodomy and the other for bestiality.[73]

In Louisiana, women were twice as likely to be defendants (that is, accused of slander or insult) as plaintiffs. This pattern presents a striking contrast to the situation in both Canada and France, where women were much more likely to be plaintiffs complaining of attacks on their honor.[74] Free Frenchwomen in New Orleans seemed to act with a degree of confidence in publicly criticizing others and even challenging authority. They, too, seem to have contributed to the colony's reputed "spirit of insubordination." For example, as mentioned earlier, Madame Bonnaud, wife of the Company storekeeper, had threatened to slap the city's engineer, Adrien de Pauger, and publicly called him a rogue (*coquin*) and mean cad (*fapin*) for his cavalier drawing of property lines.[75]

Overall, the trend in verbal violence suggests that the founder generation engaged in slander and its legal recourses more frequently than subsequent generations. I suggest that the peak of calumny cases between 1726 and 1731 relates to the fact that *engagés* and *forçats* were nearing the end of their terms of servitude and entering the ranks of the town's free populace. At the same time a reshuffling of noble and bourgeois concessionaires, planters, officials, and military officers occurred, following an exodus during the hard years of 1722–24 upon the bursting of the Mississippi Bubble. In other words, the social order was being tossed like a salad in the late 1720s. As a result, colonists scrambled for position as a new hierarchy took shape. A defensive complaint of insult and slander provides "a mirror of the social aspirations of the individual."[76] So does the offensive move of mudslinging. Some used slander to associate a rival with the ranks of former *forçats*, while others took advantage of changeovers in administrative personnel to refashion and reposition themselves. In the 1720s both Dumont de Montigny and Sieur de Chavannes used the arrival of the *ordonnateur* Delachaise in this way.[77]

Honor and reputation counted as very serious matters to France's nobility, particularly among those committed to a military career. Increasingly in the eighteenth century, honor and a good reputation were no longer guaranteed by birthright.[78] Honor had to be demonstrated by deportment and defended by the sword if need be. Maintaining membership in the ranks of *honnêtes hommes* (men of honor) required constant vigilance. The records of colonial Louisiana and Canada show that officers were sensitive to slights and quick to act in defense of their reputations. The large military presence in colonial Louisiana and a documented tension between Canadian and French officers contributed to the incidence of defamation cases in Louisiana. The attitudes of French officers in New Orleans were colored by the belief that Canadians had been "brought up, so to speak, among savages, and know little of the customs and mode of government of the kingdom." The history of enmity and mutual slander between French sub-lieutenant Dumont de Montigny and the Canadian governor Bienville illustrates this sort of tension.[79]

Overall, cases of slander and insult where both litigants came from the elite military or the slaveholding class made up a slight majority (54 percent) of all defamation cases in French colonial Louisiana. Slander cases among planters or concession employees tended to involve accusations of fraudulent business deals or the shirking of debts. Among planters and merchants, public image was perhaps even more important than it was for military officers, as financial credit depended not only on a reputation for reliable payment, but on overall social status. In 1726, when dozens of Louisiana settlers submitted a request for credit to purchase slaves, the Company of the Indies awarded credit only to "respectable" habitants whose identity could be verified.

Louisiana's verbal violence cases lend credence to the view that its colonial culture fostered "insubordination." While elite plaintiffs were more likely to file cases against elite defendants, defamation cases involving tradesmen, slaves, regular soldiers, and sailors were more likely to involve accusations that crossed class lines in Louisiana. Members of Louisiana's lower classes hurled insults against their supposed superiors, and in other cases obstinately defended their respectability against abuses from above. In Louisiana, cross-class cases were much more likely to involve lower status plaintiffs against higher status defendants.[80] Colonials of different stations used the court to fight for their place in the social hierarchy on a relatively even footing.

Examples of this type of Louisiana litigation include the case of a joiner in 1727 who sued a Company clerk for falsely accusing him of theft. In 1730 a carpenter and ship caulker took his case to court against a ship captain who falsely accused him of robbery.[81] Although they felt emboldened to take action against superiors who slandered them, tradesmen could not always escape the circular logic of class. A carpenter named Philippe Vellart complained that Le Page du Pratz (the well-known Louisiana historian who at that time ran the King's Plantation across the river from New Orleans) had falsely accused him of robbery. But the attorney general decided the case against Vellart based on his already tainted reputation as a man "known for disorder." He, rather than Le Page, was imprisoned and fined. Demonstrating the other end of this class struggle, cases brought by elites against their inferiors tended to add "insubordination" to the charges of injurious insult or slander.[82]

Cases of cross-class insults and slander occurred more frequently in the first few decades of the colony, indicative of a social landscape characterized by mobility, conflict, and resistance to new authority. By the 1740s the rate of accusations died down and tended to keep within rank, suggesting that by this time a new colonial hierarchy had begun to stabilize. Lower status individuals had less to gain and perhaps more to lose by challenging those who were now more securely established as a political and economic elite.

Although cross-class accusations dwindled during the second generation of settlement, the number of cases in which insults marked racial difference grew. These tended to be of two types. In the first, slaves or free people of color came into conflict with poor whites as individuals on their own terms. Most of these cases involved white soldiers, whom people of color had treated as social equals or inferiors. The second group of cases arose out of incidents in which freemen (of any rank) offended a slaveowner through the verbal or physical abuse of his or her slave. In these cases the owner appeared in court either as a plaintiff or as a representative for their victimized slave. The physical injuries suffered by slaves constituted an offense to the honor of the owner. Outside the civil authorities, the slaveowner was the only one with a license to abuse and the power to discipline his or her slave.

In one of the most detailed records of an exchange of insults in French New Orleans, racial overtones in the vernacular are present but subtle. In 1745 a white ship carpenter named LeMoine complained to the Superior Council that Raphael, a "*nègre libre*," and his wife Fanchon had attacked and insulted him over a borrowed tool. Raphael and Le Moine scuffled in the road by Bayou St. John. Later, Fanchon entered LeMoine's house to search for the adze and he fended her off with his sword, causing her to let out invectives, to which he responded by calling her "*une coquine*" (beggar woman or female rogue). In the street, their clash continued. She called: "Damn, come over here if you [*tu*] are brave enough!" He responded: "You [*tu*] are nothing but a whore!" "Oh, I promise you'll pay me, that you will, why you're nothing but Le Seigneur Monberaud's indentured servant [*engagé*]!" In his version of the events, LeMoine seems unnecessarily repetitive in describing Raphael and Fanchon as *nègres*, implying that this made their behavior toward him especially inappropriate. For her part, Fanchon insulted LeMoine by saying he was virtually a white slave.[83]

The only case in which an explicitly racial term was used as an insult involved a free mulatto sailor from Senegal named Etienne LaRue. In May 1747 LaRue got into an altercation with some soldiers on the streets of New

Orleans after they called out to him sarcastically, "Bonsoir, Seigneur Nég-ritte" (using the feminine form, diminutive), the sense of which is rou-ghly "Good Evening, Milady Pickaninny." He responded with "Bonsoir, Seigneur Jean Foutre," or "Good Evening, Milord Bugger" (literally "sodo-mite").[84] The combination of sexual and racial slurs ignited a fight in which LaRue's gun eventually went off. This exchange represents one of the first incidents of racial insult in Louisiana. It also carried a heavy dose of sex-ual innuendo with a challenge to each man's masculinity. When combined with evidence for an increasingly racialized system of justice beginning in the 1740s (see chapter 5), these incidents suggest the emergence of racial tensions among the laboring classes, in an as-yet-incoherent system of clas-sification and inequality.

Rogue colonialism may have produced more than the usual number of social scuffles punctuated with the epithet, "*Coquin!*" *Coquin* approxi-mates our present-day definition of *rogue*—a scoundrel or dishonest per-son. But the etymology of *rogue* in English is also significant. According to the *Oxford English Dictionary*, it originally meant "one belonging to a class of vagrants or vagabonds"—in French, those *sans aveu*, without a verifiable identity.[85] Where identities were less than certain, reputations were less than secure. The insult and defamation cases from colonial New Orleans demon-strate that the social mobility, self-fashioning, and class formation taking place were accompanied by loud contestations.

CHANGING COLOR

Native-born (creole) New Orleanians of all colors grew up in more intimate and integrated quarters than had the founder generation. At the same time, they began to form more definite ideas about "race." Through these con-cepts, they chose a segregation of the mind rather than the body. French New Orleans was a place where people of different colors and legal statuses lived side by side, cheek by jowl.

The demographic patterns in Louisiana as a whole and New Orleans as an urban center were distinct though not static. Plantation wealth became more concentrated into the hands of a few. At the same time the popula-tion ratio of slave to free declined in rural areas while it rose in the city. In 1732 enslaved people accounted for 65 percent of Louisiana's total pop-ulation. By 1766 slaves accounted for 52 percent of the colonial popula-tion (excluding Native American settlements). In New Orleans, however, the trend was reversed. Between 1726 and 1766 the enslaved population grew from 12 percent to 35 percent of the total. A rise in the slave popu-lation seen between 1726 and 1732 was largely due to importation, while growth from 1732 to 1763 has been presumed to be largely due to natural increase and the important development of urban slaveholding.[86] Between 1732 and the 1760s only one official shipment of slaves reached Louisiana directly from Africa, but the intercolonial trade (most of it outlawed) certainly contributed a small but steady supply of new laborers. Although the slave population grew steadily in the city, this rate was offset by faster natural increase among Euro-Louisianans, who had a significantly higher fertility rate as calculated by the number of children per woman. However, there are some major caveats to these figures. First, we have no idea how many slaves were smuggled into the colony after the 1740s, nor do we know to what extent unrecorded manumissions caused the ranks of the enslaved to decline. Second, we have no census data to correct for intercolonial immigration into the free population, although the growing number of residents in New Orleans who had Spanish, English, Dutch, or Irish surnames in the period from the 1740s to the 1760s suggests that this was a significant factor within the city. Finally, throughout the colony, the free population included an unknown (though likely growing) number of free people of color and urban Indians, unmarked in censuses.[87]

Most Afro-Louisianans continued to live primarily in the plantation zone around New Orleans, while the city still concentrated the colony's European residents, but by 1732 the town had ceased to look like a white enclave.[88] Planners had not anticipated the rapid growth of urban slavery, nor the unregulated movement of free people of color, runaways, and hired slaves into town. After the 1730s, as Louisiana's creole population came of age, New Orleans became a multicolored place, both in neighborhoods and within individual households.

The census of 1763 shows the evolution of a creole society in the second and third generations and its own categories of classification.[89] The slave categories remained identical to those of the 1732 census, finely divided by race, gender, and age. But by this time the ranks of the free were also finely divided. Children of the *chef de famille*, or "head of household," were identified by gender and by age (boys older and younger than fourteen years, girls older or younger than twelve), suggesting attention not only to demographic growth, but also to generational status. More important, the new category of *affranchit* (literally, "the freed") appeared for the first time on the census, subdivided into *nègres*, *négresses*, *négrillons*, and *négrittes*. The term *affranchit* suggests that freeborn people of color were not included in this category, but continued to be listed under the generic resident count. Mulattos were singled out within the ranks of the enslaved, but not among the free.

TABLE 2. New Orleans Households and Slaveholding (within town limits, excludes surrounding plantations, soldiers in barracks, and religious compounds)

	1726 n(%)	1732 n(%)	1763 n(%)
Households	237	219	363
Slaveholding households	40(7%)	82(37%)	181(50%)
Average number of slaves per slaveholding household	2.6	3.2	4.7

Note: Source for the 1726 and 1732 censuses is Maduell, *Census Tables*, 65–76, 123–41. Unfortunately, the crown's neglect of Louisiana between the 1740s and 1760s meant that no censuses were taken during this period of stabilization and natural increase in the population. For the 1763 census, see Voorhies, *Some Late Eighteenth-Century Louisianians*, 5–43; "Recensement Géneral du quartier du Detour a L'Anglois par Le Sr Prevost . . . 1763," AGI-SD, Legajo 2595, No. 4, also, 65–101.

By the late 1720s the supply of European domestic workers had dwindled as the terms of their indenture expired. African and Indian slaves replaced them. As survivors of the Law period finally began to prosper in the early 1730s, town dwellers acquired slaves as both a means and a symbol of wealth. A large staff of enslaved domestics became the new badge of elite membership.

Another reason the New Orleans slave population grew in the creole generation was that owners frequently hired out skilled slaves to work as smiths, carpenters, sailors, woodcutters, tar and pitch workers, and Indian traders. Daniel Usner observes that in New Orleans as elsewhere, "skilled black workers became a significant factor in the growth of colonial cities."[90] In 1732, 15 percent of the city's slaves lived in artisan households and 25 percent of its tradesmen lived with slaves. The Company of the Indies early on had argued for the training of slaves as artisans and sailors, claiming they cost less than the equivalent European skilled worker. Many publicly owned slaves (that is, owned by the Company or the king) were apprenticed to master craftsmen in the city to learn a trade, although some journeymen resisted sharing too much of their knowledge, for fear of being replaced.

The number of slaveowners expanded steadily after 1726, but slaveowners never constituted a majority of town residents during the French period. Urban slavery grew by two measures (table 2). The number of slaveholding households increased, and the average number of slaves living in those households also increased. In the founding years a minority of residents owned a small number of slaves each; only a handful owned more than ten. Over time, the proportion of those who owned more than ten slaves tripled. But at the same time that slave-holding became more common, the gap between wealthy and modest slave-holders in town widened. The growing prosperity of merchant-planters dramatically affected the lives of slaves in town. In 1726 most slaves lived in small households with three or fewer slaves. By 1763 most lived in households with eleven or more fellow slaves.

Free people of color were also adding to the city's diversity during the first and second creole generations. The size of the free colored population of New Orleans in the late French period has been seriously underestimated because their status represented either a dangerous or an unimportant distinction to Louisiana administrators creating the 1760s censuses. Statistics on this population, therefore, are extremely hard to come by. Historians have often cited the nineteen individuals listed in the *affranchit* category in New Orleans in 1763 as a total count for free people of color, when it really refers only to manumitted slaves, not freeborn people of color. While it may be anachronistic to separate out a group the French folded in, reading beyond the lines of the census is important if we want to understand the social, sexual, and political practices of the creole regime. It also qualifies a common argument that subsequent Spanish policies created the city's large population of free people of color by encouraging manumissions. While manumissions certainly accelerated, Spanish policies also helped create this new social group simply by "coloring" people who were already there and already free.

The strongest evidence for a significant community of free people of color in New Orleans during the French period comes from a series of four specialized censuses taken around 1770 for newly arrived Spanish governor O'Reilly. These counts were specifically designed to account for the number of *nègres libres* and *mulâtres libres* in the city. O'Reilly was apparently dissatisfied with the numbers produced by French creole assistants in the first three efforts, reporting back totals of 15, 20, and 44 respectively.[91] He finally assigned a literate free colored man to take a fourth census. Nicolas Bacus carried the title "Capitaine Moraine" (literally, Captain of the Moors) according to the document. His "List of the Number of Free Negros of New Orleans" named 195 free men of color eligible for the militia, most with French or prominent Louisiana surnames, suggesting the census reflects rooted creoles. The list omits free women of color and children, which implies that the overall size of this population was significantly larger, probably between 400 and 800 individuals.[92] Assuming that no wholesale shift in the French-speaking free colored population occurred between the 1766 census and the 1770 Bacus census, this means that instead of the modest 1–3 percent figure often reported, free people of color probably made up 10–20 percent of the city's population by the end of the French period. In fact, several of the names on Bacus's list match heads of household listed in the 1763 and 1766 French censuses, although the enumerator at that time made no note of their color. These matches occur primarily in the fourth militia district, a "back of town" neighborhood of tradesmen, taverns, the working poor, and itinerants.[93] Nicolas Bacus himself is listed in the 1766 census in this area, with no reference to his color or race. The problem for historians, and apparently for O'Reilly, is that creole Louisiana census-takers did not often mark "free black" or "free mulatto" as a category, suggesting it was not a highly relevant legal or social distinction. O'Reilly's first three failed attempts to get the figures to match what his eyes "saw" suggest either reluctance or incomprehension by Louisianans when confronted with the Spanish classification of free people according to color.

Anecdotal evidence in the notarial records bolsters the impression that a free colored population grew in New Orleans area throughout the French period. One important event that boosted the number of free people of color in the colony was the emancipation of "volunteer" slave soldiers who fought against the Natchez in 1729–30.[94] These manumitted mercenaries may have been the same individuals appearing at the Superior Council to file contracts, civil suits, or financial transactions, whom notaries occasionally and parenthetically described as *nègre libre* or *mulâtre libre*. In the 1720s Raphael Bernard, who called himself a *"negre libre,"* sued several Euro-Louisianans to collect on debts they owed him.[95] John Mingo, described as an "English free Negro" from Carolina, requested a license to marry Thérèse, a slave at the time. He signed a contract with her owner to purchase her freedom on an installment plan. He also secured assurances that their children would be free. Mingo later appeared in court to complain that his wife's owner was not honoring the agreement. Another man, François Tiocou, negotiated for the purchase of his wife Marame (sometimes rendered Marie Aram), and they hired themselves out to the public hospital in New Orleans in 1737. He was a *"negre affranchy"* who had received his freedom in return for fighting against the Natchez.[96] Mingo and other free men of color make periodic appearances in the records through contracts in which they hired themselves out. Others were business owners, such as the free woman of color Isabelle who operated a dairy concern with at least fifteen head of cattle, ran a tar-processing concern, and also owned a house on respectable Royal Street.[97]

Creole New Orleans was a hierarchical society in which slavery was a defining fact of life. Disparities in the quality of life between the legally free and unfree could be great. But these were *legal* categories tied to specific personal histories and specific documented transactions. Color and origin did not necessarily dictate social status. Legal status, class, wealth, and family connections could override these in the scramble for position and privilege. Creoles found ways to rule in which people of different colors were controlled on intimate terms rather than through a sieve of censuses and a grid of residential segregation.

Urban society, however, was distinct in Louisiana. The strategies employed in New Orleans were not necessarily those used in the predominantly black plantation belt, where enumerators marked free people of color earlier and more consistently than enumerators in town, and also broke them down by legal and color categories. In the English Turn plantation district, just across the river from New Orleans, enumerators in 1763 used the categories of "free blacks" and "free mulattos," as well as *affranchit* (distinguishing those born free from those emancipated). Census-takers in New Orleans only recorded *affranchits*. Another important difference between the downriver census and the town census was in the lead categories. None of the French-period censuses of Louisiana ever marked the head of the household and his or her family as "white" with a term such as *blanc* or *français*. The generic category into which most free people of color fell was race-neutral—*chef de famille* or *habitant*.[98] But in 1763 the English Turn census subdivided the lead category into male and female *maîtres*, or "masters," singling out slaveowners. New Orleans had no such category. Although New Orleans had begun as an intentionally segregated space in the early 1720s, by the end of the French period its racial categories were still vaguely defined among the free, and a "masterless" existence in the city was imaginable for Louisiana's free people of color. They made the town their home.

Besides emancipation of the 1729 veterans and a handful of manumissions made in wills or upon the owner's departure from Louisiana, the paths to freedom for people of color are obscure in the archives. One likely possibility is that children of enslaved mothers and free fathers were quietly manumitted without the formality of the Superior Council's approval. One example is suggestive in its subtlety. The wealthy planter Joseph Carrière was called into court in 1745 to address threats made by his son (so identified) named Monbrun. Oddly, the document, which involves a dispute between Monbrun and another man over a dogfight, never once gives Monbrun the surname Carrière, nor does it identify him as a free man of color (Monbrun could be a nickname meaning "my brown one"). This case supports the impression that in French New Orleans the rarely utilized categories *nègre libre* or *mulâtre libre* were more about class than color. Thus, these categories were not applied to a free, dark-skinned son of one of the colony's richest men. He belonged to some other, unnamed category—or less a category than a network. His familial connections clearly came to his rescue in this court case. The testimony focuses less on his wrongdoing than on his father's privilege in exempting his son from a demeaning prosecution.[99]

Historian Carl Brasseaux says the *Code Noir*'s ban on "interracial cohabitation" was "unenforced." I would add that the rules governing the legalization of manumissions were equally unenforced. Although sanctioned manumissions did occur in the French period (some legally pursued by ex-slaves themselves), they are not numerous enough to account for all the city's free people of color. One route to freedom for slaves of mixed race is suggested by a *mémoire* of 1763 by Redon de Rassac, in which he urged not only that whites and Indians be allowed to legally marry, but that every mulatto "married" to a white person be freed at the age of twenty-five. Slaves of any color were technically prohibited from marrying free whites by the *Code Noir* of 1724 and very few examples of such marriages exist in the parish records. But these are probably not the best source of evidence for such unions, which many priests found objectionable. More likely, Redon was referring to common-law or concubinage arrangements, which apparently were quite common, an illegal but licit practice.[100]

The evidence for cross-race sexual relations and family formation in the creole generation is circumstantial, an inference from the growth of the *mulâtre* category, which appears more commonly in notarial records than in the censuses. Historian Jennifer Spear discusses examples of manumissions that have the appearance of involving female companions and their children.[101] Examples, though, are few. Most manumission cases that appear in the French records come up because they are *disputed* manumissions, entering into the record upon the complaint of the former owner's creditors or heirs. In a 1738 case an owner attempted to renege on a sale because the purchaser, Capraize Mathieu (described as an indigo-maker), intended to immediately emancipate Marianne, an Indian slave. Mathieu was the plaintiff, seeking to enforce the sale, not the seller Pradel. Mathieu's strategy suggests another route to freedom, where free European men of humble station arranged to purchase women owned by wealthy slaveowners, in order to make them their wives.[102] Countless undisputed cases of a similar nature probably went unrecorded.

RISE OF A CREOLE OLIGARCHY

Through our modern eyes, the creole generations of the 1730s to 1760s could be characterized by "mixture" of various kinds, but also by segregation of a new type. Slaves, Indians, soldiers, and poor freemen continued to drink, gamble, socialize, and conduct business in the city's cabarets, although efforts to regulate these establishments were becoming more strident. While *métissage* probably contributed to slow but steady population growth among free people of color in New Orleans, the ranks of wealthy merchants and slaveholders began closing through endogamy. The *petits gens* continued to mingle, while elites began to hold themselves apart. Giving up on the difficulties of spatially segregating others in a wide-open port town, creole merchant-planters instead decided to genetically segregate *themselves.*

The New Orleans example reinforces the lesson that strategies of colonial rule involving racial ideas varied tremendously and were contingent on local conditions.[103] New Orleans may also exaggerate certain underlying patterns that have passed unnoticed elsewhere. The exaggeration, I have argued, is due to the unusually clear break between founder and creole generations caused by Louisiana's immigration gap. One implication is that strong versions of racialization and segregation are not inherently necessary to the functioning of chattel slavery. And defining who is "black" and who is not may be of secondary importance to defining who is *entitled* and who is not. Thus, the rise of the creole oligarchy in New Orleans was accompanied by *blancification* (or whitening) through endogamy and marriage alliances with the few new French officers who arrived in the colony after the 1730s. The work of defining who was a *grand* eventually evolved into defining who was "white." In other words, the elite racialized themselves. Racialization reflected the development of elite endogamy and oligarchy at least as much as it reflected the development of color-coded slavery.

As early as the 1720s French officials were arranging marriages not only with one another's families, but with families of successful planters and longtime Louisiana residents, many of them Canadians. By the 1730s French officials and ranking military officers were regularly marrying creole daughters. Members of the first creole generation, most of whose parents had immigrated between 1712 and 1723, began reaching marriageable age in the late 1730s.[104] Their children, the second creole generation, came of age in the 1750s.

Among the first-generation creoles, metropolitan power married local wealth. The second generation inherited local versions of both. For example, the legacy of the zealous *ordonnateur* Delachaise for New Orleans lies more in the creation of a powerful kinship network than in any effect his moralist policies had on the Superior Council or smuggling practices. Members of his large family married into or started branches of many prominent creole lineages. His daughter Félicité married the son of Joseph de Villars Dubreuil, an early concessionaire at Tchoupitoulas, just upriver from New Orleans. By 1746 Dubreuil had become the largest slaveholder in the colony, with over 500 bondsmen on several plantations. Even Governor Bienville's nephews, the Chevaliers de Noyan and de Chavoy, created legacies by marrying the daughters of a wealthy concession manager (Faucon-Dumanoir).[105] It is striking how many of the founding fathers of New Orleans elite creole society were rough-hewn Canadian immigrants from the early Bienville period. Men such as Claude Trépanier, François Trudeau, Joseph and François Carrière, and the four Chauvin brothers (Sieurs Chauvin, de Lery, de la Frénière, and de Beaulieu) became some of the colony's wealthiest planters and most prolific patriarchs. By the second generation of creole rule, the offspring of bootstrap *voyageurs*, noble adventurers, indentured female domestics, and an unknown number of Native American, *métis*, and African-descendant women comprised a local aristocracy of sorts. As early as 1740 one letter-writer complained of the inequality that was developing by claiming that just twenty planters owned all the slaves in the colony. Another report suggests that by 1746 "at the top of a pyramid of 800 white adult males were 25 planters with an average capital of 100,000 to 300,000 *livres*."[106]

Examining the family relationships of just one man, a member of Louisiana's final (and insurrectionist) Superior Council of 1768, provides a representative snapshot of the tightly woven genealogical order that was developing. Nicolas Chauvin de Lafrénière *fils* ("son of," or "Junior"), who held the leadership position of royal councilor and *procureur général*, had inherited a seat on the Superior Council from his father in 1749. Lafrénière Sr. was one of four Chauvin brothers of humble Canadian origin who followed another set of Canadian brothers—the LeMoyne clan of the famous founders Iberville and Bienville—to the colony.[107] Two of the Chauvins arrived on Iberville's ship *La Renommée* when it landed on the Gulf Coast in 1699. The other brothers soon followed. Three of them adopted nicknames having a seigneurial air, as if they came from landed estates, though they held no official titles. Thus they became known as Joseph Chauvin de Léry, Nicolas Chauvin de Lafrénière, and Louis Chauvin de Beaulieu. Throughout the turbulent early years of Louisiana, they remained loyal to Bienville, who bestowed favors upon them in the form of land grants, access to slaves, military posts, and positions on the Superior Council. By the mid-1730s they held over 300 slaves, making them the largest slaveholding interests in Louisiana.[108] They also reaped the rewards of marriage alliances. Lafrénière Sr. married Bienville's cousin. In the next generation, three Chauvin grandsons married three of Bienville's grand-nieces (through his sister Jeanne Catherine LeMoyne Payen de Noyan). LaFrénière Jr.'s daughter married Bienville's close grand-nephew, Jean Baptiste de Noyan, in a ceremony that was the social event of the year 1767 in New Orleans, attended by both Louisiana governors (the French Aubry and the Spanish Ulloa) and all the prominent members of the Superior Council. Noyan served with his father-in-law on the final Superior Council and shared his fate of death by firing squad in 1769. The genealogy is even more entangled than this short sketch outlines. Lafrénière and Noyan had close lateral kinship ties (as uncle, cousin, or in-law) with five of the remaining ten Superior Council members. These included descendants of Louisiana's early *intendant* Jacques Delachaise (who probably would have been horrified at the political insubordination of his heirs). Thus, the Chauvin–Le Moyne–Delachaise clan held a majority (seven out of twelve) seats on the Superior Council. Together they held a nearly parallel proportion of the colony's enslaved population.[109]

The power of this creole kinship network extended beyond the Superior Council into military and economic realms. The threat of this "syndicate" or "cabal," as some called it, was not lost on historical participants, nor were their humble roots forgotten. Ulloa, the ousted Spanish governor, reported in 1768:

> The captain of the German militia, called Villeré, is the brother-in-law of Lafrénière, and is married to the niece of D'Arensbourg, who commands at the German Coast. The captain of the Tchoupitoulas militia [a plantation settlement just upriver from New Orleans] is an individual named Léry, who is Lafrénière's first cousin; thus, the interests of Lafrénière are supported by the three companies of militia, commanded by his cousin, his brother-in-law and their relations; so that, with mere pretences to induce the militia of the town to rebel, it happens that the whole colony is put in a state of insurrection at the voice of one single man.
>
> The uncles of Noyan and Bienville [not the ex-governor but a nephew] had come from Canada to govern Louisiana, and, among the common people he brought over with him, there were four brothers . . . These four Canadians were of so low an extraction, and had so little education, that they could not write, and had come with an axe on the shoulder to live on their manual labor. The sons of these men are now the chiefs and authors of the rebellion.[110]

The upstart creole oligarchy that Ulloa so astutely maps had been fed by a gender imbalance in the founder generation of approximately six men to every European woman. French nobles committed to a life in Louisiana were willing to marry the daughters of Canadian *coureurs de bois*. The gender ratio slowly evened out over the French period, but it still encouraged class crossover in marriages, with wealthy creole sons marrying the daughters of blacksmiths and innkeepers.[111] In the third generation these descendants then married one another. In the 1750s and 1760s the mixing and crossing of *ancien régime* divisions began to give way to a new genealogical order. As in other slave societies, endogamy became increasingly common among families with large slaveholdings in order to keep property within the lineage. These marriage patterns combined with a practice carried over from France—the inheritance of public office—to help elevate bourgeois creoles to positions of power despite the original metropolitan designs against it.

Due to a gender imbalance, creole daughters of middling station had opportunities to advance their social standing by marrying the younger sons of major merchants and planters, or French officers, and many took advantage of this.[112] Of course, family formation among the city's enslaved population, craftsmen, free people of color, ex-soldiers, and petty traders was also taking place. Some unions stayed within the ranks of the working poor, but crossed ill-defined color lines. Exogamy rather than endogamy characterized the marriage patterns of creoles of the lower strata. The previously mentioned Capraize Mathieu tried to free his betrothed from slavery, while the French locksmith LeRoy and his "*negresse*" wife came to public attention not for their relationship, but because of a suspected robbery. When Frenchman François Robillard buried his son Baptiste in the New Orleans graveyard in 1727, the priest noted, "his mother is an Indian," but did not give her name.[113] Many of the sacramental records for the city's creole children omit either the father's or the mother's name; some (perhaps disingenuously) claim the parent is "unknown," suggesting the hazy legal and religious status of many relationships in the community.

"DRINKING WITH THE RUNAWAYS"

In the face of other types of fraternizing, Louisiana administrators may have thought cross-color sexual relations to be among the least of their worries. Social and economic exchanges in the cabarets and taverns of New Orleans continued to blur intended divisions of class and color. This commerce worried elites, both French and creole, throughout the French period, but their experiments and policies appear to have had negligible effects. The Superior Council issued redundant ordinances in 1725, 1746, 1751, and 1763 attempting to control the number of taverns and discourage the mixing of slaves, soldiers, and free people in these establishments. They voiced concerns about a vague "corrupting influence" on morals, but also about specific types of criminal activity these public houses encouraged. Some establishments were owned by free people of color, who offered a place for slaves to meet in the city. The *affranchitte* Jeannette held suppers at her house in the 1740s. In 1755 the merchant-planter Pradel complained that his slaves met at houses in the city owned by free blacks where plantation and town slaves met to eat, drink, and dance all night to the sound of a fiddle.[114]

A 1751 regulation reiterated an earlier effort to segregate drinking establishments, not only creating two separate canteens (military drinking halls) for the French and Swiss soldiers, but declaring that canteen owners were prohibited from "giving drinks to the inhabitants, voyageurs, sailors, Indians, or Negroes," under penalty of a heavy fine.[115] The problem persisted. In 1763 Attorney General Lafrénière claimed: "The rear of the City is infested with numbers of men without occupation . . . they are the first at the markets and are consumers instead of creators . . . they adulterate the liquors they sell and expose the slaves to violent maladies. While furnishing drink they incite them to pilfer and steal from the houses of their masters indiscriminately all they can find; the handkerchief, the towel, and empty bottles, etc., all have a price and disappear in the traffic of these clandestine taverns. The negro drinks and loses his senses. He recognizes no restraint nor the necessity of submission. He would not be violent if he did not find in these secret taverns the means to satisfy his brutal passions; what hidden pernicious disorders have resulted!"[116]

The following year Governor d'Abbadie wrote a letter to France saying, "Immoderate consumption of tafia [crude rum] has turned all the people into brutes." Interrogators in criminal trials often questioned suspects about their social drinking. Alexandre, a thirty-four-year-old Senegalese slave, admitted to drinking rum at Dusigne's tavern with his friend Jupiter, but not to passing off stolen merchandise. The testimony of a French sailor named Le Ber, who had been accused of a series of petty thefts, revealed that he spent much of his time in the woods on the edge of town, "drinking with the runaways."[117]

On 6 April 1763 the Louisiana Superior Council ordered all slaveowners to conduct a census of their slaves and submit the names and descriptions of their missing runaways to be entered into a register. A few months later the Louisiana Superior Council ordered "the expulsion from the town of all vagabonds who have no profession or trade or fixed domicile, and who cannot present certification of their virtuous existence and good morals by a person of good reputation . . . Those persons sent to the colony to work on the land, encumber the city." The new ordinance also repeated the oft-heard complaint about the problems caused by poor whites and slaves drinking together in New Orleans cabarets.[118]

Ordinances of this kind were issued periodically in the French period, often soon after the arrival of a fresh French-born administrator more in touch with the king's sense of social order than the Canadians, creoles, or naturalized French veterans running the colony. The ordinances of 1763 show the hand of Jean-Jacques d'Abbadie, who was appointed governor of Louisiana in March of that year. The expulsion of vagabonds that d'Abbadie sought in New Orleans in 1763 echoed eerily with the city's founding. At the beginning of France's move toward "confinement" in 1719, vagabonds had been rounded up from the streets of Paris and Lyon, and exiled to Louisiana. Their experience forever marked the reputation of the colony and perhaps shaped d'Abbadie's perception of New Orleans society upon his arrival. In his "observations on the character and dispositions of the inhabitants of Louisiana," d'Abbadie focused on the "disorder long existing in the colony" caused by drunkenness, laziness, and a "spirit of insubordination and independence."[119]

The methods he suggested for reinstituting social order would have been familiar to the parents and grandparents of those around him. Using a population census as a tool for social control was not new in the colony. Conducting censuses had been a regular duty for colonial administrators in the years before abandonment. The colonial population had been scrutinized, classified, mapped, counted, and recalculated almost obsessively during the chaotic years of 1721–32. The act of taking a census reflected the ambition of Louisiana administrators to know and control a colonial population of remarkable legal diversity. Enforcement of the legal status of the inhabitants had a much more direct effect upon the success or failure of the colony than any labeling of the equally diverse color spectrum would have had. Who would work the concessions? Who was on contract to build boats, repair guns, make bread? Who was free to settle small farms to feed the populace of New Orleans? Who could be forcibly mustered to build the levees to protect it? Who would stay and form families and produce new French subjects to create a demographic dam against the teeming British and restless Native Americans?

The censuses were the means through which administrators attempted to track the colonial population year to year as it scattered after disembarkment through a territory spanning thousands of miles. However, the results reveal a society rapidly evolving away from *ancien régime* designs, particularly in New Orleans. On the one hand, the enumeration of individual households in the early decades demonstrates patterns of social mobility and individual entrepreneurship. Independent-minded settlers shed legal confines and pushed open the cracks between old régime classes. On the other hand, by the time of the Spanish takeover a new social hierarchy based on wealth and an emerging kinship system had begun to solidify, with only a vestigial regard for the old lines of nobility.

A similar trend is seen with regard to race. Early administrative efforts to regulate and segregate by ethnicity and origin gave way to a society where people of diverse backgrounds mingled intimately, not only on the street but under the same roof. By the second creole generation sporadic efforts to segregate New Orleans cabarets were all that remained of the original plan for the city's architecturally enforced segregation of whites and blacks. A racial terminology did begin to develop toward the end of the period, dividing the enslaved into *nègres* and *mulâtres*, but this may have had more to do with signaling creolization or kinship than with permanently marking those of African descent. New Orleanians do not appear to have developed a strong color code for free subjects in the French period. It was by no means an egalitarian society, but there did indeed appear to be a "spirit of insubordination" against metropolitan designs for social hierarchy.

On the one hand, wealthy planters and merchants were pleased with the developing creole system, which tied status to slaveholding and commercial wealth rather than to claims of nobility that few could plausibly defend. On the other hand, the poor and the free lived in a milieu that allowed them greater mobility than was possible in France, or even in many other slave societies. There was a certain freedom to being *sans aveu*, without a verifiable identity, a *rogue* in the original sense. The same "virgin land" that made planners dream of perfect cities in the colonies meant sprawling, unmapped territories where social confinement was much more difficult to enforce than within the well-known spaces at home.

5

TENSIONS OF POWER
Law, Discipline, and Violence

In November 1725 Louisiana officials reported back to the Ministry of the Marine that they had appointed a "*nègre*" named Louis Congo as the colony's high executioner. They freed Congo and his wife from slavery in return for his public service, and granted them a small land concession on the outskirts of New Orleans, where they lived with another free black couple.[1] Louis Congo acted as the colony's public executioner for at least twelve years, from 1725 to 1737. He was the only man in the colony invested with the power to whip, brand, amputate, and torture subjects in the name of the king. His job required breaking men on the wheel and hanging them on the scaffold, be they whites, Indians, or fellow Africans.

That he was African and a former slave now seems to us imbued with symbolism and irony. Louis Congo embodied the ultimate power of the state over its subjects. However, his job title did not elevate him to the ranks of the powerful. Probably few Louisianans envied his position. In France, such men were often convicts themselves who had been spared execution or a life sentence in the galleys. In exchange, they became feared pariahs. To call someone a *bourreau*, or "executioner," was one of the strongest insults that could be hurled in eighteenth-century French. Executioner was among what anthropologist Antón Blok calls the "infamous occupations" that no one else wanted.[2]

Worse than insults, the anger directed at the individual responsible for meting out the state's punishment could be immediate and physical. In 1726 Louis Congo appears in the Superior Council records as a victim of a vicious attack in his home by three runaway Indian slaves. Eleven years later he was jumped and severely beaten again, this time by two "negro slaves" (one a runaway) near the King's Plantation. Officials took these attacks on their agent of justice seriously. In the first case, the attorney general said, "For a long time now a large troop of Indian slaves have banded together and deserted. Well-armed, they run and thieve around the city and it is feared they plan to do worse . . . let us punish the deserters with a swift blow, acting with impunity." He then went on to cite Louisiana's newly minted *Code Noir* (or Black Code, the set of laws governing slavery), specifying Articles 12, 13, and 32, which he interpreted to mean that the death penalty would be allowed in this case of aggravated desertion. Of course, Louis Congo would be the one to impose this capital punishment upon his own attackers.[3] In the 1737 case, Congo and the attorney general appealed jointly to the Council, requesting an investigation and punishment to the full extent of the law, as "the life of said Congo would not be secure if such murderous thugs [*assassins*] were tolerated." This attack was probably in retribution for a sentence Congo had carried out two weeks earlier on a baptized slave named Guala. He had been ordered to cut off Guala's ears and brand a fleur-de-lys on his right shoulder. The plantation manager had requested Guala's punishment for the crime of chronic marooning.[4]

Congo was a target of Indian and Afro-Louisiana slaves who had witnessed his administration of French justice. Perhaps they viewed him as a key instrument in the enforcement of slavery itself, and as a traitor. We have no record of vengeful attacks on Congo from members of the French majority of New Orleans, although they too were subject to his ministrations.

During his career, Louis Congo whipped "at the crossings of this town" a Frenchman named Meslun for stabbing a man who had caught him stealing bacon. The whipping proceeded despite the pleadings of Meslun's wife, who said her husband was mentally ill and addicted to strong drink.[5] In the poorly preserved criminal court records from French Louisiana, we have only two detailed records of executions performed by Louis Congo, although dozens of others are briefly mentioned in colonial correspondence. In 1728 he completed the hanging of an Indian slave named Bontemps for the crimes of aggravated desertion and robbery. In 1729 he hanged a European immigrant named Joseph Graff who had fatally stabbed his business partner.[6] It is also likely that Congo was the executioner who placed eight Bambara slaves on the wheel and an enslaved woman on the scaffold in 1731 for an alleged conspiracy to kill the French and take over the colony.[7] Congo served as the executioner for any member of the *petits gens* who posed a serious threat to the emerging local order. As in France, authorities rarely applied corporal punishment and torture to the noble and wealthy elite, although several such individuals served prison sentences in the New Orleans jail.

The executioner's slave origin may have been intended to add insult to injury for white subjects, although one may question how effective this was given the populace's disregard for the *Code Noir*. In 1720, a few years before Congo's appointment, the court-martial sentence of a soldier convicted of robbery specified that he was "to be whipped by a negro for three days," before beginning his term in the galleys. Specifying the status of the whip-wielder would be gratuitous if no social meaning inhered in the relationship between the punisher and the punished. In fact, public humiliation (such as being placed in public stocks or being forced to wear absurd clothes or placards) was a common form of punishment in eighteenth-century Europe. A mixture of humiliation and corporal punishment was also common.[8]

Louis Congo's burden was twofold. His personal freedom was purchased at the price of a rather lonely and insecure life on the edge of town, and he had to live with the fact that he played a major role in enforcing the enslavement of his former countrymen. His tenure coincides with the charter generation, a period characterized by both the application of experimental legal forms created for the colonial setting, and some of the more focused attempts by French administrators to impose the rule of law. Yet as the attacks on Louis Congo demonstrate, order and safety were not easily achieved in the colony. From its own perspective, one of the most spectacular missteps of the French state in designing colonial Louisiana was its failure to establish a police force or a system of enforcement for its laws beyond the appointment of an attorney general and a black executioner. But this lack may have been entirely intentional on the part of *local* designers, it allowed the colonial agenda to stray from the interests of absolutism. The lack of police served rogue agents such as the LeMoyne brothers and a series of later governors seduced by the smuggling economy, since presumably an independent police force would have been on the lookout for crimes against the state as well as quotidian assaults and thefts.

The end of Louis Congo's career in the late 1730s coincided with the rise of the creole regime. The local creole oligarchy that displaced the king's agents from the Company period did away with the role of "Negro executioner." Exemplary justice for slaves rather than humiliation of free subjects better served the interests of the slaveowning oligarchy.

An executioner was no longer needed because local Superior Council members had already seized the ultimate power of the state. They monopolized the means of violence by taking over the corporal punishment of slaves, as well as the physical discipline of freemen of the lower orders. Flying in the face of imperial prerogative, they promulgated laws and ignored royal decrees. As will be seen in chapter 6, this "spirit of independence" ultimately emboldened Superior Council members to rebel against Bourbon rule. Significantly, their sentences were carried out by firing squad instead of hanging because, by 1769, the colony had long been without a public executioner.

In this chapter I examine the forms that law, discipline, and political power took in French Louisiana. Both metropolitan and creole administrators experimented with law in Louisiana. Their efforts helped create a rather rancorous, insubordinate, and increasingly violent society in New Orleans, a situation to which they reacted with more laws and new strategies. Over time, the central focus shifted from efforts to control unruly free French subjects to controlling restless slaves. As the judicial and administrative seat of the colony, New Orleans provided a theater for the colony's major dramas of crime and punishment. Through an examination of the criminal record of the colony, I have found a startling rise in the rate of reported violence in the creole generations, as well as a gradual racialization in the forms of punishment. These patterns demand explanation. The most plausible causes point to the deepening tensions of slavery. During this same period, legal documents demonstrate that the local merchant-planter elite grew to act with a remarkable degree of political autonomy outside their legitimate mandates. However, despite the growing power they wielded over slaves and poor freemen, creole elites may have been the most fractious sector of local society, frequently engaging in public squabbles and bitter conflicts. One lesson to be learned from the example of French New Orleans is that colonial power has a quite complicated relationship to both law and social organization. Law as written is rarely an adequate instrument of power, and the ambitions of individual agents are frequently at odds with their own class interests. The reach for power made possible by the experimental and ambiguous nature of colonial undertakings tempted many to turn rogue.

The Misrule of Law

"The inhabitants are accustomed to a semi-wild independence, always ready to violate laws and customs," said one observer of Louisiana in 1718.[9] New Orleans was originally designed to be a French cultural island floating in the center of an Africanized plantation zone lining the banks of the lower Mississippi. This zone was cleared and carved out of a vast Indian territory of undulating forests and corn fields. Yet despite the plan for New Orleans to become a center of colonial civilization, it quickly acquired the image of a place never quite tamed, a town with seeping boundaries where "savages" of all colors lived in a "semi-wild independence."

But New Orleans as a lawless place is perhaps one of the most mislead-ing variants of the disorder trope. The town did have law. And it was the source of law for the rest of the colony. But it did not embody the same laws as France, nor were its laws static, bony things. It was a place where first metropolitan authorities and then creole elites experimented with new rules, new methods, and new subjects. These legal experiments did not nec-essarily lead to a stable, peaceful community, but that is not the same as lawlessness. It is true that New Orleans was a place of frequent conflict and violence. Conflict, however, can be legislated and institutionalized. *Ancien régime* France was itself a contentious place where the government insti-gated class conflict, and violence was a medium of social exchange. Taking a close look at the legal structures of conflict in New Orleans can help us understand the local nature of power in this society peopled by Indians, slaves, and the abandoned children of France.

Administrators in the early experimental period in Louisiana manipu-lated the thin lines between free and enslaved, white and black, to control the colony's unruly *petits gens* in the interests of the king. By the creole gen-eration of the 1730s, however, local interests overruled those of the king. And local interests, or at least those represented on the Superior Council, hinged more on the effective control of slaves than of poor white subjects. Councilors deeply invested in slaveholding took it upon themselves to pro-mulgate laws and reshape legal practices, a privilege usually reserved for the king. They began to draw a deeper line between slave and free justice. Af-ter the 1730s punishments for serious crimes by freemen (such as murder) shifted away from exemplary punishments, such as branding and break-ing on the wheel, to imprisonment and banishment.[10] For slaves, however, petty theft became serious enough to merit the public spectacle of capital punishment.

New Orleans served not only as French colonial Louisiana's administra-tive and economic center, but also as its judicial center. People traveled for hundreds of miles to have their day in court in the colony's largest town. Those accused of serious crimes in the outlying posts and settlements were transferred to New Orleans, which had both civilian and military prison chambers, as well as the instruments of "ordinary and extraordinary" tor-ture needed to draw out confessions. The colony's only public executioner lived in New Orleans. Execution days, as well as feast days and market days, were observed in the Place d'Armes. The most heinous crimes, even if com-mitted far in the backcountry, became associated with New Orleans as their final acts played out in court and in the town square. New Orleans was in many senses a "theater of violence."[11]

The judicial responsibilities of the Superior Council of Louisiana involved three jurisdictions. For civil matters and minor criminal offenses, it served as the court of first instance for residents who lived within a few days' travel of New Orleans. Residents in the more distant settlements could also travel to New Orleans to appeal a ruling by their local post commander in a civil case. Finally, all cases involving capital offenses proceeded directly to the Superior Council in its role as the high court for the colony. However, the vast majority of surviving cases handled by the Superior Council were civil in nature, involving disputes over debts, estates, and business transactions.[12]

Despite the banality of most of the Superior Council's daily business, New Orleans was perceived as the volatile center of a colonial experiment gone awry. In 1724 Louisiana's attorney general Raguet complained:

> A number of robbers and rogues . . . were convicted [and sent] to this colony . . . by orders of the king, the intent of which was to punish them by exile from France and to make them change their life. They, on the contrary, continue their wantonness and evil ways, of which we have examples every day in thefts, sedition, and conspiracies and the carrying off of ferries, boats, and sloops, not only done and fomented by these people, but by their corrupting others. Most of these malcontents stay in New Orleans . . . These sorts of idle people who have no trade debauch and entice the French domestics, Indians, and negros and get them to steal from their masters . . . Let them be exiled far from the ports.[13]

Raguet's rant became a familiar theme in French colonial New Orleans, where administrators periodically complained of the disorders and dangerous fraternizing of a multicolored underclass. Taverns and cabarets reputedly facilitated this criminal social life, so they became targets of sweeps and restrictive ordinances. In the founding generation, complaints focused most often on *forçats* and deserting soldiers. By the late 1730s maroons and slaves who roamed the city streets were no longer seen as passive accomplices corrupted by French criminals. They were equals as agents of "disorder." Fraternizing continued, and in 1763 the Superior Council issued edicts requiring slaveowners to account for their maroons and ordering "vagabonds" expelled from the city.[14]

From 1699 to 1712 Louisiana was ruled singlehandedly by a military governor. With the takeover of Crozat's company in 1712, the king issued letters patent establishing a Superior Council with responsibility for the colony's civil affairs of finance, administration, and justice. After 1722 New Orleans became the seat of the Superior Council. Although the governor sat on the Council, its sessions were overseen by the *commissaire-ordonnateur* who was also granted the office of *premier conseilleur*. The man in this role held the purse-strings of the colonial budget and was given authority over the military governor in some matters, a situation that led to endemic conflict within the colonial administration. This bicephalous leadership structure was common in French colonies at the time, and the *commissaire-ordonnateur* office was modeled after the *intendants* who governed French provinces. Many Louisianans referred to this official as the *intendant*, although technically he acted only under specific orders (or commissions), and lacked broad administrative powers. For simplicity, I have referred to this official as the *ordonnateur*, which appropriately means "the one who brings order." Many of Louisiana's *ordonnateurs*, such as Delachaise in the 1720s and Rochemore in the 1750s, arrived with a mission to "clean up" the moral and fiscal messes of Louisiana, which they often viewed as resulting from the governors' overindulgence of local interests. During Louisiana's Company period (1712–31), the *ordonnateur* made financial decisions as a representative of the Company, not the royal treasury, but the two entities were closely linked. Company men were representatives of the crown, in the sense that they served at the king's pleasure, and the Company had responsibility for the major duties of the state, such as colonization, military provisioning, policing, poor relief, public works, and the treasury.[15]

The degree of autonomy and representative power that the Superior Council acquired over time in Louisiana appears to be somewhat unusual for colonial administrations. Members frequently voted against the *ordonnateur* (many of them part of the governor's faction, others acting on their own), although this body was originally intended to serve as more of an advisory board. Other offices associated with the Superior Council were the *procureur général* (or attorney general) who functioned as the public prosecutor and legal counsel; the *greffier*, a royal notary and clerk who supervised several assistants; a bailiff who acted as town crier and summons-server; the attorney for vacant estates, who handled probate settlements and land grants; and councilors-at-large chosen from local planter-merchants and military officers. Councilors-at-large numbered three at the beginning of the period and nine by the end.[16] Technically, Louisiana's government operated under Québec, but in reality, very little correspondence occurred between the two governments. The Ministry of the Marine (the navy) had responsibility for policies and overall administration of France's colonial possessions. Most of the official correspondence between Louisiana and the metropole occurred with this ministry or, early on, with the directors of the Company. Other ministers, such as the minister of war or the minister of finance, also periodically became involved in Louisiana matters.

The most glaring structured conflict in the colony, and the source of many metropolitan complaints about Louisiana disorder, derived from the crown's own administrative design. Beginning in the late seventeenth century, French administrators decided to divide power equally in the colonies between military governors and *ordonnateurs* responsible for fiscal matters. Each had their special responsibilities and areas of veto power over the other. However, many decisions (such as how to handle trade relationships with Indian nations, or how to fortify New Orleans) involved both a military and a fiscal consideration. Rarely was one man willing to bow gracefully to the opinion or policy of the other. In addition, it was not clear who had the higher authority over large areas of civilian life, such as the regulation of private commerce or the administration of justice. An undercurrent of class tension added to the problem, as governors were usually selected from among military officers, while *ordonnateurs* originated from the professional ranks of France's "men of the robe." Nearly every pair of Louisiana's governors and *ordonnateurs* butted heads during their co-administrations. In some cases, the political fights were so fierce that the *ordonnateur* (who also served as chief justice) could be shut out of Superior Council meetings, while his close allies were rounded up and thrown in the New Orleans jail. Complaints and counter-accusations filled stacks of letters shipped to the Ministry of the Marine and well-placed contacts at court. Although similar administrative structures operated in other French colonies, the conflicts between the governor and *ordonnateur* in Louisiana were exacerbated by the fact that two out of its three long-serving governors were Canadians, not metropolitans. Bienville and Vaudreuil were northern creoles who, while loyal to the crown in military matters, tended to back local interests in civil matters.[17]

This strain between the colony's co-leaders helped elevate the importance of the Louisiana Superior Council, which the crown had originally designed as a weak advisory group. To enhance his power, the governor or the *ordonnateur* at different times created new positions on the Superior Council. Since a limited number of men from France of the proper social stature and education were available to fill these slots, officials began nominating councilors from the local merchant and slaveowning class. By the time of the 1768 rebellion, creole slaveowners and international merchants dominated the Superior Council. Technically, either the *ordonnateur* or the governor could still override any vote of the Superior Council in the name of the king, but the king was far away and each man needed political friends.

The crown had never granted the Superior Council legislative powers, yet it began issuing ordinances in the mid-1730s. As a result, the government of Louisiana became less representative of France's interests and more representative of elite local interests. Although the king technically appointed all members of Louisiana's council, by 1763 nearly half the positions were filled by creoles or men who had lived in the colony for over forty years. They included Delachaise's son and Nicolas Chauvin de Lafrénière, son of a Canadian *voyageur* who had inherited a position on the Superior Council from his father, and eventually moved up to the powerful position of *procureur général*. Other locals were Jean François Huchet de Kernion, Joseph Ducros, and Bernard Deverges.[18]

As historian Jerry Micelle remarks, "The king's will did not prevail . . . The Superior Council had never functioned in the manner prescribed by royal law, and in its mature stage it differed radically from the institution designed by the French crown." A returning colonial secretary reported to the court in 1758: "The marked independence of the inhabitants has always been their greatest vice, and the group which should be the instrument for the maintenance of the king's authority [the Superior Council] acts in truth just like the others. From this spirit of independence in all the classes, there come cabals, intrigues, and muttering."[19]

While we may not be able to uncover all the "cabals, intrigues, and muttering" that went on in French New Orleans, we can listen to loud feuds and watch for bursts of rage that punctuated the working of colonial power. Looking at conflicts and "disorder" at street level through crime statistics provides the perspective needed to see where local interests lay.

Laws, policing, and punishment were perhaps the bluntest instruments of metropolitan control over the colonies. Of course, most of Louisiana's legal structure adhered to that of France, particularly the civil code and procedures current in Paris. However, Louisiana law and order departed from French models in at least three important ways. Two changes were intentional, and one seems to have resulted from a planning oversight. The first contrast arose from the most dramatic demographic and legal difference between France and Louisiana—the presence of a significant number of slaves. In writing the *Code Noir*, crown advisers tried to anticipate new categories of crimes and problems arising from the quasi-subjecthood of slavery. Learning from experiences in Saint Domingue, they made significant changes in the Louisiana version of the law. In the creole generation, local slaveholders took the experiment further into their own hands, selectively enforcing the *Code Noir* according to common practice and writing local amendments. The second intentional modification made by metropolitan planners was to legislate lawyers out of the colony. In doing so, they hoped to curtail civil suits and challenges to political authority. The third important difference between France and Louisiana may have been unintentional. Louisiana's social engineers failed to provide for an institutional police system. In France during the eighteenth century, police forces and policing technologies were rapidly expanding, but in New Orleans law enforcement was ad hoc and understaffed.

Comparing Louisiana's *Code Noir* of 1724 with its predecessor written for Saint Domingue forty years earlier (by the influential French finance minister Jean Baptiste Colbert) provides one of the clearest examples of the ways in which French ministers built up knowledge of their colonies and adjusted their tactics with each new venture. For the Louisiana version, several articles were dropped, recombined, or modified, and two new articles were added.[20] The most significant changes entailed regulating intimate relations between blacks (*noirs*) and whites (*blancs*); controlling and limiting the free colored population; and intervening in the disciplinary regime of slavery. In the Saint Domingue code, only *concubinage* between whites and blacks was specifically prohibited. So long as the two parties were both baptized Catholics, interracial marriage *was* tacitly permitted. Further, a free man of *any* color could marry a slave woman and thereby free her. In contrast, the corresponding Louisiana article explicitly forbade marriage between whites and blacks of any station, and specified that manumission could result from marriage only in the case of a free *black* man marrying an enslaved woman. French ministers modified another article to restrict routes to freedom. In the original code, masters had the express right to free their slaves without needing to give a reason. The Louisiana version, however, dictated not only that owners had to justify a manumission, but that they had to obtain the permission of the Superior Council for it to be legal. The reason given was to prevent slaves from committing thefts to collect the funds for self-purchase. Other provisions addressed the problem of maroons. One made the freedom of free people of color much less secure by adding a new punishment: freed slaves or freeborn people of color who gave refuge to runaways could be remitted to slavery. Another new article gave permission to owners of fugitive slaves to search for them wherever they might be and to take whatever actions they deemed appropriate to regain them. Finally, the second new article prescribed specific punishments for transgressing slaves and stated who would mete these out. *Juges ordinaires* of the local jurisdiction could administer whippings, brandings, and ear-cuttings as a last resort, while only the Superior Council in New Orleans could order executions or hamstringings. Masters were prohibited from directly administering any of the more severe corporal punishments.[21]

With the Louisiana *Code Noir* of 1724, ministers attempted to design an "improved" slave society that did three things: made slavery more permanent by narrowing the chances of manumission; drew a starker color line between white and black by delegitimizing any kind of *métissage*; and intervened in the master/slave relationship in the area of corporal discipline. A major purpose of the first two changes appears to have been to prevent rapid growth in the free colored population, which in Saint Domingue threatened the slavery regime in various ways, most concretely by aiding and abetting maroons. The limits on corporal punishment expressed worries of Saint Domingue officials that an escalation in violence and abuse perpetrated by individual owners and managers threatened to destabilize the institution of slavery.[22] But the attempt to control racial slavery and its social consequences through legal instruments was a clumsy science. The volatile balance of power in a slave society such as New Orleans profoundly affected the crime rate as well as its system of justice.

Almost immediately, the differences between Saint Domingue and Louisiana rendered much of the *Code Noir* obsolete. Even though under the same crown, there were significant contrasts between colonial societies. For one, the relative demographic balance of Indians, Africans, and Europeans in lower Louisiana created an entirely different social geography from that known in the Caribbean, where those of African descent often accounted for more than 90 percent of the population. Indian slaves, whose numbers were significant in the charter generation, were not addressed in the *Code Noir*. The relations between runaways and local Indian groups presented a much greater threat of escalating *marronage* than did relations between blacks and whites. In addition, the proportionately much larger (and predominantly male) population of free, forced, and indentured French settlers presented problems for the prevention of *métissage*. Authorities who wanted a settled population of Europeans recognized that stable families were essential, but experiments in importing marriageable French women were short-lived and inadequate.[23]

The vocabulary of the *Code Noir* itself did not reflect Louisiana social categories, during either the charter generation or the creole generations. Although *noir* was occasionally used in reference to African immigrants, *nègre* was more common. *Blanc* was almost never used.[24] To further complicate things, the predominance of legal status as a form of social classification in colonial Louisiana meant, perhaps counter-intuitively, that one's degree of enslavement could blur rather than inscribe the color line.

One case dramatically corroborates the ambiguous relation between legal status and color among Louisiana's *petits gens*. Governor Bienville had convicted a French soldier to the galleys for conspiracy to desert. After his conviction, the soldier, nicknamed La Chaume (meaning "stubble" or "thatch"), was described as a *forçat* who worked as a gardener at the Natchez post. In 1743 La Chaume got into a fight with an officer's cook. The cook called for the guard to arrest him because according to the *Code Noir,* "it is not permitted for a slave [*esclave*] to strike a free man." The guard sent a *nègre* slave of the king, named Brutal (having the same meaning in French as in English), to apprehend La Chaume, who reacted by turning a knife against himself in a suicide attempt. Asked why he had done this, the Frenchman responded, "to escape slavery."[25]

Early Louisiana administrators appear to have advocated using black men, both slave (Brutal) and free (Louis Congo), to physically punish white subjects as part of a calculated "divide and rule" tactic they deployed in other realms to drive a wedge of animosity between the diverse segments of the colony's population. Governor Bienville deliberately used Native American bounty hunters against black maroons. Governor Périer sent black mercenaries after the Natchez, Chaouchas, and marooning Indian slaves. He wrote explicitly about the "great misfortune which could befall the colony" by a "union between the Indian nations and the black slaves, but happily there has always been a great aversion between them which . . . we take great care to maintain."[26] Using a black executioner against French free subjects is a sign that early administrators also feared co-conspiracies between poor whites and people of color. Desertions and mutinies carried out by interracial groups of soldiers, *forçats,* and slaves of color were common during Louisiana's early years. One of the most impressive sprees occurred in 1739, when five white soldiers, a free man of color, and at least five slaves stole large boats (*voitures* of 33 and 40 feet with rudders and oars) from Bayou St. John, raided local plantations for supplies, and escaped to Havana where they joined a growing community of Louisiana expatriates.[27]

PUNISHMENT

In the charter generation, the black-on-white penal strategy served to level the colony's *petits gens* at the same time that it attempted to cut a divide between two of the most dangerous elements of the lower orders—enslaved Africans and Frenchmen serving in the colony under their own degrees of servitude (*forçat, engagé,* soldier). It is significant that the first instance of interracial corporal punishment in 1720 preceded the large-scale importation of Africans to Louisiana by several years.[28] The work of Louis Congo and his unnamed predecessor demonstrated to the unruly colonial subject that the government (not biology nor even religion) determined who was to be free and who was to be enslaved. This message served absolutism better than statements of indivisible white superiority. Colonial administrators did not hesitate to use the threat of slavery to make subjects submissive. French *forçats* arrived with a legal status similar to that of black and Indian slaves, and were themselves known by the same term, *esclave*. Many had originally been exiled to the colony as a cheap alternative to Africans.[29]

The strategy of interracial punishment worked only to a point. After 1737 we find no further mention of a "Negro executioner." Patterns in capital punishment among slave and free, black and white, began to diverge about this time. We have detailed court records for nine executions that took place between 1740 and 1752, although the documents fail to mention who carried these out. Two executions were of soldiers. One was death by firing squad for the instigator of the "Bread Mutiny" (discussed below), the other was a hanging for attempted murder. The latter crime was committed by a soldier who had attacked two enslaved women with a bayonet while they were washing clothes in the river. A third hanging was performed in effigy for a fugitive innkeeper named Gauvain who had killed an unruly patron in a brawl (if he were to be caught, the sentence would be repeated on his person).[30] Enslaved men received the remaining six death sentences for crimes of burglary, murder, and assault. Before his hanging, Jupiter *dit* Camelle underwent torture to force him to name his accomplices in a burglary spree. François *dit* Baraca, a baptized man of the "Poulav" (Fulbe/Fulani) nation, went to the gallows in 1748 for beating his wife to death. After his hanging, the judges ordered his body put on view in the public square for twenty-four hours as "an example to others."[31]

By the 1740s exemplary forms of corporal punishment for slaves and maroons were becoming more dramatic, as well as distinct from penalties imposed on freemen for similar crimes. This trend goes hand in hand with a movement toward a greater articulation of racial categories among the creole generation. A 1742 case marks one of the first instances when *blanc* was used in a local document to describe a French Louisianan—all the more important in a case that hinged on differential treatment of black-on-white crime. Pierre *dit* Jasmin was a runaway slave who battered a French soldier at the Natchez post so severely that the attorney general considered charging him with attempted murder. Reputed to be a "bad subject" (*un mauvais*), Jasmin was asked under torture whether he knew that "a slave raising a hand to a white man deserved death." He responded that he did. After building a heavy-handed case, the attorney general asked for death by hanging. The Superior Council commuted Jasmin's sentence to ear amputation, branding, flogging, and a permanent chain around his leg. Perhaps they thought his scars would make a more lasting spectacle than execution.[32] In contrast, the Superior Council treated most white-on-white assault cases in the same period as civil suits or else limited the penalties to fines and prison terms.[33]

Charlot Kakaracou, an unbaptized slave of the "Coneda" nation (probably Akan), was condemned to death for allegedly killing a white soldier who had been poaching in his hunting territory.[34] Kakaracou's 1744 sentencing reads as follows:

> [He is] found guilty of murder, condemned to have his arms and legs broken, and to be broken on the wheel on the public square of this City, on a scaffold erected to that effect, and afterwards placed on a wheel, his face turned towards the sky, to end his life, where his body shall remain for twenty-four hours. He shall ask pardon before the main entrance of the parochial church of this City where, with a torch in hand, he shall declare that he wickedly murdered the said Pierre Olivy, for which he begs pardon of God, the King and justice.[35]

The Council added a marginal note to the official record, "that said Charlot dit Cacaracou, after having received all the blows living shall secretly be strangled." Despite this apparent act of mercy to spare Kakaracou an extremely slow death, the method of his execution was among the most horrific applied during the French period. Before Kakaracou's case, executions for individual crimes had been death by hanging.[36] The drama of his public torture and the fact of his secret strangling emphasize the exemplary nature of his case. A slave killing a white man, even a thieving soldier, represented more than an act of murder: it was an act of sedition against an emerging system of white supremacy.

Around this same time, the Superior Council increasingly began dealing with violence *against* slaves as a private civil matter.[37] In 1747, for example, when a settler with a prior criminal record was convicted of shooting and critically wounding a slave named Touta, the court did not take punitive measures, which had earlier been the practice. It merely ordered the offender to give Touta's owner a replacement slave. Simultaneously, the local government stepped back from punishing slaves for lesser crimes, returning slaves to their masters "to have administered such correction as the Master shall judge proper," as was decided in the case of maroons Mamourou and Bayou in 1748.[38] Instead of the state intervening in the relationship between slave and master, as intended in many parts of the *Code Noir*, in the creole generation local government handed over the means of force to slaveowners as a private matter. Of course, the government officials responsible for this move were themselves major slaveowners.

Officials also began to implement a new form of punishment for free people of color. The accused could be reduced to slavery for relatively minor offenses. While in 1722 a free man of color named La Roze was sentenced to flogging and six years in the galleys for stealing from the Company stores (the same punishment a white man would have received), in 1743 Jean Baptiste, a twenty-year-old manumitted man, was returned to slavery for stealing a few items of clothing from his employer. The most interesting case, however, is that of the "*negresse libre*," Jeannette. In September 1746, the Council summoned her to appear for assembling domestic slaves at her house in New Orleans for evening supper parties. The Council reprimanded her and warned her to put a stop to the gatherings. A few months later, she appeared in court on vague charges of theft and unpaid debts. The Council condemned her to become a slave once more. One suspects that the councilors were alarmed more by the assemblies of slaves and servants at her house than by any difficulties in her accounting.[39] Besides whatever social organizing her parties may have been fostering, the councilors probably suspected her of harboring runaways. In imposing these sentences upon Jean Baptiste and Jeannette, the councilors went far beyond the letter of the *Code Noir*, which stipulated this form of punishment only for free blacks who abetted runaways, not for minor property crimes.

Other legal changes in the creole generation evince a growing interest in tightening the controls of slavery. Beginning in 1738, the Superior Council required slaveowners to register a report any time one of their slaves died or ran away. The death register was designed in part to curb disciplinary excesses by masters and overseers. In these reports, owners carefully justified the "natural" or "accidental" causes of their slave's death.[40] Paralleling this effort, a new mandatory register of runaways represented an attempt to gain control over a growing maroon problem around the outskirts of New Orleans. The Superior Council began to require owners to register runaways so that they could be apprehended and punished by the government's agents or other members of the community.[41] The Council was attempting to mend a growing rift between large slaveholders, to whom most maroons technically belonged, and smallholders in both town and country whose livelihoods were more gravely affected by maroon thefts and predations. Although the new crackdown seems to have led to a few more captures in 1738 and 1739, Councilor Fazende complained in 1745 that many "*negres marrons*" were still habitually entering the city at night.[42]

The destination of runaways depended on their origin. City slaves ran to the country, or to other settlements. Some plantation slaves ran to New Orleans. As early as 1728, the governor and the *ordonnateur* complained that runaways were flocking to the city. By that time the town seems to have reached a size and a diversity that made it possible for an individual to blend into the hustle and bustle. Many runaway reports state that a missing slave was suspected of being "somewhere in the city." The runaway Guala (or Guela) had been taken to the city by a "negro belonging to Bienville," where he lived for some time before being recognized and caught. Interrogators of several slaves suspected of a rash of burglaries in the city were particularly interested in ascertaining how well they knew the city. One could circle the houses of major officials on a map, while another disclaimed any regular familiarity with the drinking houses, saying he only went there for the Sunday market. A mulatto woman named Charlotte ran to the city, where she was eventually caught hiding, half-dressed, in the bed of a ship captain. She offered her captors 100 piastres (a large sum) for her release, but they apprehended her anyway. Her owner sued the ship captain for harboring a runaway. For her part, Charlotte requested the opportunity to plead for leniency with the governor's wife on the grounds that her flight was justifiable due to her master's abuse; the customary flogging for a runaway would only compound the unfairness of her situation. Charlotte was a resourceful person who not only knew the town well, but knew the discretionary gaps in its system of justice, perhaps especially those that might offer women some measure of protection.[43]

Both slaves and slaveowners could use provisions of the *Code Noir* to their advantage, but they invoked the law selectively. Louisianans declined to enforce many of the code's articles, such as the ban on slaves carrying guns or weapons, or the ban on concubinage.[44] In his assessment of slave regulation in French Louisiana, Carl Brasseaux writes: "As slave ownership passed into the second generation of native-born Louisianans, slaveholders demanded not only greater personal control over their human property, but a greater degree of submission from their workers as well. This quiet revolution was waged through the legislative arm of the Superior Council and culminated with the appointment of a Creole slaveholder as attorney general in 1763."[45] I would add only one modification: in the streets and fields, the revolution was not so quiet. Rather, it was fought with fists, whips, and words. Punishment, except for those exemplary cases that threatened the entire system, had moved out of the king's realm, and into the sovereign domain of the slaveholder. This is perhaps one of the most telling signs of where colonial power effectively lay.

POLICE

Louisiana's councilors exercised wide discretionary powers in their judicial functions. Although the Superior Council generally followed the civil code of the *Coutume de Paris*, it virtually wrote its own criminal code.[46] In early eighteenth-century France, Enlightenment thinkers had begun to turn their attention to the problems of crime and punishment, but the French state did not implement a true criminal code—one that defined offenses, evidentiary requirements, and appropriate punishments—until the Napoleonic era. Unlike other areas in which the Bourbons expanded bureaucratic control over economic and administrative systems, the trend in law enforcement was toward greater discretionary power at the local level.[47] In this respect, practices in Louisiana adhered closely to metropolitan ones. The problem was that in a society peopled by so many "rogues"—free agents and those without verifiable identities—functionaries were handicapped. They lacked the local knowledge and "community policing" techniques their equivalents in France enjoyed. Yet the discretionary powers conferred upon the Louisiana Superior Council in judicial matters probably helped embolden members to take the law, and eventually the colony itself, into their own hands.

With the exception of the attorney general (*procureur général*) and the attorney of vacant estates (*procureur des biens vacants*) who served on the Superior Council, lawyers were barred from practicing their trade in Louisiana.[48] Planners hoped this would halt a litigious trend in French society and at the same time eliminate a group prone to challenge the authority of the king (the rebellious *parlements* of Paris and the other provinces were heavily influenced by lawyers or *avocats*). Louisiana records show that this plan, too, must be counted among the failures of the crown's experiment. Louisiana's free people were a litigious lot. By the 1740s the Superior Council considered an average of at least eleven suits per week. With a minimum of two litigants involved in each case, this meant that plausibly one out of every two free Louisianans could have been involved in a civil suit over the course of a given year. Rather than stemming the flow of litigation, eliminating lawyers and their fees placed litigants of all classes on a relatively level playing field. Complicated debt arrangements and periodic currency crises instigated many of these suits. In criminal cases, defendants and their support witnesses sometimes complained about the denial of counsel, but here, too, the unintended consequence of the ban on lawyers seems to have been that elite defendants were treated, at least procedurally, in the same manner as lower class defendants. Everyone represented themselves.[49]

In 1722 Commander Valdeterre at Dauphin Island complained that in Louisiana, "the greatest crimes remain unpunished for lack of police."[50] The commander seemed unaware that *he* was the police. The crown expected the military (both the marine troops and the Swiss mercenary regiments) to fulfill this duty. Perhaps what Valdeterre meant was that no special units or officers were assigned to assist him in this task. Rather, local post commanders such as himself (at Dauphin Island, Mobile, Kaskaskia, and so forth) were instructed to dispatch troops to pursue fugitives or quell civilian unrest on an as-needed basis. However, French soldiers were among the most common lawbreakers, and they did not police themselves very effectively.

Complaints to France about the lack of discipline among Louisiana's troops were frequent and persistent throughout the French period. Kerlérec's comments in 1757 are typical: "The twenty-four extra companies [1,200 men] which the king has seen fit to send to this colony, are made up exclusively of professional deserters and some more vicious; they have caused more harm than they have provided service. A part of them deserted; another died from the horrors of the most outrageous drunken debauchery. The rest (fortunately not a large number) are more dangerous today to the colony than the enemy himself."[51]

Nearly a dozen other mutinies and treasonable plots led by soldiers contributed to the perception of disorder in French Louisiana. In 1745 men from three companies rose up in a general mutiny in New Orleans. A soldier named Braude *dit* Dominique allegedly instigated the revolt because he was disgusted by the bread the troops had been served in their military ration. He stormed the bakery with other men in tow, stuck his knife into some old, stale bread exclaiming, "Fuck!—we don't need to eat bread like this that even dogs wouldn't want ... we must make war!" Officials panicked and within three days rushed Dominique through a speedy trial and execution by firing squad on the Place d'Armes before the assembled troops.[52] In 1758, in another dramatic mutiny case, several soldiers at the Cat Island post killed Commander Duroux and threw his naked body into the Gulf of Mexico.[53]

The majority of the colony's troublesome soldiers were garrisoned in New Orleans, but administrators only slightly modified their ad hoc approach to law enforcement there. The governor doubled as the capital's post commander, but he delegated many duties to the *major de place*, a subordinate designated to take care of military matters in town.[54] Although in the outlying posts men in similar positions administered both civil and military justice, serving as police, prosecutor, and judge, in New Orleans the *major* appears surprisingly infrequently in the records. When he does, he seems primarily to have been involved in policing the troops. The *major* served notices on military suspects and acted as prosecutor in place of the attorney general in a few courts-martial preserved in the record. In New Orleans civilian justice was left to the Superior Council, although police functions were supposed to be filled by the military. The *huissier* (often translated as "sheriff") performed duties closer to those of a court bailiff than a law enforcement officer. He served summonses and published notices of the Council, but did not take an active role in preventing or investigating criminal activity. The colony's first long-serving attorney general was one of the few individuals who appeared to be proactive on crime. In the 1720s François Fleuriau conducted sting operations on taverns, catching owners and patrons in the act of breaking the Sabbath, engaging in illegal gambling, and serving alcohol to slaves without a permit.[55] In addition to his duties as a prosecutor, he advised the Council to make arrests and issue warrants, and he led inquests and criminal investigations. Other dutiful officials (especially those newly arrived from France, who often came with a mission to reform the recalcitrant colony) attempted to apprehend and try those committing acts against the state, such as smuggling and embezzlement. The *ordonnateur* Delachaise's zeal in this area made him many enemies in the colony, including his fellow Superior Council members.

The Superior Council records make occasional references to the "guard," indicating that some soldiers were put on patrol or stand-by duty in town. These references date to the last two decades of the French period and may be related to a set of thirty-one "police" regulations that the Superior Council promulgated in 1751. These regulations mainly targeted slaves and runaways. The ordinance reinforced articles of the *Code Noir* on slave assemblies and access to the town market, in an attempt to curtail the traffic of slaves in and out of New Orleans where they frequented both black- and white-owned taverns. It also specified that drinking establishments for soldiers (called *cantines*) had to be separate from those serving the rest of the inhabitants, to discourage fraternizing between soldiers and those whom they were supposed to police.[56]

In France the military also supplied personnel for police forces in the eighteenth century, but they usually consisted of specialized units with permanent commissions for this duty. These units conducted regular patrols and developed a "professional" identity as police authorities. They also developed a set of surveillance, enforcement, and reporting techniques. Among the poor, the police had great latitude in determining guilt and meting out punishment for petty crimes. As a result, police records from busy districts in Paris are rich with much of the same type of material one would find in court records—interrogations of suspects, depositions of witnesses, summaries of evidence, and so on. In rural areas, the *prévôté* courts had similar discretionary powers. These courts had been established specifically to control the vagrant population. They tried nonresidents who had committed a crime in the community; residents were tried under a separate jurisdiction.[57]

New Orleanians almost certainly had their own practices of summary justice. Such discretionary practices often leave little record, and in any case the criminal case records from French Louisiana have been poorly preserved.[58] Certainly, surviving Superior Council records indicate that the occupancy rate at the prison was higher than the extant criminal caseload would suggest. For example, Jean, a slave arrested on suspicion of burglary, admitted that he had been arrested twice before for "quarreling," though we have no record of these occasions. In another case, goldsmith Jean Dominique Bunel was sitting in the "civilian jail" in New Orleans for defaulting on debts, but we know this only because the civil archive preserves a notarial document in which he gave power of attorney to a friend. The original arrest and judicial proceedings of a father and son from the English colonies imprisoned for the high crime of espionage are also missing from the records, although the hubbub caused by their attempted jail break a year later is documented and was the subject of transatlantic epistolary gossip.[59]

Not a single trial document survives for one of eighteenth-century Louisiana's most notorious characters. Jean Baptiste Baudreau *dit* Graveline Jr. was the bastard son of an Iberville-era Canadian who had become a planter at Bayougoula (below Baton Rouge).[60] Baudreau *fils* began his criminal career by abducting the girl of his desires (the legitimate daughter of another planter, named Huet), along with three slaves from her plantation, livestock for supplies, and a fully stocked boat. He then headed to Havana. His concerned father tracked him down and returned him to New Orleans six months later. After a stay in jail, Baudreau settled down in New Orleans and married another woman who eventually wearied of his gambling, "debauchery," and "libertine" ways. In 1752 she successfully petitioned for separation and cut him off from the family estate. Five years later he resurfaced as a "plunderer" of a Spanish shipwreck on Cat Island who allegedly persuaded four soldiers to mutiny by killing their commander and escaping to the English in Carolina, taking their booty with them. Baudreau was finally caught and broken on the wheel in 1758.[61]

Baudreau's colorful life comes to us not through the official criminal record, which is missing, but through a trail of mostly unrelated civil documents, a governor's letter, and one published travel account. To rely solely on the surviving records of prosecutions in New Orleans would give a very misleading picture of the level of crime and violence in the community.[62] Besides the problem of obvious lacunae created by lost or destroyed records, there is strong circumstantial evidence that justice in colonial New Orleans was of a summary kind, through tribunals called by military and civilian elite who exercised their judgments with relatively little legal formality. It also becomes clear that as the eighteenth century progressed, New Orleans became increasingly preoccupied with violence.[63]

Crime Statistics and Violence

At 5:45 P.M. on the evening of 3 July 1763, Nicolas Verret heard that his friend Fleury, whom he had visited earlier that afternoon, had just been killed. During the inquiry, he testified that "he ran to the place, following many other people, negroes, Indians, whites: that he saw Sieur Fleury dead . . . he did not know of any dispute, bickering or litigation of Sieur Fleury with anybody; that he had alas known Sieur Fleury as a very peaceful and quiet man." Jacques Cantrelle, the churchwarden, heard a rumor that there was a body in his garden and went to find "more than 100 persons around the dead lad." Neither he nor any of the curious townspeople claimed to know who had murdered the French clerk. The autopsy indicated that death had been inflicted by a triangular sword. The case was never solved.[64]

Like the Fleury case, the early criminal records of New Orleans themselves require patching together a puzzle with missing pieces and silent witnesses. The picture that emerges is one in which bloody and profane conflicts over the developing boundaries of race and class played an important role.

Although few studies have examined crime in early New Orleans, the topic plays directly into the debate on how "disorderly" colonial New Orleans and Louisiana were in the eighteenth century. More than any other measure, crime statistics are presumed to be an objective indicator of social "disorder." However, scholars have conveyed very different impressions, depending on their sources and orientation.[65] Although it is impossible to produce a statistically reliable set of crime rates, due to the large gaps in the archives, we can at least sketch an impression based on the surviving sample of reported crime. These reports are drawn from remnants of the criminal case books and cross-references found in the better preserved civil case books of the Louisiana Superior Council. The resulting collection provides a sample of 392 reported crimes committed between 1716 and 1763, with the majority coming from the period of best record preservation, from 1720 to 1753. The sample is primarily useful in mapping general patterns and changes within the community. It provides an idea of the range of crimes and criminals, their proportion to one another, and trends over time. Enough evidence survives to suggest that observations by historical witnesses—such as Arnaud Bonnaud, who said that crime in New Orleans posed "a notable threat to the establishment of the colony"—had some validity.[66]

Property crimes made up 37 percent of the total and included theft, burglary, embezzlement, fraud, bad debts, livestock killing, forgery, and vandalism. Violent crimes (28 percent) were dominated by assault and battery cases, but also cover assault with a deadly weapon, slave abuse, spouse abuse, child abuse, attempted murder, rape, and murder. (There were five probable rapes, and nineteen murders.) The category of moral crimes and crimes against the state (17 percent) did not involve a specific victim (except the king). Desertion cases made up the majority of this category, including instances where slave *marronage* was treated as a public crime due to aggravating circumstances, such as theft or violence. Spying, mutiny, and sedition topped the list of high crimes in this category, although smuggling (a crime against the state's commercial privileges), violating the Sabbath, and insubordination were more common offenses. Reports of sexual crimes were rare in colonial Louisiana. Besides rape (here categorized as a violent crime), allegations of sodomy, bigamy, and bestiality appear in three separate cases. Finally, defamation or "verbal violence" (18 percent) held a special place in eighteenth-century French jurisprudence. Insults, slander, and libel were verbal crimes that could literally give voice to the tensions underlying the brutality or stealth of other crimes (see discussion in chapter 4).

If we compare criminal profiles from eighteenth-century France, we see that desertion appears to be a particularly colonial type of offense. Complaints about desertion and insubordination among soldiers were constant throughout the period. In 1719 a large group of deserters actually made off with a heavily loaded brigantine (a two-masted ship, the *St. Joseph*) belonging to the Company of the Indies and headed to Havana. They were never apprehended. Almost every man who assumed the title of governor of Louisiana railed at some point against the "lack of discipline" among the colonial troops, and about their criminal propensities.[67]

Louisiana officials in the charter period tended to focus their worries on the illegal activities of the colony's poor white population, when property crime reached a per-capita peak. Besides theft, the most common accusations were price speculation, small-time smuggling, and food fraud. Cases of food fraud included using bad weights, adulterating oil or wine with water, or, in one case, butchering dogs and cats to sell as meat to the hospital. The attorney general in this last case chose a creative form of exemplary justice: "The one called Villeneuve shall be put on the 'wooden horse' and shall promenade through the town with a board on front and back saying in large letters 'eater of dogs and cats,' and he shall have a cat around his neck."[68]

As soon as slaves started to arrive in large numbers in the late 1720s, colonists began to complain about the activities of slaves and runaways— their *marronage*, petty theft, drinking, and noisome fraternizing in town. In 1729 the attorney general complained of constant chicken stealing in town perpetrated by maroons, which had recently escalated into cattle-killing.[69]

By the late 1720s New Orleans had a reputation even within Louisiana as a place where criminal passions ran wild. Responding to a letter from a friend in New Orleans in 1729, Sieur Terrisse de Ternan wrote from Illinois country that he was sorry to hear that "your capital continues to have so many murderous killings . . . that cause a tragic outpouring of blood in

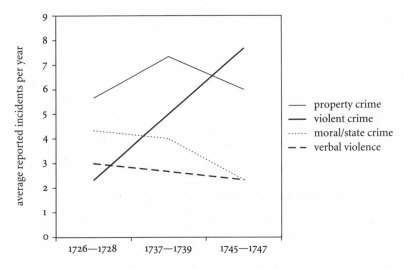

FIGURE 14. Frequency of offense types over time, from Louisiana Superior Council Records, 1726–47. [I restricted this analysis to the years of best document preservation to eliminate wild fluctuations created by record gaps. I averaged the incident rates for three sets of three years: 1726–28, 1737–39, and 1745–47 (selected for documentary completeness, not temporal spacing). Unfortunately, beyond 1747 the records are spotty to nonexistent for criminal cases, although many incidents are mentioned in colonial correspondence. Lines have not been smoothed.]

your streets." He may have been referring a series of incidents that began with "conspiracy and rioting" allegedly masterminded by German resident Pierre Schmidt in 1728. Terrisse also alluded to a "*scandale publique*" involving a man named Massy, whom he excused sympathetically on the grounds that "it is dangerous for such a gallant man to live a long time in celibacy."[70]

Toward the end of the French period, correspondents writing back to France focused their complaints on smuggling, fraud, and corruption perpetuated by slaveowners, merchants, and officials. They declined to mention that these same individuals were prone to uphold slaveholding and the colony's illegal economy through the use of direct force.

VIOLENCE

The criminal evidence from New Orleans suggests that tensions between large slaveholders, small slaveholders, and nonslaveholders could be fierce. Freemen were hardly a socially or racially unified group in the "slave society" of New Orleans. Proportionately, the ratio of violent crime to property crime appears to be relatively high, particularly during the creole regime.[71] The incidence of reported violence grew steadily and dramatically from the 1720s to the late 1740s (fig. 14). There was no sign of a slowdown in 1747, when the records become too fragmented to sample reliably. Both the number of reported violent crimes and their proportion as a percentage of all crime increased. The number of reported property crimes grew gradually, reaching a peak in the late 1730s and thereafter dropping off equally gradually into the 1740s. Reported verbal violence and moral/state crimes gradually tapered off during the first creole generation.

We can read this dramatic rise in reported violence in two ways—either violence was increasing or reporting was. The first interpretation, or some combination of the two, is the most likely for the simple reason that each of the other three types of reported crimes was declining after the 1730s. If a growing spirit of "law and order" simply led to more zealous reporting, then one would think the reporting of other crime categories should have risen as well, or at least should not have declined. As I have argued throughout this book, a number of important transitions began to take place in the late 1730s as creoles entered into their legacies and positions of influence: smuggling became institutionalized, local interests took over the Superior Council, and urban slaveholding expanded, at the same time that the socioeconomic distance between large slaveholders and nonslaveholders grew wider. A growth in violence should be added to this list of creole transitions.

Consider the pattern in assaults reported in New Orleans, for example. Only six out of the fifty assaults reported occurred in the frontier decade of the 1720s; most occurred between 1735 and 1747. Similarly, 70 percent of the homicides, infanticides, and attempted murders took place in the creole half of the sample period. The population as a whole was not growing fast enough to account for this rise, but the number of enslaved and free people of color moving into and through the city jumped noticeably in the creole generation and may have contributed to tensions. African, Afro-creole or Native American slaves made up two-thirds of the victims in murder and wrongful death cases reported in New Orleans, though they accounted for a smaller proportion of the accused.

The most common type of reported crime was committed by enlisted French soldiers against their own kind, lending some support to the view that the city's large garrison was a major source of "disorder." That the garrison served as the de facto police force did little to stem conflict within its ranks, which contributed at least 21 percent of the suspected criminal offenses in the colonial period, not counting those prosecuted in the missing court-martial records. Violent encounters within the soldiery may be significantly underreported in the archives, if the outcome of a duel on a

Monday afternoon in 1751 is any indication. Witnesses living in the back-of-town neighborhood facing the woods described seeing two men they recognized as sergeants, stripped down to their vests, dueling in a lot belonging to Gardela, the public gardener. One man received a mortal wound. They brought him to the porch of the house, where the gardener's wife Marie Querit gave him water, but he expired within a few minutes. Witnesses then said "the Guard" came to take away the body, but when the Superior Council and the *major de place* tried to investigate, no body could be found and no one claimed to know the names of those involved. Officials concluded that the dead man had been secretly buried, and they were never able to bring anyone to trial.[72]

Elite French males (military officers, merchants, major slaveholders, and high-placed bureaucrats) also committed a disproportionate number of the city's violent crimes (22 percent). They tended to focus their aggression either on enslaved men who resisted their rule or on members of their own group. Tensions within the elite group arose from Old World notions of honor, as well as New World competition. Although many members of the elite worked together to make slaveholding more secure, or to advance the position of New Orleans in the intercolonial trade network, the top stratum of society was probably the most internally divided and mutually hostile group in the colony. High-ranking officials had to watch their backs not only against political intrigue, but also against physical assault. One night on the street in 1747 a fashionable assailant, "dressed in red, with a wig and a hat drawn low over his eyes," attacked *ordonnateur* and Superior Council judge François Ange Le Normant. Le Normant suspected a noble cadet from the garrison.[73]

Enslaved men made up the next largest group of offenders (15 percent). The targets of their violence spanned the social spectrum, from other slaves (both male and female), to French artisans and elite planters. Planter François Trudeau turned a Bambara named Mazama over to public justice for "mutinous rebellion and violence." Mazama had several times threatened to kill Trudeau's wife. In another case, an owner requested an autopsy and inquiry into the poisoning of one of his slaves by another.[74] Overall, slaves accounted for 20 percent of all alleged violent offenders (men, women, and children combined), which was low in proportion to their numbers, although they made up the second largest victim group (29 percent) after lower class free males (encompassing the soldier category).[75] But as alleged perpetrators, in one area enslaved men stood out. In the reported crime sample, they committed nearly half of the homicides where the status of both victim and perpetrator can be determined, far out of proportion to their rates in other violent crimes. This finding probably reflects the fact that homicide merited the intervention of the state in the disciplinary regime, while assaults and brawls would have been handled by the slave-owner or his/her agent. In all but two of the murders allegedly committed by slaves, the victims were other slaves. The slave-on-slave cases included domestic violence, manslaughter, poisoning, and one premeditated murder. Of the two exceptions, involving a slave murdering a Frenchman, the case of Kakaracou, who killed the poaching soldier, has already been mentioned. Another case involved the murder of a French planter's son, and was said to have involved witchcraft. Sieur Corbin de Baschemin disappeared from his plantation a couple of months after a number of slaves reportedly "held a service in the negro manner . . . by which they intended to bring about the death of the said Corbin." The ritual was conducted "in the negro language" and accompanied by singing and dancing.[76]

French males of a middling status (clerks and managers, small-business owners, or those with fewer than five slaves) exercised equal opportunity in their choice of targets, attacking slaves and freemen of all statuses. They also committed one-third of all reported homicides, a disproportionately high figure for their small numbers. This may reflect the inclusion in this group of plantation overseers accused of infanticide and manslaughter of slaves, as well as tavern owners who took up arms to enforce the peace in their establishments. If guilty of all that was alleged against him, Canadian Jacques Charpentier *dit* LeRoy perpetrated the most heinous suite of crimes recorded in the French period. The plantation's owner accused his manager of committing regular slave abuse through overwork, beating, and malnutrition, as well as rape and infanticide (through the beating of a pregnant slave woman named Suzanne). Moreover, LeRoy was suspected of murdering a slave named Brunet. The Superior Council convicted LeRoy of at least one of the charges (the record does not say which), but only ordered him to quit the plantation and pay the owner 20,000 francs in compensation.[77] Notably, this case dates to 1730, when the French administration was still relatively active in the colony, and the slaveowner seems to have been cognizant of the slave protections emplaced by the *Code Noir*, though enforcement in this case may have served his own interests in rescuing his investment.

As tracked in complaints submitted to the Louisiana Superior Council, community concerns about slave abuse seem to have grown in the late 1730s and 1740s, contributing to the rise in reported crime during the period. This atmosphere is significant because the attorney general usually initiated criminal procedures only upon citizen complaint. A parallel rise in reported spousal abuse and successful petitions by women for separation of bed and board in the 1740s may stem from a related concern with controlling disciplinary excesses on the part of free French men.

Although the colonial censuses officially reported that free people of color made up no more than 3 percent of the population (and in most censuses less than 1 percent), this group accounted for 10 percent of violent offenses in the sample. A majority of these crimes were committed by free men of color against enslaved men. Some of these freemen worked as *commandeurs* (drivers or overseers) of slaves, which put them in a position where tension and conflict could brew. A free black man named Thomas was cited in an assault on a slave, in which he was described as the *commandeur* for Belair's plantation.[78] In all categories, free men of color were more than twice as likely to be offenders as victims. The numbers suggest either that free people of color accounted for a disproportionate amount of reported crime (three to ten times their share of the enumerated population), or that the free black population of New Orleans was significantly larger in the French period than census entries suggest. Since local administrators never singled out free people of color as an especially troublesome criminal element except for the habit of harboring maroons, census undercounting of free people of color is the more likely explanation (as argued in chapter 4).

Women of all classes accounted for 9 percent of the accused and 30 percent of the victims. Women's alleged violent crimes tended to be child abuse or infanticide. One case involved the complication either of mental illness or adultery, depending on whom you believe. A *negresse* of Madame Dupuy Goupillon arrived at the surgeon Baldit's house in New Orleans and thrust a half-dressed little girl (two and a half years old) into his arms, saying, "Here is your [*ton*] child that my mistress has sent you." Though not admitting paternity, Baldit sought an injunction, requesting that the husband Goupillon make arrangements to prevent exposing the child to the cruelties of such a mother who, he claimed, was crazed (*dans le fou*).[79] More commonly, women were the targets of domestic abuse. Domestic violence accounted for about one-third of the crimes against women, including two cases of enslaved women killed by their husbands. Slave women were three times more likely to be victims than aggressors.[80] Five probable rape cases appear in the records (two are discreetly ambiguous), two involving slave women and three concerning free women. Jeanneton, a slave woman owned by a *voyageur*, was imprisoned by her owner for running away and threatening to leave him. In her declaration she told her examiners she was "six weeks pregnant by him." He claimed he had only returned from Illinois eight days ago "and has not been able to obtain any service from her."[81] In another case, Jacqueline Chaumont, who was separated from her soldier husband and living alone with her child, was attacked by the *cabaretier* (bar owner) Le Gros *dit* Tendresse, who beat her severely.[82]

The gap between the number of female offenders and victims seems wide, implying a violent climate for women. Yet the Superior Council appears to have been fairly protective of women who came forward with complaints. Several separation suits based on alleged abuse by the husband were judged in the woman's favor, while a trial of an enslaved black woman for infanticide unraveled under the attorney general's scrutiny of the circumstantial evidence, even though the woman had lost consciousness during labor and could not provide her own account of events.[83] Louisiana's low female-to-male ratio in both the slave and free populations may have put women in a more favorable position than they might otherwise have had in the justice system. Because they were both rare and needed, they were considered valuable members of colonial society.

Finally, the sample of reported violence provides strikingly little evidence of conflict between lower class French men and enslaved men, suggesting either that the two groups did not often come into contact or, more likely, that such conflicts did not merit public comment except in extreme cases.

This analysis measures only those acts of violence deemed worthy of censure in the court of public opinion. Everyday acts of disciplinary violence against slaves, wives, children, and other subordinates that did not cross a hazy line of acceptability did not enter into the paper archive. But they can enter the mortuary archive. Physical anthropologists who analyzed the bodies interred at the St. Peter cemetery noticed that two men of African descent had healed "parry fractures" of the forearm, an injury so called because "this fracture often results from using the forearm defensively to ward off a blow."[84]

During excavations at the site of the civilian prison of New Orleans (built on the Place d'Armes in 1730), archaeologists found evidence of an undocumented addition to the prison made in the 1750s.[85] Neither the undocumented nature of the expansion nor its timing is surprising. Most of the stories of crime and punishment in French New Orleans have been lost, either because they took the form of summary justice and everyday violence, or because the criminal record was ultimately deemed less important to public memory than the story of property transfers. Still, from letters, rumors, and reports we can paste together a partial mosaic out of the remaining sherds and see a society experiencing a rising threshold of daily violence—a society that had reason to build a larger prison. We can see a system of justice that shifted its attention from the interests of the king to those of local slaveowners, from experimental punishments that obscured the color line to ones that scored it deeper. The king's justice demonstrated his absolute power over subjects regardless of rank, while the summary justice of Louisiana's slaveowning councilors enforced their own rising status and defended their personal dominion over individual slaves.

❧   ❧   ❧

In *ancien régime* Louisiana, the social experiment of colonial life meant that reputations were contested across all the classes, and increasingly, across an emerging racial divide. Metropolitan ministers had revised the *Code Noir* for Louisiana with the intent of creating a slave society different from that of Saint Domingue, and had banished lawyers from the colony in the hope that free society would be less contentious than in France. The outcomes of these experiments were mixed at best and, in the case of the ban on lawyers, may have had an effect opposite from what was intended. Other areas of colonial administration, such as policing, were simply not planned at all.

In the charter generation, local administrators appointed an African executioner, Louis Congo, who symbolized the near equivalency of black slaves and poor whites before the king's law. But creoles of the next generation began to worry about the fraternizing of slaves and poor Frenchmen, as well as the threat of slave rebellion. They altered their strategy in the 1740s to one in which state punishments exaggerated the differences between black and white bodies, attempting to make the former appear more "savage" by barbaric dismemberment. The increasingly creole-dominated Superior Council also introduced new legislation that amended the *Code Noir* in the interests of slaveholders. In doing so, they stepped outside the powers granted them by the king.

Over the course of the French period, public disorders of one kind or another were a constant source of hearsay headlines in New Orleans. Desertions, soldier mutinies, marauding maroons, Indian uprisings, and political melees among the colony's erstwhile rulers were not figments of the colonial imagination, although they occupied it greatly. Individual disorders in the form of crimes were as much a part of the life of New Orleans as of any other French city or American frontier, but violent encounters were reported in ever increasing frequency over the decades of transition to a creole majority. This reported violence was general, perpetrated by all, and on all, of Louisiana's inhabitants. It occurred both within the ranks of class and color, and across them. However, free French property owners perpetrated more than their share of violent acts. They lashed out against one another, as well as against the enslaved. Social mobility and ambiguous pedigrees had fostered a culture of insult and slander in the founder generation. Struggles over an emerging social hierarchy based on wealth, rather than on noble title and education, fostered a culture of violence in the creole generation. By the late 1730s cases of slander, libel, and insult were giving way to full-blown physical assaults and murders. Ironically, violence became more widespread as the tough old *forçats* faded away, supplanted by forced laborers whose darker skin was also scarred by the brand of the fleur-de-lys. Most of the violence, however, came from above.

Despite their frequent complaints about marauding maroons and insubordinate soldiers, the ways in which creole elites appropriated the state's legal apparatus and usurped the crown's monopoly on violence shows that they themselves were another type of rogue operating in colonial New Orleans. As we will see in the next and final chapter, the line between licit violence and illegitimate power had become so blurred that several leading creole slaveowners serving on the Superior Council were emboldened to think they had a right to set the political agenda. In the 1760s Louisiana became a rogue colony, a run that ended with the lives of these rogue elites before the firing squad in 1769. What had become an established colonial order was suddenly transformed into sedition and treason by a renewed imperial presence in the form of Bourbon Spain.

6

CONCLUSION
Revolt and Rogue Colonialism

Nicolas Chauvin de Lafrénière *fils* (b. 1728) is perhaps the most locally famous of the first-generation creole oligarchy. Born when the effects of the burst Mississippi Bubble were still being felt, but the devastating Natchez War of 1729 had not yet hit, Nicolas grew up in a society undergoing tremendous transition, not least of which was the effective abandonment of the colony by the French crown in the mid-1730s. Despite this imperial retreat, his father apparently valued the multi-generational cultural ties that remained with the metropole, for he sent his teenage son to pursue an education in France. Nicolas Jr. returned at the age of twenty-one to take his deceased father's place on the Louisiana Superior Council in 1749. The Atlantic was no barrier to the now wealthy Chauvin clan. After serving a few years, Nicolas returned to France for additional studies from 1752 to 1755, probably pursuing law. He then returned once again to Louisiana and acceded to the powerful position of attorney general in 1763.

Undoubtedly possessing intellectual gifts, Lafrénière was a transatlantic participant in the Republic of Letters. By the mid-eighteenth century, however, the currents of the Enlightenment had shifted away from the absolutist ideals that had helped design his native city of New Orleans. The burst of proto-scientific enthusiasm for hierarchy, observation, and rationality that had supported Louis XIV and the regency in social engineering and political experiments at home and abroad had lost ground to an increasingly discontented, philosophical, and anti-authoritarian chorus of voices led by Jean-Jacques Rousseau and Denis Diderot. Lafrénière's language shows his exposure to these thinkers during his French education. He is hailed as the leader and hero of a 1768 New Orleans revolt against the transfer to Spanish rule. His leadership was ideological as well as instrumental. Historians credit him with authoring most of the anonymous petitions and manifestos that stoked the revolt with reference to the rights of colonists and the unfair policies of the Bourbon crown. His impassioned speeches demanding the ouster of the "tyrant" Spanish governor are recorded in the minutes of the Louisiana Superior Council. His tirades against tyranny and despotism resonate with the political critiques of monarchy and colonial rule that were to be heard more loudly in the American and French revolutions to follow. Lafrénière's reported nickname, "Louis Quatorze," underscores his extravagant style and imperious self-confidence, ironically deployed against monarchy itself.[1]

Nicolas Lafrénière is an appropriate lead for our final act. He embodies the three elements of colonialism as manifested in eighteenth-century New Orleans that this book has sought to draw out: the role of the Enlightenment, the development of a creole oligarchy, and the influence of rogue agents. These conditions were also key to the making of a revolt.[2] Although the New Orleans uprising was not ultimately successful in throwing off imperial rule, understanding its contours helps place the local story within a broader context of the Atlantic world in the Age of Revolution. Explaining the revolt involves two final tasks: bringing together the arguments made in the foregoing chapters, and expanding upon the idea of rogue colonialism and its implications for our models of colonialism and revolution more generally.

Revolt

On 5 March 1766 Governor Antonio de Ulloa arrived in New Orleans with a small contingent of Spanish soldiers to begin the process of transferring the colony of Louisiana to Spain under the terms of a treaty signed four years earlier. On the dock, local officials reportedly received him indifferently. Over the next year and a half of co-governance, relations between the uptight Ulloa and independent-minded New Orleanians deteriorated. On 29 October 1768 a rowdy crowd gathered in the street outside the *ordonnateur* Foucault's house, which had become the meeting place for the technically defunct but politically active Louisiana Superior Council. Members of the crowd defiantly proclaimed their rejection of the new Spanish order. Someone began a chant exhorting French subjects to reject Catalonian "rotgut" wine. Members of Pierre Marquis's militia were there, too, supporting his call for an independent republic based on the example of his native Switzerland. These increasingly insubordinate rebels had been drinking and carousing since the day before, their numbers swelled by hundreds of German settlers and new Acadian immigrants who had come to town for the occasion.[3] Overnight, unknown vandals had spiked the town's cannons, either to weaken the garrison's ability to suppress the demonstration, or perhaps to keep wilder members of the movement from instigating a bloodbath. The number of colonists in the street who seemed prepared to advance a forceful resolution to the standoff was later estimated at over a thousand.

The Québec-born *ordonnateur* Foucault had joined forces with Louisiana creole Nicolas Chauvin de Lafrénière to resist the terms, if not the intent, of Spanish rule. The two men led the Louisiana Superior Council, Foucault as its presiding judge and Lafrénière as attorney general. Together with other councilors, merchants, and creole planters, they published critiques of Ulloa's policies and doubts about the legitimacy of the transfer. They found a ready audience among the *petits gens* who preferred the *laissez-faire* of French rule to the strictness of Spanish Catholic imperialism. Several pronouncements by Ulloa threatened to restrict customary pastimes, such as Sunday marketing (when slaves from surrounding plantations came to town), gambling, and tavern-going. But the major conflict was clearly over the nature of the local economy. In general decrees Ulloa made clear his intent to clamp down on local smuggling connections. Then, in June 1767, Ulloa impounded a ship called *Nuestra Señora de la Luz* on the charge of smuggling, overriding the Superior Council's permit to the captain to trade freely. Next, Ulloa charged a New Orleans merchant and friend of Lafrénière with dealing in contraband slaves from the Antilles.[4]

On that October day of reckoning, the renegade Council decided it had to do something to appease the crowd it had created, which was now beginning to demand far more than the malcontent merchant-planters had intended. The Council met at Foucault's house to draw up a resolution ratifying several manifestos that had already circulated through the neighborhoods, fresh off the town's new printing press (an enterprise begun by local merchant and smuggler Denis Braud in 1764). Compared to what Marquis's republican rebels wanted, their requests were conservative and entirely self-interested. Four articles of the councilors' petition demanded concessions that would effectively make New Orleans an open, free port. These were (1) that the status quo of "privileges and exemptions" for the colony be maintained; (2) that passports be issued to residents allowing them to go and trade wherever they pleased; (3) that ships of any nation be allowed to enter the river, "according to the custom which has hitherto prevailed"; and (4) that all citizens be granted "the liberty of commerce." They also proclaimed that Ulloa's rule was illegitimate because he had not registered the transfer orders with the Superior Council. He had failed to recognize local power-holders (as they imagined themselves) and local economic interests. As a result, both *les petits* and *les grands* revolted and forced the "tyrannous" Ulloa back onto his ship, bound for Havana.[5]

Louisianans enjoyed nine months of anxious political sovereignty. They had no governor and, while waiting to hear the response to their appeal to the French ministry to take back the colony, they were not even sure to which empire they nominally belonged. The Council had sent Jean Milhet, a wealthy merchant of New Orleans, to Paris as its envoy. But Milhet's request was denied, and with that, France's abandonment of the colony was finally complete. Another sort of response arrived from Spain in July 1769, in the form of a military invasion led by Ulloa's replacement, Governor Alejandro O'Reilly. O'Reilly executed, imprisoned, or exiled the elite revolutionaries, including several members of the Louisiana Superior Council. He granted amnesty to rebel *petits gens* who, he said, had been "led astray" by an ambitious few, most especially the fiery creole Nicolas Lafrénière. The *ordonnateur* Foucault pleaded that his collaboration had been a desperate attempt to placate a violent mob ready to overthrow any form of authority; as he still held an official position recognized by France, O'Reilly sent him back to Paris for reckoning. The man later dubbed "bloody O'Reilly" was harsh with creole revolutionaries. Louisiana's days of rogue colonialism ended when the heirs of its "founding father," the aging Bienville, faced the firing squad. Among those known in popular memory as the "martyrs of 1769" were his second cousin Lafrénière and grand-nephew Jean Baptiste de Noyan *dit* Bienville (nicknamed after his famous uncle).

This picaresque history of colonial New Orleans thus ends on a tragicomic note. Our most arrogant protagonist ends up before the firing squad, a reputed martyr for liberal freedoms who acted like a "Louis Quatorze" of the colonies. The irony of the confused ending, which could be read as either radical revolution or regicide, can only appeal to us in retrospect. The French Revolution was still twenty years away. Indeed, perhaps absolutism did die in the colonies first, in New Orleans in 1769. Did the historical actors view the O'Reilly invasion as the end of an era of French rule, or an alternative future cut short by Bourbon force? What died that day, the past or the future? Although the documents are of little help in answering this, a modest triumph played out in the story allows us, in good picaresque fashion, to question the social order. The people's bacchanal agitation for unrestricted trade in French wine may have been the more significant strain of revolution. The Spanish administration, despite their threats to enforce the orthodoxy of mercantilism, were soon to usher in a significant period of economic and political liberalism, known as the "Bourbon reforms." By the 1780s French wine was once again flowing freely into New Orleans taverns, as did slaves to work the now even wealthier plantations belonging to Lafrénière's heirs. Although ultimately this economic liberalization came too late to save the American colonies, it suggests that European states had learned an important lesson, that permitting liberal *material* rights to their subjects reinforced sovereignty by dampening *ideological* objections to rule.

What would our other lead characters—Marie Hachard, the young Ursuline nun; Father LeMaire, the scientist and satirist; Adrien de Pauger, the city's first engineer; Elizabeth Real, the innkeeper; St. Antoine, the African convert; Louis Congo, the executioner—have made of the Revolt of 1768? One suspects there would not have been a consensus. Marie Hachard would doubtless have been offended by the tavern rowdies and would have approved the Spanish governor's efforts to enforce Sunday Sabbath. Father LeMaire had long ago predicted this scene, the result of a jumbling of the *ancien régime* social hierarchy, and probably would have been smugly amused. He might have been personally interested in keeping up the flow of French wine, and perhaps intrigued by the intellectual justifications for the revolt. Adrien de Pauger, a fierce loyalist and ardent Catholic, would have been torn between French allegiance and the appeal of Spanish conservatism. Only Elizabeth Real actually lived to see this major event in the life of the colony. Clearly, her business depended upon the regular arrival of ship captains and their goods, so she would have been most interested in the Superior Council's efforts to preserve "customary rights" of free trade. Her longevity and prosperity had derived from it. St. Antoine's body is silent on the matter, but if we presume he was a member of the enslaved community, he may have supported the rebels because of the threatened end to the barter trade between plantation and town, which would have interrupted social life and cut off a source of modest economic independence, as well as access to St. Louis Church for Christian slaves. Freedman Louis Congo, a double exile whose services were no longer needed by the time of the revolt, would probably have been indifferent so long as he was left alone to eke out a living as a self-sufficient farmer.

The New Orleans Revolt of 1768 was by no means inevitable. Ulloa could have been more gracious and tolerant of local customs, or the councilors could have decided on a course of compromise. Perhaps it was only the eloquent harangues of the French-educated Lafrénière, or the ability to spread incendiary opinion faster through the printing press, that pushed the weight of circumstance toward a dramatic event. The revolt, however, did bring several realities of New Orleans society to the surface. On that day in October, as throughout the French period, administrators struggled to control activities on the street that their own designs had engendered. In the founder period, most of these designs had emanated from French ministers and engineers. In the creole period, they were local inventions.

During the heady days of the John Law scheme, French imperial designers had experimented with new methods of residential segregation and social recordkeeping that are striking in their precocious modernity. By the mid-1730s a new generation of creole-born New Orleans merchants and planters, some from humble (or even criminal) backgrounds, had begun to take over the reins of the colonial experiment. With the aid of sympathetic or coopted French officials, they went about restructuring the social, economic, and legal order of the colony to advance local interests—namely, slaveholding and unrestricted trade. These local interests did not necessarily coincide with those of the king, be he French or Spanish. The emerging creole oligarchy itself then struggled to control runaway slaves, soldiers, and upstart traders in a climate that continued to encourage physical and social mobility, and a degree of individualism. The oligarchy's tenuous hold on the colony revealed itself in the mob of 1,000 settlers (about one-third of the population of New Orleans) that spiked the cannons and caroused in the streets that day. What went through the minds of those who participated in the street demonstrations has largely drifted away in unrecorded memory, though minimally we know they were ready to defend their access to markets and taverns—locales of contraband bartering and unsegregated sociability.

Dissecting the anatomy of the Revolt of 1768 reveals that it was composed of at least three different sociopolitical interest groups: elite merchant-planters, represented by the Superior Council; yeoman farmers from the largely German-speaking and crypto-Protestant area just upriver from New Orleans; and the town's diverse *petits gens*, consisting of artisans, soldiers, sailors, laborers, and small-business owners. We can learn something of the role of the first group from the documents, but we have to reconstruct the roles of the other two groups from whispers and innuendoes in the archives. Still, we can make some general observations on what united these groups and also what divided them. These factors can be traced back to the conditions under which the colony was founded.

Two major factors united these sectors of the colony—the economy and a climate of relative social tolerance for free people. Since the 1730s New Orleans had developed as a de facto port of free trade in the absence of crown enforcement. The licit though illegal smuggling economy that linked New Orleanians to Mexico, the Anglo-American seaboard, and the Caribbean islands benefited the very rich as well as the very poor. Transshipments of French luxury goods for Spanish silver benefited merchant-planters. Employment in the local transportation sector and possibilities for petty trading benefited the laboring classes. And this advantage was not restricted to the legally free. Slaves and maroons played active roles in the distribution system between the colonial port and its hinterland. Some bought their freedom with their proceeds and moved into the city's multi-hued back-of-town neighborhood. The social mobility (some have called it "chaos") of the founder period did not continue unchecked. As discussed in chapter 4, a local hierarchy did develop. But overall, the physical mobility and diversity of the local population established a setting that confounded segregationist policies and obscured inherited status. These same conditions, combined with a lack of policing, weakened state controls on religious practice and morality.

Thus, the new Spanish administration intended to clamp down upon what New Orleanians had come to view as their "customary" rights and practices of free trade, quiet religious tolerance, and urban entertainments, such as drinking and gambling. As one appalled Spanish observer reported to his superiors after arriving in the city: "The principal thing about them is their habit or manner of conducting themselves, in which a libertinage and dissipation not only reigns here, it is admired, but would stun us in Spain."[6]

Also customary was a flexible approach to race and social status that the incoming Spanish administration found confusing and unacceptable. Although this customary practice might have served the interests of those among the elite creole oligarchy with Indian or African-descended kin, as well as those of the *petits gens* scrambling against any color restrictions on their rights as French subjects, slavery was clearly a fault line that separated the three major groups in the Revolt of 1768. The elite were major investors in the system; the yeoman farmers tended to be small slaveholders whose practices were often at odds with those of the major planters (and in truth they could do without slavery if needed); and most of the *petits gens* were nonslaveholders or escapees of the system. Slavery, however, is conspicuous by its absence as an issue in the revolt, probably because it was the issue most likely to fracture the fragile coalition between a "cabal" and a "mob." The Spanish trade restrictions announced by Ulloa threatened to cut off the colony's major sources for new slaves, acquired through intercolonial smuggling. Yet the military muscle that the Spanish usually lent their colonies may have appealed to owners concerned over the depredations of maroons and the threat of slave rebellion. The preservation of slavery may have been a major factor in the capitulation of most of the merchant-planters upon Alejandro O'Reilly's arrival. He appears to have calculated this in full, as "the new governor seemed to have adopted a policy of silence, permitting the massive acquisition of slaves from foreign ships."[7]

Although O'Reilly granted pardon to *petits gens* who had demonstrated in the streets, it is unlikely he was seeking a political alliance with them against the merchant-planters. Rather, his select punishment of just a few elite hotheads reasserted the natural partnership of wealth and government. He knew the Atlantic world well enough to realize that the mobility of the port town's underclass meant that if they did not like Spanish policies, they would simply move on. This is one of the major paradoxes we must add to our understanding of "the many-headed hydra," as Linebaugh and Rediker term the maritime working class.[8] The same mobility that made nationalist loyalty weak among sailors, traders, and tavern-goers (and thus made them prone to revolt) meant that they were rarely invested enough in any particular place to carry through with full-scale revolution. Revolution requires the collaboration of a group rooted to the land—be they large property owners or enslaved peasants working provision plots.

The impossibly strict economic policies of the Company of the Indies in the founder generation had helped spur contraband trade as a means of survival. This intercolonial commerce fostered a far-reaching social and cultural network and carved out a niche of relative independence from the greater Atlantic. The willingness of New Orleans to tolerate, or even perpetuate, a reputation for "disorder" actually served as a sort of signpost to traders, announcing that the port was open for business. As seen in the legal records of New Orleans dealing with trade in Veracruz and Havana, word got around within the maritime world about which ports were difficult or easy to enter, which had vigilant officials, and what bribes or strategies were customary. The reputation of New Orleans as a wild town where the rule of law was weak attracted just the right sort of people to keep trade favorable. The imposition of a Spanish custom house was viewed with dread, if only for its effects upon the town's reputation.

The theme of "disorder" operated on more levels than the economic, but it is important not to become too enchanted with it. It describes a local aesthetic, but explains little about New Orleans, then or now. "Disorder" was a trope repeated throughout various forms of literature and letter-writing related to Louisiana, and it has come to dominate images of New Orleans and its French colonial past. *Désordre* was a pervasive preoccupation of Enlightenment France, a term applied to so many aspects of daily life and public culture that it becomes difficult to have faith in its specificity. Eighteenth-century France was itself a "libertine" and "disorderly" society according to its own internal critics. In the imperial context, "disorder" could be an epithet defining the tensions between colony and metropole, between colonizer and colonized, and between creole and newcomer. One could say all colonial societies and slave societies are naturally prone to "disorder." They were difficult societies to govern, or to socially engineer. Complaints of disorder reflect the difficulty of ruling over great distances and over diverse peoples. Conflicts often followed the unsettling of social hierarchies entailed in colonization and immigration. The subsequent evolution of slavery produced (and required) gaping inequalities between slave and free, and between slaveholder and nonslaveholder, contributing to a climate of every-day violence, competition, and seething resentment. A peaceful, "orderly" slave society is an oxymoron. Although the static order/disorder trope adds little to our understanding of the kind of place New Orleans was becoming in the French period, it does suggest the need to place the town within the language and context of the Enlightenment.

New Orleans was both a product of, and a participant in, Enlightenment intellectual culture. This backwater port was an outpost of the Republic of Letters, as seen in the writings of its local *philosophes* and historians, and as seen in its observatories, laboratories, and libraries. Frenchmen and French-women came to Louisiana to collect bird feathers, describe Native American customs, conduct agronomical tests, and observe the development of the colonial experiment itself. They sent reams of reports and letters back to France that were digested and published as chapters in an accumulated, encyclopedic work of colonial *histoire*. These chapters, especially those that described the failings of Louisiana, became reference material for later im-perial efforts.

I have attempted to show the creative—and fundamentally experimen-tal—processes that went into making a new colonial society. These pro-cesses fall into two categories: idealized designs imposed by the metropole and practical solutions invented by diverse local actors. In the case of New Orleans, these categories can be characterized as rationalist absolutism and creole improvisation (or *mētis*). I have argued that the role of Enlighten-ment rationality in engineering the city in its physical, economic, and so-cial dimensions, followed by the rapid establishment of a local creole so-ciety after 1731, were major factors defining the character of New Orleans during the French regime. The original sketches drawn for New Orleans in the 1710s and early 1720s represent an experiment in colonialism that paralleled, and formed a piece of, Enlightened absolutism in France dur-ing the period of the Great Confinement. These efforts were characterized by a hyper-rationalizing effort to describe, classify, cleanse, segregate, and reorganize society according to emerging philosophical and scientific prin-ciples. Enlightened absolutism met its own obstacles in France, a struggle eventually resulting in the Revolution of 1789. But in Louisiana implemen-tation required the cooperation of a population of Canadians, Africans, Native Americans, poor Frenchmen, German Protestants, Swiss mercenar-ies, Irish privateers, Caribbean Jews, and creoles of every stripe who either lacked the cultural referents to understand the intended plan, or simply pre-ferred to improvise their own version of town life.

The original plans for New Orleans were ambitious, but they were also self-consciously experimental, reflecting a spirit of inquiry and a practical desire for knowledge. These impulses similarly characterized the social movement of the Enlightenment, which was above all a belief in intellectual solutions to worldly problems. These currents can be seen at work in the street plan for New Orleans, which represented the latest thinking in the nascent discipline of urban planning. The plans for New Orleans reflect elements of four idealized types of cities in *ancien régime* France: the fortified town, the commercial port, the garden city, and the monumental city. The city's rational and transparent street design was expected to prevent the "foul stench" of urban poverty and squalor.

The John Law mercantile experiment was an even more grandiose scheme designed to facilitate royal control, in which New Orleans played a significant part. By tying private stockholders to the public treasury, Law thought he could better manage the trade monopolies that enriched the crown. Law actively recruited noble investors, working to remove the stigma of commercial activity and to expand the social base of capitalism. New Orleans began in 1718 as a company town belonging to the Company of the Indies. Its port was to be the bottleneck through which all exports and imports would be monitored, to the benefit of the Company and the crown.

Other ministers of the king engaged in deliberate social engineering as they developed immigration policies and legal codes for Louisiana. They hoped to design a colonial society free of some of the conflicts endemic to French society. They eliminated both venality and seigneurial titles in Louisiana, limiting growth of the troublesome noble class. To quell unrest in the courts, they barred lawyers from the colony. In the early days of immigrant recruitment, Louisiana became part of the grander plan to rid France of vagabonds, criminals, and those without a verifiable identity. The *bandouliers du Mississippi* rounded up the unfortunates and shipped them to the colony as forced exiles. More than just a plan to rid France of pests, to some administrators the colonial experience was a way to provide these individuals with an opportunity for personal reform—a new approach to criminality at the time. "Enlightened" colonialism involved not only new and sometimes experimental designs for social engineering, but also new methods of social control. Early Louisiana administrators conducted some of the most detailed door-to-door censuses of the early modern era that attempted to fix the name, status, and location of colonial immigrants. Planners also attempted to control the diverse elements of the colonial population with architectural segregation. Africans were to be housed entirely apart from Europeans, and Europeans themselves were segregated in separate barracks, taverns, and settlements according to their French, Swiss, or German background, as well as their religious persuasion. The city was originally intended to be a white enclave. White/black distinctions were built into the French design of New Orleans through the *Code Noir* of 1724, modified especially for Louisiana. Sections of the code positioned the government as a mediator between the powers of the slaveholder and the limited rights of the enslaved so that the relationship would remain orderly and law-abiding. These elements of Enlightenment rationality serving absolutism played a role in making New Orleans.

But few of the plans and experiments designed for Louisiana worked out. Some were poorly conceived for the terrain, while others were resisted by the players—frequently characterized as rogues and scoundrels—who were supposed to enact them. A major source of French disappointment in New Orleans was its failure to realize the idealized plans created for it, or to respond in a predictable manner. If local residents had only cooperated, Louisiana could have been a *better* society than France. As a matter of survival in the early difficult years, New Orleanians of all ranks had to adapt to variables planners had not anticipated—from a raging river to the military superiority of Native Americans. Local deviations and creole innovations contributed to a metropolitan view of "disorder," although these adaptations may have been quite rationally suited to local conditions. For example, not until the end of the French period did local administrators finally build a version of the fortified walls that French engineers had drawn on dozens of plans for the city. Instead, throughout much of the French period, the cityscape of New Orleans was characterized by back-to-back "minifortresses" of individual lots completely enclosed by staked fences. It did not make sense for residents to invest heavily in joint defenses against external enemies because the city was already well protected by its difficult navigational approach. Internal foes—jealous neighbors or hungry cows—were more of a concern, and thus gave rise to the ubiquitous private fences.

As in France, the imposition of the Company monopoly spurred smuggling. In New Orleans, where the king and the Company had few representatives and where survival depended upon finding reliable suppliers, smuggling by individuals soon outstripped state-monopolized contraband trade with the Spanish colonies. Smuggling helped integrate New Orleans into the economy of the greater Caribbean. It also helped knit social and cultural ties to other port cities, such as Veracruz, Havana, and St. Pierre in Martinique. Trade between plantation and city brought together slaves, runaways, and poorer Frenchmen in New Orleans taverns to conduct their business, although colonial regulations constantly fretted over the commerce of these "vagrants" and "rogues." By the mid-1730s recorded ship arrivals were climbing steadily. Between 70 percent and 80 percent of this traffic cycled within the Mississippi-Caribbean region. The transatlantic trade constituted a small (though still important) minority of the city's shipping connections. It is true that Louisiana returned little to the metropole on its official trade balance, but most traders in town devoted themselves to a regional intercoastal trade that had little regard for the precepts of mercantilism. Between 1731 and 1769 New Orleans basically acted as a free port, protected by a syndicate of intermarried merchant-planters who controlled the Louisiana Superior Council and enjoyed the indulgence of pragmatic Canadian and French governors, who themselves enjoyed considerable profits from the trade.

The crown policies that shaped the peculiar profile of Louisiana's population had unintended consequences. The proportions of Canadian, African, and European immigrants created a more balanced heterogeneity in the founder generation than was the case in any other French colony, or indeed most Spanish or British colonies. Within the ranks of Europeans, immigrants arrived with widely different legal statuses, from convicts (*forçats*) to apostate refugees, vagabond soldiers, indentured servants (*engagés*), noble adventurers, and entrepreneurial bureaucrats. Immigration was then virtually cut off between 1731 and the 1760s, encouraging the relatively rapid formation of a creole society with a strong local identity. But it was a creole society with a malleable and uncertain hierarchy of class and color. By eliminating seigneurial titles as well as venality in Louisiana, ministers wanted to discourage the "ennobling" of upwardly mobile merchants and bourgeois professionals. Rather than slowing social mobility, however, this strategy seems to have had an individualizing effect that actually accelerated social climbing for many New Orleanians. Noble titles became more fashion than substance. Immigrants of both noble and common backgrounds (including some from the ranks of forced exiles and *engagés*) competed against one another for membership in an emerging merchant-planter elite defined by wealth and slaveholding. The clever entrepreneur could "buy" his or her way into this class without the benefit of family name or the politics of patronage. Self-fashioning tactics, such as the adoption of noble-sounding titles and obscured genealogies, contributed to the phenomenon of the self-made colonial elite. The process of new class formation was accompanied by acrimonious and at times violent contestation, as seen in the sample of surviving criminal records and defamation cases. For most of the French period, the colonial elite of New Orleans was a group bitterly divided about the terms of membership.

However, when the second creole generation came of age in the 1750s, endogamous marriage patterns among large slaveholding families and a system that betrothed metropolitan officials to wealthy local daughters began to close the doors on social mobility. As urban slavery grew in importance, a new social ladder emerged, with four basic rungs. The highest (*les grands*) bound together major merchant-planters with public officials and a small number of French-born noble military officers. The rest of the population (*les petits*) were divided by their relationship to slavery—small slaveholders, nonslaveholders, and slaves.

Along the dimension of race, metropolitan planners had legislated a basic division of *blanc* and *noir* in the *Code Noir* of 1724, but New Orleanians in the French period almost never used these terms in their censuses or legal documents. The special diversity of its founder population—more Indian than the West Indies, more African than New France, and in some ways more Canadian than French—made simple black/white duality a particularly poor fit. Planners had intended New Orleans to be a white enclave, but the local development of urban slavery and the opportunism of Native Americans, free people of color, and runaways attracted to the town soon erased any schemes for racial segregation. New Orleans households became increasingly diverse over the French period. Although the differences between slave and free were undeniable in colonial Louisiana, locals seem not to have viewed these different forms of legal status as clearly paralleling a classification scheme based on skin color or heredity. Early New Orleanians appear instead to have classified free people using first a hierarchy of legal statuses that ranked individuals according to their degree of servitude. In the creole period, this attention to legal status was gradually superseded by a mental map of local kinship and status, in which the background and position of free French fathers appears to have been at least as important as the color of African and Indian mothers. In the censuses, *français* and *habitant* were inclusive categories defining the legally free subject, without reference to ethnic origin or racial identification. Racial ideas were beginning to emerge more clearly in the second half of the century, but it still appears that legal and social status trumped color in the social order. As a result, the size of the French-period population called *gens de couleur libres* (a term invented under the more color-conscious regime of the Spanish) has been seriously underestimated.

Still, the local administration of justice indicates that ideas about the legal status of slaves were shifting under the creole regime. A freed African man, Louis Congo, served as the colony's public executioner for many years in early New Orleans. His services were used against Africans, Europeans, and Indians equally, and these offenders appear to have received similar punishments for similar crimes. Although Congo hardly had an enviable position, his status did seem to enhance his usefulness as a social leveler before the power of the state. With the rise of the creole merchant-planters in the 1730s, differential treatment of enslaved and free criminals began to appear, with slaves receiving more exemplary punishments in an atmosphere of spectacle. Outside of capital cases, however, local officials declined to enforce the provisions of the *Code Noir* that required the Superior Council to mediate between slaveowner and slave in the application of corporal discipline. The king's power over enslaved subjects was largely delegated to individual slaveholders, who monopolized the means of violence and practiced their own form of despotism.

The sum of these local facts means that the Revolt of 1768 represented an expressive convulsion of the forces of Enlightenment planning, creole *mētis*, and rogue colonialism. The movement arose in part from tensions imported from the *ancien régime* between ambitions for rationalist social engineering and conditions of greater social mobility—some of the same tensions that eventually led to the French Revolution. Thus, Louisiana saw the rapid rise of creoles to positions of political influence within the colonial administration, many of whom did not entirely forget their humble local roots and resented the airs of metropolitan appointees. Like the American Revolution a few years later, the New Orleans movement was a creole revolt propagated by local elites proclaiming a desire for free trade, a custom that had arisen out of economic necessity. The spark that ignited the revolt was actually an ember that had been nurtured since Louisiana's founding—the entrepreneurship of its colonial leaders and rogue agents. New Orleans was built by forces represented by three archetypes—the engineer, the creole, and the rogue. Each had a part to play in revolt, the next stage of development in the political economy of smuggling.

Historians Franklin Knight and Peggy Liss observe that throughout the Atlantic in the second half of the eighteenth century, "the device once seen as preserving imperial isolation—a monopoly of trade—now appears as a spur to the contraband that was accompanied by great transcultural contact." These contacts helped foment the American revolutions of the late eighteenth and early nineteenth centuries. To a great degree, the revolutions that swept the Caribbean in the 1790s, including the spectacular events in Haiti, began as movements to legitimize the economic independence of merchant-planters. When slaves took over these revolutions, they triumphed over their rogue rulers, but not to the benefit of the imperial state. They represented a third element in the volatile balance of colonial power.[9]

New Orleanians' contacts with other discontented colonials and masterless maroons in the Mississippi-Caribbean world brought ideas into the port that made the revolt imaginable. Their own native roguishness did, too. The reason eighteenth-century smuggling could crack open the political hegemony of empires is suggested by analysis of transnational flows today: "individuals and social groups that systematically contest or bypass state controls do not simply flout the letter of the law; with repeated transgressions over time, they bring into question the legitimacy of the state itself by questioning the state's ability to control its own territory."[10] By the time of the 1768 New Orleans Revolt, the legitimacy of Bourbon rule in Louisiana had long since been eroded by local practices. The instigators of the revolt simply crumbled the final pieces with an ideological argument that became the premise of revolutions throughout the Atlantic. It was a proclamation that colonial actors were not operating illegitimately or illicitly. Rather, the sovereignty claimed by the metropolitan state was illegitimate because it abrogated the rights and needs of its distant subjects.

Rogue Colonialism

New Orleans contributes to our understanding of colonialism in a particularly historical way, and in a more global way. The town was launched at a critical juncture in the early eighteenth century when ministers were taking a new, scholarly approach to refine strategies of rule and expand the power of the state. New Orleans was in many ways an Enlightenment experiment in which recognized tools of modern colonialism (urban planning, census-taking, natural histories, ethnographies, mapping, new criminalities, and the control of subordinates through sentiment) were under development. Such experiments in social engineering and Enlightened absolutism often failed, but the lessons derived from the famous failure of New Orleans and the Mississippi Bubble informed later colonial efforts in the nineteenth and early twentieth centuries.

The metropolitan blueprints for New Orleans represent failed experiments in early modernism. The archival impact of their idealized designs and associated data-gathering can tempt us into a false sense of clarity, preventing us from seeing more complex—and more effective—forces of colonialism. Officially endorsed maps, reports, and legal intentions have a way of obscuring the significant role played by agents who acted beyond the reach of the state and its clerical pens, or who acted in its name, but not necessarily in its interests. Their plans were not often written down in bold and incriminating ink, although snippets of correspondence can reveal their intentions and dealings.

Louisiana's very existence as an imperial project owes more to self-interested entrepreneurs such as La Salle, Cadillac, Law, and the LeMoyne brothers than to initiatives conceived within the chambers of Versailles. Without their lobbying of French ministers, it is doubtful that French interest in acquiring Louisiana as a bulwark against British expansion on the continent would have been keen enough to launch the endeavor. The argument rested on the tenuous assumption that Canada was worth protecting, a questionable premise given both the decline of the fur trade and the low opinion of *that* colony in the eyes of the French public (its reputed licentiousness and pathetic mercantile returns would be forgotten only under the shadow of Louisiana's more spectacular failures). Textbook versions of Louisiana history cite the diplomatic and strategic reasons for its establishment by the French. However, the biggest boosters of the colonial project focused on the possibilities of riches for themselves, and secondarily for the treasury. Certainly, their petitions to the court exploited the strategic political significance of the new territory within the French empire. But their actions suggest that the rhetoric was motivated by their own economic self-interest and social aspirations: they skimmed profits from the Indian trade; used the king's ships to conduct their own business; "redistributed" goods from the Company and military stores at exorbitant prices; sought licenses for private monopolies and noble titles for personal glory; assigned themselves and their loyal followers immense land grants; and set up camp along lucrative trade routes through which they brazenly engaged in contraband trade and privateering. Their sincere investment in French sovereignty is questionable, and in fact was questioned by many of their contemporaries. The "founders" of Louisiana came from a culture of military privateers and *coureurs de bois* whose livelihoods depended upon the violation of imperial law.[11]

This phenomenon of "rogue colonialism" was not unique to Louisiana. Placing New Orleans in a comparative context underscores its value as a conversation piece about the nature of colonialism and its relationship to forms of government we consider "modern." In these final pages, I will sketch out the main strands of this conversation, and also state more definitively what I mean by *rogue colonialism* and why I find it a useful idea.

My reading of early New Orleans as provided in the foregoing chapters echoes some themes in James C. Scott's work on modern state practices of "legibility" that use censuses, agronomy, and urban planning in attempts to engineer societies and economies.[12] The New Orleans example shows how colonies, particularly those designed and launched under the influence of Enlightened absolutism, served as laboratories where many of these technologies of rule were first tried out. Like Scott's examples of Brasília's urban plan and Soviet agricultural collectivization, most of the original engineering plans for the colony of Louisiana and the town of New Orleans "failed" by the measure of their own utopian ambitions. But unlike Scott's examples, Louisiana and New Orleans "succeeded" by the measure of their own adaptations.

The "early modernism" of Louisiana's colonialism was different from Scott's "high modernism" in an important way: it demanded local knowledge and allowed for major adjustments. Scott attributes large-scale social disasters to several factors, one of which is the disregard for *mētis*, or "practical knowledge, informal processes, and improvisation in the face of unpredictability."[13] In the colonial setting of Louisiana in the eighteenth century, the state's dramatic failure did not perpetrate the same human hardship or suffering that Scott identifies with more "muscle-bound" forms of late modernism, although the short-term consequences of the Mississippi Bubble were tragic. The experimental and encyclopedic impulses of the Enlightenment encouraged the *gathering* of local knowledge rather than its suppression, as well as a willingness to tinker with methods. Thus, when the grand agronomical plan for Louisiana failed (sugar and tobacco were difficult to grow and largely unprofitable in the French period), with encouragement from their correspondents in the metropole, colonists experimented with indigo, silk, wax myrtle, and rice. They found that indigo and rice were much better suited to local conditions, and the colonial economy adjusted accordingly. The original John Law plan did not include importation of African slaves, but within eight years this drastic redesign was approved in response to the demands of settlers. Another important adjustment, of course, was the "informal process" of provisioning that evolved into a full-fledged smuggling economy. The setting of Louisiana demanded many improvisational adjustments to the plan: levees and footbridges to adapt to the Mississippi's unpredictable spills, a flexible social hierarchy that accommodated mixed-race children and useful "rogues" like seafaring felons, and a justice system that expanded the power of slaveowners well beyond the king's edicts.

A legacy for scholars of modernism is the question of why and when states stopped learning from their subjects. The New Orleans example informs the present in interesting ways. New Orleans in the Enlightenment was created through a combination of rationalist planning and experimental *mētis*. But by the time of Scott's late nineteenth-century and early twentieth-century examples, state hubris—that is, faith in centrally controlled, "scientific" planning that inflexibly disregards local knowledge—was fully developed. Although many of the problems of modernity are traced back to the Enlightenment, some of its more positive features, such as an openness to new forms of knowledge, have been forgotten. One reason may be that this same experimental questioning allowed rogue colonialism to flourish, which in turn undermined the legitimacy and sovereignty of the state.

I expect that the phrases *rogue colonialism* and *rogue colony* might conjure up another term current in contemporary political vocabulary—the *rogue state*. These are three different ideas, though not unrelated. First coined in the 1970s, the term *rogue state* has enjoyed recent popularity attributable to its use by President Bill Clinton's national security adviser Anthony Lake, as a replacement for the Cold War–era *outlaw nation*. It was originally used in foreign policy circles to identify nation-states that held themselves to be immune from international law and presented a significant threat to minorities within their borders, to the stability of their region, and/or to the global order (for example, through the violation of human rights or the development of weapons of mass destruction). Both supporters and detractors of the term *rogue state* (which has since been replaced in the George W. Bush administration by *terrorist states* or *axis of evil*) agree that as used in policy circles, it identifies polities that have little regard for U.S. interests or diplomatic efforts. Prominent critics, such as Noam Chomsky, William Blum, and Jacques Derrida, have pointed out that under a "neutral" definition (defined outside policy circles), the United States is the preeminent "rogue state" in the early twenty-first century due to its military unilateralism; its disregard for the World Court and major international treaties, such as the Kyoto accords; its interference in the sovereign affairs of its Latin American neighbors; and the devastating effects of its domestic policies on minorities, particularly African Americans.[14]

Rogue colonies are like rogue states in their disregard for law and legitimacy, but instead of international law, it is the law of their own parent empire that they disregard. Examples of other rogue colonies, where local administrators or military functionaries acted with a remarkable degree of independence, if not seditious intent, include seventeenth-century Rhode Island, seventeenth-century Tortuga, eighteenth-century Uruguay, early nineteenth-century Nicaragua, Texas during its bid for independence, and even twentieth-century Taiwan from the perspective of mainland China. It is not uncommon for wars of independence to be preceded by a period of roguishness. French colonial Louisiana was not a rogue colony in this political sense until the late creole period of the 1750s and 1760s when the Superior Council adopted legislative powers for itself and then rejected Bourbon authority in an outward revolt. But by that point, it was a functioning political entity operating largely outside French law and executive mandate. Locally, Louisiana's political independence was licit though illegal, in that the legally defunct Superior Council enjoyed the general approval of public opinion, or at least that of the three diverse groups that demonstrated in the Revolt of 1768—merchant-planters, yeoman farmers, and the city's laboring freemen. It is significant that the merchant-planter creole oligarchy had assumed for itself not only law-making powers, but a monopoly on violence. This is another way to define a rogue colony—one that *acts like* an independent state.

However, the conditions of imperial isolation, ineptitude, and/or indifference that allowed *rogue colonies* to arise were not nearly so common as a more general phenomenon of *rogue colonialism*, a concept that I find more compelling and important. To explain the difference, a colony is the territorial unit politically subsumed by an outside nation-state or imperial center. The political leaders of a rogue colony do not recognize this hierarchical relationship, or in significant ways they act as if it does not exist. *Colonialism*, however, defines not just the technical facts of political and territorial hegemony, but the ideologies and practices of daily life in the colonies. In its broadest sense, colonialism is synonymous with dominant colonial culture. Following these definitions, Louisiana enjoyed a brief period as a rogue colony toward the end of the French period, but rogue colonialism was a significant factor from the beginning. My argument is that the dominant culture of some colonies, and significant minority strains within others, could be characterized by "roguishness." But this begs the next question—what is a "rogue" and what do I mean by "roguishness"?

When first recorded in the mid-sixteenth century in English, *rogue* originally meant "vagrant," but also an "independent beggar" (a connotation particularly resonant with the abandoned victims of the Mississippi Bubble). Soon this was criminalized, so that *rogue* became synonymous with "scoundrel," or a deliberately dishonest person.[15] For my purposes, I embrace both meanings. Thus, rogues can be vagrants whose origin and status are uncertain (a very common colonial condition), and/or they can be those who knowingly violate the law in pursuit of their own interests—in this case, especially those codes and blueprints meant to govern a colony. One finds rogue colonialism where rogues of either kind exert significant influence upon the moral, political, and economic life of the colony. Their influence is significant in the degree to which their identities and activities are viewed as licit, meaning socially acceptable. Rogues can be found both at the top of the colony's order and at the bottom. Given the great social mobility possible in colonial situations such as French New Orleans, we must also watch for their movement through the ranks.

Many of the actors who made up the settler colony of French Louisiana were identified by their own countrymen as "vagrants" and "beggars." Even if they did not originate from the prisons of Paris as forced exiles, the very fact of their immigration from Europe, Canada, Africa, or other parts of the Americas made their identity less fixed, less known, less "legible." This is one reason that modern census-taking seems to have originated in the colonies. From the perspective of the metropole, many of Louisiana's inhabitants, whatever their social and economic status, were under suspicion of being wandering "rogues."

The colonial undertaking offered both the individual subject and the state the possibility of a blank slate, though this shared condition caused more conflict than commonality. The uncertainty it produced contributed to the bitter rumor-mongering, defamation, and political libel to which Louisiana's elite seemed especially prone. In the founding period, leaders of the colonial venture were clearly out for their own ends, which meant that their allegiance to the state was often doubted. Iberville and Bienville knew that the Gulf Coast presented an excellent opportunity to intercept Spanish silver. Although they, along with La Salle, argued for Louisiana's potential to contribute to the treasury via this means, probably few in Versailles or Paris were naive as to their personal motivations in pushing this agenda. Rather, in real-politik terms, colonialism was a marriage of convenience between empires and rogues. The ups and downs in the careers of men such as Bienville reflect their dual reputations as "criminal despots" and highly effective colonial leaders. Bienville was recalled and then reinstated three times. This ambivalence on the part of the court demonstrates that the illegal methods Bienville employed were public knowledge, but that some ministers also found them indispensable. This relationship is not such an unusual one. As Itty Abraham and Willem van Schendel note in their overview of smuggling and globalization: "Historically the boundary of illicitness has shifted back and forth as bandits helped make states and states made bandits."[16]

Charles Tilly goes further in questioning any philosophical distinction at all between "state making" and organized crime. He says that "banditry, piracy, gangland rivalry, policing and war making all belong to the same continuum," which produced the modern nation-state as essentially a protection racket against these competing sources of depredation and violence. He identifies "the long love-hate affair between aspiring state makers and pirates or bandits" as precariously balanced on their "shared right to use violence" and the "elastic line between 'legitimate' and 'illegitimate' violence."[17] The geographical relationship between banditry and state making is more complex in the colonial situation than in the examples of European nations and their bandit-patrolled borders. However, we often see imperial states insert themselves between slaves and owners, or natives and settlers, in the same "protection racket" mode Tilly describes for governments operating between bandits and citizens. In the colonial situation, slaves/owners and natives/settlers were groups bound together in a standoff of mutual fear and threatened blood feud. States made gestures, through treaties and slave laws such as the *Code Noir*, that claimed to offer protection to both sides. This racket, which in part was motivated by a desire to ensure the return of revenues from plantations and pelts, necessitated the continuation of hostilities. Otherwise, the long-distant state would become irrelevant to those living in the colonies. But the protection the state could offer in remote colonies was logistically limited. As a result, falling back on bandits and mercenaries to deploy the means of violence or "protection" was all the more common. In Louisiana, where the military was chronically undersupplied and colonial planners failed to provide a police force, the distinction between rogue agents and state agents carried little meaning. Rogue agents held the reins of the Louisiana experiment from the beginning.

The original justification for the annexation of Louisiana and the building of New Orleans was not so much what the French state had to gain, but the fact that it did not have anything to lose by permitting the political entrepreneurship of ambitious adventurers. If they succeeded, France gained territories and revenues; if they failed, it lost only the cost of its worst soldiery (as chronic deserters and the infirm were usually sent to the colonies) and diplomatic expenses such as gifts for Indian nations (complaints to the contrary, a drop in the Versailles bucket). In this sense, the metropolitan endorsement of certain colonial projects resembled nothing so much as privateering—granting legitimacy to an activity already being conducted by private adventurers, in the name of geopolitical advancement. Thomas Gallant calls these types of men "military entrepreneurs"—men who "operating on both sides of the law significantly contributed to the formation of states in the modern world." He explains that "in situations where a central government, imperial or otherwise, was unable to impose a monopoly of violence over the means of coercion, there was a propensity for a class of men at arms whom I have called military entrepreneurs to develop."[18]

The French state's inability to impose a monopoly of violence upon either its free or enslaved subjects in Louisiana was among its most spectacular and consequential failures. In the founder generation, Governor Bienville was the dominant military entrepreneur, but he was surrounded, and often challenged, by like-minded men such as Cadillac, the Chauvin brothers, Denys St. Denis, and the rake Dumont de Montigny. In the creole generations, the force of violence shifted from the hands of these charismatic (and often ruthless) self-made men to a more anonymous creole oligarchy. The power vacuum created with de facto French abandonment of the colony in the 1730s was filled by members of an emerging class of merchant-planters who held commissions as militia commanders and whose daughters regularly married high-ranking French military officers. Both generations of colonial leaders may be thought of as rogues, or military entrepreneurs, but the founders resembled a loose group of bandits while the creoles resembled members of an organized crime syndicate.

The influential historian Eric Hobsbawm argues that the legitimate monopolization of violence by the state (an idea advanced by Weber) is a relatively recent phenomenon. He identifies it as a characteristic of the modern nation-state that evolved in tandem with, and eventually subsumed,

y. He defines "social bandits" as "peasant outlaws whom the lord
ite regard as criminals, but who remain within peasant society, and
nsidered by their people as heroes, as champions, avengers, fight-
r justice, perhaps even leaders of liberation, and in any case as men
admired, helped and supported." In Louisiana, the rogues who pro-
p‿‿d the Revolt of 1768 were *not* Hobsbawm's bandits. Neither military
entrepreneurs nor carousing urban *petits gens* qualify under his definition.
The only group that comes close are the marooned slaves who harassed the
perimeter of New Orleans, many of whom were probably viewed by the enslaved peasantry of the plantation belt as heroes and avengers. We have no
indication that they participated in the Revolt of 1768, nor evidence of what
their ideas about it might have been.[19]

The elite military entrepreneurs, however, fit another archetype proposed by Hobsbawm, that of the "robber barons." These were noble or self-
ennobled plunderers who amounted to "little more than officially licensed
bullies with a pedigree." The colonial association of his two examples seals
the match: Spanish conquistadors and Alexandre Dumas's Musketeers. The
rogue colonialism of Cortés, Pizarro, and even the Columbus clan in the
early colonization of the New World consisted of obtaining ex post facto
authorization for pillaging expeditions and one-man empires. While this
characterization of the conquistadors will not surprise anyone with a passing knowledge of Latin American history, a conceit exists that this strain
of rogue colonialism was limited to the early centuries of exploration and
piracy, or to Spanish military entrepreneurs who earned their home country
the "black legend" of colonial history. But robber barons and rogue colonialism could (and still can) flourish in many contexts. Descended from French
nobility, Alexandre Dumas had no doubt seen robber barons at work in his
native Saint Domingue in the mid-eighteenth century, where their "license
to bully" under slavery was much broader than at home. William Walker
and Cornelius Vanderbilt fought over the opportunity to run Nicaragua in
the 1850s. King Leopold II of Belgium (1835–1909) terrorized the Congo not in his capacity as a legitimate statesman, but as a private entrepreneur.

Janice Thomson historicizes the relationship between the modern
nation-state and the way in which it acquired a "legitimate monopoly on
violence." Her evidence suggests that the interrelationship between "mercenaries, pirates, and sovereigns" is a rather natural one and that their le-
galistic separation is not only a recent phenomenon, but also an exceptional
one that is difficult to maintain in practice.[20] This view invites us to recon-
sider the modern nation-state and its forms of colonialism in the nineteenth
and twentieth centuries as an aberration, a historical detour, although it also

suggests that liberal capitalism arose out of a new deal struck between out-laws and the state as a result of the Atlantic revolutions that began in the late eighteenth century. The New Orleans Revolt of 1768 was one of the first shots fired in what became a global struggle.

The rogue colonialism of Louisiana dates to the founding by the LeMoyne brothers, who in 1699 assembled a crew of freebooters or buc-caneers (*flibustiers* in French) to establish their first encampment on the northern shore of the Gulf of Mexico. They were guided there by a renowned Caribbean pirate. For the next fifty years of Bienville's long career, he en-couraged both small-time and state-sponsored smuggling. He established La Balize at the base of the Mississippi River, an example of what Janet Roit-man calls a "garrison-entrepôt" that "congeals and summarizes the military-commercial nexus." Just as "merchant-planter" must be hyphenated be-cause it is difficult to separate these economic pursuits among Louisiana's elite, it is equally difficult to separate the military and the economy. Petty officers and enlisted men were equally, and frequently, accused of dealing in contraband, piloting suspicious vessels, and reselling military issues at extortionate prices. While La Balize was the literal garrison-entrepôt for the colony, Louisiana was a figurative garrison-entrepôt for the Mississippi-Caribbean world. Despite its location on the periphery of successful plan-tation production and metal extraction in the Americas, it was an impor-tant place of business. What Roitman says of contemporary Central Africa applies to eighteenth-century New Orleans: "while etching out spaces on the margins, these sites are not marginal. Like the activities they harbor, such spaces are dependent upon commercial and financial relations that link them."[21] As this book has shown, New Orleans was actively and inti-mately connected to multiple points in the Americas, from Veracruz and Cartagena to St. Eustatius and Philadelphia. Not only was it linked to these other places, it served as a hub between them—a safe harbor and free port where merchants and traders from many nations could meet and exchange the goods their governments deemed contraband. Sometimes they met at La Balize, sometimes in a New Orleans tavern. Some considered themselves upright businessmen who followed custom if not law, while others were un-doubtedly well aware, if not proud, of their masculine banditry.

While Hobsbawm's definition of "social bandit" as a *rural* outlaw pre-cludes us from searching the urban taverns of New Orleans for their kind, there is a strong kinship between his work and that of Peter Linebaugh and Marcus Rediker, whose epic book, *The Many-Headed Hydra*, focuses on the laboring classes of the maritime Atlantic during the long Age of Revolu-tion (from the unrest of early seventeenth-century England to the end of slavery in Jamaica in 1834). Linebaugh and Rediker, like Hobsbawm, see a link between banditry and revolution, but they follow banditry from the hills of Europe to the waters and port towns of the Atlantic world. The authors also share with Hobsbawm an acknowledgment of Fernand Braudel's pioneering work on the world of the Mediterranean, in which he associated an "explosion" in banditry (especially piracy and smuggling) with the emergence of capitalism at the turn of the seventeenth century. However, it is not clear that historians of the revolutionary Atlantic have fully appreciated the complicated symbiosis between banditry, capitalism, and revolution that Braudel suggested. Rather, the romance of revolutions (even unsuccessful ones) seduces them into presenting a simple opposition between bandits and capitalism.[22]

The recurring metaphor of the "many-headed hydra" is a figure from the labors of Hercules used by writers of the Renaissance and Enlightenment to identify the dangerous underclasses. It is "an antithetical symbol of disorder and resistance, a powerful threat to the building of state, empire, and capitalism."[23] The sailors and slaves that Linebaugh and Rediker majestically raise from the depths of the archives are instantly recognizable as the same characters who made up the *petits gens* of New Orleans in the French period. They are the *forçats* and *engagés*, such as the innkeeper Elizabeth Real and the salt smuggler Joseph Le Champ *dit* La Rose, displaced by the "Great Confinement," the French version of the Enclosure Acts. They are the articulate and angry survivors of the plunder of Africa, such as Louis Congo, Etienne La Rue, and Kakaracou. Linebaugh and Rediker would suggest that the demands of the "many-headed hydra" on the streets of New Orleans in October 1768 amounted to something more politically poignant than the free flow of French wine. Their narrative paints a picture of a highly mobile, ethnically diverse, and politically restless underworld seething below the triangular trade of the Atlantic. Its members left a powder keg trail that ignited revolutions throughout the Americas from the 1760s to the 1820s. Although the hydra (being many-headed) is by its nature without a single spokesperson, we detect strains of emergent class consciousness, visions of racial equality, egalitarian and democratic bylaws, and calculated disrespect for political and religious authority. Characteristically precocious, New Orleans and its Revolt of 1768 fits like a missing puzzle piece into this montage of the revolutionary Atlantic—or almost does.

While it is tempting to imagine the maritime underclasses as romantic revolutionaries with swords drawn against capitalism, the details suggest another genre. Rather than a swashbuckling romance, a picaresque novel would be more apt, in which admirable and charming characters ultimately fail to control their own fate. To the extent that many members of the New Orleans underclass were implicated in a licit but illegal economy of smuggling, it becomes difficult to separate their interests from those of capitalism. Smuggling in the Atlantic world of the eighteenth century involved the commercial trespassing of national and imperial boundaries, the violation of legal monopolies, and the evasion of custom duties. Smuggling, then, was quintessentially the practice of free trade. Though lacking major capital and alienated from the land, many maritime *petits gens* owed their economic survival to the de facto free-market practices of the colonies, given intellectual justification by Adam Smith in his 1776 *Wealth of Nations*. Revolutions, and especially the colonial wars of independence of the long eighteenth century, were in many instances efforts to legitimate smuggling. As they succeeded, they put an end to the mercantile stage of capitalism and ushered in the first stage of economic liberalism. New Orleans shows us that colonial rogues and members of the maritime underclass were above all committed to their own free agency; they were united by and loyal to a cause to the extent that it promoted newly imagined economic rights and individual liberties of physical movement and social self-determination. The winds of change could take them in many directions. Thus, they both threatened, *and substantially collaborated in,* "the building of state, empire, and capitalism."[24]

I do not mean to say that political idealism was absent or disingenuous among actors as diverse as traders, slaves, and the landed creole elite in the revolutionary Atlantic. Nor do I mean to rescue free-market capitalism from moral critiques by linking it to romantic rogues. Far from it. Rather, the point is that the *material* meanings of liberty, and sometimes equality, for historical actors should be better accounted for. Because the results of these revolutions (the American, the Haitian, and the many Bolívar revolutions of Latin America) seem to have ultimately benefited capitalism, there has been a hindsight tendency to read propertied actors as those with material motivations and disenfranchised actors as those with idealist motivations. This oversimplifies the picture. Citizenship and membership in a new republican state may have been one means to secure economic rights, but another was to escape the territoriality of the state altogether. Some revolutionaries jumped ship, crossed borders, and inserted themselves in new frontiers, seeking agrarian or entrepreneurial self-sufficiency rather than being tied down with an investment in the transatlantic system and the shackles of citizenship. Although the main channels of mercantile capitalism created conditions of colonial dependency and plantation slavery, its coastal eddies and riptides created the conditions to overturn this global system. These currents along the periphery created alternative economies and materialized new liberties. Ultimately, they led to the end of slavery when the magical promises of the "free market" were deemed incompatible with a system of bondage. What made revolution possible was precisely the conjuncture of economic interests and idealism between the highest and the lowest creoles of the New World.

If the creation of the modern nation-state involved a complicated interdependency with bandits, then the creation of the modern capitalist economy involved a complicated interdependency with smugglers. Clear-cut divisions between outlaws and politicians, or pirates and financiers, are rarely found in real life. So we should not expect such black-and-white stories from the pages of history. As one well-known example demonstrates, the complicated relationship among criminals, economic flows, and statecraft quickly surfaces with any sustained study of organized crime. Decades of ethnographic work by Jane and Peter Schneider on the Sicilian Mafia have shown that part of what "organizes" crime is its interpenetration with government. Other distinguishing characteristics of mafiosi are that they "mediate illegal traffics or use illegal means, including violence, to gain a foothold in legal activities. To operate in this fashion, they have to be entrepreneurial, opportunistic, aggressive, capable of violence."[25] Unlike predatory bandits, who are highly mobile and often unpredictable in their patterns, mafiosi are rooted in a local area and their activities conform to a set of in-group traditions and rules. They act to protect their investments, business connections, and confidentiality while maintaining social and political ties to non-Mafia members of the society they inhabit. One of the ways they protect themselves is through in-marriage and enforced kinship fealty (both real and fictive).

The resonance of this characterization of the Mafia with the creole oligarchy of late French colonial Louisiana requires little amplification. By the 1750s a group of merchant-planters and military elite were united by a nearly closed kinship system that spanned the Caribbean and the Atlantic. They actively attempted to enforce a local monopoly on smuggling, and on slaveholding, which they backed with exemplary and extralegal violence. During the Revolt of 1768 they used their patronage debts to cultivate the sympathy and support of the working people in the streets. In France, they pulled all the political strings they had tied over the years to avoid being sent to the Bastille, or worse (and most succeeded).

Throughout this book, I have argued that we see a significant transition between the founder generation and the emergence of creole home rule in French colonial Louisiana. Although "rogue colonialism" characterized the entire period (and perhaps beyond), the bandits and robber barons of the founder period gave way to the organized syndicate of the creole oligarchy by mid-century. These references to crime are meant to highlight the complicated relationship of local agents and colonial interest groups to the imperial state in order to counteract a simplistic equation that dominates colonial studies, in which colonial power, bureaucracy, and metropolitan authority are taken as proxies for one another. I do not want to be misunderstood as equating creoles with criminals. It is time to do away with the heroes-and-villains model of historical explanation and social analysis. It distorts our understanding of the working and reworking of power, disabling us with naïveté and making it even more difficult to control our political fates. For one thing, the colonial situation strips down the pretensions of legality and legitimacy to show how fragile and murky these categories are. What was technically criminal according to metropolitan law was socially acceptable according to local custom. The state itself operates protection rackets of a questionable nature, as seen in the explicit policies of Louisiana governors to foster tensions between Africans and Native Americans and the differential treatment of elite violent offenders. Any assumed opposition between state legality and colonial criminality should be scrutinized and will probably dissolve upon close inspection. Second, there were many other creoles in the colony beyond the elite clans represented on the Superior Council, such as the maroons, *coureurs de bois*, and lady sailors who have wandered through the pages of this book. Their strategies of survival might have been viewed by metropolitan engineers as roguish deviations, but this is a testament to their creativity and spirit of independence, not to some inherent criminal character intent on doing harm to others. Third, failed revolutionaries are always defined as criminals by the government they attempted to overthrow, and as heroes by the people they attempted to liberate. The shifting relationship of colonial agents to the state is what transforms criminals into heroes, and back again. Planned or unplanned, most revolutions could probably be characterized by both blatant self-interest and heroic idealism.

We must be careful not to become too charmed by would-be revolutionaries who meet in closed chambers, as they are likely to be plotting to advance their own clannish agenda. But this is not to say we can't permit ourselves to be romanced by a few spontaneous rogues in the streets of New Orleans. In a picaresque, elements of romance, adventure, comedy, and heroic tragedy are allowed to coexist. A picaresque is not a simple story about good triumphing over evil, or the devil winning an empire. It is a more mature musing on the mishaps of fate, the follies of vanity, and the wild diversity of human nature. Like a good Mardi Gras parade, it critiques society while celebrating humanity.

A boisterous demonstration of farmers, traders, and shoemakers in the streets of New Orleans in 1768 strikes the twin notes of chagrin and merriment appropriate for the final scene of a picaresque. They defended their right to drink French wine but failed to establish a sovereign republic. As a counterpoint to the blueprints of empires and the plotting of cabals, they represent the improvisational drive and sociable independence that continues to make New Orleans *un beau désordre.*

Chronology

Glossary

concessionaire Investors under Law's scheme who were given large land grants and a share in his exclusive trade privileges. In return, they were obligated to clear the land and recruit and equip settlers to plant crops. Some *concessionaires* came to Louisiana to oversee operations, others delegated this responsibility to a manager. Concessions varied in size from a few dozen acres to thousands of acres, but in general *concessionaire* denoted a settler of high social status in the early colony.

coureur de bois Literally, "runner of the woods," referring to fur trappers and Indian traders who operated without a license.

creole Someone born in the colonies. Lacks connotations of hybridity or race that later usages acquired.

engagé An indentured servant in Louisiana, recruited during the Law period, serving a term from three to seven years for the Company or a private *concessionaire*.

forçat A forced exile. These were often criminals or military deserters, but also vagabonds, orphans, and unattached women from the prisons and hospitals of France's major cities. The term was also occasionally used to describe the subject of a *lettre de cachet*, which was a legal instrument used by individuals to have wayward family members imprisoned or exiled, usually for alleged licentious or blasphemous behavior. Criminals were often drawn from the *galériens*, those whose punishment was to be sent to the "galleys" to work for anywhere from a few years to life, sometimes on shipboard, but more commonly at onshore labor camps.

habitant Often translated as "planter," although usage indicates that *habitant* was sometimes used to refer to any colonist who owned a bit of land (*habitation*) or worked for him or herself. They usually began with a lower level of initial investment than the *concessionaires*, but many early *habitants* went on to become major planter-merchants and public figures.

ordonnateur Also called *commissaire-ordonnateur, intendant,* or *premier conseilleur.* The man in this role held the purse-strings of the colonial budget and co-governed with the military governor. The position was modeled after the *intendants* who governed French provinces.

voyageur Interchangeable with *coureur de bois,* but without the connotation of illegality; refers to traders engaged in the Indian trade.

Abbreviations

AGI-PPC   Archivo General de Indias, Papeles Procedentes de Cuba, accessed on microfilm, Historic New Orleans Collection

AGI-SD   Archivo General de Indias, Audiencia de Santo Domingo, accessed on microfilm, Historic New Orleans Collection

ANF   Archives Nationales de France

ANF-AC   Archives Coloniales section of the Archives Nationales de France, accessed on microfilm through LDS Family History Center and Historic New Orleans Collection

BNF   Bibliothèque Nationale de France

LDS   Church of Latter Day Saints, microfilm source for both Louisiana Superior Council records and Archives Nationales de France

MPA   Mississippi Provincial Archives series, published translations of selected Archives Coloniales, Archives Nationales de France documents

NONA   New Orleans Notarial Archives

SCA-LHQ   Louisiana Superior Council record English abstracts printed serially in *Louisiana Historical Quarterly*, vols. 1–26

SCR   Louisiana Superior Council original records, accessed on microfilm through LDS Family History Center and Tulane University Law Library

Notes

PREFACE

1   J. H. Ingraham, ed., *The Sunny South; or the Southerner at Home, Embracing Five Years' Experience of a Northern Governess in the Land of the Sugar and the Cotton* (Philadelphia, 1860), 322; William Darby, *A Geographical Description of the State of Louisiana, the Southern Part of the State of Mississippi, and Territory of Alabama* (New York: James Olmstead, 1817); both as quoted in Frank De Caro and Rosan Augusta Jordan, *Louisiana Sojourns: Travelers' Tales and Literary Journeys* (Baton Rouge: Louisiana State University Press, 1998), 70, 77. J. Benwell, *An Englishman's Travels in America: His Observations of Life and Manners in the Free and Slave States* (London: Binns & Goodwin, 1853), 115; Alexis de Tocqueville, *Journey to America*, ed. J. P. Mayer, trans. George Lawrence (Westport, Conn.: Greenwood, 1981), 165.

2   Shannon Lee Dawdy, *"La Ville Sauvage*: 'Enlightened' Colonialism and Creole Improvisation in New Orleans, 1699–1769" (Ph.D. diss., University of Michigan, 2003).

3   Shannon Lee Dawdy, "Enlightenment from the Ground: Le Page du Pratz' *Histoire de la Louisiana*," *French Colonial History* 3 (2003): 17–34; "La Nouvelle-Orléans au xviiie siècle: courants d'échanges dans le monde caraïbe," *Annales: histoire, sciences sociales* 62, no. 3 (2007): 663–85; "Proper Caresses and Prudent Distance: A How-to Manual from Louisiana," in *Haunted by Empire: Geographies of Intimacy in North American History*, ed. Ann Laura Stoler (Durham, N.C.: Duke University Press, 2006), 140–62; "The Burden of Louis Congo and the Evolution of Savagery in Colonial Louisiana," in *Discipline and the Other Body: Correction, Corporeality, Colonialism*, ed. Steven Pierce and Anupama Rao (Durham, N.C.: Duke University Press, 2006), 61–89; "Scoundrels, Whores, and Gentlemen: Defamation and Society in French Colonial Louisiana," in *Coastal Encounters: The Transformation of the Gulf South in the Eighteenth Century*, ed. Richmond F. Brown (Lincoln: University of Nebraska Press, 2008), 132–50.

4   Hayden White, *Metahistory: The Historical Imagination in Nineteenth-Century Europe* (Baltimore: Johns Hopkins University Press, 1973).

5   This is not to say romance has no place in scholarship. I have been moved and influenced by romantic-revolutionary works such as C. L. R. James, *The Black Jacobins:*

Toussaint L'Overture and the San Domingo Revolution, 2d ed. (New York: Vintage Books, 1963); Peter Linebaugh and Marcus Rediker, *The Many-Headed Hydra: Sailors, Slaves, Commoners, and the Hidden History of the Revolutionary Atlantic* (Boston: Beacon Press, 2000); James C. Scott, *Seeing like a State: How Certain Schemes to Improve the Human Condition Have Failed* (New Haven: Yale University Press, 1998); James C. Scott, *Domination and the Arts of Resistance: Hidden Transcripts* (New Haven: Yale University Press, 1990).

INTRODUCTION

1 This reconstruction is based upon the writings of Marie-Madeleine Hachard, from which the direct quotes are taken: *Relation du voyage des dames religieuses Ursulines de Rouen à la Nouvelle-Orléans* (Paris: Maisonneuve, 1872), 90–91. Emily Clark argues convincingly that the Ursulines saw themselves as missionaries sent to address the moral degeneracy of New Orleans, as well as the education of Indian and African women in the New World. See her *Masterless Mistresses: The New Orleans Ursulines and the Development of a New World Society* (Chapel Hill: University of North Carolina Press, 2007).

2 Pierre-François-Xavier de Charlevoix, letter of 10 January 1722, in *Journal d'un voyage fait par ordre du roi dans l'Amérique septentrionale*, 3 vols. (Paris: Rollin, 1744), 3:429–30; Caillot, "Relation du Voyage de la Louisiane ou Nouv.lle France fait par le Sr. Caillot en l'année 1730," Ms. 2005.11, Historic New Orleans Collection, fol. 104; Abbé Antoine-François Prévost, *Histoire du chevalier Des Grieux et de Manon Lescaut* (Paris: Librairie A. Colin, 1957 [1731]).

3 Frederick Cooper and Ann Laura Stoler, "Between Metropole and Colony: Rethinking a Research Agenda," in *Tensions of Empire: Colonial Cultures in a Bourgeois World*, ed. Frederick Cooper and Ann Laura Stoler (Berkeley: University of California Press, 1997), 1–56.

4 *The American Heritage Dictionary of the English Language*, 4th ed. (Boston: Houghton Mifflin, 2000).

5 Scott, *Seeing Like a State*.

6 For a reflection on the many uses of *creolization*, see E. K. Braithwaite, *The Development of Creole Society in Jamaica, 1770–1820* (London: Clarendon Press, 1971); Ulf Hannerz, *Cultural Complexity* (New York: Columbia University Press, 1992), 264–65; Kathleen Balutansky and Marie-Agnès Sourieau, eds., *Caribbean Creolization: Reflections on the Cultural Dynamics of Language, Literature and Identity* (Gainesville: University Press of Florida, 1998); Richard Price "The Miracle of Creolization: A Retrospective," *New West Indian Guide* 75 (2001): 35–64; Nicolas R. Spitzer, "Monde Créole: The Cultural World of French Louisiana Creoles and the Creolization of Modern Cultures," *Journal of American Folklore* 116 (2003): 58–59; and Stephan Palmié, "Creolization and Its Discontents," *Annual Review of Anthropology* 35 (2006): 433–56.

7 For more on the shifting historical meanings of *creole* specific to Louisiana, see Joseph G. Tregle Jr., "On That Word 'Creole' Again: A Note," *Louisiana History* 23 (1982): 193–98; and Shannon Lee Dawdy, "Understanding Cultural Change through the Vernacular: Creolization in Louisiana," *Historical Archaeology* 34, no. 3 (2000): 107–23.

8   I must admit to a certain nausea every time I hear someone refer to Louisiana culture as a "creole gumbo," though I do like my share of filé and seafood. I am made uneasy by the temptation to exoticize cultures by singling them out as hybrid, because of both the racial connotations and the colonial histories of inequality that seem always to lurk beneath the surface. I do not reject all uses of the term *hybridity*. Homi Bhabha employs *hybridity* in a unique and nuanced way to uncover the complex cultural politics of colonialism. Homi Bhabha, *The Location of Culture* (London: Routledge, 1994).

9   On generational analyses, see Bennett M. Berger, "How Long Is a Generation?" *British Journal of Sociology* 11, no. 1 (1960): 10–23; Alan B. Spitzer, "The Historical Problem of Generations," *American Historical Review* 78, no. 5 (1973): 1353–85.

10   I should note that my "founder generation" potentially includes members of Ira Berlin's Atlantic creoles, but in this study I use *creole* in the strictly local sense of "someone born in Louisiana" (see glossary). Ira Berlin, *Many Thousands Gone: The First Two Centuries of Slavery in North America* (Cambridge, Mass.: Harvard University Press, 1998).

11   In this same settlement of the war (known by Anglo–Americans as "the French and Indian War"), England received eastern Louisiana, comprising the area east of the Mississippi River excepting the "Isle d'Orleans" around the city of New Orleans. See Fred Anderson, *Crucible of War: The Seven Years War and the Fate of the Empire in British North America, 1754–1766* (New York: A. A. Knopf, 2000).

12   For an excellent overview of Louisiana's exotic reputation in American historiography and early touristic writings, see Daniel Usner, "Between Creoles and Yankees: The Discursive Representation of Colonial Louisiana in American History," in *French Colonial Louisiana and the Atlantic World*, ed. Bradley G. Bond (Baton Rouge: Louisiana State University Press, 2005), 1–21. For an understanding of the role these views have played in U.S. nationalism, see Edward Watts, *In This Remote Country: French Colonial Culture in the Anglo-American Imagination, 1780–1860* (Chapel Hill: University of North Carolina Press, 2006).

13   The last book-length treatment of French New Orleans was Marc Villiers du Terrage, *Histoire de la fondation de la Nouvelle-Orléans, 1717–1722* (Paris: Imprimerie Nationale, 1917).

14   It is impossible to do justice here to the many ways in which anthropology and history productively overlap, but for some overviews, see the following: Bernard S. Cohn, *An Anthropologist among the Historians and Other Essays* (Oxford: Oxford University Press, 1987), 18–49; John and Jean Comaroff, *Ethnography and the Historical Imagination* (Boulder, Colo.: Westview Press, 1992), 3–48; Nicolas B. Dirks, "Is Vice Versa? Historical Anthropologies and Anthropological Histories," in *The Historic Turn in the Human Sciences*, ed. Terrence J. McDonald (Ann Arbor: University of Michigan Press, 1996), 17–52.

15   Michel Foucault, *The Archaeology of Knowledge and the Discourse on Language*, trans. A. M. Sheridan Smith (New York: Pantheon, 1972); Michel De Certeau, *The Writing of History*, trans. Tom Conley (New York: Columbia University Press, 1988); Cooper and Stoler, "Between Metropole and Colony"; John Kelly, "Alternative Modernities or an Alternative to 'Modernity': Getting Out of the Modernist Sublime," in *Critically Modern: Alternatives, Alterities, Anthropologies*, ed. Bruce M. Knauft (Bloomington: University of Indiana Press, 2002), 258–86; David Scott, *Conscripts of Modernity: The Tragedy of Colonial Enlightenment* (Durham, N.C.:

Duke University Press, 2004); Frederick Cooper, *Colonialism in Question: Theory, Knowledge, History* (Berkeley: University of California Press, 2005).

16 Dipesh Chakrabarty, *Provincializing Europe: Postcolonial Thought and Historical Difference* (Princeton, N.J.: Princeton University Press, 2000), 4.

17 Scott, *Seeing Like a State.*

18 For overviews of colonial/postcolonial studies, see Bill Ashcroft, Gareth Griffiths, and Helen Tiffin, eds., *The Post-colonial Studies Reader* (New York: Routledge, 1995); Ania Loomba, *Colonialism/Postcolonialism* (New York: Routledge, 1998); Ann Laura Stoler, "Tense and Tender Ties: The Politics of Comparison in North American History and (Post)Colonial Studies," *Journal of American History* 88, no. 3 (2001): 829–65.

19 I use the terms *slave, nègre, Indian,* and so forth to reflect the historical categories understood by historical actors, not in preference to more respectful contemporary terms, such as "enslaved person," "Afro-Louisianan," "Native American," and so on, which I also use where appropriate.

20 Michel-Rolph Trouillot, *Silencing the Past: Power and the Production of History* (Boston: Beacon Press, 1997); Laurent Dubois, *A Colony of Citizens: Revolution and Slave Emancipation in the French Caribbean, 1787–1804* (Chapel Hill: University of North Carolina Press, 2006).

21 Of course, in France also ties between the monarchy and *le peuple* were loosening in the eighteenth century, with a critical turning point around 1750. I am suggesting that the process occurred a little sooner and under different conditions in Louisiana. See Arlette Farge and Jacques Revel, *The Rules of Rebellion: Child Abductions in Paris in 1750,* trans. Claudia Miéville (Cambridge: Polity Press, 1990).

22 Richard White, *The Middle Ground: Indians, Empires, and Republics in the Great Lakes Region, 1650–1815* (Cambridge: Cambridge University Press, 1991).

23 Gwynne Lewis, *France, 1715–1804: Power and the People* (Harlow, U.K.: Pearson Longman, 2004).

24 The Company was also known as the Company of the West, the Louisiana Company, or the Mississippi Company in various incarnations; I will refer to it simply as "the Company" to simplify matters.

25 Scott, *Seeing Like a State.*

26 Ibid.; Benedict Anderson, *Imagined Communities: Reflections on the Origin and Spread of Nationalism* (New York: Verso, 1991); Michel Foucault, *Discipline and Punish: The Birth of the Prison* (New York: Vintage Books, 1995).

27 Anderson, *Imagined Communities.*

28 For an overview of influential works on this topic, see Anthony D. King, "Writing Colonial Space: A Review Article," *Comparative Studies in Society and History* 37, no. 3 (1995): 541–54. Examples include the following: Zeynep Çelik, *Urban Forms and Colonial Confrontations: Algiers under French Rule* (Berkeley: University of California Press, 1997); Zeynep Çelik, Diane G. Favro, and Richard Ingersoll, *Streets: Critical Perspectives on Public Space* (Berkeley: University of California Press, 1994); Gwendolyn Wright, *The Politics of Design in French Colonial Urbanism* (Chicago: University of Chicago Press, 1991). See also chapters on planning and urbanity in Anderson, *Imagined Communities*; and Scott, *Seeing Like a State.*

29 Marc de Villiers du Terrage, *The Last Years of French Louisiana,* trans. Hosea Phillips (Lafayette: Center for Louisiana Studies, University of Southwestern Louisiana, 1982 [1903]), xii.

30 Cooper and Stoler, "Between Metropole and Colony, 6, 4.

31 Cooper, *Colonialism in Question*; Scott, *Conscripts of Modernity*.

32 Cooper, *Colonialism in Question*, 185.

33 My understanding of political modernity (or modernism) owes much to James C. Scott's *Seeing Like a State*, but here I am engaging with his work to say that the genealogy of what he calls high modernism belongs more to the practices of colonialism than to the intellectual history of Europe and its own belated capitalism. For an important critique of the modernity concept and associated terms, see Cooper, *Colonialism in Question*, 113–49. One of Cooper's main complaints concerns the Eurocentrism of most writing on modernity, and the unsatisfactory solution of locating "alternative modernities" in colonial and non-Western spaces. I agree, but still find "modernity" to be a useful shorthand for highly formalized strategies of governance and a fetishization of rationality, especially as this set of ideas and practices arose out of the crumbling ruins of the *ancien régime*.

34 I concur with David Scott, who argues that the questions we ask of history are always rooted in the politics of the present. In this case, we in the postcolonial era have been asking, "Whose fault is it?" and responding to a morally understandable quest for equity and reparations for the colonized, particularly Native Americans, Africans, and the African Diaspora. While many faults can be laid at the door of Western state powers, an assumption of penetrating and total political hegemony through colonialism simply does not fit with the historical evidence. Scott, *Conscripts of Modernity*.

35 The era of epic histories of colonialism and its "heroic" rogues is much longer than our current era of historiography as political critique, so I will mention just a few classic examples from this now buried body of work: Francis Parkman, *France and England in North America*, 9 vols. (Boston: Little, Brown, 1890–92); John Fiske, *The Discovery of America, With Some Account of Ancient America and the Spanish Conquest*, 2 vols. (Boston: Houghton Mifflin, 1892); and Jean Descola, *The Conquistadors*, trans. Malcolm Barnes (New York: Viking, 1957). Some colonial adventurers wrote their own picaresque histories, begetting a long line of colonial historiography, most notably Capt. John Smith with *The Generall Historie of Virginia, New England and the Summer Isles* (London: Michael Sparkes, 1624). For like-spirited cautions on making a vague monument out of "colonial power" or "imperialism," see Timothy Mitchell, "The Limits of the State: Beyond Statist Approaches and Their Critics," *American Political Science Review* 85, no. 1 (1991): 77–96; John D. Kelly and Martha Kaplan, "Nation and Decolonization: Toward a New Anthropology of Nationalism," *Anthropological Theory* 1, no. 4: (2001): 419–37; and several of the chapters in Craig Calhoun, Frederick Cooper, and Kevin W. Moore, eds., *Lessons of Empire: Imperial Histories and American Power* (New York: New Press, 2006).

CHAPTER 1

1 Jack Jackson, Robert S. Weddle, and Winston De Ville, *Mapping Texas and the Gulf Coast: The Contributions of Saint Denis, Oliván, and Le Maire* (College Station: Texas A&M University Press, 1990), 22, 27; Jean Delanglez, "M. Le Maire on Louisiana," *Mid-America* 19, no. 2 (1937): 127; Le Maire, Mémoire sur la Louisiane, 1718, ANF-AC, C13C 2, fol. 153.

2 Glenn R. Conrad, "Reluctant Imperialist: France in North America," in *La Salle and His Legacy: Frenchmen and Indians in the Lower Mississippi Valley*, ed. Patricia

Kay Galloway (Jackson: University Press of Mississippi, 1995), 93–105. See also Mathé Allain, *"Not Worth a Straw": French Colonial Policy and the Early Years of Louisiana* (Lafayette: University of Southwestern Louisiana, 1988).

3 Etat de la Louisiane au mois de juin 1720, ANF, Service Historique de l'Armée, ser. A1 2592, fol. 95, as cited and translated in Gwendolyn Midlo Hall, *Africans in Colonial Louisiana: The Development of Afro-Creole Culture in the Eighteenth Century* (Baton Rouge: Louisiana State University Press, 1992), 7. *Médiocre* in the French sense is closer to the meaning of "average" than its cognate in English.

4 Abbé Raynal, *A Philosophical and Political History of the Settlements and Trade of the Europeans in the East and West Indies*, trans. J. O. Justamond, 10 vols. (London: W. Strahan, 1783), book 16, p. 27.

5 *Dictionnaire de l'Académie française*, 2 vols. (Paris: J. J. Smits, 1798), 1:408.

6 Charles Gayarré, *Louisiana: Its Colonial History and Romance* (New York: Harper & Bros., 1851); Herbert Asbury, *The French Quarter: An Informal History of the New Orleans Underworld* (New York: Garden City Publishing, 1938). French historian Marcel Giraud used the term *désordre* frequently to describe Louisiana's political, financial, and moral state in his five-volume opus on the colony's first thirty-three years. More recently, Gwendolyn Midlo Hall has pointed out the failures and weaknesses of the slave regime under "the chaos of French rule," ultimately romanticizing French Louisiana as one of "the disorderly and disobedient places where creativity is born." Mark Fernandez also uses the word *chaos* to describe the early judicial system. Daniel Usner provides a nuanced portrait of the frontier economy of the lower Mississippi that failed to live up to French mercantilist speculations and instead created a network of social relations that "strayed from the norms." When speaking of the norms of slave society, Ira Berlin puts Louisiana's development in the French period into a comparative perspective, calling it one of "devolution." Jennifer Spear's studies of race and sexuality in colonial Louisiana reveal how French administrators perceived race mixture as a source of social disorder in the colony. Concentrating on the power of slaveholders, Thomas Ingersoll also addresses the order/disorder question, but weighs in on the opposite side: "this community's development was marked by order, contrary to the prevailing interpretation of early New Orleans as an anarchy." Marcel Giraud, *Histoire de la Louisiane française*, 5 vols. (Paris: Presses Universitaires de France, 1953–74); Berlin, *Many Thousands Gone*; Mark F. Fernandez, *From Chaos to Continuity: The Evolution of Louisiana's Judicial System, 1712–1862* (Baton Rouge: Louisiana State University Press, 2001); Hall, *Africans in Colonial Louisiana*; Gwendolyn Midlo Hall, "Epilogue: Historical Memory, Consciousness, and Conscience in the New Millennium," in *French Colonial Louisiana and the Atlantic World*, ed. Bradley G. Bond (Baton Rouge: Louisiana State University Press, 2005), 291–309; Jennifer Spear, "Colonial Intimacies: Legislating Sex in French Louisiana," *William & Mary Quarterly*, 3d ser., 60, no. 1 (2003): 75–98; Jennifer M. Spear, "'They Need Wives': Métissage and the Regulation of Sexuality in French Louisiana, 1699–1730," in *Sex, Love, Race: Crossing Boundaries in North American History*, ed. Martha Hodes (New York: New York University Press, 1999); Daniel H. Usner, *Indians, Settlers, and Slaves in a Frontier Exchange Economy: The Lower Mississippi Valley before 1783* (Chapel Hill: University of North Carolina Press, 1992); Thomas N. Ingersoll, *Mammon and Manon in Early New Orleans: The First Slave Society in the Deep South, 1718–1819* (Knoxville: University of Tennessee Press, 1999), xvi.

7   For a review of changing class categories in France (and debates among historians about them), see Sarah Maza, *The Myth of the French Bourgeoisie: An Essay on the Social Imaginary, 1750–1850* (Cambridge, Mass.: Harvard University Press, 2003).

8   Doris Lorraine Garraway, *The Libertine Colony: Creolization in the French Caribbean* (Durham, N.C.: Duke University Press, 2005). See also James A. Delle, "The Material and Cognitive Dimensions of Creolization in Nineteenth-century Jamaica," *Historical Archaeology* 34, no. 3 (2000): 56–72; Megan Vaughan, *Creating the Creole Island: Slavery in Eighteenth-Century Mauritius* (Durham, N.C.: Duke University Press, 2005); Peter N. Moogk, "Manon Lescaut's Countrymen: Emigration from France to North America before 1763," in *Proceedings of the Sixteenth Meeting of the French Colonial History Society, Mackinac Island, May 1990*, ed. Patricia Galloway (Lanham, Md.: University Press of America, 1992), 24–44.

9   It is impossible to do more here than gesture at the social complexities and tensions within *ancien régime* France. For a good recent overview, see Lewis, *France, 1715–1804.*

10 See, for example, Philip Pittman, *The Present State of the European Settlements on the Mississippi, with a Geographical Description of that River Illustrated by Plans and Draughts* (Cleveland: A. H. Clark Co., 1906 [1770]); and Ulloa to Grimaldi, 7 January 1767, AGI-SD, Legajo 2542.

11 Instructions pour la formation d'un établissement en Louisiane, 1722, Drouot de Val de Terre, ANF-AC, C13 A6, fol. 352. See also Gayarré, *History of Louisiana*, 1:375–76.

12 D'Abbadie to minister, 7 June 1764, ANF-AC, C13A 44, fol. 58; Noticia de los acaecimientos de la Luisiana en el año de 1768 (Ulloa to Grimaldi), Miscelánea de Ayala, XIII, Manuscritos de América, Biblioteca de Palacio (Madrid), Ms. 2827, fol. 27, as quoted in John Preston Moore, *Revolt in Louisiana: The Spanish Occupation, 1766–1770* (Baton Rouge: Louisiana State University Press, 1976), 144n3.

13 The literature on the Enlightenment is vast, but for views expanding on its intellectual diversity, skewed reputation, and social practices, see Stephen Eric Bronner, *Reclaiming the Enlightenment: Toward a Politics of Radical Engagement* (New York: Columbia University Press, 2004); Louis Dupre, *The Enlightenment and the Intellectual Foundations of Modern Culture* (New Haven, Conn.: Yale University Press, 2004); Dena Goodman, *The Republic of Letters: A Cultural History of the French Enlightenment* (Ithaca, N.Y.: Cornell University Press, 1994).

14 Roger Chartier, *The Cultural Origins of the French Revolution*, trans. Lydia D. Cochrane (Durham, N.C.: Duke University Press, 1991); Goodman, *Republic of Letters*; James Van Horn Melton, *The Rise of the Public in Enlightenment Europe* (London: Cambridge University Press, 2001); Susan Scott Parrish, *American Curiosity: Cultures of Natural History in the Colonial British Atlantic World* (Chapel Hill: University of North Carolina Press, 2006).

15 John R. Carpenter, *Histoire de la littérature française sur la Louisiane, de 1673 jusqu'à 1766* (Paris: Nizet, 1966).

16 Marcel Giraud, *Years of Transition, 1715–1717*, trans. Brian Pearce (Baton Rouge: Louisiana State University Press, 1993), 12–13. On the "science" of eighteenth-century French colonialism, see also James E. McClellan, *Colonialism and Science: Saint Domingue in the Old Regime* (Baltimore: Johns Hopkins University Press, 1992); Gilles-Antoine Langlois, "Deux fondations scientifiques à la Nouvelle-Orléans (1728–30): La connaissance à l'épreuve de la réalité coloniale," *French Colonial History* 4 (2003): 99–116. The views of McClellan and Langlois stake out a typical

division between American scholars who make claims for the success of science in the colonies and French scholars who proclaim it a failure.

17 Jackson, Weddle, and De Ville, *Mapping Texas*, 28; Giraud, *Years of Transition*, 17.

18 Charles Edwards O'Neill and Etienne-Bernard-Alexandre Viel, *Viel: Louisiana's Firstborn Author with Evandre, the First Literary Creation of a Native of the Mississippi Valley* (Lafayette: University of Southwestern Louisiana, 1991), 8. Viel (or Vielle) was often referred to simply as "Alexandre" in the documents. Marcel Giraud, *The Company of the Indies, 1723–1731*, trans. Brian Pearce (Baton Rouge: Louisiana State University Press, 1991), 216–18; Langlois, "Deux fondations scientifiques"; Jean Delanglez, "A Louisiana Poet-Historian: Dumont de Montigny," *Mid-America* 19, no. 1 (1937): 31–49. Another man, Father Laval of New Orleans, was remembered as a "professor of physics." Jonathas Darby, "Louisiana 1717 to 1751," *Louisiana Historical Quarterly* 6, no. 4 (1753): 543–67, especially 550.

19 Baron, astronomer, to Minister, 22 December 1730, ANF-AC, C13A 12, fol. 412; Samuel Wilson Jr., *The Architecture of Colonial Louisiana: Collected Essays of Samuel Wilson, Jr., F.A.I.A.*, ed. Jean M. Farnsworth and Ann M. Masson (Lafayette: Center for Louisiana Studies, 1987), 9, 262; Caillot, "Relation du Voyage de la Louisiane ou Nouv.lle France fait par le Sr. Caillot en l'année 1730," Ms. 2005.11, Historic New Orleans Collection, fol. 106. For an eighteenth-century context of Baron's astronomical activities, see Langlois, "Deux fondations scientifiques."

20 Clark, *Masterless Mistresses*; Jane Frances Heaney, *A Century of Pioneering: A History of the Ursuline Nuns in New Orleans, 1727–1827* (New Orleans: Ursuline Sisters of New Orleans Louisiana, 1993). Jean-François Benjamin Dumont de Montigny, "Mémoire De Lxx Dxx Officier Ingénieur, Contenant Les Evenemens qui se sont passés à la Louisiane depuis 1715 jusqu'a present. Ainsi que les temoignes sur les moeurs, usages et forces des divereses nations de L'Amerique Septentrionale et de ses productions," Ms., 1747, Ayer Collection, Newberry Library, Chicago, 161; Louis Hennepin, *Description de la Louisiane, nouvellement découverte* (Paris: Chez Amable Auroy, 1688); Henri de Tonti, *Dernieres decouvertes dans l'Amerique septentrionale de M. de La Sale* (Paris: Chez Jean Guignard, 1697); Carpenter, *Histoire de la littérature française*.

21 Inventory of Kolly Estate, 9 January 1730, SCA-LHQ 4, no. 4 (1921): 508; Heloise H. Cruzat, trans., "Documents concerning Sale of Chaouachas Plantation in Louisiana, 1737–1738," *Louisiana Historical Quarterly* 8, no. 4 (1925): 607.

22 Edith Dart Price, ed., "Inventory of the Estate of Sieur Jean Baptiste Prévost, Deceased Agent of the Company of the Indies. July 13, 1769," *Louisiana Historical Quarterly* 9, no. 3 (1926): 429–98.

23 Others were *Essai philosophique sur l'âme des bêtes* (1728), Prion's *Oeuvres* (1758), *Angola* (1746), and Toussaint's *Les Moeurs* (1748). I used Robert Darnton, *The Corpus of Clandestine Literature in France, 1769–1789* (New York: W. W. Norton, 1995), to identify contraband books.

24 As with most of the books in the inventory, no author is given. Two possibilities are the anonymous *Relation de la Louisianne ou Mississippi, écrite à une dame, par un officier de marine* (Amsterdam: Bernard, 1720), or the more widely known book published under the name of Henri de Tonti, *Relation de la Louisianne, et du Mississipi* (Amsterdam: Bernard, 1720).

25 Kenneth J. Banks, *Chasing Empire across the Sea: Communications and the State in the French Atlantic, 1713–1763* (Montreal: McGill-Queen's University Press, 2002), 51–52. See also Patricia K. Galloway, "Louisiana Post Letters: The Missing Evidence

for Indian Diplomacy," in *The French Experience in Louisiana*, ed. Glenn R. Conrad (Lafayette: University of Southwestern Louisiana, 1995), 322–32; Jane E. Harrison, *Until Next Year: Letter Writing and the Mails in the Canadas, 1640–1830* (Waterloo, Ont.: Wilfrid Laurier University Press, 1997).

26 A. Baillardel and A. Prioult, eds., *Le Chevalier de Pradel, Vie d'un colon français en Louisiane au XVIIIe siècle d'après sa correspondance et celle de sa famille* (Paris: Maisonneuve Frères, 1928), 63, 66.

27 André Pénicaut and Richebourg Gaillard McWilliams, *Fleur de Lys and Calumet: Being the Pénicaut Narrative of French Adventure in Louisiana* (Baton Rouge: Louisiana State University Press, 1953), 158, 166, 175; Dumont de Montigny, "Mémoire De Lxx Dxx Officier," 23–24, 129, 148, 163.

28 Antoine Simon Le Page du Pratz, *The History of Louisiana, or of the Western Parts of Virginia and Carolina: Containing a Description of the Countries that Lie on Both Sides of the River Mississippi: with an Account of the Settlements, Inhabitants, Soil, Climate, and Products* (London: T. Becket and J. S. W. Harmanson, 1774), 30; Dumont de Montigny, "Mémoire De Lxx Dxx Officier," 106, 129, 169.

29 Dumont de Montigny, "Mémoire De Lxx Dxx Officier," 78.

30 Baillardel and Prioult, *Le Chevalier de Pradel*.

31 This argument is made in Carpenter, *Histoire de la littérature française*, 15–50.

32 "Les productions de la littérature louisianaise ressemblent à des ouvrages modernes de science fiction: elles représentent un très curieux mélange des genres de la *Relation* du voyage et du roman utopique." Carpenter, *Histoire de la littérature française*, 344; Mary Louise Pratt, *Imperial Eyes: Travel Writing and Transculturation* (New York: Routledge, 1992).

33 I have found references to eighty-two different works, though I believe there may be dozens more in the French archives or scattered in obscure collections. Carpenter and Bienvenu offer nearly complete lists of the published accounts and detailed analyses of tropes in the genre. Carpenter, *Histoire de la littérature française*; Germain Joseph Bienvenu, "Another America, Another Literature: Narratives from Louisiana's Colonial Experience" (Ph.D. diss., Louisiana State University and Agricultural and Mechanical College, 1995).

34 Examples include the following: M. Vallette de Laudun, *Journal d'un voyage à la Louisiane, fait en 1720 par M.***, capitaine de vaisseau du Roi* (La Haye: Chez Musier fils & Fournier, 1768); Antoine François Laval, *Voyage de la Louisiane, fait par ordre du roy en l'année mil sept cent vingt* (Paris: J. Mariette, 1728); Chevalier de Bonrepos, *Description du Mississipi* (Rouen, 1720); Hachard, *Relation du voyage*; Chevalier de Bourgmont, "Relation du voyage du sieur de Bourgmont, chevalier de l'ordre militaire de Saint-Louis, commandant de la rivière du Missouri," in *Découvertes et établissements des Français dans l'Amérique septentrionale, 1614–1754*, ed. Pierre Margry, 6 vols. (Paris: Imprimerie Jouaust et Sigaux, 1886 [1724]), 6:389–449; and Jean-Baptiste Bénard de La Harpe, *Journal historique de l'établissement des Français à la Louisiane* (Paris: Bossange, 1831 [1720]). See Chinard's remarkably durable study for a focus on exoticism and fiction in colonial literature: Gilbert Chinard, *L'Amérique et le rêve exotique dans la littérature française au XVIIe et au XVIIIe siècle* (Geneva: Slatkine Reprints, 2000 [1918]). Also Garraway, *Libertine Colony*.

35 See Carpenter, *Histoire de la littérature française*, 233. The female reader receiving "scientific" knowledge was a common Enlightenment trope. Goodman, *Republic of Letters*.

36 Gérard Roubichou, "Trois regards sur la Louisiane au xviiie siècle," *Comptes Rendus de l'Athénée Louisianais 1974–1975* (1975): 49–57, especially 50.

37 Ibid., 50–51.

38 On the question of authorship, see Carpenter, *Histoire de la littérature française*, 212–17. Bonrepos, *Description du Mississipi.*

39 Vallette de Laudun, *Journal d'un voyage à la Louisiane.*

40 Ibid., 40.

41 Ibid., 49.

42 Ibid., 255–56.

43 Hachard, *Relation du voyage*; Marie-Madeleine Hachard, *The Letters of Marie Madelaine Hachard, 1727–28*, trans. Mildred Masson Costa (New Orleans, 1974), 20. It is difficult to know how much editorial license her father may have taken with her letters.

44 Hachard, *Letters of Marie Madelaine Hachard, 1727–28*, 21, 54–55.

45 Hachard, *Relation du voyage*, 97. The Superior Council Records fail to record a single trial for the crime of prostitution or adultery, although this may reflect a lack of enforcement zeal in this area.

46 As Robert Darnton has shown, pornographic texts were immensely popular in eighteenth-century France and often difficult to distinguish by their titles from philosophical or novelistic forms. Given the extremely heterogeneous character of colonial literature, I would not be surprised if elements of this genre, or at least of the "prurient interest" of the French public, made their way into Louisiana *mémoires* and travel accounts as well—even those written by nuns. Robert Darnton, *The Forbidden Bestsellers of Pre-Revolutionary France* (New York: Norton, 1996).

47 Abbé Prévost, *Manon Lescaut*, trans. Steve Larkin (Sawtry: Dedalus, 2001), 171.

48 Prévost, *Histoire du chevalier DesGrieux et de Manon Lescaut.* The strands of fact and fiction are further complicated by Prévost's own inclinations. A man of wide-ranging interests and literary pursuits, he compiled a collection of travel writing that the well-known Enlightenment writer Raynal later used in his even larger compendium of colonial history. Some Louisiana details and characters in *Manon Lescaut* coincide with archival sources well enough to suggest that Prévost was familiar with firsthand accounts of the colony. I am grateful to Dena Goodman for pointing out the connection to Prévost's armchair travel writing. Abbé Prévost, ed., *Histoire générale des voyages, ou Nouvelle collection de toutes les relations de voyages par Mer et par terre... pour former un systême complet d'histoire et de géographie moderne* (Paris: Didot, 1746).

49 Prévost, *Manon Lescaut*, trans. Larkin, 168.

50 Ibid., 165.

51 Ibid., 171.

52 Ibid., 172.

53 Ibid., 168–69, 174.

54 Gordon Sayre, *Les Sauvages Americains: Representations of Native Americans in French and English Colonial Literature* (Chapel Hill: University of North Carolina Press, 1997); Gordon Sayre, "Plotting the Natchez Massacre: Le Page du Pratz, Dumont de Montigny, Cheaubriand," *Early American Literature* 37, no. 3 (2002): 381–413; Patricia Galloway, "Rhetoric of Difference: Le Page du Pratz on African Slave Management in Eighteenth-Century Louisiana," *French Colonial History* 3 (2003): 1–16; Dawdy, "Enlightenment from the Ground"; Bienvenu, "Another America."

55 Defoe's book appeared in English in 1719, appropriately the same year as Dumont's first voyage to Louisiana. It was translated into French the following year. Daniel Defoe, *La vie et les avantures surprenantes de Robinson Crusoe* (Amsterdam: Chez L'Honoré & Chatelain, 1720).

56 Dumont de Montigny, "Mémoire de Lxx Dxx Officier," 2.

57 While still in the colony, Dumont began working on a long epic poem in verse entitled "L'Etablissement de la Louisiane," perhaps as a way to pass the time after his demotion as a military officer. Once he returned to France in the 1740s, Dumont went about rewriting and expanding the work in prose. A 1747 manuscript in Dumont's handwriting housed in the Ayer Collection of the Newberry Library in Chicago is the basis for my observations here (see note 21 above); few historians have had the opportunity to consult it. The Dumont work most people know is the two-volume *Mémoires Historiques sur la Louisiane* (1753), which was rewritten from the prose manuscript by M. L. L. Mascrier, a professional writer in the employ of Parisian booksellers. J. F. Dumont de Montigny and Jean-Baptiste Le Mascrier, *Mémoires historiques sur la Louisiane* (Paris: J. B. Bauche, 1753); Jean-François Benjamin Dumont de Montigny, "Poème en vers touchant l'établissement de la province de la Louisiane, connue sous le nom de Mississipi, avec tout ce qui s'est passé depuis 1716 jusqu'à 1741; le massacre des Français au poste des Natchez, les moeurs des sauvages, leurs danses, leurs religions, enfin ce qui concerne le pays en général," c. 1742, in Bibliothèque de l'Arsenal, Paris, Ms. 3459; Marc Villiers du Terrage, "Note sur un poème inédit de Dumont de Montigny décrivant les établissements du Mississipi de 1719 à 1740," *Journal de la Société des Américanistes de Paris* 11 (1914): 35–56; Marc Villiers du Terrage, "L'Etablissement de la province de la Louisiane: Poème composé de 1728 à 1742, par Dumont de Montigny," *Journal de la Société des Américanistes de Paris* 23 (1931): 273–440. For additional background on Dumont, see the introduction to a newly prepared transcription of the Newberry manuscript. Carla Zecher, Gordon Sayre, and Shannon Lee Dawdy, *Dumont de Montigny: Regards sur le monde atlantique, 1715–1747* (Quebec: Septentrion, 2008).

58 For the cultural context of Dumont's ideas about nobility, including literary performance, see Jonathan Dewald, *Aristocratic Experience and the Origins of Modern Culture: France, 1570–1715* (Berkeley: University of California Press, 1993).

59 Dumont de Montigny, "Mémoire De Lxx Dxx Officier," 132–33.

60 Ibid., 134.

61 Antoine Simon Le Page du Pratz, *Histoire de la Louisiane, contenant la découverte de ce vaste pays; sa description géographique; un voyage dans les terres; l'histoire naturelle, les moeurs, coutumes & religion des naturels, avec leurs origines; deux voyages dans le nord du nouveau Mexique, dont un jusqu'à la Mer du Sud; ornée de deux cartes & 40 planches en taille douce*, 3 vols. (Paris: De Bure, 1758). The widely available English translation is Le Page du Pratz, *The History of Louisiana*; facsimile edition with an introduction by Joseph G. Tregle Jr. (Baton Rouge: Louisiana State University Press, 1975).

62 Joseph G. Tregle, Jr., "Introduction," in Le Page du Pratz, *History of Louisiana*, xx; Antoine Simon Le Page du Pratz, *Lettre sur quelques nouveaux points d'astronomie* (Paris: Veuve Robineau, 1760).

63 Le Page du Pratz, *Histoire de la Louisiane*, 1:v, xiii–xv, 173, 265.

64 Le Page du Pratz, *History of Louisiana*, 208; *Histoire de la Louisiane*, 3:397.

65 The best known physiocrats were François Quesnay and the Marquis de Mirabeau, who first met in 1757. Ronald Meek, *The Economics of Physiocracy* (London: Ruskin House, 1962). See also Elizabeth Fox-Genovese, *The Origins of Physiocracy: Economic Revolution and the Social Order in Eighteenth-Century France* (Ithaca, N.Y.: Cornell University Press, 1976). On Louisiana's fertility and agricultural prospects, see Le Page du Pratz, *History of Louisiana*, 154 (quotation), 183–209.

66 Le Page du Pratz, *History of Louisiana*, 206.

67 In translation, see Jean Bernard Bossu, *New Travels in North America*, trans. Samuel Dorris Dickinson (Natchitoches, La.: Northwestern State University Press, 1982); Jean Bernard Bossu, *Travels in the Interior of North America, 1751–1762*, trans. Seymour Feiler (Norman: University of Oklahoma Press, 1962).

68 He speaks of "liberté" and the "droits de citoyens" and describes Kerlérec as a "despot." Bossu to unknown recipient, n.d., Affaire de la Louisiane, Bibliothèque de l'Arsenal, Archives de la Bastille, Dossier 12262, fols. 243–44v. *Mercure de France*, April 1768, Affaire de la Louisiane, Bibliothèque de l'Arsenal, Archives de la Bastille, Dossier 12262, fol. 267.

69 Letter 2, 1 July 1751, in Bossu, *Travels in the Interior*, 23–24.

70 Ibid., 24.

71 Thomas Jefferson and William Dunbar, "Description of Louisiana," in *Documents Relating to the Purchase and Exploration of Louisiana* (Boston: Houghton Mifflin, 1904), 344.

72 Light Cummings, in Bennet H. Wall and others, *Louisiana: A History* (Wheeling, Ill.: Harlan Davidson, 1997), 50; Moore, *Revolt in Louisiana*, 11. See also Stuart G. Noble and Arthur G. Nuhrah, "Education in Colonial Louisiana," *Louisiana Historical Quarterly* 32, no. 4 (1949): 759–76; Martin Luther Riley, "The Development of Education in Louisiana prior to Statehood," *Louisiana Historical Quarterly* 19, no. 3 (1936): 595–613; Roger Philip McCutcheon, "Books and Booksellers in New Orleans, 1730–1830," *Louisiana Historical Quarterly* 20, no. 3 (1937): 606–18; Roger Philip McCutcheon, "Libraries in New Orleans, 1771–1833," *Louisiana Historical Quarterly* 20, no. 1 (1937): 152–58; Giraud, *Company of the Indies*; Clark, *Masterless Mistresses*, 94, 113–17.

73 Florence M. Jumonville, "Frenchmen at Heart: New Orleans Printers and Their Imprints, 1764–1803," *Louisiana History* 22, no. 3 (1991): 279–315; Ingersoll, *Mammon and Manon*; Noble and Nuhrah, "Education in Colonial Louisiana," 771; Clark, *Masterless Mistresses*, 114–15. For estimations of literacy rates in eighteenth-century France, see Roger Chartier, "The Practical Impact of Writing," in *Passions of the Renaissance*, ed. Roger Chartier (Cambridge, Mass.: Belknap Press, 1989), 111–59, especially 112–13.

74 Quoted in Jackson, Weddle, and De Ville, *Mapping Texas*, 26.

75 Giraud, *Company of the Indies*, 299; Father Raphaël, letter, 25 July 1731, cited in Noble and Nuhrah, "Education in Colonial Louisiana," 760.

76 Bienville to minister, 15 June 1742, ANF-AC, C13A 27, fol. 27.

77 On the Capuchin–Jesuit rivalry that hindered efforts to establish a boy's school, see Charles Edwards O'Neill, *Church and State in French Colonial Louisiana: Policy and Politics to 1732* (New Haven: Yale University Press, 1966); Claude L. Vogel, "The Capuchins in French Louisiana, 1722–1766" (Ph.D. diss., Catholic University of America, 1928); Rev. Albert Hubert Biever, S.J., *The Jesuits in New Orleans and the Mississippi Valley: Jubilee Memorial* (New Orleans: Hauser Printing, 1924); and Clark, *Masterless Mistresses*.

78 Hachard, *Relation du voyage,* 97–98.

79 Riley, "Development of Education," 605; Clark, *Masterless Mistresses.*

80 Noble and Nuhrah, "Education in Colonial Louisiana"; Riley, "Development of Education"; Hachard, *Letters of Marie Madeleine Hachard,* 84; Clark, "New World Community."

81 Baillardel and Prioult, *Le Chevalier de Pradel;* O'Neill and Viel, *Viel.* Marin's son appears to have died en route or else in France. Procuration, 8 January 1745, SCA-LHQ 13, no. 3 (1930): 493; Testament of Elizabeth Real, 15 April 1771, Notary Juan B. Garic, 2:134, New Orleans Notarial Archives.

CHAPTER 2

1 Detailed accounts of the early physical development of New Orleans are provided in Marc de Villiers du Terrage, "A History of the Foundation of New Orleans, 1717–1722," *Louisiana Historical Quarterly* 3, no. 2 (1920): 157–251; Wilson, "The Vieux Carré." On the training and role of a French engineer such as Pauger, see René Chartrand, *French Fortresses in North America, 1535–1763* (New York: Osprey Publishing, 2005), 8–9.

2 Letter of 26 January 1722, in de Charlevoix, *Journal d'un voyage,* 3:438–39.

3 Pauger to Le Blond de La Tour, 14 April 1721, ANF-AC, Cartes et Plans, vol. 67, no. 5, fol. 135, pièce 13.

4 Pauger to Le Blond de la Tour, 19 August 1721, ANF-AC, C-13-A 6, fol. 139. See also Le Blond de La Tour to Commissioners of the Company, 28 April 1722, ANF-AC, C-13-A 6, fol. 316.

5 Pauger to Le Blond de la Tour, 19 August 1721, ANF-AC, C-13-A 6, fol. 139; Bienville, Pery and Fleuriau to Directors of the Company, 14 January 1724, ANF-AC · C-13-A 8, fol. 4; Pauger to Anonymous, 9 February 1724, ANF-AC, C-13-A 8, fol. 19.

6 Diron d'Artaguiette, "Journal of Diron d'Artaguiette," in *Travels in the American Colonies,* ed. Newton D. Mereness (New York: Macmillan, 1916 [1722–23]), 17. Chief Engineer Le Blond de la Tour was himself involved in another fight over a misaligned house. Raguet to Anonymous, 18 January 1722, ANF-AC, C-13-A 6, fol. 390.

7 Dubuisson was an active partner in one of the colony's largest concessions. Giraud, *Histoire de la Louisiane,* 4:245–48. Pauger was commissioned by the Company of the West to carry out other important duties. He did not, however, bear a noble title. Pauger was an army engineer who had served in the king's army since at least April 1707. He had been named captain of the Navarre Regiment and probably had seen action during the War of Spanish Succession. He received the honor of Chevalier of St. Louis just before being sent to Louisiana in 1720. His supervisor, Chief Engineer Le Blond de la Tour, was slightly older and had had a more distinguished military record as an engineer. Villiers du Terrage, "Foundation of New Orleans," 224–25.

8 Letter of 10 January 1722, in Charlevoix, *Journal d'un voyage,* 3:429–30.

9 Report on Louisiana, anonymous, n.d. (c. 1750), Louisiana Miscellany Collection, Library of Congress, Manuscripts, fol. 1493, quoted in Samuel Wilson, *The Vieux Carré, New Orleans: Its Plan, Its Growth, Its Architecture* (New Orleans: Marcou O'Leary & Associates, 1968), 37.

10   For a remarkably parallel study of urban planning in Louisiana undertaken at the same time this research was being conducted, see Gilles-Antoine Langlois, *Des villes pour la Louisiane française: Théorie et pratique de l'urbanistique coloniale au 18e siècle* (Paris: L'Harmattan, 2003). Langlois's impressive work provides much more depth and detail than space allows here, and compares New Orleans to other colonial towns, such as Biloxi and Mobile.

11   Angel Rama, *The Lettered City*, trans. John Charles Chasteen (Durham, N.C.: Duke University Press, 1996), 1.

12   On France's early policies toward Louisiana, see W. J. Eccles, *The French in North America, 1500–1783* (East Lansing: Michigan State University Press, 1998), 165–97; and Allain, *"Not Worth a Straw."*

13   Peirce F. Lewis, *New Orleans: The Making of an Urban Landscape*, 2d ed. (Santa Fe, N.M.: Center for American Places, 2003 [1976]), 39–40.

14   Gwendolyn Wright and other scholars of late colonialism have interpreted urban planning as "an expression of domination," or a physical mapping of the hegemony of the colonizer over the colonized involving the demolition and reordering of an ancient city, the addition of a separate quarter for colonial administrators, or the wholesale invention of a new city that strives toward civic modernity and architectural modernism. Planners designed monumental buildings in colonial capitals to communicate the logic of power and the mastery of control. Broad boulevards trained the line of vision toward a hierarchical landscape and open squares focused on figureheads in commemorative sculpture. The segregation of European and indigenous districts appears to be one of the most common marks of colonial urbanism. Wright, *Politics of Design*. See also Nezar Sayyad, *Forms of Dominance: On the Architecture and Urbanism of the Colonial Enterprise* (Brookfield, Vt.: Avebury, 1992); Zeynep Çelik, Diane G. Favro, and Richard Ingersoll, eds., *Streets: Critical Perspectives on Public Space* (Berkeley: University of California Press, 1994).

15   Sylvia Doughty Fries, *The Urban Idea in Colonial America* (Philadelphia: Temple University Press, 1977), 27.

16   Rama, *Lettered City*; Robert Ronald Reed, *Colonial Manila: The Context of Hispanic Urbanism and Process of Morphogenesis* (Berkeley: University of California Press, 1978); Richard L. Kagan and Fernando Marías, *Urban Images of the Hispanic World, 1493–1793* (New Haven: Yale University Press, 2000); Jay Kinsbruner, *The Colonial Spanish-American City: Urban Life in the Age of Atlantic Capitalism* (Austin: University of Texas Press, 2005); Setha M. Low, "Indigenous Architecture and the Spanish American Plaza in Mesoamerica and the Caribbean," *American Anthropologist* 97, no. 4 (1995): 748–62; Sidney David Markman, *Architecture and Urbanization in Colonial Chiapas Mexico* (Philadelphia: American Philosophical Society, 1984); Valerie Fraser, *The Architecture of Conquest: Building in the Viceroyalty of Peru, 1535–1635* (Cambridge: Cambridge University Press, 1990).

17   It seems significant that France began to build colonial towns on the Spanish model rather suddenly in the early 1700s, soon after the War of Spanish Succession, when the Bourbon family took over the Spanish throne. The new, closer working relationship of Spanish and French ministers seems to have resulted in an exchange of ideas with direct effects upon imperial strategies. I am grateful to Fernando Coronil for this suggestion.

18   John William Reps, *The Making of Urban America: A History of City Planning in the United States* (Princeton: Princeton University Press, 1965); John William Reps, *Town Planning in Frontier America* (Princeton: Princeton University Press, 1969);

Carl Bridenbaugh, *Cities in the Wilderness: The First Century of Urban Life in America, 1625–1742* (London: Oxford University Press, 1971); Howard P. Chudacoff and Judith E. Smith, *The Evolution of American Urban Society* (Upper Saddle River, N.J.: Prentice Hall, 2000); Fries, *Urban Idea*; Kenneth A. Lockridge, *A New England Town: The First Hundred Years, Dedham, Massachusetts, 1636–1736* (New York: W. W. Norton, 1970); Gary B. Nash, *The Urban Crucible: The Northern Seaports and the Origins of the American Revolution* (Cambridge, Mass.: Harvard University Press, 1986); Richard E. Foglesong, *Planning the Capitalist City: The Colonial Era to the 1920s* (Princeton: Princeton University Press, 1986), 51–52.

19   Fries, *Urban Idea*, xvii (quote), 108.

20   Hachard, *Relation du voyage*, 89–90.

21   Hugues Neveux, "Les Discours sur la ville," in *La Ville classique: de la Renaissance aux révolutions*, ed. Emmanuel Le Roy Ladurie (Paris: Editions du Seuil, 1981), 16–21; Roger Chartier, "La Ville-Chantier," in *La Ville classique*, ed. Le Roy Ladurie, 109–55, especially 110; Emmanuel Le Roy Ladurie, "De l'esthétique à la pathologie," in *La Ville classique*, ed. Le Roy Ladurie, 288–93; Langlois, *Des villes pour la Louisiane*.

22   Le Roy Ladurie, "De l'esthétique à la pathologie," 292–93; Daniel Gordon, "The City and the Plague in the Age of Enlightenment," *Yale French Studies* 92 (1997): 67–87; Nicolas Delamare, *Traité de la police: où l'on trouvera l'histoire de son établissement, les fonctions et les prerogatives de ses magistrats, toutes les loix et tous les reglemens qui la concernent, on y a joint une description historique et topographique de Paris* (Paris: M. Brunet, 1738); Jean-Louis Harouel, *Histoire de l'urbanisme* (Paris: Presses Universitaires de France, 1981); Jean-Louis Harouel, *L'Embellissement des villes: l'urbanisme français au XVIIIe siècle* (Paris: Picard, 1993).

23   Richard Louis Cleary, *The Place Royale and Urban Design in the Ancien Régime* (Cambridge: Cambridge University Press, 1999), 13, 109. Cleary dates the formalization of urban planning as a field to a 1748 competition for the design of Place Louis XV in Paris (p. 127). See also Antoine Picon, *French Architects and Engineers in the Age of Enlightenment* (New York: Cambridge University Press, 1992); and Dora Wiebenson, *The Picturesque Garden in France* (Princeton: Princeton University Press, 1977).

24   Cleary, *Place Royale*, 108.

25   Quoted in ibid., 137; see also 134–44. The term *police* in eighteenth-century French had multiple meanings, usually pertaining to a town or civic community: orderliness in appearance, social order and proper conduct, regulations and their enforcement. *Dictionnaire de l'Académie française*, 2:318. Delamare addressed all of these meanings in his work. See also Marc Antoine Laugier, *Essai sur l'architecture* (Paris: Duchesne, 1755), 121.

26   Chartier, "La Ville-Chantier," 110–12, 121; Cleary, *Place Royale*, 15. Ken Alder positions Vauban squarely within the Enlightenment in his push to make war a "science." The engineers who followed him contributed not only to the Enlightenment, Alder argues, but also, more significantly, to the French Revolution. Ken Alder, *Engineering the Revolution: Arms and Enlightenment in France, 1763–1815* (Princeton: Princeton University Press, 1997), 31–32.

27   Chartier, "La Ville-Chantier," 110.

28   Anne Blanchard, *Les Ingénieurs du roy de Louis XIV à Louis XVI: étude du corps des fortifications* (Montpellier: Université Paul-Valéry, 1979), 429, 432. See also Chartier, "La Ville-Chantier," 111–12; Pierre Lavedan, Jeanne Hugueney, and Philippe

Henrat, *L'Urbanisme à l'époque moderne: XVIe–XVIIIe siècles* (Paris: Arts et Métiers Graphiques, 1982).

29 Chartier, "La Ville-Chantier," 112–14; Josef W. Konvitz, *Cities and the Sea: Port City Planning in Early Modern Europe* (Baltimore: Johns Hopkins University Press, 1978); Robert Stein, "Measuring the French Slave Trade, 1713–1792/3," *Journal of African History* 19, no. 4 (1978): 515–21.

30 Roger Chartier refers to these as "villes-résidences." Chartier, "La Ville-Chantier," 114. Richelieu is located between Tours and Nantes.

31 Chartier, "La Ville-Chantier," 114–20; Chandra Mukerji, *Territorial Ambitions and the Gardens of Versailles* (Cambridge: Cambridge University Press, 1997); Cleary, *Place Royal*.

32 Wiebenson, *Picturesque Garden*, 3–22, 108–21; Picon, *French Architects and Engineers*, 188–90; Laugier, *Essai sur l'architecture*, 222.

33 Christopher Morris, "Impenetrable But Easy: The French Transformation of the Lower Mississippi Valley and the Founding of New Orleans," in *Transforming New Orleans and Its Environs: Centuries of Change*, ed. Craig E. Colten (Pittsburgh: University of Pittsburgh Press, 2000), 23.

34 Tristram R. Kidder, "Making the City Inevitable: Native Americans and the Geography of New Orleans," in *Transforming New Orleans and Its Environs*, ed. Colten, 7–21.

35 The margins of Lake Pontchartrain are somewhat older, dating back 2,000 to 2,500 years. Jill-Karen Yakubik and others, "Archeological Data Recovery of the Camino Site (16JE223), A Spanish Colonial Period Site near New Orleans, Louisiana" (New Orleans: Earth Search, Inc., 1996), 15–18; U.S. Department of Agriculture, "Soil Survey of Orleans Parish, Louisiana" (Washington, D.C.: USDA, 1989); Lewis, *New Orleans: The Making of an Urban Landscape*, 20–33.

36 Roger Saucier, *Recent Geomorphic History of the Pontchartrain Basin* (Baton Rouge: Louisiana State University, 1963), 6.

37 Ibid., 20, 100.

38 Robert W. Neuman, *An Introduction to Louisiana Archaeology* (Baton Rouge: Louisiana State University Press, 1984), 213; Jill-Karen Yakubik and Herschel A. Franks (with contributions by Daniel C. Weinand, Elizabeth J. Reitz, and Tristram R. Kidder), "Archaeological Investigations at the Site of the Cabildo, New Orleans, Louisiana" (New Orleans: Earth Search, Inc., 1997), 29; Marco J. Giardino, "Documentary Evidence for the Location of Historic Indian Villages in the Mississippi Delta," in *Perspectives on Gulf Coast Prehistory*, ed. Dave Davis (Gainesville: University Press of Florida, 1984), 232–57. The Natchez and Taensas Indians are also thought to be descended from Plaquemine people.

39 Acolapissa may be a variant of Quinipissa, or it may indicate that another of the *petites nations* had moved in, perhaps to take advantage of trade with the French. Giardino, "Historic Indian Villages in the Mississippi Delta," 248–49; Le Page du Pratz, *Histoire de la Louisiane*, 1:46, 82. Kidder suggests that Quinipissa and Acolapissa are probably two names for the same group. Kidder, "Making the City Inevitable," 19.

40 Yakubik and Franks, "Archaeological Investigations at the Cabildo," 29. Kidder notes that a 1718 map by Guillaume Delisle also places the Ouma in the city. Kidder, "Making the City Inevitable," 19. It is also possible that the Delisle map represents outdated information. On this topic, see Patricia Kay Galloway, "Debriefing

Explorers: Amerindian Information in the Delisles' Mapping of the Southeast," in *Cartographic Encounters: Perspectives on Native American Mapmaking and Map Use*, ed. G. Malcolm Lewis (Chicago: University of Chicago Press, 1998), 223–40.

41 Fred B. Kniffen, Hiram F. Gregory, and George A. Stokes, *The Historic Indian Tribes of Louisiana: From 1542 to the Present* (Baton Rouge: Louisiana State University Press, 1987), 55–56.

42 Pierre LeMoyne d'Iberville, *Iberville's Gulf Journal*, trans. Richebourg G. McWilliams (Birmingham: University of Alabama Press, 1980), 57.

43 Kidder, "Making the City Inevitable," 17; Saucier, *Recent Geomorphic History*.

44 Kidder, "Making the City Inevitable," 20.

45 These "towns" were centers of political and religious power, but not necessarily large residential units in the late Mississippian period. Inhabitants were dispersed in nearby satellite villages where they had easy access to their agricultural fields, as well as the ceremonial and trading center of the principal town. Tristram R. Kidder, "Mississippi Period Mound Groups and Communities in the Lower Mississippi Valley," in *Mississippian Towns and Sacred Spaces: Searching for an Architectural Grammar*, ed. R. Barry Lewis and Charles Stout (Tuscaloosa: University of Alabama Press, 1998), 123–50; Ian W. Brown, "An Archaeological Study of Culture Contact and Change in the Natchez Bluffs Region," in *La Salle and His Legacy*, ed. Galloway, 176–93; Ian W. Brown, *Natchez Indian Archaeology: Culture Change and Stability in the Lower Mississippi Valley* (Jackson: Mississippi Dept. of Archives and History, 1985).

46 As an indication of the rapid material creolization taking place in early Louisiana, Le Page purchased a sturdy, Natchez-built cabin just outside the Grand Village, while the African couple he had just bought in New Orleans lived in another, "which they built for themselves," presumably using architectural skills and aesthetics from their own culture. Le Page du Pratz, *The History of Louisiana*, 322, 27.

47 R. Barry Lewis, Charles Stout, and Cameron B. Wesson, "The Design of Mississippian Towns," in *Mississippian Towns and Sacred Spaces*, ed. Lewis and Stout, 1–21; Kidder, "Mississippi Period Mound Groups."

48 Hall, *Africans in Colonial Louisiana*, 35. Coquery-Vidrovitch provides a *longue durée* history of urbanization in Africa that critiques scholars who have too universally characterized colonizers as having cities and the colonized as having villages. I believe this also applies to many archaeologists' and historians' choice of words in describing Native America. Catherine Coquery-Vidrovitch, "The Process of Urbanization in Africa (from the Origins to the Beginning of Independence)," *African Studies Review* 34, no. 1 (1991): 1–98.

49 For additional background on indigenous African urbanity, European forts, and creole ports in West Africa, see Christopher R. DeCorse, *West Africa during the Atlantic Slave Trade: Archaeological Perspectives* (London: Leicester University Press, 2001); Christopher R. DeCorse, *An Archaeology of Elmina: Africans and Europeans on the Gold Coast, 1400–1900* (Washington, D.C.: Smithsonian Institution Press, 2001); Paul Wheatley, "The Significance of Traditional Yoruba Urbanism," *Comparative Studies in Society and History* 12, no. 2 (1970): 393–423; Derwent Whittlesey, "Dakar and the Other Cape Verde Settlements," *Geographical Review* 31, no. 4 (1941): 609–38; Joseph O. Vogel, ed., *Encyclopedia of Pre-Colonial Africa: Archaeology, History, Linguistics, and Environments* (Walnut Creek, Calif.: Alta Mira Press, 1997); W. Raymond Wood, "An Archaeological Appraisal of Early European

Settlements in the Senegambia," *Journal of African History* 8, no. 1 (1967): 39–64; Christopher Winters, "Urban Morphogenesis in Francophone Black Africa," *Geographical Review* 72, no. 2 (1982): 139–54.

50 Ira Berlin, "From Creole to African: Atlantic Creoles and the Origins of African-American Society in Mainland North America," *William and Mary Quarterly*, 3d ser., 53, no. 2 (1996): 259. See Berlin, *Many Thousands Gone*; Donald R. Wright, *The World and a Very Small Place in Africa* (Armonk, N.Y.: M. E. Sharpe, 1997).

51 Berlin, *Many Thousands Gone*; Peter Mark, "Constructing Identity: Sixteenth- and Seventeenth-Century Architecture in the Gambia-Geba Region and the Articulation of Luso-African Ethnicity," *History in Africa* 22 (1995): 307–27; Sylvie Kandé, *Terres, urbanisme et architecture "créoles" en Sierra Leone: XVIIIe–XIXe siècles* (Paris: L'Harmattan, 1998).

52 La Tour to Commissioners of the Company, 13 September 1722, ANF-AC, C-13-A 6, fol. 339.

53 De La Harpe, *Journal historique*, 81; Le Blond de La Tour to Commissioners of the Company, 20 August 1722, ANF-AC, C-13-A 6, fol. 321; King to Bienville and Salmon, 2 February 1732, in *Mississippi Provincial Archives 1704–1743: French Dominion*, ed. Dunbar Rowland and A. G. Sanders, vol. 3 (Jackson: Mississippi Department of Archives and History, 1932), 563 (hereafter cited as MPA 3); Vergès to Rochemore, 24 August 1760, ANF-AC, C-13-A 42, fol. 134.

54 Instructions pour la formation d'un établissement, 1719, Drouot de Valdeterre, ANF-AC, C-13-A 6, fol. 352. Pauger wrote that the annual floods "rendered the town impracticable and cause the most dangerous illnesses there." Pauger to Directors of the Company, 3 January 1724, ANF-AC, C-13-A 8, fol. 9.

55 Dubreuil to Minister, 27 June 1740, ANF-AC, C-13-A 25, fol. 268.

56 Morris, "Impenetrable But Easy," 34–38; Wilson, "Vieux Carré," 15–20, 30–32, 38.

57 Morris, "Impenetrable But Easy," 35. Curiously, two recent environmental histories of New Orleans entirely neglect the colonial period, instead picking up the story with the Louisiana Purchase of 1803. Since the concepts of levee-building and the maintenance of a clear urban/rural border were initiated in the French period, this omission is peculiar, except that it may reflect a more general problem in Louisiana historiography in which Americanist scholars are uncomfortable with the French and Spanish sources from the colonial era. Ari Kelman, *A River and Its City: The Nature of Landscape in New Orleans* (Berkeley: University of California Press, 2003); Craig E. Colten, *An Unnatural Metropolis: Wresting New Orleans from Nature* (Baton Rouge: Louisiana University Press, 2005).

58 *MPA 3*, 594, 638 (quote).

59 Morris, "Impenetrable But Easy," 25; Eléonore Oglethorpe, Marquise de Mézières, to Jean Gravé de La Mancelière, 12 June 1721, Rosemond E. and Emile Kuntz Collection, Tulane University Special Collections, Tulane University, New Orleans.

60 Sugar's success had to wait until 1795, when planter Etienne de Boré introduced skilled slaves from Saint Domingue who knew more efficient methods for planting and processing cane, as well as varieties more suitable to Louisiana.

61 Usner, *Indians, Settlers, and Slaves*.

62 Pauger to Le Blond de La Tour, 14 April 1721, ANF-AC, Cartes et Plans, vol. 67, no. 5, fol. 135, pièce 13.

63 Dumont de Montigny, "Mémoire De Lxx Dxx Officier," 142.

64 Morris, "Impenetrable But Easy," 32, 23.

65 Complete technical data on faunal identifications, biomass, MNIs (minimum number of individuals), and so forth are presented in Shannon Lee Dawdy et al., "Greater New Orleans Archaeology Program End of Federal Fiscal Year Report 2001–2002," (New Orleans: College of Urban and Public Affairs, University of New Orleans, 2002), 26–66.

66 Usner, *Indians, Settlers, and Slaves*, 149–218; Hall, *Africans in Colonial Louisiana*, 201–12.

67 Milk production from the sheep/goat is inferred because individuals were found only in rural contexts in proportions and ages suggesting butchering for herd control rather than meat production. In terms of local adaptation, a similar trend is seen in the grain diet. The founder generation tried quixotically to plant wheat in Louisiana's subtropical zone, with predictable failure. Nevertheless, women in New Orleans were said to be particularly troublesome when they could not obtain wheat flour to make the bread to which they were accustomed. Although wheat importation became a major factor in the New Orleans economy, locals did adopt American corn into their diet, apparently with greater alacrity in the creole generation. They also experimented with rice flour, making a sort of rice bread with it that locals accepted but to which newer French immigrants objected. As the rice itself and knowledge regarding its cultivation seems to be a contribution made by African slaves, the recipe for rice bread may be of African origin. See Hall, *Africans in Colonial Louisiana*, 121–24.

68 Instruction pour M. Perrier, ingénieur en chef de la Louisiane, 14 April 1718, in Pierre Margry, *Découvertes et établissements des français dans l'ouest et dans le sud de l'Amérique Septentrionale (1614–1754)*, vol. 5 (Paris: D. Jouaust, 1876), 606–7.

69 The shores of the river and lake follow unfamiliar contours and the map is upside down, showing Lake Pontchartrain to the south of the city. Perrier appears never to have made it to Louisiana. He was replaced by Le Blond de la Tour.

70 "Account of Jonathas Darby," *Records of the American Catholic Historical Society of Philadelphia* 10 (June 1899): 201.

71 On New Orleans maps, see Wilson, "Vieux Carré."

72 Pauger to Directors of the Company, 3 January 1724, ANF-AC, C-13-A 8, fol. 10.

73 Hachard, *Relation du voyage*, 89–90; Wilson, *Architecture of Colonial Louisiana*, 1–23, 221–60; Malcolm Heard, *French Quarter Manual: An Architectural Guide to New Orleans' Vieux Carré* (New Orleans: Tulane School of Architecture, 1997), 18–20. A similar architecture of two-story, gallery "manor houses" arose at the same time in the West Indies, giving the style its name. Builders in New Orleans may have been influenced by Caribbean architecture, but the synchronicity suggests that New Orleans was simply the northern fringe of a world sharing a material culture. For an example of the half-timber charter-generation buildings, see figure 2 in chapter 1, above.

74 This was the same writer who complained about "negro cabarets" and the town's uncontrolled borders. Report on Louisiana, quoted in Wilson, "Vieux Carré," 37.

75 Such as Le Page's articles in the *Journal Oeconomique*; and De Montigny and Le Mascrier, *Mémoires historiques sur la Louisiane*.

76 Thierry, "Plan de la ville la Nouvelle Orleans capitale de la province de la Louisiane, 1758," Historic New Orleans Collection, Williams Research Center, acc. no. 1939.8.

77　Richard Wade and others have suggested that the brick walls surrounding urban compounds in cities such as New Orleans and Charleston helped control the movement of slaves. But given the great mobility of slaves commented upon in colonial New Orleans, walls were not an effective means of control. Richard C. Wade, *Slavery in the Cities: The South, 1820–1860* (New York: Oxford University Press, 1964). See also George J. Castille and others, "Archeological Excavations at Esplanade Avenue and Rampart Street, New Orleans, Louisiana" (Baton Rouge: Coastal Environments, Inc., 1982); Kenneth E. Lewis, *Camden: A Frontier Town in Eighteenth-century South Carolina* (Columbia: University of South Carolina, 1976). For caveats on reading too much symbolism into the urban landscape, see Shannon Lee Dawdy, "Ethnicity in the Urban Landscape: The Archaeology of Creole New Orleans," in *Archaeology of Southern Urban Landscapes*, ed. Amy L. Young (Tuscaloosa: University of Alabama Press, 2000), 127–49.

78　Vaughan, *Creating the Creole Island*.

79　A. J. B. Johnston, *Control and Order in French Colonial Louisbourg, 1713–1758* (East Lansing: Michigan State University Press, 2001).

80　Ibid., 101. Johnston also notes the striking visual parallels in the original plans for Louisbourg and New Orleans.

81　Procès-verbal of Bienville, Salmon, de Noyan, and Bizoton, 12 July 1734, ANF-AC, C-13-A 18, fol. 176.

82　Johnston, *Control and Order*, 77–82, 107–10.

83　Ibid., 81.

84　Villiers du Terrage, *Last Years of French Louisiana*, 52–53.

85　Wilson, "Vieux Carré," 16; Procès-verbal of Bienville, Salmon, de Noyan, and Bizoton, 12 July 1734, ANF-AC, C-13-A 18, fol. 176; Harry Gordon, "Journal of Captain Harry Gordon," in *Travels in the American Colonies*, ed. Newton D. Mereness (New York: Macmillan, 1916 [1766]), 464–89, especially 483.

86　Arlette Farge, *Fragile Lives: Violence, Power and Solidarity in Eighteenth-century Paris* (Cambridge, Mass.: Harvard University Press, 1993), 18–19.

87　Johnston, *Control and Order*, 63.

88　Wilson, "Vieux Carré," 26–32.

89　Report on Louisiana, quoted in Wilson, "Vieux Carré," 37.

90　Villiers du Terrage, *Last Years of French Louisiana*, 118–29, 378–406; De Vergès to Rochemore, 12 August 1760, ANF-AC, C-13-A 42, fol. 135; Kerlérec to Minister, 15 August 1760, ANF-AC, C-13-A 42 fol. 64. The imprisonment and investigation records of the Louisiana Affair comprise several hundred pages housed at the Bibliothèque de l'Arsenal in Paris, which holds the surviving records of the Bastille. Most of them are concerned with Kerlérec's enemies whom he had imprisoned for slander and libel before he himself was exiled from Paris for abuse of office and suspicion of smuggling. Louisiana Affair, Bibliothèque de l'Arsenal, Archives de la Bastille, Dossiers 12262, 12249, 12507, and 12705. See also Hervé Gourmelon, *Le Chevalier de Kerlérec: l'affaire de la Louisiane* (Paris: By the author, 2003), a curious *essai de réhabilitation*.

91　Langlois, *Des villes pour la Louisiane*, 211. For examples of other French colonial towns in this mold, see Lavedan, Hugueney, and Henrat, *L'Urbanisme à l'époque moderne*, 231–32, figs. 681, 711–12, and 716.

92　Evarts Boutell Greene and Virginia Draper Harrington, *American Population before the Federal Census of 1790* (Gloucester, Mass.: P. Smith, 1966). Taylor counts any community over 2,500 as urban. Only four cities in British North America numbered more than 5,000 in 1760: Philadelphia, Boston, New York, and Charleston. George Rogers Taylor, "Urban Growth Preceding the Railway Age," *Journal of Economic History* 27, no. 3 (1967): 309–39.

93 Interestingly, the Sicilian Mafia, another rogue political economy, is credited with having a tremendous influence on the urban development of Palermo, with the anti-Mafia campaign measuring its recent successes by the implementation of historic preservation plans. Jane C. Schneider and Peter T. Schneider, *Reversible Destiny: Mafia, Antimafia, and the Struggle for Palermo* (Berkeley: University of California Press, 2003).

94 Daniel Gordon describes a similar failure of modern urban planning to prevent disease in Marseille during the same time period (1720s). He argues that the literature arising from this experience contributed to early *philosophe* critiques of urbanism. Gordon, "City and the Plague."

CHAPTER 3

1 Louisiana State Museum, Notarial Records, Deverges no. 92766, Ducro no.10433.
2 Elizabeth Real may be the same woman identified as "Marie Real" on the passenger list of the *Marie*, which left France for Louisiana on 23 May 1718. This woman was also from Oléron; she is listed as an indentured employee of none other than the historian (then concessionaire) Le Page du Pratz. Glenn R. Conrad, *First Families of Louisiana*, 2 vols. (Baton Rouge: Claitor's, 1970), 1:8.
3 Marriage contract, 30 April 1739, SCA-LHQ 6, no. 3 (1923): 501; Inventoire de Sr. François Goudeau, 29 May 1759, SCR. Madame Real actually wrote two wills: Marin Testament, 27 April 1769, Notary E. Deverges Act 10358/Ducros Act 10433; and Real Testament, 15 April 1771, Notary Jean Baptiste Garic Act 2/134, NONA. On artifacts, see Shannon Lee Dawdy, "Madame John's Legacy (160R51) Revisited: A Closer Look at the Archaeology of Colonial New Orleans" (University of New Orleans, 1998), tables C-1 and C-2.
4 In 1736 Marin delivered a load of muskets to Florida; in 1737 he was on a trade expedition to the "Coast of Spain" (probably Cartagena area); and in 1738 he made a voyage to Havana. Power of attorney, [n.d.] 1736; maritime accounts, 6 March 1737–15 July 1738; court summons, 4 November 1737 and 3 January 1738, SCA-LHQ 5, no. 3 (1922): 386, 391–92, 420. In the census of 1727 Madame Real's household was listed with only two occupants—herself and her child. Presumably she informed the census taker that her husband was away on business, but he was not enumerated. Charles R. Maduell Jr., *The Census Tables for the French Colony of Louisiana from 1699 through 1732* (Baltimore: Genealogical Publishing Co., 1972), 94.
5 Sale, Francisco Goudeau to Santiago Lemelle, 12 September 1776, J. B. Garic notary, NONA; Santiago Lemelle to Rene Beluche, 30 July 1778, J. B. Garic notary, NONA; George Washington Cable, "Tite Poulette," in *Old Creole Days* (New York: Charles Scribner's Sons, 1883), 213–43.
6 Kerlérec to Rouillé, 8 March 1753, ANF-AC, C13A 37, fols. 34–38; in *Mississippi Provincial Archives: French Dominion, 1749–1763*, ed. Dunbar Rowland, A. G. Sanders, and Patricia Kay Galloway, vol. 5 (Baton Rouge: Louisiana State University Press, 1984), 123 (hereafter cited as MPA 5).
7 Usner, *Indians, Settlers, and Slaves.*

8   The relationship of New Orleans to Cap Français is akin to what Louis Pérez describes for Santiago de Cuba and Havana: "The west flourished as a result of the official presence, in defense of colonial policy; the east flourished as a result of the official absence, in defiance of colonial policy." Louis A. Pérez, *Cuba: Between Reform and Revolution* (New York: Oxford University Press, 1995), 41.

9   For background on French mercantilism, see Allain, *"Not Worth a Straw"*; John Garretson Clark, *New Orleans, 1718-1812: An Economic History* (Baton Rouge: Louisiana State University Press, 1970); John Robert McNeill, *Atlantic Empires of France and Spain: Louisbourg and Havana, 1700-1763* (Chapel Hill: University of North Carolina Press, 1985); Charles Woolsey Cole, *Colbert and a Century of French Mercantilism* (Hamden, Conn.: Archon Books, 1964).

10   In two major contributions to Louisiana's early economic history, John Clark focuses on official, international trade relationships and the export of cash crops, while Daniel Usner focuses on the informal and local aspects of the economy, as well as its social dimensions. Clark dismisses the importance of illicit commerce, while Usner concentrates on the terrestrial Indian trade. Clark, *New Orleans, 1718–1812*; Usner, *Indians, Settlers, and Slaves*.

11   Most freshwater routes ran approximately north-south, the largest arteries being the Mississippi, Red, Ouachita, Missouri, Tombigbee, and Alabama Rivers, which connected the Great Lakes to the Gulf of Mexico. With a few exceptions (notably near New Orleans through Bayou Manchac and Lake Pontchartrain), east-west routes were overland, with paths connecting English Carolina to New Mexico.

12   J. Duboys, *Recueils de Reglemens, Edits, Declarations et Arrêts, Concernant le Commerce, l'Administration de la Justice, & la Police des Colonies Françaises de l'Amerique & les Engagés, avec le Code Noir et l'Addition Audit Code* (Paris: Les Libraires Associez, 1744–45).

13   Clark, *New Orleans, 1718–1812*; Usner, *Indians, Settlers, and Slaves*, 31, 63, 121, 130, 164, 181, 184–85, 199–202, 215, 250.

14   Contract, 7 January 1737, SCA-LHQ 8, no. 4 (1925): 688; acknowledgment by Sr. Claude Reynaud dit Avignon, 6 August 1739, SCA-LHQ 7, no. 2 (1924): 354.

15   Examples of women's involvement in the colonial economy abound in the notarial documents. Usner, *Indians, Settlers, and Slaves*, 267; obligation, 18 December 1743, SCA-LHQ 12, no. 3 (1929): 494; declaration, 28 July 1730, SCR. Louboey to Maurepas, 23 June 1740; in *Mississippi Provincial Archives: French Dominion, 1729-1748*, ed. Dunbar Rowland, A. G. Sanders, and Patricia Galloway, vol. 4 (Baton Rouge: Louisiana State University Press, 1983) (hereafter cited as MPA 4), 170–71. Sale, 26 November 1743, SCA-LHQ 12, no. 3 (1929): 473; "Agreement between a free negro . . . and Sr. Francois Trudeau," 20 August 1736, SCA-LHQ 8, no. 3 (1925): 489; contract by free Negro, 10 March 1739, SCA-LHQ 6, no. 2 (1923): 306.

16   Usner, *Indians, Settlers, and Slaves*, 71, 103, 123. In 1758 William Perry reported that "he saw Numbers of Indians in Town, fifty or sixty in a Gang." William Perry, "New Orleans in 1758, Being the Experiences of William Perry, an American Seaman, Held in 'Jayl' There as a French Prisoner of War," *Louisiana Historical Quarterly* 5, no. 1 (1922 [1758]): 56. On the licit and illegal workings of the Mississippi trade, see Cécile Vidal, "Antoine Bienvenu, Illinois Planter and Mississippi Trader: The Structure of Exchange between Lower and Upper Louisiana," in *French Colonial Louisiana and the Atlantic World*, ed. Bond, 111–33.

17   Bienvenu, "Another America, Another Literature," 198–269.

18 May Rush Gwin Waggoner, ed., "Mémoire of Jean Béranger," in *Le Plus Beau Pais du Monde: Completing the Picture of Proprietary Louisiana, 1699–1722* (Lafayette: Center for Louisiana Studies, 2005), 150–99, especially 189 (quote).

19 Nancy Maria Miller Surrey, *The Commerce of Louisiana during the French Régime, 1699–1763* (New York: Columbia University Press, 1916), 75–76. Local shipbuilding and repair businesses also thrived. See "Contract to Build a Ship in New Orleans, 1769," *Louisiana Historical Quarterly* 9, no. 4 (1926 [1769]): 593–97; contract to build boat, 9 March 1739, SCA-LHQ 6, no. 2 (1923): 305–6; Clark, *New Orleans, 1718–1812*, 23, 57.

20 Anonymous [Jonathas Darby], "Louisiana 1717 to 1751."

21 A much-needed history of the Mississippi-Caribbean world inspired by French historian Fernand Braudel's magnum opus on the Mediterranean would encourage us to consider environment, technology, and trade over the long term (*la longue durée*) in the region. Such an approach would help us mend an exaggerated break between the prehistoric and historic periods of American history, or the divide between archaeology and history. In the absence of epic in our present-day historiography, I offer here a Braudelian microhistory of the site of New Orleans and the factors that the city's founders undoubtedly took into account as they planned its economic future. Fernand Braudel, *The Mediterranean and the Mediterranean World in the Age of Philip II*, trans. Siân Reynolds (London: Collins, 1972).

22 Evidence points to a relationship between southeastern Mississippian groups and cultures in the Huesteca and Veracruz regions of Mexico during the period A.D. 1000–1400. For a discussion of this evidence, see Dawdy, "La Ville Sauvage," 111–19.

23 Banks, *Chasing Empire across the Sea*, 87–94; Usner, *Indians, Settlers, and Slaves*, 233–34. See also Vidal, "Antoine Bienvenu."

24 Banks, *Chasing Empire*, 84–87; Maduell, *Census Tables*, 95–96.

25 Memoir on Louisiana, Bienville to Ministry of the Colonies, 1726, in MPA 3:510. Bienville continues: "[I]n the future a very considerable commerce could be carried on with the Spaniards. One could not have for that purpose a more fortunate situation than that of Louisiana. It is only two hundred leagues distant from Havana on one side and from Tampico on the other, only three hundred leagues from Veracruz and Campeche. It is true that all the avenues to these posts are carefully guarded by the vessels that the King of Spain maintains there for the express purpose of keeping smugglers away and that the different governors have the precise orders of his Catholic Majesty strictly observed, but that will not continue forever . . . I do not know whether even at present a means of rendering the governors more tractable might not be found" (517).

26 On the navigational access of the delta, see Delachaise to Directors of the Company of the Indies, 18 October 1723; in *Mississippi Provincial Archives: French Dominion, 1701–1729*, ed. Dunbar Rowland and A. G. Sanders, vol. 2 (Jackson: Mississippi State Department of Archives and History, 1929) (hereafter cited as MPA 2), 380. Samuel Wilson Jr., "Early Aids to Navigation at the Mouth of the Mississippi River," *Proceedings of the United States Naval Institute* 70 (1944): 278–87. Barataria is *baraterie* in French, *barratry* in English. Although named after the Spanish term, the bay acquired its name during the French period. See, for example, agreement, 22 November 1738, SCA-LHQ 6, no. 1 (1923): 142; "Interrogation du nègre François Cariton," 14 April 1751, SCR.

27 Gordon, "New Orleans and Bayou St. John in 1766," 19–20.

28   Bienville recommended in 1726: "As the post of The Balize is the most handy for the commerce with the Spaniards it is necessary to have there a clerk who understands this commerce and knows the Spanish language" (MPA 3:504).

29   Bienville and Salmon to Maurepas, 12 May 1733, in MPA 3:604. In 1743 a new ordinance prohibited French merchants from traveling to Florida in order to better direct cash flows to New Orleans. Clark, *New Orleans, 1718–1812*, 141–44.

30   Allan J. Kuethe, "Havana in the Eighteenth Century," in *Atlantic Port Cities: Economy, Culture, and Society in the Atlantic World, 1650–1850*, ed. Franklin W. Knight and Peggy K. Liss (Knoxville: University of Tennessee Press, 1991), 13–39; McNeill, *Atlantic Empires of France and Spain*; John Robert Fisher, *Commercial Relations between Spain and Spanish America in the Era of Free Trade, 1778–1796* (Liverpool: Centre for Latin-American Studies, University of Liverpool, 1985); Banks, *Chasing Empire*, 166 (quote). One observer in 1751 noted that an enterprising Louisiana planter "frequently brings in horses and mules, which are sold to the Spaniards on the Islands at the same price as negroes." Anonymous [Darby], "Louisiana 1717 to 1751," 566.

31   Robert Sidney Smith, "Shipping in the Port of Veracruz, 1790–1821," *Hispanic American Historical Review* 23, no. 1 (1973): 5 (quote); Stanley J. Stein and Barbara H. Stein, *Silver, Trade, and War: Spain and America in the Making of Early Modern Europe* (Baltimore: Johns Hopkins University Press, 2000); Guadalupe Jiménez Codinach, "An Atlantic Silver Entrepôt: Veracruz and the House of Gordon and Murphy," in *Atlantic Port Cities*, ed. Knight and Liss, 149–67; Javier Ducasse Ortiz de la Tabla, *Comercio exterior de Veracruz, 1778–1821: Crisis de dependencia* (Seville: Escuela de Estudios Hispano-Americanos de Sevilla, 1978); Jackie R. Booker, *Veracruz Merchants, 1770–1829: A Merchant Elite in Late Bourbon and Early Independent Mexico* (Boulder, Colo.: Westview Press, 1993).

32   Julius Sherrard Scott III, "The Common Wind: Currents of Afro-American Communication in the Era of the Haitian Revolution" (Ph.D. diss., Duke University, 1986), 29, 28 (quotes); Duclos to Pontchartrain, 25 October 1713, in MPA 2:100. By small, Duclos probably means ships under 100 tons. Most regular transatlantic ships were rated for at least 100 tons (although the voyage was possible in ships as small as 60 tons), and 250 tons was closer to average. The size of the ships coming through New Orleans, when recorded, ranged from 25 to 250 tons, but most were two-masted vessels of various sail designs (brig, brigantine, schooner, snow) that fell within the range of 35–70 tons.

33   Caillot, "Relation du Voyage de la Louisiane," fol. 106.

34   These ships in some cases appear several times in the Superior Council records. See entries for 16 January 1735, 12 June 1735, 2 May 1736, 25 June 1736, 17 November 1736, 1 January 1737, 31 January 1737, 3 August 1737, 4 November 1737, 22 November 1737, 27–28 November 1737, 27 October 1738, 26 March 1739, 10 March 1740, 5 May 1740, 25 October 1740, 2 February 1741, 4 September 1743, 20 September 1743, 14 December 1743, 8 February 1745, 15 February 1745, 1 June 1745, 14 June 1745, 2 March 1747, 1 May 1747, 8 May 1747, 23 March 1748, in volumes of SCA-LHQ, from 5, no. 2 (1922) through 19, no. 2 (1936).

35   Kris E. Lane, *Pillaging the Empire: Piracy in the Americas, 1500–1750* (Armonk, N.Y.: M. E. Sharpe, 1998), 167; D'Iberville, *Iberville's Gulf Journals*, 24; Mémoire of Béranger, n.d. [c. 1724], ANF-AC, C13A 4, fol. 91 (on praise for Bienville, see fol. 93); Maduell, *Census Tables*, 2; Marcel Giraud, *Reign of Louis XIV, 1698–1715*, trans. Brian Pearce (Baton Rouge: Louisiana State University Press, 1974), 91.

Iberville had requested fifty "flibustiers venant de Saint-Domingue." Letter from
Iberville, n.d. [c. 1698], ANF-AC, C13A 1, fols. 83–90.

36 D'Artaguette to Minister, 18 August 1708, ANF-AC, C13A 2, fols. 327–40; Pontchartrain to Bienville, 10 May 1710, in MPA 3:145; Hubert to Conseil, n.d. [c.
1718], ANF-AC, C13A 1, fols. 47–62; D'Artaguette to Minister, 8 September 1712,
ANF-AC, C13A 2, fols. 799–802.

37 Projet pour la Royalle Compagnie des Indes au Sujet de commerce de Mexique,
n.d. [between 1718 and 1728], ANF-AC, C13C 4, fols. 167–75v; letters patent of
the king, October 1727, ANF-AC, Series A 25, fols. 83v-90.

38 For recent work on this subject, see Knight and Liss, eds., *Atlantic Port Cities*;
Lance Raymond Grahn, *The Political Economy of Smuggling: Regional Informal
Economies in Early Bourbon New Granada* (Boulder, Colo.: Westview Press, 1997);
Lane, *Pillaging the Empire*; Jorge Miguel Viana Pedreira, "Contraband, Crisis, and
the Collapse of the Old Colonial System," *Hispanic American Historical Review*
81, nos. 3–4 (2001): 739–44; Ernst Pijning, "A New Interpretation of Contraband
Trade," *Hispanic American Historical Review* 81, nos. 3–4 (2001): 733–38; and Nu-
ala Zahedieh, "The Merchants of Port Royal, Jamaica, and the Spanish Contraband
Trade, 1655–1692," *William and Mary Quarterly*, 3d ser., 43, no. 4 (1986): 570–93;
Linebaugh and Rediker, *Many-Headed Hydra*.

39 Usner and Clark acknowledge that smuggling activity was high in New Orleans
after the British acquired nearby West Florida in 1763. While the legal ambiguity
of the transfer period probably encouraged smugglers, I believe illegal trade had
grown steadily from Louisiana's earliest days and that the "spike" in references to
smuggling in the 1760s, almost all of which derive from English sources, represents
a period of intelligence-gathering by the British about their new neighbors. Clark,
New Orleans, 1718–1812, 122, 147, 164; Usner, *Indians, Settlers, and Slaves*, 268–75.

40 W. A. Cole, "Trends in Eighteenth-Century Smuggling," *Economic History Review*, 2d ser., 10 (1958): 395–410; Hoh-Cheung Mui and Lorna H. Mui, "'Trends
in Eighteenth-Century Smuggling' Reconsidered," *Economic History Review* 28,
no. 1 (1975): 28–43; Grahn, *Political Economy of Smuggling*, xv; Waggoner, ed.,
"Mémoire of Jean Béranger," 191.

41 For a detailed chart of recorded ship arrivals, see Dawdy, "*La Ville Sauvage*," 133.
Nothing like a customs or port register exists for French Louisiana, so the data have
been culled from multiple sources. I have compiled ship arrivals drawn from correspondence to the French ministries along with incidental references in Louisiana
Superior Council records. The latter occurred when financial transactions regarding cargo or civil matters of passengers and crew were entered into the notarial or
civil court records. These records provide a better sample of ships that made the
complete journey up to New Orleans (or that stopped over at La Balize long enough
for crew members to make the journey to town in a pirogue). Neither source lists
ships making brief stops at La Balize or in the Barataria marsh, the favored method
of Spanish colonial ships. A typical example of the notarial entries is the registration of a business partnership between New Orleans merchant Gerard Pery and
shipowner Antoine Chapelet for outfitting *Les Deux Amis* for trade "at Pensacola,
Havana, and Veracruz." Another is a receipt for cargo paid by Layssard Brothers
in 1745 for goods coming from *La Superbe* of Martinique, described as "at present
in the port of New Orleans." The account record of an unidentified New Orleans
merchant shows a running tab between 1743 and 1745 to Don Renato, "payable
on his return from Cartagena." Partnership, 10 March 1740, SCA-LHQ 10, no. 2

(1927): 269; deposit in registry, 30 May 1745, SCA-LHQ 14, no. 1 (1931): 117–18; memoranda of merchandise, 5 November 1745, SCA-LHQ 14, no. 4 (1931): 592.

42   Vaudreuil cited in Clark, *New Orleans, 1718–1812,* 142, 147. During this same period (1740s-early 1750s), the entire deerskin trade is estimated at 100,000 livres; tobacco and indigo combined at 120,000; with tar, pitch, and lumber making up most of the rest of 80,000 (see Usner, *Indians, Settlers, and Slaves,* 246–47); Darby, "Louisiana 1717 to 1751," 567.

43   Banks, *Chasing Empire,* 169–77; Ann Pérotin-Dumon, "Cabotage, Contraband, and Corsairs: The Port Cities of Guadeloupe and Their Inhabitants, 1650–1800," in Knight and Liss, *Atlantic Port Cities,* 58–86.

44   Mercantile instructions, 29 October 1742; sailing orders, 31 October 1742, both in SCA-LHQ 11, no. 2 (1928): 307; bill, 25 September 1743, SCA-LHQ 12, no. 1 (1929): 157. Cargo of *Lion d'Or,* 22 September 1743; Fernando de Bustillo to Elie Rasteau, 23 September 1743, both in SCA-LHQ 12, no. 1 (1929): 154; letter to Jean Baptiste Garic and excerpts of others, 9 March 1748, SCA-LHQ 19, no. 2 (1936): 493.

45   Instructions, 2 July 1745, SCR, fols. 1–2.

46   Testimony on brandy cargo, 29–30 December 1723, SCA-LHQ 1, no. 1 (1917–18): 227–28. An almost identical case involved the ship *L'Éléphant* in 1725. Verdict of restitution and sentence in confiscation, 10 October 1725, SCA-LHQ 2, no. 4 (1919): 474–75; examination of Thomas Desarsy, 6 September 1724, SCA-LHQ 1, no. 2 (1917–18): 244; testimony on shipwreck of *La Bellone,* 2 April 1725, 17–26 April 1725, SCA-LHQ 2, nos. 1–2 (1919): 118, 196–202; motion for investigation, 3 April 1724, SCA-LHQ 1, no. 3 (1919): 236.

47   Ruling, 27 March 1724, SCR, fols. 1–2. In this case, the Council made no effort to follow through by deposing crew members or tracking down the ship's original cargo. See also Heloise Cruzat, "Sidelights on Louisiana History," *Louisiana Historical Quarterly* 1, no. 3 (1918): 123.

48   The case comprises seventeen entries in the Louisiana Superior Council records between 2 and 24 September 1729, transcribed in Henry P. Dart, "The Smuggler St. Michel," *Louisiana Historical Quarterly* 7, no. 3 (1924): 371–413.

49   Despite his Irish name, Macmahon was described in the documents as a native Frenchman. Dart, "Smuggler St. Michel," 384 (quote), 385, 401–3.

50   Ibid., 382, 385–87, 392, 394, 397 (quote).

51   Ibid., 389 (quote), 390, 394–97, 406–7, 412–13. The split in the Council represents one instance of a repeated pattern of political dissension among the colony's political elite that put the governor and the *ordonnateur* on opposite sides. Only now has it become clear that smuggling was one of the main issues that divided officeholders. See Villiers du Terrage, *Last Years of French Louisiana;* Allain, *"Not Worth a Straw";* Giraud, *Company of the Indies, 1723–1731.*

52   Conrad, *First Families of Louisiana,* 2:148. Apparently unaware of local happenings, the Company approved Macmahon's appointment (probably recommended by Governor Périer), and he acquired the new title "General Storekeeper of European Merchandise in Louisiana." This, of course, put him in charge of his own confiscated merchandise from the *St. Michel.* The outcome of the original court proceedings gave him back his ship, but not its cargo. Within five months of his appointment to the Council, MacMahon was outfitting his ship for another voyage to Mexico out of the mingled stores of the Company warehouse. Henry P. Dart,

"Laurent MacMahon," *Louisiana Historical Quarterly* 10, no. 4 (1927), 522–24; Dart, "Smuggler St. Michel," 381; Ory to Périer, 1 November 1730, in MPA 4:50 (quote).

53 Périer and La Chaise to Directors of the Company, 18 August 1728, ANF-AC, C13A 11, fols. 100–101; "Lettre des Négots de la Nouvelle Orléans," 6 May 1759, ANF-AC, Series F3, vol. 25, fols. 101–6; Banks, *Chasing Empire*, 211–14. Clark provides biographical sketches of businessmen Paul Rasteau and Bancio Piemont that show them engaged in both legitimate transatlantic trade and greater Caribbean smuggling. Clark, *New Orleans, 1718–1812*, 88–106. Liss and Knight note that the archive "does not usually permit a clear differentiation between legal and illegal traders" (*Atlantic Port Cities*, 9).

54 De Meyère was of French nationality but has a common Dutch (and sometimes Jewish) surname. This first de Meyère case is translated and transcribed by Henry P. Dart, "A Case in Admiralty in Louisiana 1741," *Louisiana Historical Quarterly* 7, no. 1 (1924): 5–19.

55 Gerald *déclaration*, 31 July 1741, SCR. For summaries of other documents referred to, see the following: memorandum of account, 14 July 1741; notices to witnesses, 20 July 1741; court notice and testimonies, 28 July 1741, 1 August 1741, 2 August 1741, 5 August 1741; decree, 5 August 1741; prosecution for libel, 8 August 1741; conclusions of *procureur général*, 2 September 1741, all in SCA-LHQ 11, no. 1 (1928): 122–31.

56 Juan Ignace de Estemburu to Gerard Pery, 22 May 1743, SCR, fols. 1–3, especially fol. 2 (quote); "Traduction de la lettre qu'ecrit M. Pery," 29 May 1743, SCR, fols. 1–2. For details of the case, see petition to the Governor of Veracruz, 28 February 1743; memorandum on brandy, 13 March 1743; letter of Pedro Dascubenia to Gerard Pery, 14 March 1743, all in SCA-LHQ 11, no. 3 (1928): 483, 485. Inventory of effects of de Meyère, 10 July 1743; petition for citation of de Meyère, 10 July 1743; judgment of Pery vs. de Meyère, 13 July 1743, all in SCA-LHQ 11, no. 4 (1928): 629–30, 634. Report by arbiters, 29 November 1743; petition by de Meyère, 26 December 1743, both in SCA-LHQ 12, no. 3 (1929): 478–79, 496. Declarations of Jacques de Meyère and others, 26 December 1743, SCR, fols. 1–8. In general, *interlope* means "clandestine," but in French nautical terminology it also refers to a smuggling vessel. The other captains giving testimony were Pierre Cádiz of St. Pierre, Martinique, Henry Maget of Spain, Jean Delaporte of La Rochelle, and Louis Pierre Senet, whose ink-stained place of origin appears to read "St. Croix." All attest to the difficulty of conducting business in Veracruz at the time, and the high cost of bribes, or "the gifts one is obliged to make" (fol. 5). Senet later on appears as a resident merchant in New Orleans. The long-lived Captain Cádiz made a voyage from Martinique to New Orleans in 1751 and attempted to smuggle slaves into the city in 1768. Bill for freight, 21 October 1751, SCA-LHQ 21, no. 4 (1938): 1225; Villiers du Terrage, *Last Years of French Louisiana*, 151n31.

57 Diron d'Artaguette to Maurepas, 8 May 1737, in MPA 1:346–47.

58 Letter of Diron d'Artaguette with abstracts of letters to him from Bienville, Fleuriau, and Gerald, 26 October 1737, SCR, fols. 1–16. Bienville was well aware of the need to cover his tracks in official correspondence. He wrote two letters giving completely contradictory orders to Diron d'Artaguette regarding the handling of Olivier. The first, which supported the arrest, was duplicated for the benefit of the Ministry, but the second, private letter expressed dismay over the commander's proceedings against Olivier, who would, no doubt, "be condemned to the

galleys for three years." Bienville was well aware that accepting foreign goods in Louisiana was a punishable crime as viewed by the metropole, but he did not want to enforce this rule against a "hardworking" colonist. Diron d'Artaguette to Maurepas, 24 October 1737, ANF-AC, C13A22, fols. 233–43v, in MPA 4:144–45. See also Diron d'Artaguette to Maurepas, 8 May 1737, in MPA 1:343–45.

59 Suit of J. B. Prevost, 3 April 1743; petition to M. de Salmon, 12 April 1743; petition to suspend seizure, 9 April 1734; petition of Captain Charles Le Roy, 17 April 1743; defense of Charles Le Roy, 19 April 1743; decision, 1 June 1743, all in SCA-LHQ 11, no. 3 (1928): 488–99.

60 Salmon to Maurepas, 6 March 1741, ANF-AC, C13A 26, fols. 115–19.

61 A partisan letter reports: "[h]is wife is capable of a lower commerce than that one. She has business with everybody here and she forces the merchants and individuals here to take charge of her merchandise to sell it at the price that she fixes. She has a warehouse at her house of all sorts of stuff . . . Her husband is not ignorant of it. He gets a good revenue from it, and that is the motive of all his desires and his occupations." Michel to Rouillé, 20 July 1751, in MPA 5:101.

62 D'Erneville to Berryer, 15 March 1760, ANF-AC, C13A 42, fols. 179–86v, in MPA 5:243. While the Spanish merchants were welcome at La Balize, the English seem to have preferred the beaches of the Gulf Coast. Another smuggling prosecution case from Mobile resulted in the seizure of the English ship *Marguerite* and its cargo. The ship purchaser at auction was none other than local smuggler Philippe Olivier. Crémont to Maurepas, 24 February 1734; Diron d'Artaguette to Maurepas, 24 October 1737, both in MPA 4:130–33, 144–45; Diron d'Artaguette to Maurepas, 8 May 1737, in MPA 1:343–45; Kerlérec to Rouillé, 8 March 1753, ANF-AC, C13A 37, fols. 34–38, in MPA 5:123.

63 Kerlérec to Minister, 17 September 1758, ANF-AC, C13 A 40, fols. 62–63v; petition of Broutin, 3 September 1763, SCA-LHQ 25, no. 4 (1941): 1137.

64 Technically, privateering involved the seizure of ships from an enemy country during wartime. Privateers operated with the approval of and sometimes a specific license from their home government and had to obey international rules of war regarding treatment of prisoners and national rules for the distribution of bounty. Pirates used the same methods as privateers to tail, trap, and board ships and seize their cargoes, but their activities were illegal, if not violent, and they swore allegiance to no state. Smuggling means simply outlawed trade involving prohibited relationships and/or trafficking in contraband goods.

65 Petition, 16 September 1745, SCA-LHQ 14, no. 4 (1931): 575; copy of muster roll, 13 July 1762, SCA-LHQ 24, no. 1 (1941): 221–22; translation of diverse sales, 13 July 1762, SCA-LHQ 24, no. 1 (1941): 222–26; settlement, 25 April 1763, SCA-LHQ 24, no. 4 (1941): 1196–97; petition, 28 May 1763, SCA-LHQ 24, no. 4 (1941): 1228–29; Perry, "New Orleans in 1758"; Villiers du Terrage, *Last Years of French Louisiana*, 102–18. Memorandum of argument, 5 August 1763; answer to petition, 5 August 1763, both in SCA-LHQ 25, no. 3 (1942): 843–46. The 13 July translation document notes that Captain Matuticte (also spelled Mathutique) was known "in civil life" as Monsieur Lonet. His crew was multinational and multiracial, including Spanish colonials, French colonials, and a free mulatto.

66 Philippe François Bart to Louis Billouart de Kerlérec, 6 July 1759, from private collection of Kerlérec's correspondence, cited in Villiers du Terrage, *Last Years of French Louisiana*, 116; Perry, "New Orleans in 1758," 57. Most of the thirteen ships Perry observed during his ten-month stay in the city were from Philadelphia and

Rhode Island. See William S. McClellan, *Smuggling in the American Colonies at the Outbreak of the Revolution with Special Reference to the West Indies Trade*, vol. 3 (New York: Moffat, Yard & Co., 1912), 50–51. The planter Darby reported the arrival of another "shipload" of Jamaican slaves in 1749. Darby, "Louisiana 1717 to 1751," 567. Louisiana's slave population may have been regularly reinforced by smuggled imports from the Caribbean, although official dockets record only a handful of shipments after the 1730s.

67 Villiers du Terrage, *Last Years of French Louisiana* 103–18, 378–406; Bibliothèque de l'Arsenal, Affaire de la Louisiane, Archives de la Bastille, Cat. 12262. See also Gourmelon, *Le Chevalier de Kerlérec, 1704–1770*.

68 *Négociants* of New Orleans to Kerlérec, 29 April 1759, from private collection of Kerlérec's correspondence, cited in Villiers du Terrage, *Last Years of French Louisiana*, 150.

69 Licencias de Barcos, in AGI-PPC, Legajo 188A, Expediente 2, fol. 6 (fourteen items dated 1769).

70 For example, the work of David Hancock and coauthors Linebaugh and Rediker maps the transatlantic connections of financial elites that drove the burgeoning capitalist system, as well as members of the underclass who fought back to redefine the terms of their participation. Although often politically opposed, both groups identified themselves as "citizens of the world." David Hancock, *Citizens of the World: London Merchants and the Integration of the British Atlantic Community, 1735–1785* (Cambridge: Cambridge University Press, 1995); Linebaugh and Rediker, *Many-Headed Hydra*.

71 Forstall had immigrated from Martinique to New Orleans in the early 1740s. Clark, *New Orleans, 1718–1812*, 97–99; Henry P. Dart, "The Wreck of *La Superbe* in the Gulf of Mexico en Route from Veracruz to New Orleans, May, 1745," *Louisiana Historical Quarterly* 11, no. 2 (1928): 179–208; Baillardel and Prioult, *Le Chevalier de Pradel*.

72 Officials also said that African sailors were easier to provision, since they did not demand expensive French imports, such as wine and wheat flour. Usner, *Indians, Settlers, and Slaves*, 228–32; Berlin, *Many Thousands Gone*, 17–28; Heloise H. Cruzat, "The Documents Covering the Criminal Trial of Etienne La Rue, for Attempt to Murder and Illicit Carrying of Arms," *Louisiana Historical Quarterly* 13, no. 3 (1930): 377–90.

73 The ship was returning to New Orleans from Veracruz when the captain lost his bearings and became stranded on a sandbar, losing the ship's cargo. *La Superbe*'s Captain Grenier, a suspected smuggler, had been hired by the Superior Council to procure flour. Charmion Clair Shelby, ed., "Grenier's Journal of His Voyage to Veracruz, 1745," *Louisiana Historical Quarterly* 21, no. 3 (1938): 629–68; Dart, "Wreck of *La Superbe*."

74 Investigation of thefts, 23–30 March 1741, SCA-LHQ 10, no. 4 (1927): 574–76; succession of Ferchaud, 23 September 1739, SCA-LHQ 7, no. 2 (1926): 363; procuration, 24 April 1736, SCA-LHQ 8, no. 2 (1925): 289.

75 Nevertheless, intensive excavations at early French colonial sites in Alabama have turned up over 100 coins, most of them Spanish reales. George W. Shorter Jr., "Status and Trade at Port Dauphin," *Historical Archaeology* 36, no. 1 (2002): 135–42, especially 136. See also Gregory A. Waselkov, "Intercolonial Trade and Smuggling on Gulf of Mexico, c. 1700–1720," paper presented at the twentieth annual meeting of the French Colonial Historical Society, 1994.

76 More important than single artifacts symbolizing foreign contact is a consistent pattern. On French-period archaeological sites, at least 5 percent of the ceramic assemblages comprise Spanish pottery such as Marine Ware, Spanish Olive Jar, and different types of majolicas. A majority of the last-named appear to be of Spanish colonial manufacture, such as the Puebla polychrome traditions from Mexico exported out of Veracruz. In addition, British-made ceramics make up 5–10 percent of the assemblages. Jacqueline S. Olin and others, "Compositional Analysis of Glazed Earthenwares from Eighteenth-Century Sites on the Northern Gulf Coast," *Historical Archaeology* 36, no. 1 (2002): 79–96; Jill-Karen Yakubik, "Ceramic Use in Late-Eighteenth-Century and Early-Nineteenth-Century Southeastern Louisiana" (Ph.D. diss., Tulane University, 1990).

77 Shorter, "Status and Trade at Port Dauphin," 137.

78 Caillot, "Relation du Voyage de la Louisiane," fol. 106.

79 Ibrahima Seck, "The Relationships between St. Louis of Senegal, Its Hinterlands, and Colonial Louisiana," in *French Colonial Louisiana and the Atlantic World*, ed. Bond, 265–90, especially 272.

80 Scott, "Common Wind;" Linebaugh and Rediker, *Many-Headed Hydra*.

81 Session of the Superior Council and Judgments, 9 March 1748; declaration by fugitive Negroes, 22 March 1748, both in SCA-LHQ 19, no. 2 (1936): 489, 497, 503. Usner, *Indians, Settlers, and Slaves*, 241.

82 Scott, "Common Wind," 9.

83 Inns or "hostels" were distinguished from taverns by offering accommodation. Taverns offered food and drink, but cabarets and canteens only served alcohol. Edwin Davis, *The Story of Louisiana* (New Orleans: J. F. Hyer Publishing, 1960), 94 (quote); Henry P. Dart, "Cabarets of New Orleans in the French Colonial Period," *Louisiana Historical Quarterly* 19, no. 3 (1936): 578–83.

84 Kerlérec to Duval, n.d.; Kerlérec to Duval, 3 September 1764, both in Bibliothèque de l'Arsenal, Archives de la Bastille, Dossier 12262, fols. 24–28.

85 Janet Roitman, "The Garrison-Entrepôt: A Mode of Governing in the Chad Basin," in *Global Assemblages: Technology, Politics, and Ethics as Anthropological Problems*, ed. Aihwa Ong and Stephen J. Collier (Malden, Mass.: Blackwell, 2005), 417–36.

86 Itty Abraham and Willem van Schendel, "Introduction: The Making of Illicitness," in *Illicit Flows and Criminal Things: States, Borders and the Other Side of Globalization*, ed. Willem van Schendel and Itty Abraham (Bloomington: Indiana University Press, 2005), 1–37, especially 7 (quote). See also Katherine E. Browne, *Creole Economics: Caribbean Cunning under the French Flag* (Austin: University of Texas Press, 2004), especially 43–80; Janet Roitman, "Productivity in the Margins: The Reconstitution of State Power in the Chad Basin," in *Anthropology in the Margins of the State*, ed. Veena Das and Deborah Poole (Santa Fe: School of American Research, 2004), 191–224.

87 Willem van Schendel, "Spaces of Engagement: How Borderlands, Illegal Flows, and Territorial State Interlock," in *Illicit Flows and Criminal Things*, ed. Schendel and Abraham, 38–68, especially 61 (quote).

88 Janet Roitman, *Fiscal Disobedience: An Anthropology of Economic Regulation in Central Africa* (Princeton: Princeton University Press, 2005), 6.

89 Browne, *Creole Economics*.

90 In Martinique the white creole elite called Békés were also the most vocal advocates for independence from France, on economic grounds. Ibid., 35.

CHAPTER 4

1   Douglas W. Owsley and others, "An Archaeological and Physical Anthropological Study of the First Cemetery in New Orleans" (Baton Rouge: Louisiana State University, 1985).

2   Saint Anthony is often depicted holding the Christ child in the same position or holding a book while receiving a vision. The back side of the other medal is too corroded to make out. The archaeologists do not mention the placement of the objects within the coffin. Ibid., 83–86, 160, 165.

3   The *Code Noir* of 1724 instructed slaveowners to baptize infant slaves and to encourage catechism and conversion among adults, though enforcement was left to the inclination of the slaveowner. The law also required them to bury baptized slaves with Catholic services. Carl A. Brasseaux, "Slave Regulations in French Louisiana," in *French Experience in Louisiana*, ed. Conrad, 209–25. On the early participation of people of color in the religious life of New Orleans, see Clark, *Masterless Mistresses*; and John Bernard Alberts, "Origins of Black Catholic Parishes in the Archdiocese of New Orleans, 1718–1920" (Ph.D. diss., Louisiana State University and Agricultural and Mechanical College, 1998).

4   Berlin, *Many Thousands Gone.*

5   As physical race types were constructed during a later era, I prefer terms that reference a presumed recent geographical ancestry: African, European, and Indian (meaning Amerindian) and the adjectives derived from them. It should be borne in mind that although the skeletons of these individuals may indicate dominant phenotypes associated with one of the major continents at the time that racial notions became fixed in the modern era, the actual birthplaces of these individuals could have been anywhere in the Atlantic world, including Canada and the Caribbean. Physical anthropologist Doug Owsley studied 31 skeletons recovered from the site and assigned ancestry to 18, based on cranio-facial measurements. Using his terms, he identified 13 "Negro," 2 "White," 2 White-Negro, and 1 White-Indian individual. Many of the "Negro" men's skeletons bore dramatic bone spurs caused by repeated, strenuous muscle use. The limited number of artifacts associated with the burials suggests a lower socioeconomic profile of the dead. All the coffins were simple, cypress-wood boxes, devoid of hardware and ornamentation. No remains of clothing survived except for a single bone button. The area exposed during modern construction consisted of two rectangular sections measuring 11.1 by 38.7 meters and 21.4 by 26.9 meters. Due to the disturbed conditions, it was impossible to determine chronology of the burials. Owsley and others, "First Cemetery in New Orleans," 67–68, 100, 163.

6   Spear, "Colonial Intimacies," 75–98. I would add that the censuses and church marriage registers are of little help: the former because of evasive racial categories, and the latter because they may not include interracial unions of freemen, who would likely not have sought religious approval precisely because it would have been denied.

7   Michel Foucault, *Discipline and Punish: The Birth of the Prison* (New York: Vintage Books, 1995), 144.

8   Rebecca Scott uses the phrase "degrees of freedom" to refer to the segmented hierarchy of citizenship that existed legally and practically in the post-Emancipation period. In the French colonial period, one could argue that servitude rather than

freedom was the norm for subjects (and one can further elaborate a distinction between subjects and citizens), so that a segmented hierarchy of rights and privileges corresponded to "degrees of servitude." Rebecca J. Scott, *Degrees of Freedom: Louisiana and Cuba after Slavery* (Cambridge, Mass.: Harvard University Press, 2005).

9 For an overview of French policies toward Louisiana, see Allain, *"Not Worth a Straw."*

10 On the politics of the Louisiana Superior Council, see Giraud, *Company of the Indies, 1723–1731*; and Villiers du Terrage, *Last Years of French Louisiana.*

11 Spear, "Colonial Intimacies;" Brasseaux, "Slave Regulations in French Louisiana"; Bienville and Salmon to Minister, 17 April 1734, ANF-AC, D2A 51, fols. 117v–18. On early German immigration, see Marcel Giraud, *La Louisiane après le système de Law, 1721–1723*, vol. 4 (Paris: Presses Universitaires de France, 1974), 154–67; Glenn R. Conrad, "Alsatian Emigration to Louisiana 1753–1759," in *French Experience*, ed. Conrad, 163–73; Reinhart Kondert, *The Germans of Colonial Louisiana, 1720–1803* (Stuttgart: Hans-Dieter Heinz Akademischer Verlag, 1990); Hartmut Lehmann, Hermann Wellenreuther, and Renate Wilson, *In Search of Peace and Prosperity: New German Settlements in Eighteenth-century Europe and America* (University Park: Pennsylvania State University Press, 2000); and James Pritchard, "Population in French America, 1670–1730: The Demographic Context of Colonial Louisiana," in *French Colonial Louisiana and the Atlantic World*, ed. Bond, 175–203, 198.

12 James D. Hardy Jr., "The Transportation of Convicts to Colonial Louisiana," *Louisiana History* 7 (1966): 207–20; Glenn R. Conrad, "Emigration Forcée: A French Attempt to Populate Louisiana, 1716–1720," in *Proceedings of the Fourth Meeting of the French Colonial Historical Society*, ed. James J. Cooke (Washington, D.C.: University Press of America, 1979), 57–66; and Carl A. Brasseaux, "The Image of Louisiana and the Failure of Voluntary French Emigration, 1683–1731," in *French Experience*, ed. Conrad, 153–62.

13 For more on this, see Dawdy, "Enlightenment from the Ground."

14 Louis XV acquired this plantation from the Company of the Indies when it surrendered its charter in 1731. Slaves at the plantation were employed on public works projects in New Orleans, tasks associated with shipping, and raising of a small amount of indigo and tobacco.

15 Le Page du Pratz, *History of Louisiana*, 381–82. Compare Le Page du Pratz, *Histoire de la Louisiane*, 3:342.

16 In Louisiana the private Swiss mercenary regiment outfitted by Colonel Karrer arrived in 1731 and made up approximately one-fifth of the New Orleans garrison during the French period. See David Hardcastle, "Swiss Mercenary Soldiers in the Service of France in Louisiana," in *French Experience*, ed. Conrad, 368–77.

17 By some estimates, Law ended up transporting 7,000 Europeans and 2,000 Africans. Giraud, *Histoire de la Louisiana française*, 3:26. Pritchard provides a comparative overview of demographics in the French colonies during this period, concluding that there was no French template for immigration or population ratios. Pritchard, "Population in French America, 1670–1730."

18 Farge and Revel, *Rules of Rebellion*; James D. Hardy, "Transportation of Convicts to Colonial Louisiana," in *French Experience*, ed. Conrad, 115–24; Conrad, "Emigration Forcée."

19 Mortality rates for *galèriens* hovered around 50 percent due to disease and malnutrition. Françoise de Person, *Bateliers: contrebandiers du sel XVIIe–XVIIIe siècle* (Rennes: Editions Ouest-France, 1999), 105–6. See also André Zysberg, *Les Galériens: vies et destins de 60,000 forçats sur les galères de France, 1680–1748* (Paris: Editions du Seuil, 1987). Convicts had been sent in small numbers to New France since the seventeenth century and its reputation likewise suffered as a result, but proportionately this immigration paled in comparison to the Louisiana effort. Moogk, "Manon Lescaut's Countrymen."

20 The song "L'Aventure de Quoniam" relates the story of a man whose wife was the object of a public official's affection; as a result of his jealous rage, the husband was exiled by *lettre de cachet* to Louisiana, a convenient arrangement for the lovers. Several verses highlight the tragedy of being sent to Mississippi. Emile Raunié and Hipopolyte Rousselle, *Chansonnier historique du XVIIIe siècle*, 10 vols. (Paris: A. Quantin, 1879–84), 3:17–24.

21 Bienville to the Council of the Marine, 20 October 1719, ANF-AC C13A 5, fol. 276v.

22 Report of Raguet to Council, 2 September 1724, SCR.

23 Ingersoll, *Mammon and Manon*, 13; Hardy, "Transportation of Convicts," 122. See also Conrad, "Emigration Forcée"; Mathé Allain, "L'Immigration française en Louisiane," *Revue d'histoire de l'Amérique française* 28 (1975): 555–64; Mathé Allain, "Manon Lescaut et Ses Consoeurs: Women in the Early French Period, 1700–1731," in *Proceedings of the Fifth Meeting of the French Colonial Historical Society*, ed. James J. Cooke (Lanham, Md.: French Colonial Historical Society, 1980); Paul LaChance, "The Growth of the Free and Slave Populations of French Colonial Louisiana," in *French Colonial Louisiana and the Atlantic World*, ed. Bond, 204–43; Daniel H. Usner Jr., "From African Captivity to American Slavery: The Introduction of Black Laborers to Colonial Louisiana," in *French Experience*, ed. Conrad, 183; and Hall, *Africans in Colonial Louisiana*, 6–8. On the end of this recruitment policy, see Attorney General Raguet, 2 September 1724, SCA-LHQ 1, no. 3 (1917–18): 243; and Delachaise to Directors of Company of the Indies, 6 September 1723, in MPA 2:317–19. Despite the apparent consensus of historians about the dismal prospects of *forçats*, the only evidence in the primary documents I have been able to find to support this is a caustic statement made four decades after the mass migration saying that "their laziness and licentiousness resulted in their destruction." "Feuille au roi," 1 July 1760, ANF-AC, C13A 42, fols. 168–74, quoted in Hall, *Africans in Colonial Louisiana*, 25.

24 Usner, *Indians, Settlers, and Slaves*, 32. See also Giraud, *Years of Transition*. Three available ship lists from the Law period alone identify 222 salt and tobacco smugglers. Twenty-three percent of all those condemned to the French galleys from 1715 to 1748 were salt smugglers. Albert LaPlace Dart, trans., "Ship Lists of Passengers Leaving France for Louisiana, 1718–1724," *Louisiana Historical Quarterly* 21, no. 4 (1938): 965–78; and Zysberg, *Galériens*.

25 Marie-Hélène Bourquin, "Le Procès de Mandrin et la contrebande au XVIIIe siècle," in *Aspects de la contrebande au XVIIIe siècle*, ed. Marie-Hélène Bourquin and Emmanuel Hepp (Paris: Presses Universitaires de France, 1969), 1–37.

26 Dart, "Ship Lists of Passengers," 976–77. People became *contrebandiers du sel* either by manufacturing their own, transporting salt without a license or payment of duties, or peddling it on the black market. Sailors, tavern keepers, and female

peddlers worked in a tightly knit underground economy. *Bandouliers* were often poor fishermen identified by colorful nicknames. The salt tax was despised by many in France (Saint-Simon among others), and it became one of the hot-button issues of the Revolution. Person, *Bateliers*; Vaudreuil and Michel to Rouillé, 20 May 1751, in MPA 5:82–83; Dutertre procuration, 23 September 1737, SCR.

27 Emmanuel Hepp, "La Contrebande du tabac au XVIIIe siècle," in *Aspects de la contrebande*, ed. Bourquin and Hepp, 39–42.

28 These are translated and transcribed, with some errors and omissions, in Conrad, *First Families of Louisiana*; Maduell, *Census Tables*; and Jacqueline K. Voorhies, *Some Late Eighteenth-century Louisianians: Census Records, 1758–1796* (Lafayette: University of Southwestern Louisiana, 1973).

29 Nicole Castan, "Summary Justice," in *Deviants and the Abandoned in French Society*, ed. Robert Forster and Orest Ranum (Baltimore: Johns Hopkins University Press, 1978), 111–56; and André Zysberg, "Galley Rowers in the Mid-Eighteenth Century," in *Deviants and the Abandoned*, ed. Forster and Ranum, 83–110.

30 Comparable censuses in the metropole were not conducted until the mid-1750s. David I. Kertzer and Dominique Arel, "Censuses, Identity Formation, and the Struggle for Political Power," in *Census and Identity: The Politics of Race, Ethnicity, and Language in National Censuses*, ed. David I. Kertzer and Dominique Arel (New York: Cambridge University Press, 2002), 1–42, especially 7; C. James Haug, "Manuscript Census Materials in France: The Use and Availability of the Listes Nominatives," *French Historical Studies* 11, no. 2 (1979): 258–74, especially 259.

31 Spanish colonials developed a color-based code much earlier than the French, who tended to exaggerate ethnic "character" differences over phenotype. Nicholas Hudson, "From 'Nation' to 'Race': The Origin of Racial Classification in Eighteenth-Century Thought," *Eighteenth-Century Studies* 29, no. 3 (1996): 247–64. Peabody dates the regular usage of race concepts in French domestic law to the second half of the eighteenth century. Sue Peabody, *"There Are No Slaves in France": The Political Culture of Race and Slavery in the Ancien Régime* (New York: Oxford University Press, 1996).

32 Le Page du Pratz, *History of Louisiana*, 376–77. Cohen also contrasts the views of colonists with those of urban metropolitans, the former often having more complicated ideas of race. William B. Cohen, *The French Encounter with Africans: White Response to Blacks, 1530–1880* (Bloomington: Indiana University Press, 1980).

33 Jennifer Spear, "'Whiteness and the Purity of Blood': Race, Sexuality, and Social Order in Colonial Louisiana" (Ph.D. diss., University of Minnesota, 1999), 145. For discussions of Louisiana's evolving racial classification into the Spanish and American periods, see also Virginia R. Domínguez, *White by Definition: Social Classification in Creole Louisiana* (New Brunswick, N.J.: Rutgers University Press, 1986); and Kimberly S. Hanger, *Bounded Lives, Bounded Places: Free Black Society in Colonial New Orleans, 1769–1803* (Durham, N.C.: Duke University Press, 1997).

34 "La Louisiane: Recensement des habitants et concessionaires . . . 1721," ANF Series G^1 464. Note that in eighteenth-century French, accents and orthography are inconsistent. I have left them the way they appear in the documents (e.g., *negre* instead of *nègre*).

35 They were living in barracks, so were not heads of households. This was the first and only time *forçats* were separately identified in a census.

36 The censuses of 1726 and 1727 used the same categories for individual households, adding only the amount of land under cultivation for the rural settlements in 1726

and a "head count" for pigs in 1727. Recensements, 1 January 1726, July 1727, ANF Series G¹ 464.

37 "Recensement de la Louisiane," 1731; "Recensement General de la Ville de la Nlle. Orleans," January 1732, ANF Series G¹ 464.

38 According to Hall's research, 5,761 Africans destined for the colony were loaded onto ships between 1719 and 1731. Hall, *Africans in Louisiana*, 60.

39 The human categories were the following: men bearing arms (*hommes portant armes*), women and marriageable girls (*femmes ou filles à marier*), children (*enfans*), orphans (*orfelins*), Negro male slaves (*esclaves nègres*), Negro female slaves (*esclaves negresses*), Negro slave boys (*esclaves negrillons*), Negro slave girls (*esclaves negrittes*), male Indian slaves (*esclaves sauvages*), female Indian slaves (*esclaves sauvagesses*), mulatto male slaves (*esclaves mulâtres*), and mulatto female slaves (*esclaves mulatresses*).

40 Between the censuses of 1727 and 1732, New Orleans went from being a company town to a king's town dominated by the military. After the Natchez Indian rebellion of 1729, the Ministry of the Marine beefed up the New Orleans garrison to 400 men. Soldiers made up a significant majority (65 percent) of the "free" male populace in 1732, though their legal status resembled something much closer to a form of bondage. At the end of the French regime, they accounted for about 36 percent. See Dawdy, "*La Ville Sauvage*," app. B, 379–81.

41 Maduell, *Census Tables*, 88, 92–93.

42 Ibid., 123–41.

43 LaChance concurs in this interpretation, LaChance, "Growth of the Free and Slave Populations," 214. Indenture contracts ranged from three to seven years.

44 These totals represent civilian censuses plus estimates of the New Orleans garrison for the given year. I have strictly followed census-takers' definitions of the New Orleans district, meaning that surrounding plantations were excluded, and the nearby Gentilly and Bayou St. John *faubourgs* were included. I have recalculated the totals from the original tally sheets. The 1721, 1726, and 1732 censuses are grouped chronologically (no folio numbers) in ANF Series G¹ 464. The 1763 census is found in AGI-SD, Legajo 2595, No. 4, fols. 64–101.

45 Deciding whether to bound New Orleans as the limits of its street grid or to include all or part of the surrounding plantation zone can drastically alter the statistical portrait of French colonial Louisiana, leading to large discrepancies. Authors have given the total population of New Orleans in the year 1732 variously as 623, 890, 1,276, or 4,564. This also results in extremely different color ratios, depicting New Orleans as a place with either a black majority of 80 percent or a black minority of 28 percent. Compare, for example, Giraud, *Company of the Indies*, 201; Hanger, *Bounded Lives, Bounded Places*, 12; Ingersoll, *Mammon and Manon*, 18; LaChance, "Growth of the Free and Slave Populations," 218; Marc de Villiers du Terrage, *Histoire de la fondation de la Nouvelle-Orleans, 1717–1722* (Paris: Imprimerie Nationale, 1917), 122. LaChance is the most conservative, keeping estimates to the civilian population within the city's street grid. Again, my figures include the estimated garrison population, which was not counted in the censuses but which I believe to be a significant factor in demographic estimates.

46 These characterizations and those that follow in this section are based on a database I created for 300 New Orleans property owners from the 1728 and 1731 maps, which were then cross-referenced to censuses, passenger lists, church records, Superior Council Records, and administrative correspondence. For complete entries

and citations, see Dawdy, "*La Ville Sauvage,*" app. C, 382–409. The base maps used were "Plan de la Ville de la Nouvelle Orleans telle quelle était en Mai 1728," and "Plan de la Nouvelle Orleans telle quelle estait au mois de decembre 1731," signed by Gonichon, ANF-AC. The main sources used to create the database were the following: abstracts of Louisiana Superior Council, published in *Louisiana Historical Quarterly* (vols. 1–26); documentary indexes published in *New Orleans Genesis*, including those of the "Black Boxes" (an incomplete index of the Superior Council Records) and St. Louis Cathedral baptism, death, and marriage records; *Mississippi Provincial Archives*, vols. 1–5; Voorhies, *Some Late Eighteenth-century Louisianans*; Maduell, *Census Tables*; Gwendolyn Midlo Hall, *Databases for the Study of Afro-Louisiana History and Genealogy, 1699–1860* (CD-ROM) (Baton Rouge: Louisiana State University Press, 2000); Conrad, *First Families*; Carl A. Brasseaux, *France's Forgotten Legion: Service Records of French Military and Administrative Personnel Stationed in the Mississippi Valley and Gulf Coast Region, 1699–1769* (CD-ROM) (Baton Rouge: Louisiana State University Press, 2000); and Archives Nationales (France), *Inventaire des archives coloniales correspondance à l'arrivée en provenance de la Louisiane* (Paris: Archives Nationales, 1976).

47 I was able to trace the origin of about one-third (n = 111) of these property owners. Of these, 30 percent came to Louisiana from Canada (n = 33). The rest arrived from Europe on ships that embarked between 1717 and 1721. I would not, of course, argue that there was no social mobility in France. Many scholars have argued that the accelerated movement from the merchant-professional class to nobility and from the "fourth estate" into some tier of the bourgeoisie was the major factor precipitating the French Revolution. I am simply making a claim about relative mobility: if it is one measure of modernity, then the colonies were more modern than the metropole in the eighteenth century. See Lewis, *France, 1715–1804*; Maza, *Myth of the French Bourgeoisie*.

48 One might think "Né." is equivalent to *né*, meaning "born," referring to a birth name. However Gonichon occasionally varied his list with a full spelling, such as no. 57, "Au nommé Coupard." Thus, *Né.* was actually an abbreviation rather than a word. It was also used before obviously acquired nicknames ("Né. La Liberté" or "Né. Grandjean"). Nicole Castan says that even among France's working class, the key to respectability was being rooted within a village or town network. Thus, a carpenter or farmer who was well known and well respected in the community probably would not have been described as *nommé*. His genealogy was known. Nicole Castan, "Summary Justice," in *Deviants and the Abandoned*, ed. Forster and Ranum, 111–56.

49 Marcel Giraud, *The Reign of Louis XIV, 1698–1715*, trans. Joseph C. Lambert (Baton Rouge: Louisiana State University Press, 1974), 35–41.

50 Joseph G. Tregle, Jr., "Creoles and Americans," in *Creole New Orleans: Race and Americanization*, ed. Arnold R. Hirsch and Joseph Logsdon (Baton Rouge: Louisiana State University Press, 1992), 137. Tregle says even Iberville used it, though he didn't live long enough to know any Louisiana creoles. In the administrative correspondence from the colony, the term becomes routine by around 1740. See, for example, letter of Edmé-Gatien Salmon, 25 April 1741, ANF-AC, C13A 26, fols. 138–39, cited in Hall, *Africans in Colonial Louisiana*, 175.

51 Dumont de Montigny, "Mémoire De Lxx Dxx," 36.

52 Ibid., 41–44. This could have been a seigneurial title associated with his extended family (he comes from a family of lawyers and priests), but Dumont was clearly

never the heir of an estate. The "de Montigny" nickname appears to have been adopted after a relative. Certainly the ambiguity of the seigneurial-sounding name would have worked in Dumont's favor. See Carla Zecher, Gordon Sayre, and Shannon Lee Dawdy, eds., *Dumont de Montigny: Regards sur le monde atlantique, 1715–1747* (Québec: Septentrion, 2008).

53 Natalie Zemon Davis, *The Return of Martin Guerre* (Cambridge, Mass.: Harvard University Press, 1983).

54 Brasseaux, "France's Forgotten Legion," xi.

55 Although many records indicate a name is an alias by preceding it with *dit* or *nommé*, this is not always the case. Individuals are sometimes listed by their birth name, sometimes by one or more nicknames. This brings to archival work perhaps more than the usual number of frustrations and "aha!" moments when tracking individuals.

56 Report of Raguet to Council, 2 September 1724, SCR.

57 Summons of witnesses, 24 September 1723, SCA-LHQ 1, no. 1 (1917–18): 113. Petition to recover beer account, 4 December 1724; petition for judgment, 20 December 1724, both in SCA-LHQ 1, no. 3 (1917–18): 255. For the rest, see Dawdy, "*La Ville Sauvage*," app. C, 382–409.

58 Maduell, *Census Tables*, 5. See also several entries in the Louisiana Superior Council records for the following dates: 26 January 1744, 28 January 1744, 29–30 May 1745, 5 June 1747, 7 October 1747, 12 January 1748, 16 August 1752.

59 Examination of runaway slaves, 16 January 1741, SCA-LHQ 10, no. 4 (1927): 567; Jasmin proceedings, 9, 13, 16, 20 January 1742, SCA-LHQ 11, no. 2 (1928): 288–92; Baraca murder case, 9 February–4 May 1748, SCA-LHQ 19, no. 2 (1936): 471–78; and Jupiter and Alexandre proceedings, 20 February–21 March 1744, SCA-LHQ 12, no. 4 (1929): 663–74, and 13, no. 1 (1930): 120–23. For many more examples of slave naming and renaming practices, see Hall, *Databases for the Study of Afro-Louisiana History*.

60 Maduell, *Census Tables*, 20–21.

61 Twenty percent is remarkably close to the number reported by a memorialist of 1721 who tallied the immigrants sent to Louisiana, and noted that 18 percent of them were *forçats*. This is further evidence that the long-circulating idea that *forçats* suffered a greater mortality rate than other immigrants is not well founded. "Mémoire sur l'etat actuel ou est la colonie de la Louisiane," n.d. [after 1721], ANF-AC, C13C 1, fol. 329. See also Dawdy, "*La Ville Sauvage*," 379.

62 Again, the source for these microhistorical profiles is the database presented in Dawdy, "*La Ville Sauvage*," app. C, 382–409, which lists the many documentary sources used to build each biographical sketch.

63 Baker says that about one-fifth of 512 women on surviving passenger lists were *forçats*. I came to the estimate of 250 by assuming missing passenger lists had the same proportion. Vaughan B. Baker, "Cherchez les Femmes: Some Glimpses of Women in Early Eighteenth-century Louisiana," in *French Experience*, ed. Conrad, 482. For Marie Baron, see Conrad, *First Families of Louisiana*, 1:28, 2:80.

64 Later, an Afro-creole girl named Marie Jeanne Françoise was living in his house and was baptized in 1729.

65 Quote from Périer to Raguet, 15 February 1729, ANF-AC, C13 A 12, fol. 354v.

66 In a 1785–86 sample of New Orleans church burial records, Owsley and others found that the average age of death for adults was 43.59 years, with no statistically significant differences by race among adults. Owsley and others, "First Cemetery in New Orleans," 114–15.

67 Milon to Council, 16 September 1730, SCR; [Darby] petition for honorable amends, 1 August 1730, SCA-LHQ 5, no. 1 (1922): 85.

68 Between 1722 and 1753 a total of sixty-one verbal violence cases were recorded as prosecuted offenses in the Superior Council Records, or constituted part of the defense for retaliatory action in the case of assault. For a more detailed presentation of Louisiana's defamation cases, see Dawdy, "Scoundrels, Whores, and Gentlemen."

69 Rules against registering titles of nobility, pardon, or concession without special permission, 5 October 1748, SCA-LHQ 20, no. 1 (1937): 233.

70 Philip B. Uninsky, "Violence, Honor, and Litigation: Injures et Voies de Fait in Pre-Revolutionary Rouen," *New York University Journal of International Law and Politics* 23, no. 3 (1991): 867–904, especially 876.

71 See, for example, Landerneau v. Lacour, 29 and 31 March, 1749; Chancelier declaration, 2 March 1747; LeMoine declaration, 28 January 1745; Balcourt declaration, 6 October 1736; Baldit to Council, 17 August 1729; information concerning Rousseau v. La Court, 13 June 1725; Louis Brouet declaration, 10 June 1737; LeMoine declaration, 28 January 1745, all in SCR.

72 Peter N. Moogk, "'Thieving Buggers' and 'Stupid Sluts': Insults and Popular Culture in New France," *William & Mary Quarterly*, 3d ser., 44, no. 1 (1979): 3–38; Hughes LeCharney, "L'Injure à Paris au XVIIe siècle: un aspect de la violence au quotidien," *Revue d'histoire moderne et contemporaine* 36 (1989): 559–85. See also Julius R. Ruff, *Crime, Justice and Public Order in Old Regime France: The Sénéchaussées of Libourne and Bazas, 1696–1789* (Dover, N.H.: Croom Helm, 1984). On the reputation of Louisiana's female immigrants, see Allain, "Manon Lescaut et Ses Consoeurs."

73 Although the *Code Noir* technically prohibited the testimony of slaves against free people except in unusual circumstances, councilors seem to have had little hesitation to use slave testimony in Louisiana. For details of the bestiality case, see Dawdy, "*La Ville Sauvage*," 290–91; criminal case of André Baron, 12 August—6 October 1753, SCA-LHQ 22, no. 3 (1939): 861–87.

74 André LaChance, "Une étude de mentalité: les injures verbales au Canada au XVIIe siècle (1712–1748)," *Revue d'histoire de l'Amerique française* 31, no. 2 (1977): 229–38; Moogk, "'Thieving Buggers.'"

75 Pauger to Le Blond de la Tour, 19 August 1721, ANF-AC, C-13-A 6, fols. 140r–v.

76 LeCharney, "L'Injure à Paris," 568.

77 Delachaise to Directors of the Company of the Indies, 8 March 1724, in MPA 2:337–38; Périer to Raguet, 15 February 1729, ANF-AC, C13 A 12, fol. 354v.

78 For more on this important aspect of eighteenth-century French culture, see Yves Castan, *Honnêteté et relations sociales en Languedoc, 1715–1780* (Paris: Plon, 1974); LeCharney, "L'Injure à Paris"; Uninsky, "Violence, Honor, and Litigation."

79 Letter of Raphael, 12 March 1726, ANF-AC, C13A 10, fol. 41; Dawdy, "Scoundrels, Whores, and Gentlemen."

80 In Louisiana, these made up about half, or 47 percent, of all cross-class cases. For greater detail and an explanation of how class membership was assigned, see Dawdy, "*La Ville Sauvage*," 273–75.

81 Bouet v. Sieur and Dame LaGoublaye, 16 July 1727, SCA-LHQ 3, no. 4 (1920): 223; Milon v. Marchand, 13 March 1730, SCA-LHQ 4, no. 4 (1921): 516.

82 Petition to prosecute, 18 May 1729, SCA-LHQ 4, no. 3 (1921): 333. On insubordination, Dalcour v. Dupuy Planchard, 22 February 1727 and 7–8 March 1727,

SCA-LHQ 3, no. 3 (1920): 435–38; De Verteuil v. Semson, 12–13 October 1726, SCA-LHQ 3, no. 3 (1920): 418–19. Conrad, *First Families of Louisiana*, 1:28; 2:80.

83   This translation is the best I could make out of an unpunctuated stream of excited narrative: After the exchange of insults, her five or six children then followed him down the street, pelting him with sticks. As he had to pass by their house on the way to his worksite, he requested the Superior Council to intervene. We have no record of their response. LeMoine declaration, 28 January 1745, SCR.

84   Cruzat, "Documents Covering the Criminal Trial of Etienne La Rue." My translations differ from Cruzat's. I have tried here to translate both for the meaning and intensity of the term. *Foutre* is a very strong term, equivalent to "fuck/fucking" in English. *Seigneur* had the meaning of "lord" in the feudal sense, whereas *Sieur* was a polite, but more general form of address.

85   William Little, H. W. Fowler, and J. Colson, eds., *The Shorter Oxford English Dictionary*, 3d ed. (Oxford: Clarendon Press, 1964), 1748.

86   Census data is from ANF Series G^1 464 and AGI-SD, Legajo 2595, No. 4, fols. 64–101. The peak of the African slave trade to Louisiana occurred 1727–29, most passing through New Orleans. Hall, *Africans in Colonial Louisiana*, 60.

87   These are "settlement" population estimates that exclude Native American communities that dominated the territory as a whole. Estimates by modern racial categories are approximate because the correlation between race/color and status was neither identical nor always recorded. The 1731–32 census counted 2,109 free people (mostly European) and 3,926 enslaved *nègres* and *sauvages* in Louisiana. In 1766 there were 5,556 free and 5,940 enslaved. Voorhies, *Some Late Eighteenth-century Louisianians*; Maduell, *Census Tables*, 163. LaChance has made an effort to calculate both the growth rate of New Orleans and the relative natural increase rates of the European and enslaved populations. LaChance, "Growth of the Free and Slave Populations," 228–32.

88   In 1732 New Orleans was home to 40 percent of Louisiana's European population; in 1766, 30 percent.

89   "Recensement Général fait a la Nouvell Orleans . . . 1763," AGI-SD, Legajo 2595 No. 4, fols. 64–101.

90   Usner, "From African Captivity to American Slavery," 189.

91   "Liste des négres libres établit tant à 4 lieuës de cette ville . . . y ceux de la ville"; "Etat de mulatres et negres libres"; "Rolle des mulatre libre de la Nlle. Orleans"; "Liste de la quantité des naîgre libre de la Nlle orleans faite par moi, nicolas Bacus, Capitaine Moraine," all in AGI-PPC, Legajo 188A, Expediente 2, all undated but appended to fol. 5 dated 1770.

92   Nicolas Bacus went on to receive recognition for military action against the British in the campaign of 1779–80 and also had several sons who were active in the free black militias in later decades. See Hanger, *Bounded Lives, Bounded Places*, 128–30. In 1769 O'Reilly brought with him from Cuba 160 militiamen from the *moreno* and *pardo* militias. However, these were clearly not the men counted by Bacus. Rather, his is a list of French creole free people of color. Almost all the individuals on his list had French surnames, about half of which match those of prominent slaveholding families in Louisiana (Vilars, Carière, Maxant, Dreux, Lafrénière, and so forth). Some had names suggestive of Louisiana Indian heritage, such as Jean and Laurent Panis, Petit Colas Maxant, Louis Colas, and Jean Penssacola. Many others bore seemingly created names, a few suggesting African heritage (Joseph

Congoliver, François Moor, Joseph Don Don, Pierre Lafriquen). On the Cuba militias, see Hanger, *Bounded Lives, Bounded Places*, 118–20.

93 In the fourth district of the 1766 census I have identified twenty-five possible matches, most of which occur in two spatial clusters, suggesting they were neighbors. Examples include the following: Hardy, Sarpy, Caffin/Coffigny, Maxent, Major/La Major, Colles/Colas. See "Padron y Lista de las quatro Compañias de Milicianos y habitantes en la Ciudad por Quarteles segun Revista passada en 27 de Mayo 1766," AGI-SD, Legajo 2595 [reel 59], fols. 17–23v.

94 Proposition to free Negroes for military merit, 13 May 1730, SCA-LHQ 4, no. 4 (1921): 524.

95 Raphael Bernard was well educated. He penned and signed his own petition. See petition of recovery, 9 May 1724; court sentence, 10 May 1724; and restitution, 26 July 1724, all in SCR.

96 Marriage license, 28 November 1727, SCR. Her owner was another Englishman who had settled in French Louisiana, Jonathas Darby. Tiocou's former owner was Kolly, a major concessionaire who was killed in the 1729 uprising. Diocou to Council, 28 June 1737; Tiocou, "Obligation à L'hopital," 12 July 1737, both in SCR. Others were freed for fighting in the Chickasaw wars of the 1730s and 1740s. See Brasseaux, "Slave Regulations."

97 Agreement for hire of free Negroes, 21 October 1729. In this agreement, Mingo arranged to hire out both himself and Thérèse to the noble *forçat* Chavannes (discussed above). See also contract between Dr. Prat and Pierre Almanzor, 2 March 1737, SCA-LHQ 9, no. 1 (1926): 115; contract, 7 January 1737, SCA-LHQ 8, no. 4 1925): 688; and acknowledgment by Sr. Claude Reynaud dit Avignon, 6 August 1739, SCA-LHQ 7, no. 2 (1924): 354.

98 "Recensement Géneral du quartier du Detour a L'Anglois par Le Sr Prevost . . . 1763," AGI-SD, Legajo 2595, No. 4, fol. 104. Both Hall and LaChance agree that the French censuses seriously undercount free people of color. Hall interprets this to mean that most "passed" into white society. In contrast, Ingersoll says that the number of free blacks was small and New Orleans had a rigid racial hierarchy from its early years. Hall, *Africans in Colonial Louisiana*, 239; Ingersoll, *Mammon and Manon*, 79; LaChance, "Growth of the Free and Slave Populations of French Colonial Louisiana."

99 Provenché declaration, 23 February 1745, SCR.

100 Brasseaux, "Slave Regulations," 214; Redon de Rassac to Minister, 15 August 1763, ANF-AC, C13A 43, fol. 377. One example of free people seeking ratification of a manumission is Marie, "negresse ve [widow] du nommé Gorgé son mary nègre" who petitioned the Council to confirm the freedom granted to her by Governor Bienville. Marie to Council, 4 June 1735, SCR.

101 Spear, "Colonial Intimacies." It should be emphasized that in the French period *mulâtre* was a term used almost exclusively to describe slaves, not free or freed people. In contrast to later periods and other colonial contexts, *mulatto* was not a term substituted for "free person of color."

102 Petition for binding contract, 29 October 1738; remonstrance, 8 November 1738; Pradel to Councilor, 9 November 1738; declaration, 13 November 1738; all in SCA-LHQ 6, no. 1 (1923): 138–40. See also several court actions instigated by creditors of DeCoustilhas, a long-time Louisiana resident who emancipated many of his slaves in his will. Louisiana Superior Council entries on 4 March 1739, 19 and 22 August 1743, 10–14 September 1743, 3 September 1746, 8–11 April 1747, SCR.

103 For work influential on this topic, see Stoler, ed., *Haunted by Empire.*

104 Ingersoll found that the average age of Louisiana brides at marriage was 15.65 years and that fully half of his sample of 62 were unions contracted with twelve- to fifteen-year-old girls. Ingersoll, *Mammon and Manon*, 58. See also Spear, "Colonial Intimacies."

105 Giraud, *Company of the Indies*, 272–76; Ingersoll, *Mammon and Manon*, 41–48.

106 LaChance, "Growth of the Free and the Slave Populations," 226. LaChance cites both the 1740 and 1746 *mémoires*; they are ANF-AC, C13C 1, fol. 375, "Sur l'état de cette colonie, ses productions et les avantages qu'on en peut retirer"; and ANF-AC, C13A 30, fols. 241–56, "Mémoire sur la Louisiane," 1746.

107 One observer called them "miller's sons," and the Le Moynes were said to be "miller's grandsons," but it is difficult to tell if this is a literal or figurative assignation of their status as millers were demeaned in early modern Europe. Gary B. Mills, "The Chauvin Brothers: Early Colonists of Louisiana," *Louisiana History* 15 (1974): 117–31, especially 124.

108 See entries under their names in Glenn R. Conrad, *A Dictionary of Louisiana Biography* (New Orleans: Louisiana Historical Association, 1988). Maduell, *Census Tables.*

109 There is more to this genealogy, and an incestuousness to business relationships as well, mapped out helpfully by Emilie Leumas in "Ties That Bind: The Family, Social, and Business Associations of the Insurrectionists of 1768," *Louisiana History* 47, no. 2 (2006): 183–202.

110 Cited in Charles Gayarré, *History of Louisiana*, 5th ed., 4 vols. (Gretna, La.: Pelican Publishing, 1974 [1851–1902]), 2:234.

111 As Ingersoll notes, "the town's white population intermarried across the barriers of social status that discouraged such marriages in France." Ingersoll, *Mammon and Manon*, 41.

112 The gender ratio of free European men to free European women in New Orleans stood near 2:1 in the early period, declining gradually, but was still at 1.7:1 in 1777. Many historians have discussed the gender ratio and its presumed effects on marriage and *métissage* in New Orleans. See Kimberly S. Hanger, "Household and Community Structure among the Free Population of Spanish New Orleans, 1778," *Louisiana History* 30 (1989): 63–79; Spear, "Colonial Intimacies"; Hall, *Africans in Colonial Louisiana*, 10; Hanger, *Bounded Lives, Bounded Places*, 22, table 1.3.

113 Conrad, *First Families.*

114 Dart, "Cabarets of New Orleans in the French Colonial Period"; reports by Fleuriau, 1 and 5 November 1725 and 21–22 December 1725, SCA-LHQ 2, no. 4 (1919): 480–81, 484. Jeanette Negresse Libre, 3 September 1746; Fleurieau to Council, 8 April 1747, both in SCR. Baillardel and Prioult, *Chevalier de Pradel*, 260.

115 Lease of taverns, 24 August 1746, SCA-LHQ 16, no. 3 (1933), 509; "Réglement sur la police des cabarets, des esclaves, des marchés en Louisiane," 18 February–1 March 1751, ANF-AC, C13A 35, fols. 39–52v.

116 Lafrénière report, 3 September 1763, SCR (the original appears to have been misplaced or never microfilmed in LDS-SCR series); translated in Dart, "Cabarets of New Orleans," 581.

117 D'Abbadie to Minister, 7 June 1764, ANF-AC, C13A 44, fols. 58–62; Jupiter and Alexandre proceedings, 20 February–21 March 1744, SCA-LHQ 12, no. 4 (1929): 663–74, and 13, no. 1 (1930): 120–23; Le Ber case, 22 February 1749, 25 September 1749, SCA-LHQ 20, no. 2 (1937): 493, 515.

118 Edicts of Superior Council, 6 April 1763, 3 September 1763, ANF-AC C13A 43, fols. 304–7v, 310–13v.

119 Edict of Superior Council, 3 September 1763, ANF-AC, C13A 43, fols. 310–13v; D'Abbadie to Minister, 7 June 1764, C13A 44, fol. 58.

CHAPTER 5

1   Diary entries [probably by Delachaise], 21 November 1725, ANF-AC, C14A9, fols. 267–75. The 1727 census recorded Louis Congo living on his plot of land along with an associate named M. de Shautes (Des Hautes?), and their wives. They are listed as "Negros" and "workmen." Maduell, *Census Tables*, 95.

2   Moogk, "'Thieving Buggers'"; Antón Blok, *Honour and Violence* (Malden, Mass.: Blackwell, 2001).

3   Report of *procureur général*, 17 August 1726, SCR. The attackers may have been the *"esclaves sauvages"* Jean Guillory and Bontemp, two years later remanded to *"l'executeur de haute justice."* Congo assisted Bontemps to the scaffold, while Guillory received *"battre de verges"* (flogging or beating) in prison. Condemnation, 14 June 1728, SCR.

4   "François et Louis déclaration," 24 January 1737, SCR. *Assassin* could mean both "killer" and "ruffian." In response to the question of whether he knew that marooning was punishable, Guala responded "that he knew well but that his master beat him often and did not give him enough to eat." "Interrogatoire de nègre Guala," 10 January 1737, SCR. See also *Procureur Général* to Council, 4 January 1737; "Condamnation du nègre Guala," 12 January 1737, SCR.

5   Meslun was also banished from New Orleans in perpetuity. He was probably a discharged soldier. He had two nicknames, "Loranger" and "Bourguignon." "Procès criminal," 29 May 1728, SCR. See also motion for trial, 22 May 1728; and petition of mercy, 24 May 1728, both in SCA-LHQ 4, no. 4 (1921): 484.

6   Capital sentence on Indian slave, 14 June 1728, SCA-LHQ 4, no. 4 (1921): 489; petition for voiding of will, 20 July 1729, SCA-LHQ 4, no. 2 (1921): 339. Another man, *"l'executeur dit la Lanceur"* (the Launcher or the Quick One), performed the first recorded public execution in the Place d'Armes. His ethnic origin is unknown. In 1723 a slave named Napi was condemned to hang for killing his wife. The sentence provided that he first be offered baptism. He received a brief stay of execution because the gallows were still being built. "Condamnation d'un Nègre appartenant à Sieur Delery," 1 October 1723, SCR.

7   Unfortunately, the trial records for this dramatic event in New Orleans are missing, although the proceedings are mentioned in letters by officials. "Chronologie des mouvements," 21 and 28 July 1731, fols. 85–93; and Beauchamp to Maurepas, 5 November 1731, fols. 197–201, both in ANF-AC, C13A 13.

8   Court-martial sentence, 23 February 1720, SCA-LHQ 1, no. 1 (1917–18): 106. On humiliation, see Malcolm Ross Greenshields, *An Economy of Violence in Early Modern France: Crime and Justice in the Haute Auvergne, 1587–1664* (University Park, Pa.: Pennsylvania State University Press, 1994).

9   Brirassac de Beaumont, quoted in Marc Villiers du Terrage, *Les dernières années de la Louisiane française* (Paris: Guilmoto, 1903), 16.

10 For example, René Meslier was convicted of assault and revolt in 1747 and sentenced to the galleys. St. François and his wife were suspected of murder, along

with other "scandalous behavior," and were banished to Saint Domingue. Similar crimes by whites committed in the founder generation had been punished more severely. Petition and inquiry, 19–22 April 1747, SCA-LHQ 18, no. 1 (1935): 183–85; petition from *procureur général*, 21 September 1763, SCA-LHQ 25, no. 4 (1942): 1148–49.

11 Arlette Farge and André Zysberg, "Les Théâtres de la violence à Paris au XVIIIe siècle," *Annales: économies, sociétés, civilisations* 34, no. 5 (1979): 984–1015.

12 In New Orleans the local post commander designate (the *major de place*) was superseded by the Superior Council for judicial functions except in the case of disputes among soldiers and in court-martial cases. Technically, civilians had a final appeal option with the Council of Versailles, but realistically few could exercise it.

13 Raguet to Council, 2 September 1724, SCR.

14 Edicts of Superior Council, 6 April 1763, 3 September 1763, ANF-AC, C13A 43, fols. 304–7v, 310–13v.

15 The distinction between colonial company and royal administration is particularly hazy in the period of Louis XIV and the regency. Colbert, the most influential of Louis XIV's ministers, created his own colonial company and promoted the expansion of others overseas. Clark makes a useful distinction between different kinds of colonial companies and their responsibilities: "Nominally, the purpose of most companies was to promote commerce in stipulated parts of the world, but this frequently involved the organizations in paramilitary activities in which they served as a political arm of the state ... A distinction may be made between the purposes of the East India Company ... and those of the companies which came and went in New France and those engaged in Louisiana. Although the former were organized strictly for trading purposes, the latter were compelled to devote a portion of their resources to development and settlement." Clark, *New Orleans, 1718–1812*, 13n5. On Colbert, see Allain, *"Not Worth a Straw."*

16 For more on Louisiana's governance, see James D. Hardy Jr., "The Superior Council in Colonial Louisiana," in *Frenchmen and French Ways in the Mississippi Valley*, ed. John Francis McDermott (Urbana: University of Illinois Press, 1969), 87–101; Donald Jile LeMieux, "The Office of 'Commissaire Ordonnateur' in French Louisiana, 1731–1763: A Study in French Colonial Administration" (Ph.D. diss., Louisiana State University and Agricultural and Mechanical College, 1972); Jerry A. Micelle, "From Law Court to Local Government: Metamorphosis of the Superior Council of French Louisiana," in *French Experience in Louisiana*, ed. Conrad, 408–24.

17 Villiers du Terrage, *Last Years of French Louisiana*; Giraud, *Reign of Louis XIV*; Giraud, *Company of the Indies*; Allain, *"Not Worth a Straw"*; Micelle, "From Law Court to Local Government."

18 Because France made venality (or the purchase of offices) illegal in Louisiana, the ascent of creoles to power mainly came about through marriage and political patronage. This stands in contrast to the Spanish colonies where there was a long tradition of office purchase. See Mark A. Burkholder and D. D. Chandler, *From Impotence to Authority: The Spanish Crown and the American Audiencias, 1687–1808* (Columbia: University of Missouri Press, 1977).

19 Micelle, "From Law Court to Local Government," 419–20; Thiton de Silègue to Minister, 12 December 1761, ANF-AC, C13A 42, fol. 249.

20 For a point-by-point comparison, see Dawdy, *"La Ville Sauvage,"* 238–39. These royal edicts were published in Duboys, *Recueils de Reglements*, 135–56. Also repro-

duced in Louis Sala-Molins, *Le Code Noir, ou Le calvaire de Canaan* (Paris: Presses Universitaires de France, 1987); and on the Web site of the Bibliothèque Nationale de France.

21 Louisiana Article 33. Additional articles retained from the Saint Domingue code prohibited the killing or torture of slaves by owners (rights reserved for judicial authorities). These provisions offer a contrast to the practices of slave law in the British colonies and United States. See Alan Watson, *Slave Law in the Americas* (Athens: University of Georgia Press, 1989); Thomas D. Morris, *Southern Slavery and the Law, 1619–1860* (Chapel Hill: University of North Carolina Press, 1996).

22 Clarence J. Munford and Michael Zeuske, "Black Slavery, Class Struggle, Fear and Revolution in St. Domingue and Cuba, 1785–1795," *Journal of Negro History* 73, nos. 1–4 (1988): 12–32; Carolyn E. Fick, *The Making of Haiti: The Saint Domingue Revolution from Below* (Knoxville: University of Tennessee Press, 1990).

23 Spear, "'They Need Wives.'"

24 According to the 1762 *Dictionnaire de L'Académie Française* (4th ed.), *nègre* was used in the sense of identifying someone from a nation, although in this case only in the most general way; the entry further states that the term was most often used as the equivalent for *esclave*. This usage suggests that the term means someone of African ancestry whose legal status is that of a slave. In comparison, the same source states that the substantive *noir*, as a reference to a person, was used only in opposition to *blanc*. The first emphasizes legal status, while the second stresses racial difference. It is interesting to note that neither word had appeared in the 1694 edition of the dictionary.

25 "Procès verbal," 18 June 1743, SCR.

26 "Mouvements des Sauvages . . . par M. de Périer," January 1731, ANF-AC, C13A 13, fol. 87. Translation suggested in Hall, *Africans in Colonial Louisiana*, 103. Hall discusses this policy in more detail on pages 89–106.

27 An abandoned boat they left behind was described as "bathed in blood," though it is not clear whether it was human or animal blood. Aufrere declaration, 16 October 1739, SCR. See also declaration by fugitive Negroes, 22 March 1748, SCA-LHQ 19, no. 2 (1936): 503–4.

28 Court-martial sentence, 23 February 1720, SCA-LHQ 1, no. 1 (1917–18): 106. By 1720 only two official slave ships had arrived in Louisiana, and Europeans still far outnumbered Africans. Most slavers arrived between 1726 and 1731. Hall, *Africans in Colonial Louisiana*, 59–60.

29 Many *forçats* were serving life terms. As with black and Indian slaves, the labor of *forçats* could be bought and sold, and they were subject to the physical discipline of their assigned overseers (the crown being their "owner"). They were also branded with a fleur-de-lys to mark the permanence of their status (a visual similarity to chronic maroons, who were also marked thus). The key difference was that their children did not inherit slavery. During this time in France, the association of skin color with slave status was neither fixed nor exclusive. Sue Peabody shows that slavery was not even a stable legal status—under a customary doctrine that said slavery was illegal in France, black slaves from the colonies who traveled to the metropole successfully sued for emancipation. Only in the late eighteenth century did French law begin to clearly distinguish the status of subjects by race alone. Instead of prohibiting the immigration of slaves, a new law in 1777 prohibited the immigration of *noirs*, thereby stemming the growth of a domestic free black

population while preserving the liberty principle. Peabody, *"There Are No Slaves in France."*

30 In the Gauvain case, the documents are complete with an autopsy of the victim. Justice moved slowly. When the sheriff (*huissier*) went to serve notice on the suspect, his wife reported he had left the house six or seven days earlier. "Jugement a Gauvain," 19 April 1741; "Exposé de Cendret," 5 November 1740; Fleuriau to Council, 5 November 1740; "Interrogatoires," 7 November, 1740, all in SCR.

31 The Bad Bread Mutiny, 12–14 July 1745, SCA-LHQ 14, no. 2 (1931): 263–67; criminal trial, 8 June 1752, SCA-LHQ 21, no. 2 (1938): 567–73; Des Essarts, 5–11 November 1740, SCA-LHQ 10, no. 3 1927): 434–35; confrontation, 8 February 1741, SCA-LHQ 10, no. 4 (1927): 569; *procureur général's* conclusions, 19 April 1741, SCA-LHQ 10, no. 4 (1927): 580; criminal prosecution, 15 February–14 March 1744, SCA-LHQ 12, no. 4 (1929): 663–74; interrogation, 21 March 1744, SCA-LHQ 13, no. 1 (1930): 122–23; murder case, 9 February–4 May 1748, SCA-LHQ 19, no. 2 (1936): 471–78.

32 Interrogation of *nommé* Pierrot *dit* Jasmin, 9 January 1742, fol. 3, SCR. The soldier had his jaw broken and eye detached. See Fleuriau to Council, 9 January 1742; "Prise de corps," 9 January 1742; "pour quoy il est prisonnier . . ." 9 January 1742; "Déclaration contre Pierre dit Jasmin," 13 January 1742; "Recollement des temoins contre Pierre dit Jasmin," 16 January 1742; "Confrontations du nommé Pierre dit Jasmin," 16 January 1742; "Information contre Pierre dit Jasmin," 16 January 1742; "Interrogatoire de Pierre dit Jasmin," 16, 20 January 1742; "Requeste de Fleuriau," 20 January 1742; "Condamnation du nommé Pierre dit Jasmin," 20 January 1742, SCR.

33 See, for example, documents pertaining to Jahan v. Carrière, 2, 26, and 29 November 1743, SCA-LHQ 12, no. 3 (1929): 474–77; and Bardon v. Beaupre, 16 September 1743, SCA-LHQ 12, no. 1 (1929): 149; judgment, 29 November, 1743, SCA-LHQ 12, no. 3 (1929): 485.

34 In the Twi dialect of Akan, "Kaka" is a common male first name meaning "born on Wednesday." "Racou" is the second part of the name with another meaning, usually corresponding to birth order, birthplace, family lineage, or a nickname descriptor (possibly a corruption or variant of Daku, for "eleventh child"). See Kofi Agyekum, "The Sociolinguistics of Akan Personal Names," *Nordic Journal of African Studies* 15, no. 1 (2006): 206–35.

35 This trial occupied the Superior Council from 15 February to 28 March 1744. The original documents of this case are in poor condition. The translation is a slightly corrected version of what appears in criminal trial of Jupiter, SCA-LHQ 12, no. 4 (1929): 662–74, and 13, no. 1 (1930): 120–24.

36 The one exception was a sailor keelhauled in the early years for theft. I am here speaking of individual crimes, rather than group rebellions or mutinies, which seemed to demand gruesome spectacle throughout the period, whether the instigators were slaves, Indians, or European soldiers. In 1757 four soldiers mutinied and killed their commanding officer. One committed suicide to escape his sentence, two were broken on the wheel, and a Swiss soldier was placed alive in a coffin and sawed in half. His head and hands were cut off and "his body exposed for a week on the gallows." But even in this area, the punishments meted out to slaves continued to escalate. In 1795 the heads of twenty-three slaves accused of conspiracy to revolt were cut off and placed on posts along the river between New Orleans and Pointe Coupée. For an account of this conspiracy and the reaction, see

Hall, *Africans in Colonial Louisiana*, 343–80; Dawdy, "Burden of Louis Congo." A letter from Kerlérec describing the 1757 mutiny is quoted in Villiers du Terrage, *Last Years of French Louisiana*, 86.

37 Brasseaux, "Slave Regulations in French Louisiana." A similar pattern is seen in the British colonies, although they were in the process of fine-tuning an entirely separate legal code and court process for enslaved criminals, a step that Louisiana did not take until the American antebellum period. Donna Spindel, *Crime and Society in North Carolina, 1663–1776* (Baton Rouge: Louisiana State University Press, 1989); Philip J. Schwarz, *Slave Laws in Virginia* (Athens: University of Georgia Press, 1996); Alan D. Watson, "North Carolina Slave Courts, 1715–1785," *North Carolina Historical Review* 60, no. 1 (1983): 24–36.

38 Sens v. Malborough, 16 December 1747, SCA-LHQ 18, no. 4 (1935): 995, and 1 March 1748, SCA-LHQ 19, no. 2 (1936): 485. The accused, Estienne Daigle *dit* Malborough, had assaulted a roofer and his wife in New Orleans in 1736. Report in registry, 19 June 1736, SCA-LHQ 8, no. 2 (1925): 296. For the 1748 case, see criminal session, 24 June 1748, SCA-LHQ 19, no. 4 (1936): 1095–96.

39 The above-mentioned Jean Baptiste and Jeannette probably knew one another well, if they were not family. They had been owned by the same man, named Coustilhas, who freed them both in his will. Some outstanding creditors of the estate, however, contested the Coustilhas manumissions, which suggests that their unusual punishment was actually a shady legal maneuver to settle the estate. See Jeanette *negresse libre*, 3 September 1746; Fleuriau to Council, 8 April 1747, both in SCR. On the Coustilhas manumissions, see entries in Superior Council records for 19 and 22 August 1743, 10–14 September 1743, 3 September 1746, and 8–11 April 1747.

40 These registries were obviously begun in response to a local ordinance now missing from the record, though a similar one for the runaway registry was reissued in 1763. Examples that describe the cause of death: "aged about 100 years, a savagess . . . she died of a lingering illness, having always been infirm"; and Marianne, a fifty-year-old Afro-Louisiana woman who "had been ailing with a chronic infirmity." See 17 October 1739, SCA-LHQ 19, no. 3 (1936): 753; 25 February 1739, SCA-LHQ 6, no. 2 (1923): 301. One wonders how a woman could have been "always infirm," yet lived to be 100 under the conditions of slavery.

41 Examples of these include Famussa, who ran away from Madame Dalcour, "for no cause but the runaway habit," and Fabou, who ran away supposedly out of embarrassment because of a love triangle. Runaway register entry, 18 May 1740, SCA-LHQ 10, no. 3 (1927): 414; 25 August 1740, SCA-LHQ 10, no. 3 (1927): 426. Anecdotal evidence supports a rise in *marronage* during the creole generation. Bienville sent Native American mercenaries after maroons in the neighboring woods in the late 1730s; one caught was La Fleur, who "had been a maroon for a very long time" and who survived by killing and eating wandering livestock on scattered plantations below the city. He was interrogated about his "*bande*," of which Papa Congo, Pierrot, Jeanet, and Québra were members. Fleuriau to Council, 11 April 1738; and "Interrogatoire de La Fleur," 11 April 1738, both in SCR. In 1739 maroons Antoine and Vulcaine were accused of *grand marronage* and theft. Chaperon declaration, 7 November 1739, SCR.

42 Letter of Fazende, 17 February 1745, SCR. In 1744 there had also been complaints of cattle-killing by "the King's negros"; Delisle Dupart declaration, 18 May 1744, SCR. Many of the slaves in New Orleans were publicly owned, first by the Company of the Indies and later by the king. This "public" ownership seems to have given

slaves a greater opportunity not only for *marronage*, but for a degree of autonomy in the city and elsewhere. Many of the "king's slaves" lived on their own, working at various trades. For additional examples of *marronage* in this period, see Hall, *Africans in Colonial Louisiana*, 143–48.

43 Périer and Delachaise, 30 March 1728, ANF-AC, C13A 11, fols. 97–100; 15 March 1745, SCA-LHQ 14, no. 1 (1931): 96; motion, examination, and sentence of run-away slave, 4, 10 and 13 January 1737, SCA-LHQ 5, no. 3 (1922): 386–88; interrogations, 9 June 1748–24 June 1748, SCA-LHQ 19, no. 4 (1936): 1090–96; testimonies and inquiries, 15–24 June 1751, SCA-LHQ 20, no. 4 (1937):1122–31.

44 Documents indicate many slaves had guns for hunting and for tracking down Indians and maroons. A rare complaint about gun possession involved a slave boy who shot another, but the concern was only that they were too young for the responsibility. D'Auseville declaration, 14 December 1739, SCR.

45 Brasseaux, "Slave Regulations," 220.

46 The *Coutume de Paris* was the common law of Paris chosen for Louisiana, from among a crazy-quilt of Roman and Gallic customs in the different regions of France. For an overview of the code, see Hans W. Baade, "Marriage Contracts in French and Spanish Louisiana: A Study in 'Notarial' Jurisprudence," *Tulane Law Review* 53 (1978): 3–92.

47 On this theme, see Alan Williams, *The Police of Paris, 1718–1789* (Baton Rouge: Louisiana State University Press, 1979); Farge and Zysberg, "Les Théâtres de la violence;" Ruff, *Crime, Justice and Public Order in Old Regime France*.

48 The *procureur général* served as the public prosecutor and chief counsel. The post of attorney of vacant estates was created to handle the tangled affairs of abandoned concessions and estate settlements. Other colonists with legal training served as notaries and helped clients draft petitions, though they were barred from appearing in court. Kerlérec complained of one Bellot who "is no doubt one of a number of people practicing law at the courthouse, practitioners of which the king, by his instructions forbids governors to permit in his colonies." Kerlérec to Minister, 24 April 1759, ANF-AC, C13A 41, fol. 16. Translation suggested in Villiers du Terrage, *Last Years of French Louisiana*, 103.

49 Examination procedures were similar to those in France where a series of interrogations, reinterrogations, and confrontations between the accused and witnesses were performed, following the "Ordonnance du Roy pour les matieres criminelles . . . August 1670" (Bibliothèque Nationale, Catalog 40806). In France defendants of means could hire a lawyer to present evidence of their innocence.

50 "Instructions pour la formation d'un établissement en Louisiane . . . par Drouot de Valdeterre," 1722 (before 9 December), ANF-AC, C13A 6, fol. 452. Translation from Villiers du Terrage, *Last Years of French Louisiana*, 22.

51 Kerlérec to Minister, 22 October 1757, ANF-AC, C13A 39, fols. 284–85. Bienville had voiced similar complaints. Bienville to Council of the Marine, 20 October 1719, ANF-AC, C13A 5, fol. 276v. See also Vaudreuil and Michel to Rouillé, 20 May 1751, in MPA 5:83.

52 Favrot declaration, 13 July 1745; Tixerant declaration, 13 July 1745; DeBenac to Council of War, 14 July 1745; and "Condamnation de Braude," 14 July 1745, all in SCR.

53 Bossu, *Travels in the Interior of North America*, 177–82. Although the trial records are lost, Governor Kerlérec also described this case in his correspondence. See Villiers du Terrage, *Last Years of French Louisiana*, 86.

54 The term has sometimes been mistranslated as "mayor." New Orleans had no such office in the French period. It has also been translated as "town major," which is closer.

55 See Fleuriau's reports on rounds he made during high mass on All Saints Day and the Feast of Saint Thomas. Inspections, 1 and 5 November 1725, 21–22 December 1725, SCA-LHQ 2, no. 4 (1919): 480–81, 484.

56 "Réglement sur la police des cabarets, des esclaves, des marchés en Louisiane," 28 February—1 March 1751, ANF-AC, C13A 35, fols. 39–52. Brasseaux links these regulations to a panic in 1748 caused by maroon raiding in the *bas de fleuve* area below New Orleans. Brasseaux, "Slave Regulations," 219.

57 Farge and Zysberg, "Les Théâtres de la violence"; Castan, "Summary Justice"; Dennis Charles Rousey, *Policing the Southern City: New Orleans, 1805–1889* (Baton Rouge: Louisiana State University Press, 1996), 16–19.

58 Since New Orleans lacked a dedicated police force or a *prévôté* court, we do not have a set of arrest records and summary justice comparable to those of France. What we do have are remnants of criminal cases brought to formal trial before the Superior Council and references to major crimes made in civil documents. It is possible that the *major*, or even the *huissier*, played a more active role in law enforcement and summary justice than the court record indicates. Kerr observes that in French New Orleans, "cases were tried orally with only brief records kept of the proceedings." Although this may have been true for some petty crimes, the overall criminal court record has been substantially thinned by document loss and archival culling. Occasionally, the criminal court docket appears well preserved for a run of consecutive weeks, where one finds cases comprising dozens of related documents. Derek N. Kerr, *Petty Felony, Slave Defiance, and Frontier Villainy: Crime and Criminal Justice in Spanish Louisiana, 1770–1803* (New York: Garland Publishing, 1993), 11.

59 Interrogation, 22 February 1744, SCA-LHQ 12, no. 4 (1929): 666; procuration, 14 January 1763, SCA-LHQ 24, no. 3 (1941): 788; "Attempted Escape of John and Josiah Hayward, Father and Son, in 1744, from the Prison in New Orleans Where They Had Been Detained Since Two Years," *Louisiana Historical Quarterly* 9, no. 3 (1926): 361–84.

60 He may have been half Indian, possibly Choctaw. Bossu notes that Baudreau *fils* spoke their language and that he had been made "a member of their nation." His father had arrived with Iberville in 1698 and lived to a very old age, although Bossu's claim that he was 118 years old in 1762 is probably exaggerated. Bossu, *Travels in the Interior*, 181, 220.

61 Mademoiselle Huet also returned. The council held her responsible for her own "seduction," which had resulted in two children. She was denied damages and remained unmarried. The "abducted" slaves were an eighteen-year-old *negresse* named Jeanneton, her five-year-old daughter, and a sixteen-year-old Indian. "Ignace Petit Déclaration," 26 January 1744, SCR; "Ordonne de saisir," 28 January 1744, SCR. See also Superior Council entries for 29–30 May 1745, 5 June 1745, 7 October 1747, 12 January 1748, 16 August 1752; and Kerlérec to unknown recipient, 28 October 1757, from private collection, quoted in Villiers du Terrage, *Last Years of French Louisiana*, 86. See also Bossu, *Travels in the Interior*, 179–81.

62 Of nineteen known murders committed between 1722 and 1763, we have trial records for only four; of fifty known assaults, we have trial records for only eigh-

teen, and most of these are incomplete. More dramatically, we have no trial or conviction records of major incidents, such as the Bambara slave conspiracy of 1731. Gaps in the archive suggest that the criminal case record was kept separate from that of civil hearings and notarial matters. The latter appear to have been much better preserved due to the custodial mandate inherited with the office of notary. By the 1740s the Louisiana government had separated these functions architecturally with a "civic chamber" at the government house and a "criminal chamber" attached to the civilian prison next to the church on the Place d'Armes. The records for procedures taking place in these two locations may have been stored separately and the criminal records perhaps fell victim to fires, renovations, or neglect. Yakubik and Franks, "Archaeological Investigations at the Site of the Cabildo."

63 Surviving documents refer to a Register of the Prison and a Register of Criminal Sessions, but no such registers or document series remain among the 11,748 items in the Superior Council records. The Register of Prisons was mentioned in a 1753 bestiality case when the suspect was transferred from Mobile to New Orleans. King v. Baron, 5 October 1753, SCA-LHQ 22, no. 3 (1939): 886. The Registry of Criminal Sessions is listed in the estate inventory of Michel Rossard, who was clerk of the Louisiana Superior Council from approximately 1723 to 1736. One lot of items is described as "Papers of the Registry: A Registry of Criminal Sessions, from folio 1 to folio 32, included: two Registers of Civil Sessions, in one covering up to folio 132 from January 4, 1718 to December 19, 1728; another covering up to folio 137 from January 8, 1729 to November 5, 1735; Register of the Sessions of the Admiralty . . . a Register serving for registration of commissions, rulings and ordinances of the Superior Council up to and including folio 95; a Register of Deliberations," and so on. Rossard inventory, 25 May 1736, SCA-LHQ 8, no. 2 (1925): 291. For a provenance history of the Superior Council's records and their notarial connection, see Henry Putney Beers, *French and Spanish Records of Louisiana: A Bibliographical Guide to Archive and Manuscript Sources* (Baton Rouge: Louisiana State University Press, 1989), 9–15.

64 Original not microfilmed. For a near complete translation, see Fleury inquest, 3 July–1 August 1763, SCA-LHQ 25, no. 2 (1942): 552–57.

65 Based on his reading of colonial correspondence, French historian Villiers du Terrage held the view that in Louisiana "there was hardly a month that went by without an execution." Thomas Ingersoll, in contrast, interprets the (remnant) crime records of the Louisiana Superior Council to mean that crime rates were low in the French colony and that "capital punishment and judicial torture of white people were almost unheard of because serious crimes were almost never committed by them . . . In New Orleans, as in most colonies, white people were generally able to police themselves." Hardy makes the most in-depth sounding of the surviving documents, though he concludes that the Superior Council "did little work" in its criminal court capacity, "for few criminal cases came before it, although ample evidence exists to demonstrate that Louisiana colonists were far from peaceful or orderly." Villiers du Terrage, *Last Years of French Louisiana*, 57; Ingersoll, *Mammon and Manon*, 64; Hardy, "Superior Council," 95.

66 Declaration of Bonnaud, 28 May 1723, SCR. I stress that the sample is one of *reported crimes* from several sources. The sample is *not* limited to the total number of prosecutions in the Superior Council records (though these are included), nor is it equivalent to arrests or convictions.

67   For analysis of moral and state crimes in France, see Ruff, *Crime, Justice and Public Order*, 146–81. In 1742 French administrators were still trying to resolve the case of the stolen ship."Enquête," 10 September 1742, SCR.

68   "Condamnation de le no*mmé* Villeneuve," 10 September 1723, SCR. The "wooden horse" was a type of wooden vault made with an uncomfortable peak in the center, upon which the condemned would sit while exposed to public ridicule.

69   The investigation led to the arrest and interrogation of several Bambara slaves (Changereau, François, Pierrot, and Sabany). "Requeste du procureur général," 5 September 1729, SCR. See also criminal procedures, 5 September 1729, SCA-LHQ 4, no. 3 (1921): 347–48.

70   Letter of Terrisse de Ternan, 13 October 1729, SCR. Schmidt's crimes were *"desertion, complots et attroupements."* Summons, 4 June 1728, SCR. A woman named Jeanne Carroy Vincent, wife of a soldier, was also suspected of being a ringleader; they supposedly convinced a number of soldiers and *engagés* to steal a longboat and desert. The phrase used is *aller aux Anglais,* but as this is a colloquialism that means "to slip away," it is not certain the English colonies were their destination (an English version of this colloquialism is "to take a French leave"). Several of the principal accused are shown as New Orleans property owners in 1728. Over twenty witnesses were called in this well-documented case that includes several verbatim interrogations. That of Sieur Langlois is the best preserved. "Interrogatoire de Sr. Langlois," 1 June 1728, SCR. See also interrogations, 1–3 June 1728, SCA-LHQ 4, no. 4 (1921): 486–88.

71   For a more detailed discussion of the numbers and how they were arrived at, see Dawdy, *"La Ville Sauvage,"* 264–71. There is a long tradition of characterizing southern society in general as violent, arising from observations of antebellum dueling, white-on-black violence in the post–Civil War era, and gun violence in the twentieth century. Only a few studies have looked at antebellum or colonial crime rates. Those that have done so note a high incidence of white-on-white assaults and other violent crimes in comparison to northern cities. Few authors, however, have offered a convincing explanation for this phenomenon; most fall back either on the concept of "southern honor" making people hotheaded or the notion that the violence used to discipline slaves was contagious. This topic requires a historical sociology that has yet to be done. See James M. Denham, *A Rogue's Paradise: Crime and Punishment in Antebellum Florida, 1821–1861* (Tuscaloosa: University of Alabama Press, 1998); Edward L. Ayers, *Vengeance and Justice: Crime and Punishment in the 19th-Century American South* (New York: Oxford University Press, 1984); Robert M. Saunders, "Crime and Punishment in Early National America: Richmond, Virginia, 1784–1820," *Virginia Magazine of History and Biography* 86, no. 1 (1978): 33–44; Jim Rice, "'This Province, So Meanly and Thinly Inhabited': Punishing Maryland's Criminals, 1681–1850," *Journal of the Early Republic* 19, no. 1 (1999): 15–42; Spindel, *Crime and Society in North Carolina, 1663–1776;* and Michael Stephen Hindus, *Prison and Plantation: Crime, Justice, and Authority in Massachusetts and South Carolina, 1767–1878* (Chapel Hill: University of North Carolina Press, 1980).

72   "Information sur un duel et al mort de Servin," 23 June 1751, SCR. See also good translations in the following: inquiry, testimonies, and *procès verbal,* 23 June 1751; and criminal session, 3 July 1751, SCA-LHQ 20, no. 4 (1937): 1127–29. For tabular results of these statistics, see Dawdy, *"La Ville Sauvage,"* 275.

73   Le Normant declaration, 24 March 1747, SCR.

74   Recommendation of *procureur général*, 27 September 1729, SCR; declaration of Bonnaud, 21 October 1729, SCR.

75   This contrasts sharply with the Spanish era, when "slaves and the increasing population of free men of color dominate the criminal statistics in Spanish Louisiana." Kerr, *Petty Felony, Slave Defiance, and Frontier Villainy*, 211.

76   Examples of domestic violence include the case of Baraca, mentioned earlier, and that of "Papa" who killed his wife Helene with "*un coup de hache*" (a blow with an axe). Murder case, 9 February–4 May 1748, SCA-LHQ 19, no. 2 (1936): 471–78; Brosset declaration, 1 April 1745, SCR. For the witchcraft case, see Fleuriau to Council, 9 September 1743, SCR. See also a letter of Corbin's father in which he suspects a slave named Pompé. Bachemin to unknown recipient, 26 June 1743, SCR.

77   One document describes his crimes as arising simply "from a mean spirit . . . [he] satisfies his violent passion by mistreating the Negros." Declaration of D'Ausseville, 5 September 1730, SCR. The owner refers to violations of the *Code Noir* and asks that slaves be brought in for testimony. See also examination, 17 January 1730; Letter of D'Auseville, 6 April 1730; D'Auseville to Roy, 29 April 1730, all in SCA-LHQ 4, no. 4 (1921): 510, 518, 521. Petition to prosecute, 30 August 1730; petition to reinforce prosecution, 7 September 1730; testimony, 18 September 1730, all in SCA-LHQ 5, no. 1 (1922): 89, 92, 94.

78   Although Thomas was a free man, the plaintiff slaveowner still sought redress from employer Belair rather than Thomas. "Plainte du Sr. de Blanc contre Belair," 29 December 1731, SCR. Another case involving two free men of color suggests that people with this status settled together as neighbors, although relations were not always tranquil. A free man of color named Le Gros was terrorized by another free black neighbor who killed his turkey cocks and made daily threats because he thought Le Gros was meddling in his marriage. Gros declaration, 17 May 1745, SCA-LHQ 14, no. 1 (1931): 113.

79   Declaration of Baldit, 21 June 1735, SCR. It is notable that the unnamed enslaved woman used the familiar form of speech (*tu*) with Baldit.

80   One exception was an unnamed slave woman belonging to Sieur Latticolais who nearly "strangled" a planter's nephew after he threw a brick at her wandering pig. Judice declaration, 10 April 1747, SCR.

81   Sexual abuse of slaves, as well as concubinage, were explicitly outlawed by Louisiana's *Code Noir*, a fact of which Jeanneton seemed to be aware, though one assumes enforcement was rare. Pierre Garsont [Garçon] and L'Eveillé declaration, 29 June 1737, SCR.

82   There was a free man of color named Le Gros living in New Orleans in 1745, but it is unclear whether this was the same man. Chaumont to Council, 30 January 1745; Gros *negre libre* declaration, 17 May 1745, SCR.

83   For examples of separation suits, see answer and defense of Membrede, 2 September 1745, SCA-LHQ 14, no. 4 (1931): 572–73; session of Superior Council, 4 July 1744, SCA-LHQ 13, no. 1 (1930): 141; case of infanticide, 14 July 1748–1 July 1749, SCA-LHQ 19, no. 4 (1936): 1112–16.

84   Owsley and others, "Archaeological and Physical Anthropological Study of the First Cemetery in New Orleans," 128.

85   Yakubik and Franks, "Archaeological Investigations at the Site of the Cabildo." Besides architectural features, deposits from the French period were nearly void of artifacts, due to repeated phases of demolition and rebuilding on the site.

CHAPTER 6

1 Villiers du Terrage, *Last Years of French Louisiana,* 112n33, 183n25; Moore, *Revolt in Louisiana,* 146.

2 The events of 1768 are sometimes referred to as a rebellion, but I prefer to call them a revolt. Although both *rebellion* and *revolt* are defined as short-lived and ultimately unsuccessful rejections of political authority, the etymological root of *rebellion* is "war" while that of *revolt* is a "turning away." Although arms were displayed during the New Orleans events, not a single drop of blood was shed until the conspirators were punished. *Rebellion* also has a connotation of an uncontrolled and spontaneous movement, while *revolt* encompasses the possibility of a planned, but failed, revolution. The 1768 events followed a slow buildup over years and appear to have been planned (and even voted upon) by the local Louisiana Superior Council.

3 The crown had long feared that Protestantism would lead to republicanism, a fear that the heavy German presence in the revolt may justify. See Bertrand Van Ruymbeke, "'A Dominion of True Believers Not a Republic for Heretics': French Colonial Religious Policy and the Settlement of Early Louisiana, 1699–1730," in *French Colonial Louisiana and the Atlantic World,* ed. Bond, 83–94. The first Acadian immigrants (ancestors of the Cajuns), refugees of an expulsion by the British in what is now Nova Scotia, arrived in Louisiana in 1764. They are one of several French-speaking immigration streams to Louisiana, but due to their late arrival are not strongly associated with the French colonial period. See Carl A. Brasseaux, *The Founding of New Acadia: The Beginnings of Acadian Life in Louisiana, 1765–1803* (Baton Rouge: Louisiana State University Press, 1997).

4 Moore, *Revolt in Louisiana,* 107–8, 157–58; Villiers du Terrage, *Last Years of French Louisiana,* 306–7, 319–20.

5 For more details of the revolt, see Moore, *Revolt in Louisiana;* and Carl A. Brasseaux, *Denis-Nicolas Foucault and the New Orleans Rebellion of 1768* (Ruston, La.: McGinty Publications, 1987). For full French transcriptions of many documents related to the uprising, see Gayarré, *Histoire de la Louisiane,* 2:146–381; and Villiers du Terrage, *Last Years of French Louisiana.* For text of the petition, see Gayarré, *Histoire de la Louisiane,* 2:167–68. A rare copy of the latter, printed on Braud's press, is owned by the Lauinger Library of Georgetown University, Washington, D.C., and carries the title *Mémoire, des habitans et negocians de la Louisianne, sur l'événement du 29 octobre 1768.*

6 Clemente Saldaña, quoted in Vincente Rodríguez Casado, "Costumbres de los habitants de Nueva Orleans en el comienzo de la dominación española," *Revista de Indias* 2, no. 4 (1941): 176–79.

7 Seck, "Relationships between St. Louis of Senegal, Its Hinterlands, and Colonial Louisiana," 274.

8 Linebaugh and Rediker, *Many-Headed Hydra.*

9 Peggy K. Liss and Franklin W. Knight, "Introduction," in *Atlantic Port Cities,* ed. Knight and Liss, 10; Peggy K. Liss, *Atlantic Empires: The Network of Trade and Revolution, 1713–1826* (Baltimore: Johns Hopkins University Press, 1983); Laurent Dubois, *Avengers of the New World: The Story of the Haitian Revolution* (Cambridge, Mass.: Belknap Press, 2004).

10 Abraham and Van Schendel, "Introduction: The Making of Illicitness," 14.

11   On the LeMoynes as soldiers of fortune, see Nellis M. Crouse, *LeMoyne D'Iberville: Soldier of New France* (Baton Rouge: Louisiana State University Press, 2001 [1954]). Although Crouse's account was intended to idolize Iberville, it is difficult to conclude from the facts presented that the LeMoynes were not freebooters above all else, beginning with campaigns in Canada against the Hudson's Bay Company posts motivated by the opportunity to capture a privateer's share of the season's fur harvest. On the fur trade, see W. J. Eccles, *Essays on New France* (Oxford: Oxford University Press, 1987), 79–96, 110–25; Yves Zoltvany, "New France and the West, 1701–1713," *Canadian Historical Review* 46 (1965): 301–22; Richard Weyhing, "Cadillac's Vision and Dubuisson's Dilemma: The Founding of Detroit, The 'Fox Massacre' and the Impasses of Early Modern Empire in French North America," unpublished paper, University of Chicago, Department of History, 2006. On moral views of Canada, see Peter Moogk, *La Nouvelle France: The Making of French Canada, a Cultural History* (East Lansing: Michigan State University Press, 2000), 87–120; and Gilles Havard, *Empire et Métissages: Indiens et Français dan le Pays d'en haut, 1660–1715* (Montreal: Septentrion, 2003). Havard names some aspects of rogue colonialism the "Cadillac syndrome," after that early Louisiana governor's renowned corruption and personal despotism. Saadani also remarks that Cadillac "was working mainly for his own personal interests, which were not necessarily those of the colony." Khalil Saadani, "Gift Exchange between the French and Native Americans in Louisiana," in *French Colonial Louisiana and the Atlantic World*, ed. Bond, 43–64, especially 55. Seck notes that traders in Senegal were also notorious for graft and smuggling. Seck, "Relationships between St. Louis of Senegal," 265.

12   Scott, *Seeing Like a State*. For a thoughtful critique of Scott's work that also suggests capitalism and nonstate actors be considered as part of the "plan" of modernism, see Fernando Coronil, "Smelling like a Market," *American Historical Review* 106, no. 1 (2001): 119–29.

13   Ibid., 6.

14   Steven Mufson, "Threat of 'Rogue' States: Is It Reality or Rhetoric?" *Washington Post*, 29 May 2001, A1; Noam Chomsky, *Rogue States: The Rule of Force in World Affairs* (Cambridge, Mass.: South End Press, 2000); William Blum, *Rogue State: A Guide to the World's Only Superpower* (Monroe, Maine: Common Courage Press, 2005); Jacques Derrida, *Rogues: Two Essays on Reason* (Stanford, Calif.: Stanford University Press, 2005).

15   C. T. Onions, ed., *Oxford English Dictionary* (Oxford: Clarendon Press, 1964). The same source says there is no evidence of an etymological connection with the French adjective *rogue*, meaning "arrogant."

16   Abraham and van Schendel, "Making of Illicitness," 7.

17   Charles Tilly, "War Making and State Making as Organized Crime," in *Bringing the State Back In*, ed. Peter Evans, Dietrich Rueschemeyer, and Theda Skocpol (Cambridge: Cambridge University Press, 1985), 169–91, especially 170 and 173 (quotes).

18   Thomas W. Gallant, "Brigandage, Piracy, Capitalism, and State-Formation: Transnational Crime from a Historical World-Systems Perspective," in *States and Illegal Practices*, ed. Heyman, 25–61, especially 40 (quote).

19   Eric Hobsbawm, *Bandits*, 4th ed., revised and expanded (New York: New Press, 2000 [1969]), 20, 42. Antón Blok offered many thoughtful critiques and expansions

of Hobsbawm's work on banditry, to which Hobsbawm responded in this revised fourth edition. See essays reprinted in Blok, *Honour and Violence*, especially 14–43.

20   Janice E. Thomson, *Mercenaries, Pirates, and Sovereigns: State-building and Extraterritorial Violence in Early Modern Europe* (Princeton: Princeton University Press, 1995). Rogue colonialism ends up looking an awful lot like postcolonialism, or at least present-day examples of postcolonial societies struggling to establish a rule of law, where entrepreneurialism trumps social planning and the line between legitimacy and criminality in both political and economic realms is difficult to draw because no one monopolizes violence. As Jean and John Comaroff state about the postcolonial condition, there is "something inherent in the unfolding conjuncture everywhere of violence, sovereignty, il/legality, modernity." What are we to make of this echo between eighteenth-century New Orleans and the postcolonial present? If there is a kinship between rogue colonialism and postcolonialism, can we make any forecasts based on the Louisiana example? One might be that we are simply in a period of transition when the relationship between the bandit and the state is being redefined. Another could be that where one state loses interest or nerve, the bandits prepare the way for another to enter, and a new kind of empire takes over. A third is that a rogue period precedes revolution. Jean Comaroff and John L. Comaroff, "Preface," in *Law and Disorder in the Postcolony*, ed. Jean Comaroff and John L. Comaroff (Chicago: University of Chicago Press, 2006), vii.

21   Roitman, "Garrison-Entrepôt: A Mode of Governing in the Chad Basin," 418. See also Roitman, *Fiscal Disobedience*. On Louisiana military profiteering, see Usner, *Indians, Settlers, and Slaves*, 250–52.

22   Hobsbawm, *Bandits*; Linebaugh and Rediker, *Many-Headed Hydra*; Braudel, *Mediterranean and the Mediterranean World in the Age of Philip II*. See also Tilly, "War Making," 173.

23   Linebaugh and Rediker, *Many-Headed Hydra*, 2.

24   Ibid.

25   Schneider and Schneider, *Reversible Destiny*, 46. See also Jane Schneider and Peter Schneider, *Culture and Political Economy in Western Sicily* (New York: Academic Press, 1976); Blok, *Honour and Violence*, 87–102; Raimondo Catanzaro, *Men of Respect: A Social History of the Sicilian Mafia* (New York, Free Press, 1992).

Index

The letter *t* following a page number denotes a table; the letter *f* denotes a figure.

crime (*cont.*)

    moral crimes/crimes against the state; calumny cases and, 171–72; desertion, 152, 199–200, 210; mutiny and sedition, 200, 202, 206, 210; smuggling, 116, 122–28, 207; spying, 210; property crimes; burglary, 201, 204, 207, 209; cattle rustling/killing, 208, 209, 210; 298n41, 298n42; debt, 203, 208–9; embezzlement, 209; forgery, 209; fraud, 112, 173, 209–10; theft, 193, 202–3, 209–10; vandalism, 209; punishment, 190–91, 193, 200–4, 297n36; rates and statistics, 209–17, 301n65; taverns and, 186; verbal violence, 210; violent crimes; assault/battery, 201; increase in, discussed, 211–17; murder, 201–2, 213–14; rape, 209, 215. *See also* executioner; executions; insults and slander; prison

criminality: and colonialism, 245

Crozat, Antoine, 14, 116, 146, 194; company charter, 116

Crusoe, Robinson, 51

Cuba, 110, 113, 120t, 291n92; Havana, 110, 120t, 200, 274n8; Havana, as destination for criminals and runaways, 208, 210; Havana, as trade partner with New Orleans, 102, 107, 113, 119, 226, 229; Santiago de Cuba, 113, 274n8

Curaçao, 120t, 121

d'Abbadie, Jean-Jacques, 186–87

Darby, Jonathas, 87, 170, 292n96; views on trade, 107–8, 119

Darby, William, xv

Darnton, Robert, 262n46

D'Artaguette, Diron, 65, 115, 126–27, 279n58

Dauphin Island, 14, 205

Davis, Edwin, 134

Davis, Natalie Zemon, 164

De Batz, 106

debt, 127, 205; slander and, 173. *See also under* crime

Delachaise, Jacques, 123–24, 160, 169, 172, 182, 184, 207

Delamare, Nicolas: *Traité de la police*, 70–71

Delisle brothers, 35

demographics, 3, 7, 12, 92, 96, 151, 156–57; city limits and, 287n45; racial categories and, 291n87; slave to free, ratio of, 175–76. *See also* censuses and census-taking

deserters and desertion, 150, 163, 194, 302n70. *See also under* crime

De Soto, Hernando, 74

de Tocqueville, Alexis, xv

Dictionnaire de l'Académie française, 28

Diderot, Denis, 219

disease, 2, 51, 82, 97

disorder (*désordre*): as trope for New Orleans, 28–31, 226–27

drawing and painting, 51–52, 65–66, 88

Druout de Valdeterre, 40, 81–82, 205

Dubois, Laurent, 11

Dubreuil, Claude Joseph Villars, 81, 182–83

Dubuisson, Sieur, 64, 65

Duc d'Orléans, Philippe, 14, 15, 33

Duclos, 114

Dumanoir (Faucon-Dumanoir), Jean Baptiste, 123, 125, 183

Dumas, Alexandre, 240

Dumont de Montigny, Jean-François Benjamin, 35, 37, 83, 163, 168, 172; as *forçat*, 51; *histoire* of, 51–52; letters of, 40; *mémoire* of, 39; as party to slander case, 173; poetry of, 263n57

education, 56–60; of boys, 57–60; of girls, 58–59

Elmina, 80

emancipation, 296n29

emigrants, 146, 152. *See also forçats*

Emile (Rousseau), 37

engagés. See indentured servants

engineers: in France, 13, 71; in Louisiana, 88; as representation of Enlightenment, 11; training, 13. *See also* Broutin; Le Blond de la Tour; Pauger; Perrier; Vauban

England, 241, 255n11; attacks on Louisbourg, 92, 95; colonial cities of, 69, 272n92; expansion in North America, 233; invasion of Havana, 113; mercantilist policies of, 103; slave laws

intendant, 195
Isabelle, 104

Jamaica, 29, 107, 119, 120t, 129; slaves
from, 129, 281n66
Jeanneton, 215
Jeannette, 185, 203
Jefferson, Thomas: *Account of Louisiana*,
56
Jesuits, 41, 59
Jews and Judaism, 227; exclusion of Jews,
145
Johnston, A. J. B., 92–93
Journal d'un voyage à la Louisiane
(Vallette de Laudun), 44–45
Juffure, 80

Kerlérec, Louis Billouart, Chevalier de,
94, 129, 134; plans for fortifications,
95; recalled to France, 95; smuggling,
concerns about, 101, 128; smuggling,
involvement in, 55, 127–30
King George's War. *See under* wars and
military engagements:
kinship, 231; cemeteries as maps of,
140; networks among the elites, 182–
84
Knight, Franklin, 232

Labuissonnière, Madame, 106
LaChance, Paul, 292n98
La Chaume, 199–200
Lafrénière, Nicolas Chauvin de, 183, 186,
197, 219–22
Lake Pontchartrain, 75, 78, 79, 107, 108,
268n35
Lamesse, Jan (Le Flamand), 164
Langlois, Gilles, 96
La Rochelle, 121
La Rue, Etienne, 131, 174
La Salle, René-Robert Cavelier, Sieur de,
14, 32, 45, 86
Laugier, Marc Antoine, 74
Law, John, 2, 14–15, 27, 47, 101, 150,
228; tobacco monopoly, 153. *See also*
Company of the Indies; Mississippi
Bubble
laws and regulations, 198–200, 228; in
British colonies, 298n37; *Coutume de*

Paris, 299n46; effect of slaves on, 197.
See also Code Noir; legal status
lawyers: banning of, 67, 145, 197, 205,
228
Le Ber, 186
Le Blanc, Claude, 39, 163
Le Blond de la Tour, Pierre, 39, 65, 81, 88,
265n7
legal status: as principle of social organization, 142–44, 155, 187, 231, 296n24;
racial categories and, 179–80, 199–200,
296n29. *See also* class
Le Havre, 72
Le Maire, Father, 25–26, 57, 223; description of social order, 29; writings of, 25,
35
Lemelle, Santiago, 101
Lemoine, 174
LeMoyne brothers. *See* Bienville; Iberville
Le Normant, François Ange, 213
Le Page du Pratz, Antoine-Simon, 35, 39,
49, 78, 173; *Histoire de la Louisiane*,
52–54; *Plan du Camp des Negres*, 149;
plantation planning, 146–48; views on
the Natchez, 79; views on race, 155
L'Esprit des loix (Montesquieu), 37
letters and letter-writing, 32–33, 38–42;
as accumulation of knowledge, 16–17;
censorship, 40; from French vs. English
colonies, 38; as literature, 41. *See also*
Republic of Letters
lettres de cachet, 12, 151, 163
Lettres d'une Péruvienne (Grafigny), 37
levees, 53, 270n57; levee system, effects
of, 82
Lewis, Gwynne, 14
Lewis, Peirce, 67
libel, 22, 55, 164, 171, 210, 238, 272n90;
prosecution for, 279n55. *See also* insults and slander
Linebaugh, Peter, 133, 226; *The Many-
Headed Hydra* (Linebaugh and
Rediker), 241–42, 281n70
Liss, Peggy, 232
literacy, 56–57, 59
literature, 17; banned books, 37; letters
as, 41; of Louisiana, discussed, 42–49;
travel writing, 54
Lobry, 124

Locke, John: *An Essay on Human Understanding*, 37
London, 69
Londonderry, Ireland, 120t
Lorient, 72–73; as home port of the Company of the Indies, 73
Los Adayes, 108
Louis XIII, 13
Louis XIV, 13–14, 73; imperial aspirations of, 71; as patron of architecture, 70; as patron of intellectualism, 13
Louis XV, 8, 14
Louisbourg, 72; compared to New Orleans, 92–94, 96
"Louisiana Affair," 96, 130
Louisiana: Its Colonial History and Romance (Gayarré), 28
lumber: trade in, 278n42

Macmahon, Laurent, 123–24, 278n52
Madame John's Legacy (house), 84, 101. *See also* Real Pascal Marin, Elizabeth
Mafia (Sicilian), 244; Palermo and, 273n93
magic, 214
major de place, 206, 295n12
Mali, 80
Manchac, 108
Mandeville, Marigny de, 55
Manon Lescaut. See Histoire du chevalier DesGrieux et de Manon Lescaut
manumission, 178–81, 292n102; *Code Noir* provisions, 198; 298n39; of slave soldiers, 179, 292n96
Many-Headed Hydra, The (Linebaugh and Rediker), 241–42, 281n70
maps and mapmaking, 35, 88, 90; as urban planning, 158–62
Mardi Gras. *See* carnival
Marin, François, 100, 114, 132
market: slave access to, regulation of, 104, 207
maroons and runaways, 186, 190, 194, 203–4, 240, 298n41, 299n44; census of, 186, 203; economic activity, 86; Native Americans and, 199–200; smuggling, 224; urban population of, 176, 231. *See also* slaves
Marquis, Pierre, 220

marriage: age at, 293n104; *Code Noir* and, 181, 198; contracts, 57; endogamy among creole elites, 182–85, 230; exogamy among nonelites, 184–85; as means of attaining elite status, 295n18; separations, 208, 214, 216. *See also* kinship; oligarchy
Marseille: disease in, 273n94
Martinique, 114, 136–37; Békés, 282n90; St. Pierre, black market of, 119–20; St. Pierre, as trade partner with New Orleans, 102, 119–20, 120t, 229
Mathieu, Capraize, 181, 185
Mauritius, 29; compared to New Orleans, 92
Mazama, 213
Mazarin, 13
medicine, 17; medical uses of plants, 35; metaphors of city and, 70
Mediterranean and the Mediterranean World in the Age of Philip II, The (Braudel), 275n21
mercantilism, 101; discussed, 103–7; lifting of restrictions, 117–18; smuggling and, 152
merchants (*négociants*) and merchant-planters, 125, 145; circum-Caribbean networks, 131; as smugglers, 130. *See also under* oligarchy
Mercier, Louis-Sebastien: *Tableau de Paris*, 70
Mercure de France, Le, 37, 43, 55, 66
mētis, 227, 235; defined, 5; Revolt of 1768 and, 232; rogue colonialism and, 5–6; subsistence economy and, 83
métis, 5, 105, 183
métissage, 182, 199, 293n112
Mexico, 120t; Campeche, 108, 111, 120t, 121, 129, 275n25; Mississippian groups and, 275n22; smuggling and, 113, 126; trade, 102, 110; Veracruz, 58, 110; Veracruz, as trade partner with New Orleans, 102, 107, 108, 113, 119, 120t, 121, 226, 229, 279n56
Meyère, Jacques de, 106, 125–26
Mézières, Marquise de, 83, 84
Micelle, Jerry, 197
"middle ground," 12

sexual relations, 199; *Code Noir* prohibitions, 303n81. *See also métissage*
ships and sailing; arrivals, 118, 277n41; destinations, 119–20; "king's ships," 102, 121, 128, 234; navigation, 109–11; ports of origin, 119–20; routes; in the Gulf of Mexico, 109f, 110; to New Orleans from the Gulf of Mexico, 108; ships based in New Orleans, 101, 114–15; types and sizes of ships, 110–11, 114–15, 276n32; *interlope* (smuggling vessel), 279n56; lighters, 111; *pirogues*, 102, 106, 109, 110, 114, 133; wrecks, 112, 122
silver: mines in Illinois country, 43; Spanish/Mexican silver, importance in trade, 113, 116, 119, 121, 132, 224, 238
Sister Stanislas. *See* Hachard, Marie-Madeleine
slander. *See* insults and slander
slaves and slavery, 31, 83, 142, 143, 185, 194, 207; African slaves, 146, 155, 177; as artisans and craftsmen, 177; censuses and, 154–55; conspiracies of, 190, 297n36; crime and, 210, 213–15; desertions, 200; economic activity of, 104, 131, 133, 207; housing of, 92, 146–49, 161; Indian slaves, 155, 177, 189; legal status of slaves, 231; literacy of, 57; maritime trade and, 133; nicknames and, 165–66; punishment of, 193, 202, 231–32, 297n36; as sailors, 131; slander and, 174; smuggling and, 224, 226–27; testimony of slaves, 290n73; urban population of, 157–58, 175–78, 212, 230–31, 272n77, 298n42; as wealth, 162. *See also Code Noir*; emancipation; laws and regulations; manumission; *specific individuals*
slave trade, 73, 80, 103, 106, 132–33, 296n28; smuggling and, 132–33; Spanish restriction of, 221; transatlantic, 107, 281n70
Smith, Adam: *Wealth of Nations*, 243
smoking, 52, 153
smuggling, 16, 115–34, 212, 229, 277n39; archaeology and, 132; capitalism and, 244–45; contraband, 106, 121, 122, 127, 152–53, 226; defined, 103;

280n64; enforcement, 122–28, 207; as free trade, 243; French government sanction of, 116; importance to economy, 224; methods, 117, 129; New Orleans as base for, 106; salt smugglers, 3, 151–53, 167, 285n24, 285n26; during Seven Years' War, 128–29; slave trade and, 132–33; Spanish restriction of, 130–31, 221; terrestrial, 133–34; tobacco smugglers, 3, 117, 150, 151–53, 168, 285n24. *See also* Balize, La; Bienville, Jean-Baptiste LeMoyne de; crime; England; Iberville, Pierre LeMoyne d'; Kerlérec, Louis Billouart; maroons; mercantilism; merchants; Mexico; revolution; rogue colonialism; ships and sailing; slaves; Superior Council of Louisiana; trade; Vaudreuil
social mobility, 182–83: in colonies vs. metropole, 288n47. *See also* capitalism
soldiers, 14, 142, 143, 156, 185, 200, 224; barracks of, 93, 148; criminal activity of, 205–6, 212–13; economic activity, 133–34; insults and, 174; literacy of, 57; manumission of slave soldiers, 179; mercenaries, 200; mutinies, 206; nicknames, 164; as percentage of New Orleans population, 287n40; as police, 205, 207. *See also under* Swiss
Soubagnier (Sabannier), 168
Spain and the Spanish, 31; administration, restrictions imposed on New Orleans, 221, 225; colonial urban planning, 68–69; conquistadors, 240; educational efforts in New Orleans, 56; involvement in Louisiana economy, 102, 106
Spear, Jennifer, 140, 181, 258n6
spying, 129, 298, 210
Stoler, Ann, 17
Superbe, La, 131–32
Superior Council of Louisiana, 8, 65, 82, 220; composition of, 196; criminal case records, 300n58, 301n63; independence of, 195–97, 236; judicial function of, 145, 193–95, 204–6, 295n12; La Balize and, 112–13; legislative function of, 145, 193, 196–97; regulation

vieux carrés, 70
Villiers du Terrage, Marc de, 17; on crime
 rate, 301n65
violence: in southern U.S., 302n71
Virginia, 83
Vitruvius: *Ten Books on Architecture*,
 68
Voltaire: *Oeuvres*, 37
voyageurs, 105, 157, 183, 249

Wade, Richard, 272n77
wars and military engagements: Chickasaw War I (1736), 51, 292n96; Chickasaw War II (1739–1740), 51, 292n96;
 King George's War, 118; Natchez Wars,
 27, 79, 95, 100, 132, 168–69, 287n40;
 Pensacola War, 51; Seven Years' War
 (French and Indian War), 8, 95, 128;
 War of Jenkins' Ear, 112; War of Spanish Succession, 265n7, 266n17

Wealth of Nations (Smith), 243
West Florida. *See under* Florida
wheat, 271n67, 281n72; trade in, 104,
 132. *See also* food
White, Hayden, xvii
Williamsburg, 69
wine, 102, 220, 281n72; black market,
 132; fraud, 210; as item of trade, 104,
 105, 106, 113, 115, 122, 222
women, 150; abuse of, 214, 216; brides,
 average age of, 293n104; characterizations of, 45–46, 56, 171; economic
 activity of, 100–1, 132, 106; education,
 58–59; as *forçats*, 289n63; legal status,
 144; literacy, 57, 59; ratio of women to
 men, 184, 199, 216, 293n112; violent
 crime and, 215–16.
Wright, Gwendolyn, 266n14

Xavier, Nicolas, 156